A Dictionary of the Bible & Christian Doctrine in Everyday English

A Dictionary of the Bible & Christian Doctrine in Everyday English

Second Edition

J. Wesley Eby
George Lyons
Al Truesdale

Beacon Hill Press of Kansas City
Kansas City, Missouri

Second edition 2004

ISBN 083-412-0860

Printed in the
United States of America

Cover Design: Paul Franitza

Library of Congress Cataloging-in-Publication data

A dictionary of the Bible and Christian doctrine in everyday English / J. Wesley Eby, George Lyons, Albert Truesdale.—2nd ed.

p. cm.

ISBN 0-8341-2086-0 (pbk.)

1. Bible—Dictionaries. 2. Theology, Doctrinal—Dictionaries. I. Eby, J. Wesley. II. Lyons, George. III. Truesdale, Albert, 1941-

BS440.D52 2004

220.3—dc22

2003025784

10 9 8 7 6 5 4 3 2 1

Contents

PREFACE

In 1983 Jerry Appleby, who was then the ethnic/urban coordinator at the International Center of the Church of the Nazarene, approached us (plus the late Nancy Clark) about the possibility of developing a simplified dictionary of the Bible and Christian doctrine. At that time, Rev. Appleby envisioned a relatively small book that would include definitions of some basic biblical and doctrinal terms. These definitions were to be of particular interest and use by pastors and teachers of people in the United States whose knowledge of and proficiency in English were limited.

On this basis, we assumed, at first, that the dictionary would be quite brief and would be used by a relatively small group of people. But as the work progressed, its potential for use by Christian workers worldwide became clearer. As we surveyed the field, we found that dictionaries such as we were developing were virtually nonexistent.

Consequently, as work on this volume continued and its range of users broadened, the scope of definitions was greatly enlarged. But even as the nature of the dictionary changed, we did not lose sight of those for whom it was initially intended.

We have tried to produce a dictionary that puts the results of sound theological and biblical research into everyday English for today's average layperson. Those people whose own expertise and language proficiency is beyond the level at which this dictionary is written should find it useful in explaining the Bible and Christian doctrine to others less schooled. It can also help those who are not Christians to better understand the meaning of the Christian faith. This dictionary can be used as a companion to Bible and doctrinal study. Or it can be used by itself for a basic, systematic study of Christian doctrine. This can be done by following the biblical and topical cross-references at the end of the dictionary entries.

This second edition is a major revision of the first one. Almost 350 new entries have been included. Of these there are 250 new definitions and almost 100 cross-referenced terms. Many of the definitions in the first edition have been rewritten or expanded. Cross-references and biblical references have been carefully researched, resulting in numerous modifications.

Our prayer is that this dictionary will be an important resource through which people can better understand and follow the gospel of Jesus Christ. We hope this volume will help people within the Wesleyan tradition to gain a better understanding of other parts of the Christian faith. We also hope that we have clearly stated the basic ideas of Wesleyanism.

Al Truesdale
Emeritus Professor of Philosophy and Religion and Christians Ethics
Nazarene Theological Seminary

George Lyons
Professor of Biblical Literature
Northwest Nazarene University

J. Wesley Eby
Mission Education Coordinator, Nazarene Missions International
World Mission Division

Acknowledgments

We wish to acknowledge with gratitude the many people who have had a part in the production of both editions of this volume. First, we are indebted to the initial 40-plus contributors. Their articles have undergone considerable change, which is, in part, because the character of the dictionary has changed considerably since its early stages.

Second, we wish to express special appreciation to the following who played major roles in one of the editions of this volume: Raymond W. Hurn, general superintendent emeritus; William M. Greathouse, general superintendent emeritus; Jerry Appleby, former ethnic/urban coordinator, Church of the Nazarene; the late M. A. "Bud" Lunn, former president of Nazarene Publishing House; Ray Hendrix, director of World Mission Literature Ministries (formerly Publications International); and Bonnie Perry, director of Beacon Hill Press of Kansas City. Each of these people in his or her own way has expressed enthusiastic support for this project.

Third, countless others have helped with the seemingly endless details necessitated by a work of this nature. We thank those who worked at computer terminals, checked scripture and word references, and performed numerous meticulous tasks that arose during the tedious editorial process.

Next we remember with thanksgiving the dedicated labors of the late Nancy Clark, one of the editorial team of the first edition. Nancy's genuine concern for new immigrants to America along with her boundless energy added a special dimension to our editorial committee.

Last, we express deep gratitude to our families who were solidly supportive even though it meant many hours and days of separation, especially in writing the first edition.

Guidelines Used in the Preparation of This Dictionary

Grammar

The editors have written the dictionary definitions in common, everyday English. They have purposely avoided scholarly, theological terminology. In addition, they have observed specific guidelines related to the grammar of English based on principles taken from the field of English as a second/foreign language. In applying these guidelines, simplicity of language was the intent. The editors have sometimes had to sacrifice style to obtain easy-to-read-and-understand English.

Vocabulary

Controlled or limited vocabulary is essential in simplifying materials linguistically. Thus, the editors have worked with a vocabulary list of about 2,500 words. The carefully researched list includes the work of Dolch, Thorndike, Stone, Fry, Dale, and Eeds. Various studies have shown that the 3,000 most common words in any language account for 90 percent of the words in its adult literature. Therefore, the words in the book are, for the most part, the ones most frequently used in English. Several specialized words, of course, (for example, *biblical, divine,* and *missionary*) have been added because of their high-frequency use in a resource book of this nature.

Pronunciation

One common pronunciation has been given for each term. The resource for most pronunciations has been *Merriam Webster's Collegiate Dictionary,* Tenth Edition, © 1998.

The pronunciations have been written in a simplified symbol system that uses only the letters of the English alphabet rather than one of the pronunciation keys in common use today. The accented syllables are shown in uppercase letters (capitals), while unaccented syllables are in lowercase. Thus, the word *adoration* is symbolized in the dictionary as AD-uh-RAY-shun. See the Pronunciation Key on page 14.

Dictionary Entry Features

The dictionary entries contain the following features:

1. *Dictionary Term*

   The word or phrase that is defined and sometimes explained or cross-referenced is printed in large, bold type for easy identification.

2. *Pronunciation*

   The way the dictionary entry is commonly pronounced is provided in a simplified, alphabetic form within parentheses.

3. *Part of Speech*

The part of speech or how the term is usually used in English is provided. This grammatical label (for example, noun, proper noun, noun phrase, verb, adjective, and so on) gives the user helpful information about the grammatical structure of the term, that is, its usual function in English discourse.

4. *Definition*

A definition of how the term is used in the Bible or in Christian doctrine is given for most terms. (Some terms are cross-referenced to other entries for definition or explanation.) Sometimes a general definition of the term is given when it is needed for comparison or contrast. For more important terms, an explanation is provided that goes beyond a simple definition. This additional information will expand and enhance the understanding of the defined term.

All definitions and explanations are written in complete sentences. This differs from the usual format in most dictionaries, which define words in phrases or subordinate clauses.

5. *Bible References*

For most terms, references in the Bible are provided where the term itself or the concept can be found. The editors strongly believe that the Word of God must be read and studied along with the definitions to have a complete understanding of the terms.

6. *Cross-references*

Most entries have cross-references where additional, helpful information can be found. These are indicated by the word *See*. Many of the cross-referenced terms are used in the definition or explanation itself. Also, some terms that have the same or similar meanings are cross-referenced to one or more entries to avoid redefining those entries.

7. *Map References*

Numerous geographical place names are referenced to the maps in the appendix. This map information will help in acquiring a geographical sense of where significant events occurred or in locating important places.

8. *Time Line References*

A few terms are referenced to a historical time line (chronology) in the appendix. This information will help in acquiring a sense of when significant events occurred and when important people lived.

The maps and time line are from the *Today's English Version*. The American Bible Society gave permission for their use, for which the editors are grateful.

On the opposite page is a sample of a dictionary entry that contains summarized information about each feature.

How to Use This Dictionary

Dictionary Term
The word or phrase that is defined is printed in a large, bold size.

Pronunciation
The way the term is pronounced is written in an easy form. It uses only the letters of the English alphabet.

Part of Speech
The part of speech in the English language is provided. It shows the usual function of the term in English.

Edom (EE-dum) *proper noun:*

1. Edom was another name given to Esau. The name Edom in Hebrew means "red."
2. Edom was also the name of the nation made up of the descendants of Esau. The people were called Edomites. The soil in the land of Edom was red in color. Edom is called Idumea in the New Testament.

Genesis 25:19-34; 35:1-43

See **Arab, Edom (map 4), Esau, Hebrew, New Testament**

Definition
A definition is given of how the term is used in the Bible and Christian doctrine. Sometimes a general definition of the term will be given.

Bible References
Verses in the Bible are given where the term or idea can be found.

Cross-References
Other terms in the dictionary are usually given. These cross-references will give more help in understanding the defined term.

Map References
Some terms will refer to a map or time line. The maps and time line in the appendix will give more help in understanding the term.

PRONUNCIATION GUIDE

Vowels

Symbol	Key Words	Usual Spellings
ay	age, day	a, ai, ay
a	ask, back	a
ah	father, ox	a, o
aw	auto, saw	au, aw
ee	each, sea	e, ee, ea, ey, y
e	egg, bed	e
air	air, bear	air, are, ear
er	her, bird, fur	er, ir, ur
ie	ice, pie, my	i, ie, y
i	inch, sit	i
oh	oat, nose	o, oa, oe, ow
ew	new, moon	u, ew, oo, ue
oo	good, bush	oo, u
ou	out, cow	ou, ow
oy	oil, boy	oi, oy
yew	use, human	u
u or uh*	up, just, sofa	u, a, e, i, o

Consonants

Symbol	Key Words	Usual Spellings
b	boat, cab	b, bb
ch	church, match	ch, tch
d	day, dad	d, dd
f	foot, wife	f, ff, ph, gh
g	gate, big	g, gg
h	hand, behind	h, wh
j	joy, page	j, g, dg
k	king, music	k, c, ck, ch
ks	box, sacks	x, cks
kw	queen, equal	qu
l	life, hill	l, ll
m	man, ham	m, mm
n	new, son	n, nn, kn
ng	drink, sing	n, ng
p	pig, cap	p, pp
r	race, year	r, rr, wr
s	sun, face	s, c, ss, sc
sh	sheep, fish	sh, ch, ti
t	teach, mat	t, tt
th	thin, bath	th
th (underlined)	this, bathe	th
v	vine, give	v
w	win, away	w
y	you, lawyer	y
z	zeal, breeze	z
zh	treasure, azure	s, z

*Same as the schwa sound found in many dictionaries.

A a

Aaron (AIR-un) *proper noun:*

Aaron was the older brother of Moses. He was also a brother of Miriam. God chose him and his descendants to be the priests for the Hebrew people.

Exodus 4:10-17; 28:1-43

See **Hebrew, Miriam, Moses, priest, tabernacle, temple**

Abel (AY-bul) *proper noun:*

Abel was the second son of Adam and Eve. He was the first shepherd. He was killed by his brother Cain who hated him. He was also a brother of Seth.

Genesis 4:1-9; Hebrews 11:4

See **Abel (time line), Adam, Cain, Eve, Seth, shepherd**

Abijah (uh-BIE-juh) *proper noun:*

1. Abijah was the name of several biblical persons, both male and female. For example, Abijah was a son of the prophet Samuel (1 Samuel 8:1-2). Abijah was also the mother of King Hezekiah (2 Kings 18:1-2).

2. Abijah was the second king of Judah, the Southern Kingdom. He was also called Abijam. He was the son of Rehoboam and the father of Asa. He was an evil king just as his father, Rehoboam, was (1 Kings 14:31; 15:1-8).

See **Abijah (time line), Asa, biblical, god, Hezekiah, Judah, king, Rehoboam, Samuel**

abomination (uh-BAHM-uh-NAY-shun) *noun:*

An abomination is an act or thing that is very sinful or unclean. It offends and disgusts God and believers. Idols and false worship are examples of abominations. Places that were made unclean by abominations had to be cleansed or destroyed.

Deuteronomy 7:25; Proverbs 28:9; Revelation 17:4-5

See **abomination of desolation, cleanse, God, idol, unclean, worship**

abomination of desolation (uh-BAHM-un-NAY-shun uv DES-uh-LAY-shun) *noun phrase:*

Abomination of desolation was the name given an idol someone placed in the Temple. Any idol was an abomination to God. This idol was called an *abomination of desolation* because it made the Temple unclean. The Temple had to be cleansed before the people could worship there again.

The phrase *abomination of desolation* is found in the Book of Daniel. Daniel predicted that the Temple would become unclean. This happened in 168 B.C. An evil king of Syria placed an idol in the Temple. But the Temple was made clean again by the Maccabees a few years later. The Jewish people still celebrate this cleansing during the Festival of Dedication or Hanukkah.

The phrase *abomination of desolation* is also used in the Gospels. Jesus predicted that the Temple would be made unclean again. He said that God would cause the Temple to be destroyed. This would be His judgment for the sins of the people of Israel. The soldiers of Rome entered the Temple and destroyed it in A.D. 70.

Daniel 8:13; 9:27; 11:31; 12:11; Matthew 24:15; Mark 13:14

***See* abomination, dedication, festival, God, Hanukkah, idol, Maccabees, prophesy, Syria (map 9), temple, unclean**

Abraham (AY-bruh-HAM) *proper noun:*

Abraham was the great ancestor of the Hebrew people. He was one of the patriarchs. He lived about 2000 B.C. The name Abraham meant "father of many people." God gave him the name Abraham when he had no children. Abraham and his wife Sarah had their son, Isaac, when they were very old. Abraham trusted the promise of God. God considered him a righteous man.

The New Testament often uses Abraham as the example of a man of faith. Paul said that people who trust in God alone for salvation are *sons of Abraham.*

Genesis 12:1-20; John 8:31-59; Romans 4:1-25; Hebrews 11:8-12

***See* Abraham (time line), Chaldea, faith, Hebrew, Isaac, Jew, Moriah, patriarch, Paul, righteous, Sarah**

Abraham's bosom (AY-bruh-HAMZ BOO-zum) *noun phrase:*

Abraham's bosom is a phrase used to describe the comfort God gives in heaven. The bosom is the chest of a person. To be in *Abraham's bosom* was to be close to Abraham. This was a great honor.

Jesus used *Abraham's bosom* in the story of the rich man and Lazarus (Luke 16:19-31). Jesus said that poor Lazarus died and went to heaven. There, he sat next to Abraham at a feast. He received comfort from Abraham.

***See* Abraham, heaven, Lazarus**

abstain (ab-STAYN) *verb:*

To abstain is to do without or avoid something. Christians are told in the Bible to abstain from all evil.

Acts 15:20, 29; 1 Thessalonians 4:3; 5:22; 1 Timothy 4:3; 1 Peter 2:11

***See* abstinence, Christian, evil**

abstinence (AB-stuh-nuns) *noun:*

Abstinence is choosing to do without or to avoid something. Christians are to avoid all evil. This is one form of abstinence. A person may also abstain from something that is not evil. That is, people may deny themselves of something as a spiritual discipline. A person might do without food for a time. This abstinence is called fasting. Total abstinence is the practice of refusing to drink any alcohol.

Acts 27:21

See **abstain, discipline, fast, temperance, wine**

abyss (uh-BIS) *noun:*

An abyss is a deep pit. The Bible uses the word *abyss* to describe where wicked people go when they die. Thus it is a term for hell.

Luke 8:31; Romans 10:7; Revelation 9:1-11; 11:7; 17:8; 20:1-3

See **Hades, heaven, hell**

accursed (uh-KERST)

1. *adjective:* Accursed describes something that God will destroy. People in the Old Testament sometimes destroyed things that they took in war. They burned these things as a sacrifice to God. The things that they took were said to be accursed.

2. *noun:* The accursed are people who will be separated from God in hell unless they repent.

Joshua 6:17; Romans 9:3; 1 Corinthians 12:3; Galatians 1:8-9

See **curse, God, hell, judgment, repent, sacrifice**

Acts (AKTS) *proper noun:*

Acts is the name of a book in the New Testament. Its full title is the Acts of the Apostles. The book tells the story of the Early Christian Church. It especially stresses the work of the Holy Spirit through the Church.

Peter and Paul are the most important human characters in the story. The book starts with the return of Jesus back to heaven. It tells how the Church carried out its mission of witnessing for Jesus. It ends with Paul in prison in Rome. Most scholars say that Luke wrote Acts.

See **apostle, ascension, Christian, Holy Spirit, Luke, Paul, Peter**

Adam (Ad-um) *proper noun:*

Adam was the name of the first man God created. The name Adam means "man" in Hebrew.

Genesis 2:4—5:5

See **Adam (time line), creation, Hebrew, man, Old Testament**

admonish (ad-MAHN-ish) *verb:*

To admonish is to warn someone kindly. The purpose of admonishing is to warn against error and harm. The Bible admonishes Christians to avoid everything that would harm their faith in Christ.

Acts 20:31; Romans 15:15; 1 Corinthians 4:14; Colossians 1:28; 3:16; 1 Thessalonians 5:12, 14; 2 Thessalonians 3:15

See **disciple, faith, obedience, righteousness**

Adonai (AD-uh-NIE) *proper noun:*

Adonai is one of the names for God in the Old Testament. The word *Adonai* comes from a Hebrew word that means lord. In the Old Testament, Adonai refers to both God and to human rulers or lords. The use of Adonai by the Jews occurred most often late in the Old Testament period.

Many Jews used Adonai to refer to God instead of using God's personal name, Yahweh. The Jews used Adonai out of respect for God. They did not want to misuse the word *Yahweh.*

***See* Elohim, God, Lord, Old Testament, worship, Yahweh**

adopt (uh-DAHPT) *verb:*

To adopt is to make a child one's own son or daughter. This happens by law and not by birth. The adopted person has all the rights and duties of a child by birth.

God adopts people spiritually when they trust Christ for salvation. They become God's children. Christians are adopted into the family of God.

***See* adoption, child of God, Christian, family of God, salvation**

adoption (uh-DAHP-shun) *noun:*

Adoption is an act that makes a person a member of a new family. This happens by law.

Adoption describes part of the new relation sinners have with God after He forgives them. Sinners who trust Christ for salvation are no longer separated from Him. They become children of God. Spiritual adoption is by grace, not by law.

Romans 8:15, 23; 9:4; 2 Corinthians 6:14—7:1; Galatians 4:5; Ephesians 1:5

***See* adopt, born again, child of God, conversion, election, forgiveness, grace, justification, new birth, reconciliation, redemption, regeneration, salvation**

adoration (AD-uh-RAY-shun) *noun:*

Adoration is the devotion and love that people give to God. It describes the feelings that people have toward God. It is reverence and respect. People show adoration in prayer and worship.

***See* fear, God, love, praise, prayer, reverence, worship**

adultery (uh-DUL-ter-ee) *noun:*

Adultery is the sexual act, done willingly between people not married to each other. At least one of these people is married to another person. The Bible says that adultery is a very serious sin.

The Bible sometimes uses adultery in a religious sense. Adultery may also refer to the worship of idols by the people of God. This means they no longer worship God as the one true God.

Exodus 20:14; Leviticus 18:20; Deuteronomy 22:22; Hosea 1:2; 2:1-23; Matthew 5:27-28; 19:3-9; 1 Corinthians 6:9

***See* divorce, faithful, fornication, God, idol, immoral, marriage, Ten Commandments**

Advent (AD-vent) *proper noun:*

Advent means "coming." The Advent season celebrates the birth of Christ when He first came to earth. It includes the four Sundays just before Christmas.

The Second Advent is the second coming of Christ. This is still in the future.

Matthew 1—2; Luke 1—2; Philippians 2:6-11; 1 Thessalonians 4:3—5:11; Revelation 1:1-9; 22:6-21

See **Christ, eschatology, incarnation, parousia, Second Coming**

adversary (AD-ver-SAIR-ee) *noun:*

An adversary is an enemy. The Bible calls Satan *the adversary*. Satan is the enemy both of God and God's people.

Deuteronomy 32:27; 1 Samuel 29:4; 1 Kings 11:14, 23, 25; Psalm 109:20, 29; Luke 21:15; 1 Corinthians 16:9

See **advocate, devil, enemy, Hades, Satan**

advocate (AD-vuh-kut) *noun:*

An advocate is a person who speaks or writes in behalf of another. For example, a lawyer is an advocate who speaks in behalf of a person.

The Greek word for advocate is translated "paraclete." The Book of 1 John describes Jesus as an advocate with God for sinners. The Gospel of John describes the Holy Spirit as the Paraclete.

John 14:16, 26; 15:26; 16:7; 1 John 2:1

See **adversary, Comforter, Holy Spirit, 1 and 2 and 3 John, Paraclete, sin, sinner**

Aelia Capitolina (EE-lee-uh KAP-uh-tuh-LEE-nuh) *proper noun:*

See **Jerusalem**

affection (uh-FEK-shun) *noun:*

An affection is a fond feeling toward someone or something. Affection makes people hold closely what they love.

Christ has a great affection for His Church. Christians are to have the same kind of affection for one another.

An affection may also be evil. For example, greed and lust are evil affections.

2 Corinthians 7:13-16; Philippians 1:8-11

See **agape, covet, emotion, love, lust, mind, passion, will**

affliction (uh-FLIK-shun) *noun:*

See **suffering**

agape (ah-GAH-pay) *noun:*

Agape means love. It is the most often used Greek word for love in the New Testament. John uses it when he says: "God is love" (1 John 4:8). Paul used *agape* when he described what Christian love is like. It is a love that is given whether or not it is returned.

Matthew 22:34-40; Luke 10:27; John 3:16; 21:15-19; Romans 12:9; 1 Corinthians 13:1-13; 2 Timothy 4:10; 1 John 2:15

See **affection, Great Commandment, hate, holiness, love, lust, perfect love, redemption**

agnostic (ag-NAHS-tik) *noun:*

An agnostic is a person who claims not to know whether or not God exists. God may or may not exist. There are not enough reasons for believing or not believing. An agnostic is open to belief.

Psalms 14; 19; Acts 17:23; Romans 1

See **atheism, belief, faith, God, knowledge, skepticism, skeptic**

Agrippa (uh-GRIP-uh) *proper noun:*

Herod Agrippa was the name of a Roman ruler in Palestine. He is mentioned in the Book of Acts. The New Testament calls him simply Agrippa. His great-grandfather was Herod the Great. The apostle Paul was once on trial before him.

Acts 25:13—26:32

See **Acts, apostle, Herod, New Testament, Paul**

Ahab (AY-hab) *proper noun:*

Ahab was the seventh king of Israel, the Northern Kingdom. He was the son of Omri. He and his wife, Jezebel, led the people of Israel to worship false gods. The prophet Elijah condemned Ahab and Jezebel as wicked leaders.

1 Kings 16:29—22:40

See **Ahab (time line), Baal, Elijah, god, idol, Israel, Jezebel, Omri**

Ahasuerus (uh-HAZ-yew-REE-us) *proper noun:*

See **Xerxes**

Ahaz (AY-haz) *proper noun:*

Ahaz was a king of Judah, the Southern Kingdom. He was the son of Jotham. He was known as an evil king. He worshiped idols and even sacrificed his own son.

2 Kings 16:1-4; 2 Chronicles 28:1-5

See **Ahaz (time line), Baal, god, Hinnom, idol, Jotham, Judah, king, pagan, sacrifice**

Ahaziah (AY-huh-ZIE-uh) *proper noun:*

1. Ahaziah was the sixth king of Judah, the Southern Kingdom. He was the son of Jehoram and Athaliah, Ahab's daughter. He was known as an idol worshiper. He was king for only a short time. (2 Kings 8:25-29; 9:27-29)

2. Ahaziah was the eighth king of Israel, the Northern Kingdom. He was the son of Ahab and Jezebel. He worshiped the false gods of Jezebel. He was king for only a year. (1 Kings 22:51-53)

See **Ahab, Ahaziah (time line), Athaliah, Baal, god, idol, Israel, Jehoram, Jezebel, Judah, king**

alabaster (AL-uh-BAS-ter) *noun:*

Alabaster is a soft white stone. Vases or jars are sometimes made from alabaster.

People put perfume in alabaster jars. A woman broke an alabaster jar and poured perfume on the head of Jesus.

Matthew 26:7; Mark 14:3; Luke 7:37-38; John 12:3

See **anoint, Jesus**

Alexander the Great (AL-ig-ZAN-der thuh GRAYT) *proper noun phrase:*

Alexander the Great was a famous Greek ruler. He once ruled all the lands around the Mediterranean Sea. His armies brought him to power during the 300s B.C. He led Greece in defeating Persia. His kingdom was divided among his generals after his death. The families of two of these generals ruled in Egypt and Syria. Palestine was ruled by Egypt or Syria until the time of the Maccabees.

See **Alexander the Great (time line), Egypt (map 2), Greece, Greek, Maccabees, Mediterranean Sea (maps 1, 11), Palestine, Persia, Syria (map 4)**

alien (AY-lee-un) *noun:*

An alien is a foreigner or stranger. Aliens are people who live away from their homelands.

God told His people in the Old Testament to be kind to aliens. He reminded them that they were once aliens in Egypt.

Exodus 22:21; 23:9-13; Deuteronomy 10:12-22; 24:17-21

See **alienate, alienation**

alienate (AY-lee-uh-NAYT) *verb:*

Alienate means to separate someone from his country, family, friends, or home.

All people belong to God. They were created by Him. But people have become alienated from God because they are sinners. God wants sinners to return to Him and worship Him. God made this possible through His Son, Jesus Christ.

Colossians 1:21-23

See **alien, forgiveness, reconcile, reconciliation, sin, sinners**

alienation (AY-lee-uh-NAY-shun) *noun:*

Alienation means "separation." Alienation is being and feeling like a stranger. Alienation may be by force or by choice.

Sin causes people to experience alienation from God. God overcomes this alienation by saving people from their sins. He reconciles them to himself.

Sin also causes alienation among people. The love of God can overcome this alienation. Jesus Christ loves the Church and makes it the family of God. Alienation has no place in His family. Christians should show other people how to overcome alienation.

Job 19:13-21; Ephesians 2:11-22; 4:17-18; 1 Peter 2:9-10

See **alien, church, reconciliation, redemption, salvation, sin, unity**

Allah (AL-uh or AH-luh) *proper noun:*

Allah is the Arabic word for God. Allah may refer to the God of the Bible. Allah also may refer to the God of the Koran, which is the sacred book of Islam. Christians who speak Arabic may refer to God as Allah.

See **Arab, Islam, monotheism**

alleluia (AL-uh-LEW-yuh) *interjection:*

See **hallelujah**

alpha and omega (AL-fuh and oh-MAY-guh) *noun phrase:*

Alpha and omega are the first and last letters of the Greek alphabet. The New Testament says that Jesus Christ is the Alpha and Omega. This means that He is the beginning and the end. He is the eternal Son of God. He is the Creator of the world. He will also bring the final redemption of His people.

Isaiah 44:6; 48:12; John 8:48-58; Colossians 1:15-20; Revelation 1:8; 21:6; 22:13

See **Christ, Creator, eternal, Greek, Jesus, redemption, Yahweh**

altar (AWL-ter) *noun:*

An altar is a place of sacrifice to a god. Altars in the Old Testament times were used to offer sacrifices to God. This was an act of worship. The most important altar to the God of Israel was at the Temple in Jerusalem. People who worshiped false gods also made altars to worship them.

The Christian life is an act of worship to God. This replaces the altar of the Old Testament. Christians serve God as "living sacrifices" to Him (Romans 12:1-2).

The altar is the place in some churches where the priest celebrates Mass. An altar in some churches is a rail where people kneel to pray. The altar is a special place where people meet God. People kneel there to ask God to forgive their sins. People receive Communion and join the church at the altar. Sometimes people are married or baptized there.

The phrase *family altar* is the worship time practiced by many Christian families in the home. Families usually pray and read the Bible together during this time of family devotions.

Genesis 8:20; 2 Samuel 24:15-25; Matthew 5:23-24; Acts 17:23; Romans 12:1-2; 1 Corinthians 5:6-8; 10:14—11:1

See **church, devotions, Mass, prayer, priest, sacrifice, sanctification, sanctuary, temple, worship**

altar call (AWL-ter KAWL) *noun phrase:*

See **invitation**

Amaziah (AM-uh-ZIE-uh) *proper noun:*

Amaziah was a king of Judah, the Southern Kingdom. His father was Joash. Amaziah was a good king for many years. However, he did not obey God completely. He worshiped the pagan gods of the Edomites.

2 Kings 14:1-5; 2 Chronicles 25:1-4

See **Amaziah (time line), Edom, god, Joash, Judah, king, pagan**

ambassador (am-BAS-uh-der) *noun:*

An ambassador is a person who represents one government to another one. Ambassadors speak and act for their leaders or nations. It is an honor to be an ambassador.

Christians are ambassadors for Christ. They represent the kingdom of God to the world. They invite sinners to turn to God.

2 Chronicles 32:31; Ezekiel 17:11-21; Romans 1:1-6; 2 Corinthians 5:17—6:10; Ephesians 6:10-20

See **alienation, apostle, Christ, elder, evangelist, God, messenger, reconcile, reconciliation, servant, sinner**

amen (AY-men or AH-men) *interjection:*

Amen is from a Hebrew word that means "Yes, it is true." *Amen* means that a person agrees with what someone else says or prays. It can mean "Let it be so." Prayers usually end with *amen.*

People sometimes say *amen* in response to something a preacher says in a sermon. This means that they agree very much with what is said.

Jesus often began His messages with *amen.* He meant that what He was going to say was a very important truth. Sometimes this *amen* is translated "verily," "truly," or "I tell you the truth."

Psalms 41:13; 106:48; Matthew 5:18; 6:9-13; John 1:51; 3:3; 5:19; 2 Corinthians 1:18-22; Revelation 5:11-14; 7:9-12

See **message, prayer, sermon, truth**

American Standard Version (uh-MAIR-uh-kun STAN-derd VER-zhun) *proper noun phrase:*

The *American Standard Version* is a modern translation of the Bible. Scholars wrote it around 1900 to make the King James Version more modern. Its abbreviation is ASV.

See **Bible, translation, version**

amillennialism (AH-muh-LEN-ee-ul-IZ-um) *noun:*

See **millennium**

Amish (AHM-ish) *proper noun:*

See **Anabaptist**

Ammon (AM-un) *proper noun:*

Ammon was the name of a nation related to the people of Israel. Ammon was a son of Abraham's nephew Lot. They were enemies of Israel. A person from Ammon was called an Ammonite. The land of Ammon was east of Israel.

Genesis 19:36-38; Deuteronomy 2:19-20; 23:3-6

See **Abraham, Ammon (map 7), Ammonites (map 3), Arab, Israel, Lot**

Amon (AY-mun) *proper noun:*

Amon was a king of Judah, the Southern Kingdom. He was the son of Manasseh. He was king for only a short time. He was an idol worshiper like his father.

2 Kings 21:19-26

See **Amon (time line), god, idol, Judah, king, Manasseh**

Amorite (AM-uh-riet) *proper noun:*

See **Canaanite**

Amos (AY-mus) *proper noun:*

1. Amos was a prophet in the Old Testament. He lived during the 700s B.C. Amos was a farmer from Tekoa (tuh-KOH-uh), a country village in Judah.

Amos traveled to the Northern Kingdom of Israel. There he saw a few very rich people and many very poor people. The rich were selfish and not at all fair with the poor. Amos spoke out against this lack of justice in Israel. He also saw that the people were very religious. But their religion did not cause them to live right. He called upon the people to repent and obey God.

2. Amos is a book in the Old Testament. It is one of the Minor Prophets. It contains the messages of Amos to Israel.

See **Amos (time line), Israel, Judah, justice, messenger, Old Testament, prophet, religion, religious, repent, right**

Anabaptist (AN-uh-BAP-tist) *proper noun:*

The Anabaptists were a group of Christians who formed part of the Protestant Reformation. They were named Anabaptists by those who opposed them. The Anabaptists believed that only adult believers in Christ should be baptized. Thus, they rejected the practice of infant baptism. They stressed the need for Christians to live a life of piety.

Anabaptists believed that church and state should be separate. Only the Bible was accepted as the law of the church. What the state demanded was not accepted as the law of the church. They would not take part in a church supported by the state.

Anabaptists believed that Christians should not go to war or serve in the army. Many countries viewed them as enemies of the state.

Anabaptists were persecuted by other Protestants and by Roman Catholics. Most of their early leaders were killed. Today, the Anabaptist tradition is being continued by the Baptists, Mennonites, and Amish.

See **baptism, Baptist, Mennonite, pacifism, piety, Protestant, reformation, Roman Catholic**

Ananias (AN-uh-NIE-us) *proper noun:*

Ananias was the name of three different men in the Book of Acts.

1. Ananias was an early disciple in Jerusalem. He and his wife, Sapphira, died after they lied (Acts 5:1-11).

2. Ananias was an early disciple in Damascus. He prayed for Saul to get his sight back (Acts 9:10-19).

3. Ananias was the high priest when Paul was questioned by the Sanhedrin (Acts 22:30—23:11).

See **Damascus (map 8), disciple, Jerusalem (map 10), priest, Sanhedrin, Saul**

Andrew (AN-drew) *proper noun:*

Andrew was one of the 12 disciples of Jesus. He was a brother of Simon Peter. He brought his brother to Jesus.

Matthew 4:18; 10:2-4; John 1:35-42

See **apostle, disciple, Jesus, Peter**

angel (AYN-jul) *noun:*

An angel is a messenger from God. Messengers in the Bible can be either heavenly or human. Angels give words of warning or hope. Heavenly angels are spirits.

The Bible refers to two different groups of angels: seraphim and cherubim. Two angels are named in the Bible: Michael and Gabriel.

Genesis 1:31; 3:24; Psalms 29:1; 89:6; Isaiah 6:1; Daniel 8:16; Luke 1:19, 26; 9:26; 2 Thessalonians 1:7

See **cherub, Gabriel, messenger, seraph**

anger (ANG-ger) *noun:*

Anger is an emotion expressing a strong feeling of dislike. It is caused by something felt to be wrong.

The writers of the Bible refer to the anger of man and of God. Human anger may be good or bad. Anger against wrong can result in good. Anger that seeks to hurt people is wrong. The anger of God expresses His strong dislike for sin.

Exodus 32:1-35; Hosea 6:1-6; 11:1-9; Zechariah 10:1-5; Mark 3; Galatians 5:18-23; Ephesians 4:25—5:2; Colossians 3:5-17

See **forgiveness, hate, love, wrath**

Anglican (ANG-gli-kun) *proper adjective:*

Anglican describes the Episcopal Church of England. *Anglican* comes from a word meaning "English." The Anglican church is one of the four major divisions of Christianity.

See **Christianity, church, episcopal**

animism (AN-uh-MIZ-um) *noun:*

Animism is a kind of religion. It believes that spirits live in nature and natural objects. Animism is the belief that all natural objects have souls. Animists believe that these souls should be respected and worshiped. The spirits can hurt people who do not treat them properly. But the spirits can be made to help people through magic and other means. People who practice animism are called animists.

See **magic, religion, soul, spirit, worship**

animist (AN-uh-mist) *noun:*

See **animism**

annunciation (uh-NUN-see-AY-shun) *noun:*

An annunciation is an announcement. An annunciation gives important news to people. There are many annunciations in the Bible. The Annunciation usually refers to a very special announcement made to Mary, the mother of Jesus. An angel told Mary that she would be the mother of Jesus. Jesus would be the Messiah. An angel announced this news to Mary.

Roman Catholics celebrate the Feast of the Annunciation of the Blessed Virgin Mary on March 25.

Genesis 6:7; 12:1-3; 1 Samuel 13:13-14; Jeremiah 15:1-9; Luke 1:26-38

See **angel, Jesus, Luke, Mary, Messiah, Roman Catholic, virgin**

anoint (uh-NOYNT) *verb:*

To anoint is to put oil on objects or persons. Sometimes perfume was used for anointing. Anointing in the Bible was done most often for religious purposes. Sometimes oil was used as a medicine. Sometimes it was used to make a person look more beautiful.

Kings, priests, and prophets were anointed before taking office. This was a sign of their call to serve God (Exodus 28:40-43; 1 Samuel 10:1; 16:1-13).

The Hebrew people of the Old Testament expected a great king to come. They called this king the Messiah. *Messiah* means "the anointed one" in the Hebrew language. *Christ* means "the anointed one" in the Greek language. Jesus was the Christ or the Messiah who came.

Psalms 2:2; 18:50; Daniel 9:25-26; John 1:41; 4:25; James 5:13-18

See **Christ, healing, inspiration, king, Messiah, oil, priest, prophet**

antichrist (AN-ti-KRIEST) *noun:*

Antichrist means "against Christ" or "instead of Christ." An antichrist denies that Jesus is the Christ. Anyone who claims to be Christ is an antichrist. The Antichrist is the great enemy of Jesus Christ.

2 Thessalonians 2:1-12; 1 John 2:18, 22; 4:3; 2 John 7; Revelation 13:1-18

See **Christ, eschatology, evil, false prophet, tribulation**

Antioch (AN-tee-ahk) *proper noun:*

Antioch was the name of two different cities referred to in Acts.

1. Antioch was the capital city of Syria. Disciples were first called Christians there (Acts 11:19-26; 13:1-3).

2. Antioch was an important city in Pisidia in Asia Minor (Acts 13:14-50).

See **Acts, Antioch (map 9), Asia Minor (map 11), Christian, disciple, Pisidia (map 9), Syria (map 8)**

apocalypse (uh-PAHK-uh-lips) *noun:*

The Apocalypse is the Book of Revelation.

There are other Jewish and early Christian writings like the Book of Revelation. They contain strange visions about the end of the present, evil age. These are sometimes called *apocalypses.*

Apocalypses say that God will destroy evil and set up His kingdom. They were written to give hope to believers.

See **apocalyptic, eschatology, evil, prophet, revelation, vision**

apocalyptic (uh-PAHK-uh-LIP-tik) *adjective:*

Apocalyptic describes a special kind of Jewish and Christian writings and religious beliefs. These writings and beliefs are called apocalyptic because they are similar to the Apocalypse.

Most apocalyptic writings appeared after the Exile. The Jews then were ruled by foreign kings who did not worship the God of Israel. They would not listen to the prophets of God.

Thus, the voice of God seemed to be silent. God seemed to be far away, and things only went from bad to worse. The Messiah had not come as Israel had expected. The persecuted people of God lost all hope for the present evil age. Apocalyptic writers offered them hope for the future. God would destroy all evil and bring history to an end.

The Books of Daniel and Revelation are apocalyptic. The teachings of Jesus and the letters of Paul were influenced by apocalyptic beliefs. But early Christian apocalyptic convictions were different from Jewish apocalyptic beliefs in many ways. Christians believed that the end had already begun with the coming of Jesus Christ. He was already bringing about the future purposes of God for the world. And Christians believed that they were to work with Him as agents of salvation.

Luke 17:20-21; Acts 2:14-42; 1 Corinthians 15:20-28, 57-58; 2 Corinthians 4:16—5:21; 1 Thessalonians 4:13—5:11; 2 Peter 3:1-13

See **apocalypse, Daniel, eschatology, exile, hope, Israel, Messiah, prophesy, prophet, revelation, salvation, Second Coming**

Apocrypha (uh-PAHK-ruh-fuh) *proper noun:*

The Apocrypha is a group of religious books not included in the Protestant Bible. These books were written by Christian and Jewish writers. Some Jews thought the books should be included in the Bible. Thus, the Roman Catholic Bible includes some of the Apocrypha. Most Protestants believe the Apocrypha is not inspired by God.

See **authority of Scripture, Bible, canon, catholic, inspiration, Protestant, Roman Catholic**

apologetics (uh-PAHL-uh-JET-iks) *noun:*

Apologetics explains the Christian faith to people who do not believe. Apologetics answers questions about Christian beliefs. It also responds to attacks against Christianity.

Examples of apologetics in the Bible are Acts 2:14-36; 17:22-32; 1 Peter 3:15.

See **belief, doctrine, faith, theology**

apostasy (uh-PAHS-tuh-see) *noun:*

Apostasy means turning away from a religious faith. Christians commit apostasy by giving up their faith in Christ and His way. Apostasy is more serious than simply failing to obey Christ. People who commit apostasy no longer want to obey Christ. Apostasy is worse than backsliding. To commit apostasy is to reject one's religious faith completely.

Acts 21:20-21; 2 Thessalonians 2:3; Hebrews 5:11—6:12

See **backslide, blasphemy, faith, reprobate**

apostle (uh-PAHS-ul) *noun:*

An apostle was a special kind of minister. The risen Christ called certain people to be apostles. Their mission was to preach so that people would become disciples of Jesus Christ. Therefore, apostles were a type of missionary. They included Paul, the disciples of Jesus, and a few others.

Matthew 28:16-20; Acts 1:1—2:42; Romans 1:1-6; 16:7; 1 Corinthians 9:1-27; Galatians 1:1, 11—2:10; Ephesians 4:11-16

See **disciple, gift, Great Commission, minister, missionary**

Apostles' Creed (uh-PAHS-ulz KREED) *proper noun phrase:*

The Apostles' Creed is a short statement of the Christian faith. It has been used by Christians for many centuries. It is accepted by Protestant, Roman Catholic, and Eastern Orthodox churches. The Apostles' Creed is said in many church services as a confession of faith.

See **belief, confession, creed, Eastern Orthodoxy, faith, Nicene Creed, Protestant, Roman Catholic**

Aquila (uh-KWIL-uh or AK-wuh-luh) *proper noun phrase:*

Aquila was a Jew who was friend of the apostle Paul. He and his wife, Priscilla, were tentmakers. They helped Paul in his ministry in Europe and Asia Minor. Aquila is always mentioned along with his wife in the New Testament.

Acts 18:1-3, 18-19, 24-26; Romans 16:3; 1 Corinthians 16:19; 2 Timothy 4:19

See **apostle, Asia Minor, Europe, Jew, ministry, Paul, Priscilla**

Arab (AIR-ub or AY-rab) *proper noun:*

An Arab was a person living in the desert south and east of Palestine. The Hebrew word for Arab first meant "desert."

Some Arabs were descendants of Lot, the nephew of Abraham (Genesis 19:30-38). Other Arabs were descendants of Abraham by his wives Keturah and Hagar (Genesis 25). Still other Arabs were descendants of Esau (Genesis 36). Arabs were Gentiles who were closely related to the people of Israel. Most Arabs today speak the Arabic language.

See **Abraham, Esau, Gentile, Hagar, Hebrew, Ishmael, Israel, Keturah**

Aram (AIR-um) *proper noun:*

See **Syria**

Aramaic (AIR-uh-MAY-ik) *proper noun:*

Aramaic was the language of most Jews in Palestine during the time of Jesus. Jesus probably preached in Aramaic. It was a language very similar to Hebrew. The Jews began to use Aramaic while they were in exile in Babylon. Some short sections of the Old Testament were first written in Aramaic. This language is still spoken in parts of Israel.

See **Babylon, exile, Hebrew, Jesus, Old Testament, Palestine**

Ararat (AIR-uh-rat) *proper noun:*

Ararat is the name of the mountain on which Noah's ark came to rest. Mount Ararat is located in eastern Turkey.

Genesis 8:4

See **ark**

archaeology (AHR-kee-AHL-uh-jee) *noun:*

Archaeology is the study of human records from the past. These records include writings, tools, pottery, coins, weapons, and buildings. Scholars study these records to learn how people lived in the past. Archaeology helps scholars to know more about biblical times.

See **Bible**

Areopagus (AIR-ee-AHP-uh-gus) *proper noun:*

The Areopagus is a hill in Athens, Greece. It means "hill of Ares," which was named for the Greek god of war. The Areopagus is often called Mars Hill.

One time the apostle Paul preached on the Areopagus (Acts 17:16-34). He talked to the Greeks about their altar to an unknown god. Paul told them about the true God whom they were worshiping in ignorance.

See **altar, apostle, Athens (map 11), God, god, Greek, Paul, worship**

ark (AHRK) *noun:*

An ark is a boat or a box.

1. The ark of Noah was a large boat (Genesis 6—8). God told Noah to build the ark. Noah, his family, and all kinds of animals went into the ark. It saved them from the great Flood. It came to rest on the mountain named Ararat.

2. The ark of the covenant was a special box (Exodus 25:10-22; 37:1-10). God told Moses to build this ark. The ark of the covenant had three pur-

poses. The Ten Commandments and sacred things were kept in it (Hebrews 9:1-5). It served as a sign of the presence of God (Numbers 10:35-36; 1 Samuel 4:1-7; 1 Chronicles 15—16). The cover of the box was called the *mercy seat*. It reminded Israel of the mercy of God (Exodus 25:10-22). The ark of the covenant was first used by the Israelites in the Tabernacle in the wilderness. It was later kept in the Temple in Jerusalem. The ark of the covenant does not exist today.

***See* Ararat, cherub, covenant, flood, holy of holies, Jerusalem, mercy seat, tabernacle, Ten Commandments, veil**

ark of the covenant (ARHK uv thuh KUV-uh-nunt) *noun phrase:*

***See* ark, mercy seat**

Armageddon (AHR-muh-GED-un) *proper noun:*

Armageddon is the symbolic name given the final battle between God and evil (Revelation 16:16). God will win this battle and set up His kingdom.

Armageddon was the name of a large valley in northern Israel. The Bible usually calls this valley Jezreel. The Greek word for Jezreel is Esdraelon. The valley is located near the mountain of Megiddo. Armageddon in Hebrew means "mountain of Megiddo."

Judges 5:19; 2 Kings 9:27; 23:29

***See* eschatology, Israel, Jezreel, kingdom of God, Megiddo (map 4)**

Arminianism (ahr-MIN-ee-un-IZ-um) *proper noun:*

Arminianism is the doctrinal ideas developed from the teachings of James Arminius. It differs from Calvinism in certain important ways. For example, Arminianism believes that Jesus Christ died for all people. Thus anyone may be saved. It also teaches it is possible for Christians to lose their salvation and be lost.

***See* James Arminius, Calvinism, eternal security, freedom, lost, Protestant, Reformed tradition, salvation, Wesleyanism**

Arminius, James (ahr-MIN-ee-us, JAYMZ) *proper noun phrase:*

James Arminius is the name of a Dutch Protestant leader. He lived during the late 1500s. He opposed certain teachings of Calvinism.

***See* Arminianism, Calvinism, Protestant, Reformed tradition**

armor (AHR-mer) *noun:*

Armor was the covering once used to protect the soldier's body in battle. Armor was made of leather and metal. It usually included a helmet, a shield, and body covering.

God protects Christians against the attacks of the devil. The Bible calls this the armor of God.

1 Samuel 17:54; 2 Kings 3:21; Romans 13:12; 2 Corinthians 6:7; Ephesians 6:10-18; 1 Thessalonians 5:8-10; 1 Peter 5:8

***See* devil, Satan**

Articles of Faith (AHR-ti-kulz uv FAYTH) *proper noun phrase:*
Articles of Faith are short statements of Christian beliefs. Each article states one belief. For example, one article may state what Christians believe about Christ. Another article may state what Christians believe about the Scriptures.

Most denominations have listed their Articles of Faith. These articles tell what Christians in those denominations believe.

See **church, creed, denomination, doctrine, faith, manual**

Asa (AY-suh) *proper noun:*
Asa was the third king of Judah, the Southern Kingdom. He was the son of Abijah. He was king for 41 years. Asa was a righteous king. He showed his people how to worship the true God.

1 Kings 15:9-24; 2 Chronicles 14—16

See **Abijah, Asa (time line), Judah, righteous, worship**

Ascension (uh-SEN-shun) *proper noun:*
Ascension is the event when Jesus Christ returned to heaven. This happened after God raised Him from the dead. Now Jesus Christ reigns with His Father in heaven.

Ascension Day is the sixth Thursday after Easter on the Christian calendar.

Luke 24:50-51; Acts 1:9-10; 2:29-36

See **Easter, heaven, Jesus, resurrection**

Ashdod (ASH-dahd) *proper noun:*
Ashdod was one of five main cities of the Philistines. It was located near the Mediterranean Sea in the southwest part of Israel.

One time the Philistines defeated the Israelites. The Philistines brought the ark of the covenant to Ashdod. They put it in the temple of one of their gods. The people of Ashdod suffered a plague. Then they returned the ark to Israel. See 1 Samuel 5:1-12.

Joshua 11:22; 15:46-47; 2 Chronicles 26:6

See **ark, Ashdod (map 4), god, Israel, Mediterranean Sea, Philistine, plague, temple**

Asher (ASH-er) *proper noun:*

1. Asher was one of the 12 sons of Jacob. His descendants became one of the 12 tribes of the nation of Israel.

2. Asher was the name of the land occupied by the tribe of Asher.

Genesis 30:12-13; Joshua 19:24-31

See **Asher (map 3), Israel, Jacob, Old Testament, tribes of Israel**

Asherah (ASH-er-uh) *proper noun:*
Asherah was a false goddess of the people of Canaan. She was the mother of the god Baal. The people of Canaan believed that Asherah helped

make the crops grow. They also believed that she helped women to have many children.

Idols of Asherah were also called Asherah. The King James Version always translates the Hebrew word for Asherah *grove.*

Exodus 34:13; Judges 3:7; 1 Kings 16:29-33

See **Ashtaroth, Baal, Canaan, idol, idolatry, Ten Commandments**

Ashkelon (ASH-kuh-lahn) *proper noun:*

Ashkelon was one of five main cities of the Philistines. It was located near the Mediterranean Sea in the southwest part of Israel. Several of the Old Testament prophets made prophecies about Ashkelon.

Judges 1:18; 14:19; Jeremiah 25:17-20; 47:5-7; Amos 1:8; Zephaniah 2:4, 7; Zephaniah 9:3-5

See **Ashkelon (map 4), Israel, Mediterranean Sea, Philistine, prophecy, prophet**

Ashtaroth (ASH-tuh-rahth) *proper noun:*

Ashtaroth was a false goddess of the people of Canaan. She was a wife of the god Baal. Idols representing her were also called Ashtaroth. She was always represented as a naked female. The plural of Ashtaroth is Ashtareth.

See **Asherah, Baal, Canaan, idol, idolatry, Ten Commandments**

Asia Minor (AY-zhuh MIE-ner) *proper noun:*

Asia Minor is a peninsula in western Asia between the Mediterranean and Black seas. Today the country of Turkey is located in Asia Minor.

The apostle Paul visited Asia Minor on all three of his missionary trips. Three of the letters Paul wrote were sent to churches in Asia Minor. These letters, which are books in the New Testament, are Galatians, Ephesians, and Colossians.

See **Asia Minor (map 11), apostle, Colossians, Ephesians, Galatians, Mediterranean Sea, missionary, Paul**

Assemblies of God (uh-SEM-bleez uv GAHD) *proper noun phrase:*

The Assemblies of God is a Protestant, evangelical denomination. This church accepts the basic doctrines of the Christian faith. Its doctrines are found in its "Sixteen Fundamental Truths." It is best known for its special teaching about the Holy Spirit. It teaches that the proof of being baptized with the Holy Spirit is speaking with tongues. This is the first sign of the baptism, but not the only one. It also teaches that the gifts of the Spirit are very important.

See **Charismatic Movement, denomination, evangelical, fundamentalism, gift, Holy Spirit, Protestant, tongue**

assurance (uh-SHOOR-uns) *noun:*

Assurance is the certain knowledge of salvation. People may know that God has saved them. The Holy Spirit lets people know this. The Holy Spirit also helps people love God and others.

Romans 4:21-22; 8:14-17; Ephesians 2:4-10; 1 Thessalonians 1:4-8; Hebrews 10:22; 1 John 3:14-18; 4:13-21; 5:6-15

See **God, good works, Holy Spirit, salvation**

Assyria (uh-SEER-ee-uh) *proper noun:*

Assyria was a large nation in northern Mesopotamia. It was located to the north and east of Palestine. Its capital was Nineveh. Assyria was a very powerful nation. It ruled most of that part of the world between 1000 and 600 B.C.

Genesis 2:14; 2 Kings 15:19—20:6; 23:29; Ezra 6:22; Nehemiah 9:32

See **Assyria (map 6), Jonah, Mesopotamia, Nahum, Nineveh, Palestine**

astrology (uh-STRAHL-uh-jee) *noun:*

Astrology is a belief in the power of the stars and planets. Some people think that the stars and planets control their lives. They think astrology predicts the future.

The Bible does not approve of astrology. The Bible says that God made and controls the stars and planets. Therefore, people should trust God for their future. Jesus Christ frees people from false beliefs like astrology.

Galatians 4:8-9; Colossians 1:15-20

See **creation, fatalism, freedom, magi, principalities and powers**

ASV *abbreviation:*

ASV is an abbreviation for the *American Standard Version* of the Bible.

See **American Standard Version, Bible, translation, version**

Athaliah (ATH-uh-LIE-uh) *proper noun:*

Athaliah was a queen of Judah, the Southern Kingdom. She was the daughter of Ahab and Jezebel. She was the wife of Jehoram and the mother of Ahaziah. She was an evil ruler. She introduced the worship of Baal during the reigns of her husband and son. When Ahaziah was killed, Athaliah made herself the queen.

2 Kings 11:1-20; 2 Chronicles 22:10-12; 23:1-21

See **Ahab, Ahaziah, Athaliah (time line), Baal, god, Jehoram, Jezebel, Judah**

atheism (AY-thee-IZ-um) *noun:*

Atheism is the belief that there is no God. One who believes there is no God is an atheist.

Psalms 14:1; 53:1

See **agnostic, belief, God, skepticism, skeptic, theism**

atheist (AY-thee-ist) *noun:*

An atheist is a person who accepts atheism. An atheist believes that God does not exist.

See **atheism, skepticism, skeptic**

Athens (ATH-unz) *proper noun:*

Athens is the capital city of the country of Greece today. In Bible times,

Athens was an important city. It was a center of trade, culture, and religion for hundreds of years. The people of Athens worshiped a group of gods. They built many temples in which to worship these gods.

The apostle Paul visited Athens on two of his missionary trips. He preached a sermon in the Areopagus or Mars Hill in Athens.

Acts 17:15-16; 21-23; 18:1

See **Athens (map 11), Areopagus, apostle, god, Greece, idol, missionary, Paul, worship**

atonement (uh-TOHN-munt) *noun:*

Atonement is the act that provides or makes possible salvation and reconciliation. It is also a doctrine that explains how God forgives people their sins.

Sacrifices were the way atonement for sin was made in the Old Testament. The Day of Atonement or Yom Kippur (YOHM kuh-POOR) was a special, holy day for Israel. The people confessed their sins each year on this day. The priests offered animal sacrifices for them. This was a sign of the mercy and forgiveness of God.

Jesus Christ gave His life as the one true sacrifice for the sin of the world. His death is now the means of atonement.

Leviticus 16:15-16; Isaiah 38:17; Micah 7:19; Mark 10:45; John 3:16-17; Romans 3:26; 5:6-11; 2 Corinthians 5:21; Philippians 2:5-8; 1 Peter 1:18-19; 1 John 2:2

See **Christ, doctrine, expiation, forgiveness, Jesus, mercy seat, propitiation, ransom, reconciliation, sacrifice, salvation**

attribute (AT-ruh-byewt) *noun:*

An attribute is a quality of God. Attributes describe who God is and what He does. God has many attributes. For example, God is holy, loving, just, eternal, sovereign, omnipotent, omnipresent, and omniscient.

Exodus 3:14; 29:43; Leviticus 10:3; Psalms 19:9; 90:2; Isaiah 6:3; 11:5; 40:12-18; 66:1; Matthew 19:26; John 5:26; Acts 7:48-49; Romans 11:33-34; Hebrews 6:18; James 1:13, 17; Revelation 4:11; 16:5

See **eternal, God, holy, immortality, just, love, omnipotence, omnipresence, omniscience, sovereign**

Augustus (au-GUS-tus) *proper noun:*

Augustus was the name of a ruler of the empire of Rome. He was the ruler when Jesus was born. He was one of the Caesars.

Luke 2:1

See **Caesar, Jesus, Rome (map 11)**

authority of Scripture (uh-THOR-uh-tee uv SKRIP-cher) *noun phrase:*

The authority of Scripture is its right to be accepted and obeyed by people. Scripture tells about how God revealed himself in the past. It tells who He is and what He has done. It tells what He has done to redeem people. It tells how He wants people to live in relation to Him and other people. It tells people all that is necessary for salvation.

Christians believe that God inspired the writing of the Bible. Any doctrine that does not agree with Scripture should be rejected by Christians.

2 Timothy 3:14-17

See **Bible, canon, conservative Christianity, fundamentalism, inerrant, inspiration of the Bible, rule of faith and practice, salvation, Scripture, truth, word**

awakening (uh-WAY-kuh-ning) *noun:*

Awakening is the stopping of sleep. This can refer to being awakened from normal sleep (Psalm 139:18).

Awakening may refer to other types of *sleep*. For example, the new birth is the awakening from the sleep of sin (Isaiah 51:17; Romans 13:11-14). Resurrection is the awakening from the sleep of death (Psalm 17:15; Isaiah 26:19; Daniel 12:2; John 11:11).

The Great Awakening was a time of great revival in the history of the Church.

See **born again, church, death, eternal life, new birth, resurrection, revival**

Azariah (AZ-uh-RIE-uh) *proper noun:*

Azariah was a common name in Old Testament times. There are more than 20 men in the Bible with this name. The most important Azariah was king of Judah. He is better known as Uzziah.

See **Judah, Uzziah, Uzziah (time line)**

B b

Baal (BAY-ul or BAYL) *proper noun:*

Baal was the name of a false god worshiped by the people of Canaan. He was a male god.

The word *Baal* means lord. The most important part of Baal worship was immoral sex.

God warned the people of Israel to be faithful to Him. God said that He was their true Lord. But Israel often yielded to the temptation to worship Baal. Israel was punished for this sin.

Judges 2:11-15; 1 Kings 18:16-40; 2 Chronicles 33:1-20

See **adultery, Asherah, Canaan, fornication, idol, idolatry, immoral, temptation, Ten Commandments**

Baasha (BAY-uh-shuh) *proper noun:*

Baasha was the third king of Israel, the Northern Kingdom. He became king by killing Nadab. He ruled for 24 years. His son Elah became the next king.

1 Kings 15:27—16:6

See **Baasha (time line), Elah, Israel, Nadab**

Babel (BAY-bul or BAB-ul) *proper noun:*

Babel was another name for the city of Babylon (Genesis 10:10; 11:9). It was the place where a tall temple tower was built. It was known as the Tower of Babel or Tower of Babylon.

Babel means "gate of the gods." The temple tower was the attempt of people to reach God through their own works. The people began to speak many different languages here. Thus Babel refers to the divisions among the people caused by these different languages.

Genesis 11:1-9

See **Babylon, God, temple, tongue**

Babylon (BAB-uh-lun) *proper noun:*

Babylon was the capital city of a great kingdom of southern Mesopotamia. Its beautiful hanging gardens were one of the seven wonders of the ancient world.

Babylon was also the name of the powerful kingdom whose capital was Babylon. Babylon was also called Babylonia, and the people were called Babylonians. Nebuchadnezzar II (NEB-yew-kud-NEZ-er) was the greatest king of Babylon. He made Babylon the leading power in the Middle East after Assyria's fall. He led Babylon in destroying Jerusalem and its Temple in 586 B.C. Later Babylon was defeated by Persia in 539 B.C. (2 Kings 24:10—25:28; Daniel 1:1—5:31).

Babylon became a symbol of the strong and evil enemy of the people of God. Babylon reminded early Christians of the power of Satan in the world. His power was great but his final destruction was certain.

Some early Christians called Rome *Babylon* (1 Peter 5:13; Revelation 14:8; 18:2).

See **Assyria, Babel, Belshazzar, Chaldea, Darius, God, Jerusalem, Mesopotamia, Middle East, Nebuchadnezzar, Persia, Rome, Satan**

backslide (BAK-SLIED) *verb:*

To backslide means to turn from following Jesus Christ. Backsliding includes the choice of a person not to obey God. Backsliding may lead to apostasy. Christians who backslide may be lost. But backsliders who repent can once more become followers of Jesus Christ.

Jeremiah 3:22; 8:5; Matthew 24:10-12; Colossians 1:22-23; Hebrews 2:1-3

See **apostasy, Arminianism, Calvinism, disciple, eternal security, faith, obedience, predestination, Wesleyanism**

balm (BAHM or BAHLM) *noun:*

Balm was a medicine made from a certain bush or small tree. The bush or small tree grew in Gilead (GIL-ee-ud), a place in Palestine. This medicine was called the *balm of Gilead.* People believed the balm of Gilead could help heal wounds.

Sometimes Jesus is spoken of as the Balm of Gilead. This is a way of describing Jesus as the Healer. Jesus Christ heals people of the disease of sin. Jesus Christ also has the power to heal sick people.

Genesis 37:25; Jeremiah 46:11; 51:8

See **Gilead (map 7), healing, Jesus, Palestine**

baptism (BAP-tiz-um) *noun:*

Baptism is an important practice of the Christian faith that uses water. A person may be put under the water and quickly brought up again. This is called immersion. Or water may be sprinkled or poured on a person. The place in some churches where people are baptized is called a baptistry.

Baptism is a sacrament observed by most Christian churches. It is a sign and seal of saving grace. It is a symbol that God has made the sinner clean. Baptism is a public testimony that the person has received Christ as his Savior. In some countries, baptism means that now one belongs to the Christian community.

See **church, faith, grace, immersion, new birth, pouring, sacrament, salvation, sign, sprinkling, testimony**

baptism with the Holy Spirit (BAP-tiz-um with <u>th</u>uh HOH-lee SPIR-ut) *noun phrase:*

Baptism with the Holy Spirit is the way that entire sanctification happens. The Holy Spirit makes believers clean from original sin. God gives them this baptism by faith. It is also called entire sanctification and filled with the Spirit.

Matthew 3:11-12; Acts 1:1-5; 2:1-4, 32-47; 10:44-45; 15:8-9; Romans 5:1-5; 8:3-4. See also 1 Corinthians 12:13 and Titus 3:5-6

See **Charismatic Movement, Christian perfection, entire sanctification, holiness, original sin, Pentecostalism, perfect love, sanctification**

Baptist (BAP-tist)

1. *proper noun:* Baptist is the name of a certain group of Christian denominations. There are about 30 different Baptist denominations in Canada and the United States. The largest is the Southern Baptist Convention.

Members of Baptist denominations are called Baptists. Baptists may disagree among themselves on many aspects of Christian doctrine. For example, they hold a number of different views about election. But they do generally agree on these points.

a. They strongly believe in the authority of Scripture. The Bible is more important than any church tradition or government.

b. Baptists believe in religious freedom. They believe that people should be free to worship God as they pleases. The state should not take this freedom away.

c. Baptists believe that babies should not be baptized. Only adult believers should be baptized. Most Baptists baptize only by immersion.

d. Baptists believe that each local church should be free from outside control. Baptists do not submit to church governments that are above the local church. Ministers are ordained by local churches.

2. *proper adjective:* Baptist describes a person, belief, or practice of Baptists. It also identified John the Baptist as one who baptized.

See **Anabaptist, baptism, Christian, church, denomination, doctrine, immersion, John, polity**

barbarian (bahr-BAIR-ee-un) *noun:*

A barbarian was someone who did not speak Greek in New Testament times. Barbarians were people whose culture was not Greek or Roman.

Romans 1:14; 1 Corinthians 14:11; Colossians 3:11

See **Gentile, Greek, New Testament, Rome**

Barnabas (BAHR-nuh-bus) *proper noun:*

Barnabas was a member of the Early Christian Church. He and Paul were sent on a missionary trip to the Gentiles. He also went on a missionary trip with Mark.

Acts 4:36-37; 11:22-30; 13:1-3

See **Cyprus, Gentile, Mark, missionary, Paul**

Bartholomew (bahr-THAHL-uh-myew) *proper noun:*

Bartholomew was one of the 12 disciples of Jesus Christ. He was probably the same person as Nathanael (John 1:45-46).

Matthew 10:2-4

See **apostle, disciple, Nathanael**

bear false witness (BAIR FAWLS WIT-nes) *verb phrase:*

To bear false witness means to tell a lie about a person. Bearing false witness or testimony can harm other people. The Bible says that bearing false witness is wrong. One of the Ten Commandments is against bearing false witness.

Exodus 20:16; Deuteronomy 19:18; Proverbs 6:19

See **Bible, lie, Ten Commandments**

Beatitudes (bee-AT-uh-tewdz) *proper noun:*

The Beatitudes are some of the sayings of Jesus (Matthew 5:3-12; Luke 6:20-23). The word *beatitude* means being blessed or happy.

The Beatitudes describe the character of a Christian believer. They also describe the blessings and joys of the Christian life.

Other sayings in the Bible that give blessing may also be called beatitudes.

Psalm 1:1

See **bless, joy, Sermon on the Mount**

Beelzebub (bee-EL-zee-bub) *proper noun:*

Beelzebub is another name for Satan in the New Testament. Beelzebub was one of the false gods of the people of Palestine in Old Testament times.

2 Kings 1:2; Matthew 10:25; 12:24-27

See **demon, devil, idol, idolatry, New Testament, Old Testament, Palestine, Satan, tempt, temptation**

Beersheba (beer-SHEE-buh) *proper noun:*

Beersheba was a city in southern Palestine in the Negev desert. Abraham, Isaac, and Jacob all lived in Beersheba for a time. Later, it was a religious center during the Kingdom of Israel. The saying "from Dan to Beersheba" indicates the northern and southern limits of David's kingdom (Judges 20:1; 1 Samuel 3:20; 2 Samuel 3:10; 17:11; 24:2, 15; 1 Kings 4:25; 1 Chronicles 21:2).

Genesis 21:31-33; 22:19; 26:23-25, 32-33; 28:10; 46:1-5; 2 Kings 23:8

See Abraham, Beersheba (maps 3, 4, 7), David, Isaac, Israel, Jacob, Negev

beget (buh-GET or bee-GET) *verb:*

To beget means to produce a child. A parent begets a child.

Job 38:28; Psalm 2:7; Isaiah 45:10; Hebrews 1:5

See **genealogy**

belief (buh-LEEF or bee-LEEF) *noun:*

A belief is what a person considers to be true. It is knowledge based on faith.

The central Christian belief is that Jesus Christ is Lord. This belief is necessary for salvation.

John 3:16; 9:35; 11:27; Romans 4:3; Galatians 3:6; James 2:19

See **Christ, Christian, faith, Jesus, Lord, salvation**

believer (buh-LEEV-er or bee-LEEV-er) *noun:*
A believer is a person who trusts in Jesus for salvation. A believer accepts Jesus as the Savior of the world. A believer is a Christian.
Mark 16:16; John 3:15; 5:24; Romans 3:26; 1 John 5:1
See **born again, Christian, disciple, faith, salvation**

Belshazzar (bel-SHAZ-er) *proper noun:*
Belshazzar was a king of Babylon during the time of the Exile. He is known for receiving a handwritten message on a wall during a banquet. Daniel interpreted for Belshazzar what the meaning of the message. That night Belshazzar was killed (Daniel 5:1-30).
See **Babylon, Daniel, exile, interpretation**

Belteshazzar (BEL-tuh-SHAZ-er) *proper noun:*
Belteshazzar is the Babylonian name for Daniel (Daniel 1:7).
See **Babylon, Daniel, exile**

benediction (BEN-uh-DIK-shun) *noun:*
A benediction is a special kind of blessing. It is the blessing of God upon His people. Ministers of God speak words of blessing upon believers. The final prayer in a worship service is often called a benediction.
See **Beatitudes, bless, prayer**

Benjamin (BEN-juh-mun) *proper noun:*
1. Benjamin was the youngest of the 12 sons of Jacob. His descendants became one of the tribes of the nation of Israel.
2. Benjamin was the name of the land occupied by the tribe of Benjamin.
Genesis 35:16-18; Joshua 18:11-28
See **Benjamin (map 3), Israel, Jacob, tribes of Israel**

bereave (buh-REEV) *verb:*
To bereave means to take away something of value. The word *bereave* is most often used when a death happens. People are bereaved when some-one they love dies.
Genesis 27:45; 42:36; 43:14; Leviticus 26:22; Ezekiel 5:17; 36:12
See **death**

Bethany (BETH-uh-nee) *proper noun:*
Bethany was the name of a small town in Palestine. It was located near Jerusalem. It was the town where Lazarus, Mary, and Martha lived.
Mark 11:11; Luke 19:29; John 11:1
See **Bethany (map 8), Jerusalem, Lazarus, Martha, Mary, Palestine**

Bethel (BETH-ul) *proper noun:*
Bethel was a town north of Jerusalem. Abraham lived at Bethel for a time. There he built an altar and worshiped God (Genesis 12:6-9). Jacob had his dream of a ladder to heaven at Bethel (Genesis 28:10-19). The tabernacle

with the ark of the covenant was at Bethel for a long time (Judges 20:26-27). Bethel is mentioned many times in the Old Testament.

Genesis 13:3; 31:13; 35:1-8, 15-16; Joshua 7:2; Judges 1:22-23; 1 Samuel 7:15-16

See **Abraham, altar, ark of the covenant, Bethel (maps 3 and 4), Jacob, Jerusalem, tabernacle, worship**

Bethlehem (BETH-luh-hem) *proper noun:*

Bethlehem was a town about five miles south of Jerusalem. King David was from this town. Jesus was born in Bethlehem.

1 Samuel 16:1-13; Micah 5:2-4; Matthew 2:1-12; Luke 2:1-7

See **Bethlehem (map 7), David, Jerusalem (map 7), Jesus**

Bethsaida (beth-SAY-uh-duh) *proper noun:*

Bethsaida was a town on the northern shore of the Sea of Galilee. It was the home of Peter, Andrew, and Philip (John 1:44; 12:21). It was the place of Jesus' miracle of feeding the 5,000 (Luke 9:10).

Matthew 11:20-24; Mark 8:22-25

See **Andrew, Bethsaida (map 8), Galilee, Jesus, miracle, Peter, Philip**

betrayal (buh-TRAY-ul or bee-TRAY-ul) *noun:*

The betrayal was the act in which Judas turned Jesus over to His enemies. Judas betrayed Jesus with a kiss. Judas is sometimes called the betrayer.

Matthew 26:47-50; 27:3-10; John 18:1-9; 1 Corinthians 11:23

See **Christ, Jesus, Judas, kiss**

Bible (BIE-bul) *proper noun:*

The Bible is the holy book of Jews and Christians. The Bible of the Jews includes only the Old Testament. The Christian Bible includes both the Old and New Testaments. The Roman Catholic Bible contains the Old and New Testaments plus the Apocrypha.

The Bible contains books written by many different writers. It tells the story of how God worked with His people. It tells the story of salvation. Believers consider the Bible the inspired Word of God.

The Bible has been translated into about 2,000 different languages. There are also many English versions.

Acts 17:11; Romans 1:2

See **Apocrypha, Christian, inspiration, inspiration of the Bible, New Testament, Old Testament, Scripture, version, word**

biblical (BIB-li-kul) *adjective:*

Biblical describes a person, belief, or practice that is found in the Bible. For example, a biblical doctrine is one that is supported by Scripture.

See **Bible**

birthright (BERTH-RIET) *noun:*

A birthright was the special right the Hebrew people gave an oldest son. The birthright included several things. The oldest son received a special blessing from his father. That son inherited twice as much as his brothers. He also became the leader of his family after his father died.

Genesis 25:31-34; Exodus 22:29; Deuteronomy 21:17; 2 Chronicles 21:3

See **bless, firstborn, Hebrew, inheritance, right**

bishop (BISH-up) *noun:*

Bishop is a title for a church leader. The bishop was the pastor of a church in New Testament times. Bishops were sometimes called *elders*. Later, a bishop was a leader of a group of churches. Some denominations call their leaders *bishops*.

1 Timothy 3:1-19; Titus 1:7

See **church, clergy, elder, pastor**

blasphemy (BLAS-fuh-mee) *noun:*

Blasphemy means to speak evil of God. It shows that a person is an enemy of God. Blasphemy is an act or word by which a person denies that God is God.

Matthew 12:31; 26:65

See **curse, evil, God, holy, reverence, unpardonable sin**

bless (BLES) *verb:*

To bless means to praise someone. It also means to wish happiness for someone.

To bless God means to praise Him. To bless people may mean to make them happy. It may also mean to ask God to give His grace to them.

A blessing sometimes means a prayer before a meal. It praises and thanks God for the food. It also asks Him to give grace through the food.

A blessing may be what someone does that blesses another person. Someone who is blessed has received the grace of God.

Genesis 2:3; 12:3; Psalms 103:1; 104:1; Hebrews 6:14

See **birthright, Beatitudes, benediction, grace, praise**

blessing (BLES-ing) *noun:*

See **bless**

blood (BLUD) *noun:*

Blood is the red fluid that is necessary for life in the physical body. The blood of animals was part of Old Testament sacrifices.

Jesus Christ bled and died on the Cross. He gave His life and blood to save people from their sins. His blood makes salvation possible. The blood of Christ refers to His death by which people are saved.

Leviticus 17:11; Romans 3:23-25; Ephesians 1:7

See **atonement, Christ, Jesus, life, reconciliation, redemption, sacrifice, salvation, save**

blot out (BLAHT OUT) *verb:*

To blot out means to remove. To blot out sin is to remove sin or cleanse from sin.

Nehemiah 13:14; Psalm 51:1, 9; Jeremiah 18:33

See **cleanse, expiation, forgive, propitiation, sin**

Boaz (BOH-az) *proper noun:*

Boaz was the name of a man in the Old Testament. He married Ruth. Their son was the grandfather of David. Thus, Boaz was an ancestor of Jesus Christ.

Ruth 2—4

See **David, Ruth**

body (BAH-dee) *noun:*

A body is the form of a person. The physical body was created by God. It will become old and die (2 Corinthians 4:7—5:10). God will give Christians spiritual bodies at the resurrection.

A body may also be a group of people. Christians are the Body of Christ (1 Corinthians 12:12-31; Ephesians 4:4-13).

1 Corinthians 3:16-17; 6:15-20

See **Body of Christ, Christian, eternal life, human, person, resurrection, soul, spirit**

Body of Christ (BAH-dee uv KRIEST) *proper noun phrase:*

The Body of Christ is the Church. The Body of Christ includes the whole community of believers. Each Christian has a place to fill in the Body of Christ. The Spirit helps Christians work together as a unit. He helps them do the work of God in the world. Christ lives in the world today through His Church.

Romans 12:4-5; 1 Corinthians 12:27; Ephesians 4:12

See **believer, Christ, church, community, incarnation, Jesus, Lord, Spirit**

bondage (BAHN-dij) *noun:*

Bondage is slavery. People in bondage have lost their freedom.

The Old Testament says that Israel was often in bondage. The nations of Egypt, Assyria, and Babylon made slaves of the people of Israel. Then the Israelites could not do as they wished. They lost their freedom.

The New Testament tells us that sin makes people its slaves. Bondage to sin causes people to disobey God. Their bondage makes it easier to sin than to do right.

Legalism is another kind of bondage. Sin makes the law like a slave master.

Jesus Christ can make people free from bondage.

Exodus 6:9; Ezra 9:8; Jeremiah 34:10; Romans 7:8-21

See **Assyria, Babylon, exile, freedom, Israel, legalism, New Testament, Old Testament, sin, slave**

Book of Life (BOOK uv LIEF) *proper noun phrase:*

The Book of Life is a record in heaven. In this book, the names of the righteous are written (Psalm 69:28; Philippians 4:3; Revelation 22:19). It is sometimes called the Lamb's Book of Life. The Book of Life means eternal salvation for all people who are born again.

See also **Job 40:7; Psalm 40:7; Daniel 7:10; Malachi 3:16; Luke 10:20; Hebrews 12:23**

See **born again, eternal, heaven, Lamb of God, righteous, salvation**

born again (BOHRN uh-GEN)

1. *verb phrase:* To be born again means to become a Christian. To be born again is really to be born from above. This means that God, not man, causes this birth or new life to happen. God gives believers a new start. He gives them a spiritual or new birth. God frees people from their old lives of sin.

2. *adjective phrase:* Born again describes a person who is a Christian. Evangelical Christians believe that the new birth is necessary for salvation. Right ideas about Jesus Christ are not enough. God must change the lives of people. They must be born again.

John 3:3-8

See **believer, Christ, Christian, conversion, evangelical, faith, Jesus, new birth, regeneration, salvation**

Branch (BRANCH) *proper noun:*

Branch is a title for the Messiah. The Old Testament says that the Messiah will be a descendant of David. David was the son of Jesse. The family of Jesse was like a tree that had been cut down. The Messiah would be like a new branch of that tree. It would grow where the tree had been. The Messiah would give a new start to Israel (Isaiah 11:1-16).

Jesus said that He was like a vine that gave life to the branches. His disciples were like branches that grew from Him (John 15:1-8).

Isaiah 4:2; Jeremiah 23:5; 33:15; Zechariah 3:8; 6:12

See **Christ, David, disciple, Israel, Jesus, Messiah, prophesy**

bread (BRED) *noun:*

Bread is a kind of food. It is usually made with wheat flour. Bread in the Bible may also mean any kind of food.

Jesus Christ is called the *Bread of Life* (John 6:35-58). He is the Source of life and growth for Christians.

Genesis 18:6; Matthew 6:11

See **Christ, Christian, edify, growth in grace, leaven, life, unleavened bread**

breath of life (BRETH uv LIEF) *noun phrase:*

The breath of life was the gift of life from God to man at creation (Genesis 2:7). This gift made humans alive. Humans depend on God for life.

Genesis 1:30; 6:17

See **creation, human, life, soul, spirit**

bride (BRIED) *noun:*

A bride is a recently married woman.

God is referred to as the Bridegroom and Israel as the Bride in the Old Testament. Christ is referred to as the Bridegroom and the Church as the Bride in the New Testament. The Church is the Bride of Christ.

Genesis 34:12; 1 Samuel 18:22-27; Isaiah 62:1-5; Jeremiah 2:2; John 3:29; Revelation 19:7; 22:17

See **bridegroom, Christ, church, marriage, marriage supper of the Lamb**

bridegroom (BRIED-GREWM) *noun:*

A bridegroom is a recently married man. The New Testament calls Jesus a *bridegroom.* The Church is His Bride. Christ loves the Church and has a close relation with it.

Matthew 9:15; 25:1-10; Ephesians 5:25-57

See **bride, Christ, church, Jesus, marriage, marriage supper of the Lamb**

brimstone (BRIM-STOHN) *noun:*

Brimstone is a type of hot, melted rock. Brimstone was used for divine judgment. For example, the wicked cities of Sodom and Gomorrah were destroyed by brimstone.

Genesis 19:24-25; Isaiah 30:29-33; Revelation 21:5-8

See **divine, judgment, Sodom and Gomorrah**

brother (BRUH-<u>th</u>er) *noun:*

A brother is a male who has the same parents as another person. It also means a person who has the same ancestors, heritage, or purpose as others.

The New Testament teaches that all Christian believers are brothers of one another. Brother in the New Testament often refers to both male and female. God is the common Father of all believers. He gave them new life through Jesus Christ, His Son. Thus, Christians have been adopted into the family of God. They are heirs of the riches of God.

Jesus said that His disciples were His brothers.

See **adoption, believer, disciple, father, God, Jesus, New Testament**

Buddha (BEW-duh) *proper noun:*

See **Buddhism**

Buddhism (BEW-diz-um) *proper noun:*

Buddhism is a religion that arose in India in the 500s B.C. The founder of Buddhism was Gautama Buddha. Gautama (GOW-tuh-muh) was his family name. Buddha means "the Enlightened One." This means that he thought he had found the true meaning of life.

The Buddha taught how to be free from suffering in his "Four Noble Truths."

There are two main kinds of Buddhism: Mahayana (MAH-huh-YAH-nuh) and Theravada (THAIR-uh-VAH-duh). Buddhism has many followers, most of them in Eastern countries.

See **idol, idolatry, polytheism, religion**

burden (BER-dun) *noun:*

A burden is something heavy to carry. It can mean a task that is not easy to do. A burden may also be some form of oppression, punishment, debt, or guilt.

The guilt of sin is the burden that a sinner must carry. Christ can free a sinner from this burden.

A person may choose to carry or share the burden of another. The New Testament teaches that Christians should help one another with their problems. They share the burdens of another in this way. Thus, they follow the example of Christ.

Galatians 6:1-5

See **Christ, guilt, sin**

burning bush (BERN-ing BOOSH) *noun phrase:*

The burning bush was a bush Moses saw in the desert. It did not burn up. God spoke to Moses out of the bush.

Exodus 3:1-4; Acts 7:30

See **call, Egypt (map 2), Exodus, Israel, Moses, revelation, Yahweh**

C c

Caesar (SEE-zer) *proper noun:*

Caesar was the title of the ruler of Rome during the time of Jesus. A Caesar was a type of king.

Matthew 22:21-22; Luke 2:1; Acts 25:8, 11-12

See **Augustus, king, Rome, Rome (map 11)**

Caesarea (SES-us-REE-uh) *proper noun:*

Caesarea was the name of two cities in the New Testament. Both were named for a Caesar.

1. Caesarea in the Book of Acts was a seacoast city in western Palestine. The rulers from Rome lived there. Paul was put in prison there for preaching the gospel (Acts 23:23—27:1).

2. Caesarea Philippi (FIL-uh-pie) in the Gospels was a city in far northern Palestine. Peter made his great confession there that Jesus was the Christ (Matthew 16:13-20).

See **Acts, Caesar, Caesarea (map 8), Caesarea Philippi (map 8), confession, gospel, Palestine (map 8), Peter, Rome**

Cain (KAYN) *proper noun:*

Cain was the oldest son of Adam and Eve. He killed his brother Abel because he hated him.

Genesis 4:1-9

See **Abel, Adam, Eve**

Caleb (KAY-lub) *proper noun:*

Caleb was one of the 12 spies who were sent to explore Canaan. Caleb and Joshua believed that God would help the Israelites to capture the land. The others feared the giants there.

Numbers 13:2, 6, 30-33

See **Canaan, Israel, Joshua**

call (KAWL)

1. *noun:* A call is the invitation that God gives to people. The call of God to salvation is for everyone. But God has also chosen certain people to serve Him in special ways. This choice is a call or vocation, such as a call to preach or to be a missionary.

2. *verb:* To call means to invite someone. God calls all Christians to serve Him. He helps them do what He asks.

Mark 2:17; Luke 14:13; Romans 1:1, 6; 1 Corinthians 1:1-2, 9; Galatians 1:15; Ephesians 4:1, 7-13; Hebrews 9:15

See **ministry, mission, missionary, preach, salvation, service, vocation**

Calvary (KAL-vuh-ree) *proper noun:*

Calvary is the Latin name of the place where Jesus was crucified. Calvary is also called Golgotha. It was outside the wall of the city of Jerusalem. Jesus died on Calvary.

Matthew 27:33; Mark 15:22; Luke 23:33; John 19:17; Hebrews 13:12

***See* crucifixion, crucify, Golgotha, Jerusalem (map 10)**

Calvin, John (KAL-vin, JAHN) *proper noun phrase:*

John Calvin was a main leader of the Protestant Reformation. He lived in the city of Geneva, Switzerland.

***See* Calvinism, Protestant, Reformation**

Calvinism (KAL-vun-iz-um) *proper noun:*

Calvinism is the doctrinal ideas taught by the followers of John Calvin. A Calvinist is a person who accepts the beliefs of Calvinism. Calvinism does not follow the teachings of John Calvin in every detail. Calvinism differs from Arminianism in some important ways. For example, Calvinism believes that God chooses only certain people to become Christians. It also teaches that all those who are chosen will become and remain Christians.

***See* Arminianism, John Calvin, election, eternal security, propitiation, Protestant, Reformed tradition, sinning religion, sovereign, Wesleyanism**

Cana (KAY-nuh) *proper noun:*

Cana was a small village near Nazareth. Jesus did his first miracle there at a wedding (John 2:1-11). It was the home of Nathanael (John 21:2).

John 4:46-54

***See* Cana (map 8), Jesus, miracle, Nathanael, Nazareth, Nazareth (map 8)**

Canaan (KAY-nun) *proper noun:*

1. Canaan was a man in the Old Testament. He was a grandson of Noah. He was the father of the Canaanites.

2. Canaan is the part of Palestine west of the Jordan River. It was the land promised by God to Abraham and his descendants.

Genesis 9:20-27; 10:6; 12:5-6; 24:3, 37; Joshua 3:10

***See* Canaan (map 3), Canaanite, Noah, Old Testament, Palestine**

Canaanite (KAY-nuh-niet) *proper noun:*

A Canaanite was a person who lived in the land of Canaan. The Canaanites were descendants of Canaan, a grandson of Noah. The Israelites were not Canaanites.

There were many different tribes of Canaanites. They included the Jebusites, Hivites, Hittites, and Perizzites. Sometimes the Bible refers to the Canaanites as Amorites.

Genesis 10:5-19; Joshua 10:1-43; 24:11; 1 Samuel 7:14; 1 Kings 9:20-21

***See* Canaan, Hittites, Hivites, Israel, Israelites, Jebusites, Noah, Perizzites**

canon (KAN-un) *noun:*

Canon was the guide used for deciding which books belonged in the Bible. It also means the list of all the books of the Bible. The word *canon* comes from Hebrew and Greek words that mean "a measure" or "list."

The Church agrees that God inspired the Scriptures. The authority of Scripture is based on this inspiration. The canon includes those books that the Church believes God inspired.

The Protestant canon includes 66 books. The Old Testament of Protestants includes the same books as the Hebrew canon. The Old Testament of Roman Catholics includes also the books of the Apocrypha. All Christian Bibles contain the same New Testament books.

See **Apocrypha, authority of Scripture, Bible, inspiration, inspiration of the Bible, New Testament, Old Testament, Protestant, Roman Catholic**

canonical (kuh-NAH-ni-kul) *adjective:*

Canonical describes something that is related to the Bible. Canonical usually refers to a book of the Bible. It may also refer to a truth that the Bible teaches.

See **Bible, canon, truth**

Canticles (KAN-ti-kulz) *proper noun:*

See **Song of Solomon**

Capernaum (kuh-PER-nee-um) *proper noun:*

Capernaum was a town located on the northern shore of the Sea of Galilee. It was the center of Jesus' ministry in the region of Galilee (Matthew 4:13; Mark 2:1). Jesus did many miracles in Capernaum. Matthew was from Capernaum (Matthew 9:1, 9-13).

Matthew 8:5-13; 11:20-24; Mark 2:1-12; Luke 4:31-41; 10:13-16

See **Capernaum (map 8), Galilee, Jesus, Matthew, ministry, miracle**

captivity (kap-TIV-uh-tee) *noun:*

See **exile**

Carmel (KAHR-mul) *proper noun:*

Carmel is a mountain range in northern Israel near the Mediterranean Sea. On Mount Carmel, the prophet Elijah had a contest with the prophets of Baal (1 Kings 18:16-40).

See **Baal, Carmel (map 4), Elijah, Mediterranean Sea**

carnal (KAHR-nul) *adjective:*

The word *carnal* comes from a Greek word that means "of the flesh." God made the human body. Thus, the human body is not sinful by itself. But the word *flesh* is used sometimes in the New Testament to mean people's fallen nature. This fallen nature is opposed to God. This is the carnal, fleshly, or sinful nature.

The Bible calls a person carnal who resists God's way. Such persons seek to have their own way. This carnal nature makes it easy for sinners to disobey God. The carnal nature is also called carnality. But Christians also feel the influence of the carnal mind. The carnal nature or carnality is cleansed when Christians are entirely sanctified.

Romans 7:14; 8:6; 15:27; 1 Corinthians 9:11; 2 Corinthians 10:4; Hebrews 7:16

See **depravity, entire sanctification, fall, flesh, indwelling sin, mind, nature, original sin, sanctification, sin, sinful nature**

carnality (kahr-NAL-uh-tee) *noun:*

See **carnal, mind, nature**

catechism (KAT-uh-KIZ-um) *noun:*

A catechism is a special way of teaching the doctrines of the Christian faith. It is usually done in the form of questions and answers. A catechism is often used to prepare children for confirmation.

See **Christian, church, confirmation, denomination, doctrine, faith**

catholic (KATH-uh-lik) *adjective:*

Catholic describes something that is general or universal. Catholic refers to the entire Christian Church. The catholic Church is the Church in all places. It includes all people who say Jesus is Lord. A Roman Catholic is a person who belongs to the Roman Catholic church.

Ephesians 4:4-6

See **Body of Christ, Catholicism, church, Roman Catholic**

Catholicism (kuh-THAHL-uh-SIZ-um) *proper noun:*

Catholicism refers to the Roman Catholic church. It includes the doctrine, practices, and system of Catholic Christianity. This church is sometimes known as Roman Catholicism.

See **catholic, doctrine, Roman Catholic**

celebrate (SEL-uh-brayt) *verb:*

To celebrate is to honor a special day or event. For example, the people of Israel praised God by having festivals. Believers celebrate by praising God and rejoicing.

Christians honor the death of Christ by celebrating Holy Communion.

Exodus 10:9; 23:14; Leviticus 23:32, 39, 41; Joshua 5:10; Psalms 145:7; 148:1-14; Matthew 26:18; 1 Corinthians 11:17-26

See **festival, Holy Communion, Israel, Passover, praise, worship**

centurion (sen-CHOOR-ee-un or sen-TOOR-ee-un) *noun:*

A centurion was a leader in the army of Rome. He was in charge of 100 soldiers.

The Synoptic Gospels tell about a centurion who saw Jesus die on the Cross. This centurion believed that Jesus was the Son of God.

Matthew 8:5-13; 27:54; Mark 15:39; Luke 7:1-10; 23:47; Acts 10:1-48; 27:31

See **cross, Rome, Synoptic Gospels**

Cephas (SEE-fus) *proper noun:*

Cephas in Aramaic means "rock" or "stone." Jesus gave this name to one of His disciples. Cephas in Greek is Petra, which is the better-known name of the disciple Peter.

Matthew 16:13-18; John 1:40-42; 1 Corinthians 1:12; Galatians 1:18; 2:6-14

See **Aramaic, disciple, Jesus, Peter**

ceremony (SAIR-uh-moh-nee) *noun:*

A ceremony is a celebration of a religious or other special event. A ceremony follows a regular form or order. The Passover festival is an important ceremony for Jews. The Lord's Supper is an important ceremony for Christians.

Exodus 12:25-26; 13:5; Numbers 9:3; Hebrews 9:10, 13, 21; 13:9

See **celebrate, festival, liturgy, ritual, sacrifice**

Chaldea (kal-DEE-uh) *proper noun:*

Chaldea was a country that was a part of Babylon in southern Mesopotamia. Often Chaldea and Babylon were referred to as the same country. Another name for Chaldea was Chaldees. The people were called Chaldeans.

Abraham lived in the city of Ur in Chaldea. He left Ur to follow God's command to go to Canaan.

Genesis 11:28, 31; 15:7; Ezra 5:12; Job 1:17; Isaiah 50; Ezekiel 23:14-17; Acts 7:4

See **Abraham, Babylon, Babylonia (maps 1, 6), Canaan, Mesopotamia, Ur (map 1, 6)**

character (KAIR-ik-ter) *noun:*

Character is the usual way a person is and acts. It is the moral quality of a person. The character of a person may be good or bad. For example, *faithful* describes the character of Abraham.

A character is a person in a story. For example, Abraham is the main character in Genesis 12—25.

Genesis 15:1-6; John 8:39-59; Romans 4:1-25; Galatians 3:6-29; Hebrews 11:8-10

See **Abraham, attribute, faithful, morality, nature, person**

chariot (CHAIR-ee-ut) *noun:*

A chariot was a kind of cart for carrying people or things. It usually had two wheels, and it was pulled by horses.

Chariots in Bible times were often used in war. The Hebrew prophets warned their people not to trust in chariots. This meant that people should not trust in their own military power (Isaiah 31:1). Sometimes *chariots* refer to the power of God to defend His people (2 Kings 6:15-19; Isaiah 66:15-16).

2 Kings 2:11; Acts 8:26-31, 38

See **Hebrew, prophet**

charismatic (KAIR-iz-MAT-ik)

1. *adjective:* Charismatic describes someone or something as gifted, especially by the Holy Spirit. For example, the judges in the Old Testament

were charismatic leaders. The word *charismatic* is from the Greek word that means "gift."

2. *noun:* A charismatic is someone who is a part of the Charismatic Movement.

See **Charismatic Movement, gift, Holy Spirit, judge**

Charismatic Movement (KAIR-iz-MAT-ik MEWV-munt) *proper noun phrase:*

The Charismatic Movement is a religious movement that began in the 1950s. The Charismatic Movement began in the United States in the older denominations. It began as a revival of the gifts of the Spirit in these denominations. The Charismatic Movement stresses baptism *in* the Holy Spirit for believers. It teaches that this is the beginning of the Spirit-filled life. This baptism in the Spirit gives power for witness and ministry.

The Charismatic Movement greatly stresses the gift of speaking in tongues or glossolalia. Many say this is the sign that the Christian is filled with the Holy Spirit. The Charismatic Movement claims that speaking in tongues is a way of speaking to God. People who speak in tongues speak to God in a language they do not know. Such people say that the Holy Spirit gives the language. Someone else must explain or interpret what is being said.

Charismatics especially practice speaking in tongues or glossolalia in times of prayer. They believe it is a form of praise to God. But they also stress other gifts of the Spirit such as healing and prophecy.

Some members of the Charismatic Movement do not stress speaking in tongues. They see it as only one sign of the baptism with the Holy Spirit.

The Charismatic Movement is sometimes called Neo-Pentecostalism or Charismatic Renewal. Pentecostal denominations are part of the Charismatic Movement.

See **baptism with the Holy Spirit, gift, glossolalia, Holy Spirit, Pentecostalism, praise, prayer, revival, tongue**

charity (CHAIR-uh-tee) *noun:*

Charity comes from a Latin word that means "love." The King James Version of the Bible uses *charity* for *love*. Today charity means sharing possessions with someone who is in need.

1 Corinthians 13:1-3

See **agape, Bible, compassion, compassionate ministries, King James Version, love, version**

cherub (CHAIR-ub) *noun:*

A cherub is a kind of angel. (Cherubim is the plural form of cherub.) Cherubim are often special messengers of God. Images of cherubim were placed at the ends of the ark of the covenant.

Genesis 3:24; Exodus 25:10-22; 26:1; Numbers 7:89; 2 Samuel 22:11; Psalms 18:10; 80:1; Ezekiel 10:1-18

See **angel, ark, covenant, mercy seat, seraph**

cherubim (CHAIR-uh-bim) *plural noun:*

See **cherub**

chief priest (CHEEF PREEST) *noun phrase:*

See **high priest**

chief publican (CHEEF PUB-li-kun) *noun phrase:*

See **publican, Zacchaeus**

child of God (CHIELD uv GAHD) *noun phrase:*

Every person is a child of God because God created all people. But sin has separated people from their heavenly Father. Sin makes them the children of Satan. Sinners must repent of their sins. They must be born again through the Spirit of God. Then they are adopted into the family of God. They become His children in a special way.

Exodus 4:22; Isaiah 64:8; Hosea 1:10; Matthew 3:17; 5:9; Luke 3:38; Acts 17:28; Romans 9:26; Galatians 3:26; 1 John 3:1-3

See **adoption, creation, new birth, Satan, sin, Spirit**

children of Israel (CHIL-drun uv IZ-ree-ul) *noun phrase:*

The children of Israel are the descendants of Jacob. God changed the name of Jacob to Israel. So his children were called the people of Israel or Israelites. They were called the Jews after the Exile.

Genesis 32:28; 49:1-28; Exodus 12:40-42; Joshua 13:7—14:3; 1 Kings 12:16-24

See **exile, Israel, Jacob, Jew**

Chinnereth (KIN-uh-rith) *proper noun:*

See **Galilee**

Christ (KRIEST) *proper noun:*

Christ comes from the Greek word that means "Messiah." In Hebrew, Messiah means "the Anointed One." Christians believe that Jesus is the Christ. Thus He is often called Jesus Christ.

Matthew 16:16, 20-21; Luke 4:16-20; 9:18-20; John 1:40-41; Acts 2:36; 9:22; 2 Corinthians 5:16-21

See **anoint, Christian, Jesus, Messiah**

Christ Jesus (KRIEST JEE-zus) *proper noun:*

See **Jesus Christ**

Christian (KRIS-chun)

1. *proper noun:* A Christian is a person who has received Jesus Christ as Savior and Lord. Evangelicals believe that a person becomes a Christian only by being born again. Christian may mean a person who just accepts Christianity. Such a person might not be born again.

2. *proper adjective:* Christian describes someone or something related to Jesus Christ or Christianity. For example, a Christian believer is someone

who trusts Jesus as his Savior. A Christian doctrine is a belief accepted by Christians.

Acts 11:26; 26:28; 1 Peter 4:16

See **born again, Christ, Christianity, disciple, doctrine, evangelical, Lord, Savior**

Christian perfection (KRIS-chun per-FEK-shun) *noun phrase:*

Christian perfection is a term used in the Holiness Movement for entire sanctification. It means to be made perfect in love toward God and people. Christian perfection is a work of God's grace in the believer.

The experience of entire sanctification makes it possible for Christians to please God. God helps them to do His will. He makes it possible for them to obey the Great Commandment. They can love God completely, and they can love other people as themselves. It is only in this way that Christians can be called perfect.

Christian perfection is not total perfection. Only God is perfect in this way. It is not the perfection of angels. It is not the perfection man and woman had before the Fall, nor human perfection. Christians still make mistakes. They can still fall into sin. But they can be restored if they will turn to God quickly for forgiveness. Christian perfection allows for growth in grace.

Matthew 5:43-48; 22:37-40; Romans 12:9-21; Philippians 2:5-11; 3:10-15; Hebrews 6:1

See **angel, entire sanctification, fall, Great Commandment, growth in grace, holiness, perfect love, perfection, sin**

Christian Restorationism (KRIS-chun RES-tuh-RAY-shun-iz-um) *proper noun phrase:*

Christian Restorationism is an effort to return Christianity to what it was in New Testament times.

Christian Restorationism is a religious movement that began in America early in the 1800s. Thomas and Alexander Campbell were important in the beginning of Restorationism. The leaders of Christian Restorationism wanted Christians to follow the example of the Early Church. They believed that differences among denominations were made by humans. So they rejected all creeds. They said that creeds had divided the church. They said that Christians should base their beliefs on the New Testament.

A number of churches grew out of Christian Restorationism. Two of these are the Disciples of Christ and the Church of Christ. Another one is the Church of God based in Anderson, Indiana (U.S.A.). This is a Wesleyan church. These groups do not think of themselves as denominations.

See **Christianity, creed, denomination, New Testament, Protestant**

Christianity (KRIS-chee-AN-uh-tee) *proper noun:*

Christianity is the religion based on the teachings of Jesus Christ and His followers. One central teaching of Christianity is that Jesus Christ is the Son of God. He alone is the Lord and Savior of the world.

Christianity includes four main groups. These are the Roman Catholic, Eastern Orthodox, Anglican, and Protestant churches.

See **Anglican, Christ, Christian, church, Eastern Orthodox, Lord, Protestant, Roman Catholic, Savior, Son of God**

Christmas (KRIS-mus) *proper noun:*

Christmas is the day that celebrates the birth of Christ. The term Christmas means "Mass of Christ." Protestants and Roman Catholics celebrate Christmas on December 25.

Matthew 1—2; Luke 1—2; Galatians 4:4

See **Advent, Bethlehem, Christ, magi, Mass, Protestant, Roman Catholic, Virgin Birth, wise men**

Christology (kris-TAHL-uh-jee) *proper noun:*

Christology is the doctrine about the person of Jesus Christ. It explains who He is in relation to God and humans. Christians believe that Christ is fully God and fully human.

See **Christ, God, Holy Spirit, Immanuel, Incarnation, Jesus, Lord, Messiah, Son of God, Son of Man, Trinity, Virgin Birth**

Chronicles (KRAH-ni-kulz) *proper noun:*

First and Second Chronicles are books in the Old Testament. They are two of the history books. They tell the story of the kings of united Israel. They also tell the story of the kings of the Southern Kingdom of Judah. King David, King Solomon, and the story of the building of the Temple are very important in Chronicles.

See **Bible, David, Israel, Judah, 1 and 2 Kings, Old Testament, Solomon, temple**

church (CHERCH) *noun:*

The word *church* comes from an old English word that means "belonging to the Lord." The Greek word for church means "the people called together." The people who worship God together in the name of Christ are the Church.

The Church is the community of those who believe that Jesus is Lord. They have trusted Him for salvation. The Church was called into existence by Christ. He is its Lord. He builds the Church. The Church is the people of God who are doing His work in the world.

Protestants believe that the Church exists wherever the gospel is preached. The Church exists also wherever the sacraments are correctly celebrated.

The word *church* is used in a number of other ways. Church is the name given to a place where Christians gather to worship. Thus church may refer to a building. Church sometimes means an organized community of Christian believers. Thus church may refer to a Christian denomination or local congregation.

The New Testament describes the Church in many important ways. The

Church is the Body of Christ. It is the new or true Israel of God. It is the family of God. It is the Bride of Christ. It is the temple of the Holy Spirit.

Matthew 16:18; 18:15-17, 20; 26:31; Luke 12:32; John 10:16; Acts 2:43-47; Romans 12:1-21; 1 Corinthians 3:9-17; 9:7; 12:13; 16:19; 2 Corinthians 1:1-2; Ephesians 4:1; 5:24, 27; Colossians 1:24-29; 1 Peter 2:5-8

***See* apostle, believers, Body of Christ, Bride of Christ, catholic, Christ, Christian, community, denomination, family of God, Greek, holy, Israel, Jesus, Lord, New Testament, Protestant, salvation, temple, worship**

church growth (CHERCH GROHTH) *noun phrase:*

Church growth means the growth of churches. Church growth also means a group of ideas about how to help the church grow.

Many denominations emphasize church growth.

Acts 2:46-47; 8:1-40; 10:1-48; 13:48-52

***See* Acts, church, church plant, denomination, edification, Pentecost**

Church of Christ (CHERCH uv KRIEST) *proper noun phrase:*

***See* Christian Restorationism**

Church of England (CHERCH uv ING-glund) *proper noun phrase:*

***See* Anglican, episcopal**

Church of God (CHERCH uv GAHD) *proper noun phrase:*

The Church of God is the name of two Protestant denominations. The Church of God (Anderson) has it headquarters located in Anderson, Indiana. It is a Wesleyan denomination. The Church of God (Cleveland) has its headquarters in Cleveland, Tennessee. It is a Pentecostal denomination.

***See* Christian Restorationism, denomination, Pentecostalism, Protestant, Wesleyanism**

Church of Jesus Christ of Latter Day Saints (CHERCH uv JEE-zus KRIEST uv LAT-er DAY SAYNTS) *proper noun phrase:*

***See* Mormon**

Church of the Nazarene (CHERCH uv thuh NAZ-uh-reen) *proper noun phrase:*

The Church of the Nazarene is a Protestant denomination. It arose from the 19th-century Holiness Movement in the U.S.A. Three small Holiness denominations united to form the Church of the Nazarene. One group from the East in the United States and another group from the West united in 1907. A group from the South united with the larger group in 1908. This happened at Pilot Point, Texas. Phineas Bresee was a major leader. Other Holiness groups have united with the Church of the Nazarene since then. Today, the international headquarters are located in Kansas City, Missouri.

The Church of the Nazarene bases its theology on the Bible and the rich history of Christian doctrine. The church names John Wesley of England as the main source for the doctrine of entire sanctification. The Holiness Movement in America also shaped the Church of the Nazarene.

Members of the Church of the Nazarene believe that God is Triune. They believe in the deity of Christ. They teach that the Old and New Testaments are inspired by God. They believe that the Church is the Body of Christ. They believe that Christ will return to fulfill His kingdom.

Nazarenes believe that Christ forgives the sinner who repents and the person is born again. The person's sins are forgiven and that person becomes a new creation. Nazarenes believe that Christians should love God completely. Jesus Christ makes this possible. This is why the doctrine of entire sanctification is important for them. The members believe that all Christians should be sanctified completely. Jesus Christ sanctifies the person who wants to love God completely. This is called entire sanctification. The Holy Spirit help Christians live a holy life.

Nazarenes believe that Christians should love their neighbors as themselves. They teach that Christians should work for justice in the world. Members of this denomination support missionaries and efforts to evangelize the world. Nazarenes believe that Christians should do deeds of mercy to others. They teach that members should accept high moral standards that agree with God's will

See **Body of Christ, born again, compassion, compassionate ministries, deity, denomination, entire sanctification, evangelize, holiness, Holiness Movement, inspiration of the Bible, justice, mercy, new birth, Protestant, repent, repentance, sanctify, theology, trinity, triune, Wesley, Wesleyanism**

Churches of Christ in Christian Union (CHERCH-iz uv KRIEST in KRIS-chun YEW-yun) *proper noun phrase:*

The Churches of Christ in Christian Union is a Protestant denomination. The Churches of Christ in Christian Union are a part of the Wesleyan tradition. The denomination gives special importance to missionary work.

The Churches of Christ in Christian Union was started in 1909. The main offices are located in Circleville, Ohio.

See **denomination, missionary, Protestant, Wesleyanism, tradition**

church plant (CHERCH PLANT) *noun phrase:*

A church plant is an effort to start a new Christian congregation. A minister or layperson who starts a new congregation is called a church planter.

The apostle Paul was a church planter. He started several churches in Asia Minor and Macedonia, such at Ephesus, Philippi, Corinth, and Thessalonica.

See **Asia Minor, church, church growth, congregation, Corinth, Ephesus, Macedonia, Map 11, minister, Philippi, Thessalonica**

circumcise (SER-kum-siez) *verb:*

To circumcise means to cut off the loose skin of the penis. The Hebrew people circumcised their baby boys as a religious ritual. This act was a sign that they belonged to God.

Genesis 17:10-14; Deuteronomy 30:6; Jeremiah 9:25-26; Acts 7:8; 15:1-13; Romans 4:11; Galatians 5:2-3; 6:15

See **circumcision, covenant, ritual, sign**

circumcision (SER-kum-SI-zhun) *noun:*

Circumcision is the act of circumcising. It had a special religious meaning in the Bible. Circumcision was the sign of the covenant between God and the descendants of Abraham. It showed that they belonged to God.

The circumcision sometimes means the Jews, who were circumcised. Their circumcision set them apart from the Gentiles, who were not circumcised.

The Bible also uses the word *circumcision* to mean a spiritual act. The circumcision of the heart is an act done by God. He removes the nature that makes it easy for the people to disobey Him. God does this so they can obey Him and love him completely.

Genesis 17:9-14; Deuteronomy 10:12-16; 30:6-8; Jeremiah 9:23-26; Acts 7:51-53; Romans 2:25-29; 4:9-12; Galatians 2:3-10; 5:1-12

***See* Abraham, circumcise, covenant, depravity, Gentile, Jew, nature**

cleanse (KLENZ) *verb:*

The word *cleanse* means to make clean or pure. The Bible uses the word *cleanse* in a number of ways.

Physical cleansing washes away all kinds of dirt (Leviticus 14:33-57; Matthew 6:17; 15:1-20; 1 Peter 3:21).

Another kind of cleansing happens in religious ceremonies. This kind of cleansing makes something fit to be used by God. For example, the priests in the Old Testament cleansed the Temple by removing idols (2 Chronicles 29:15-19).

Spiritual cleansing is forgiveness of sin by God. God cleanses sinners from the guilt of sin when they receive His forgiveness (1 John 1:9). Wesleyanism believes that God also cleanses Christians from the carnal nature in entire sanctification.

***See* carnal, ceremony, entire sanctification, forgiveness, guilt, idol, nature, priests, pure, regeneration, ritual, sin, unclean, Wesleyanism**

clergy (KLER-jee) *noun:*

Clergy means those who have been ordained for special religious service. Clergy refers to ministers, priests, and rabbis. The Christian clergy includes pastors, evangelists, some missionaries, and some teachers of religion. Clergy are special ministers who help equip the entire Body of Believers for service.

The word *clergy* in Greek means "called." Most clergy believe that they have been called by God to their special ministry.

Isaiah 61:1-7; Luke 3:23; 2 Corinthians 3:3; 5:18; 6:3; Galatians 2:8; Ephesians 4:11-12; 2 Timothy 4:5

***See* call, deacon, evangelist, laity, minister, ministry, missionary, ordain, pastor, preach, priest, rabbi, service**

Colosse (kuh-LAH-see) *proper noun:*

Colosse was a town in Asia Minor in New Testament times. A church there was started by a fellow worker of Paul named Epaphras (Colossians 1:7; 4:12).

See **Asia Minor, Colosse (map 11), Epaphras, Paul**

Colossians (kuh-LAHSH-unz) *proper noun:*

1. The Colossians were people who lived in the city of Colosse. The apostle Paul wrote a letter to the Christian converts in that city.

2. Colossians is the name of a book in the New Testament. It is one of the epistles.

Colossians was written by Paul to the Christians at Colosse. The letter gives the advice of Paul to correct certain problems in the church. False teachers had taught that Christ was not the only Savior. They held that people also had to worship angels and follow certain legalistic rituals.

See **angel, apostle, Asia Minor (map 11), church, Colosse (map 11), convert, epistle, legalism, New Testament, Paul, ritual, Savior**

Comforter (KUM-fer-ter) *proper noun:*

The Comforter is a title given to the Holy Spirit. The Bible uses the word *Comforter* and *advocate* for the Greek word translated *paraclete.* Jesus is called a Paraclete (1 John 2:1-2). Jesus also calls the Holy Spirit *another Comforter.*

The Holy Spirit continues the work that Jesus began while He was on earth. He helps Christians know who Jesus is. The Holy Spirit helps believers. He comforts and encourages them.

John 14:16, 26: 15:26; 16:7-11

See **advocate, conviction, Holy Spirit, Jesus, Paraclete**

commandment (kuh-MAND-munt) *noun:*

A commandment is a statement of the will of God. It tells the way that God wants His people to live. The Ten Commandments are the most important statements of the will of God in the Bible. Jesus commanded His disciples to love God completely. He commanded them to love their neighbors also. This is called the Great Commandment.

Exodus 20:1-7; Leviticus 19:4-37; Matthew 22:34-40; John 15:12-17; Romans 13:8-10; 1 John 2:3-11; 3:23-24

See covenant, Great Commandment, law, love, Ten Commandments, Torah, will

communion (kuh-MYEWN-yun) *noun:*

See **Eucharist, Holy Communion, koinonia, Lord's Supper**

community (kuh-MYEW-nuh-tee) *noun:*

A community is a group of people who share something in common. For example, people in a church may be called a Christian community. They share a common faith in Jesus Christ as Lord. They also have the same basic beliefs about God. Religious orders are sometimes called communities.

See **Christ, church, faith, Jesus, koinonia, Lord, religious**

Community of Christ (kuh-MYEW-nuh-tee uv KRIEST) *proper noun phrase:*

See **Mormon**

compassion (kum-PA-shun) *noun:*

Compassion is partly an emotion caused by love. But compassion is more than this. People feel sorry for others with needs. Compassion involves *feeling with* another person. A person with compassion shares in the suffering of hurting people.

The New Testament says that Jesus felt *compassion* for people. He hurt inside when He saw the pain of others. This feeling led Jesus to help people.

Compassion also means acting in the best interests of a needy person. Real compassion requires us to do something to relieve suffering.

Acts of compassion usually involve meeting the physical needs of people. Physical needs may include health, clothing, housing, education, and jobs. We may show compassion by giving money to provide food and clothing for needy people. Compassion may mean providing medical help to sick people. It may mean teaching people how to read and write. It may involve training people without work in new skills.

Compassion may also involve meeting the spiritual needs of people. Sometimes churches neglect people for various reasons. Sometimes churches neglect people because they are of a different race. At times, it is because people are very poor. Or it may be because they live in a distant land. It may be because they live in a dangerous neighborhood. It may be because the people are very sinful. Christian compassion requires us to help everyone we can in every way we can.

In summary, compassion is a love for mercy and justice.

Deuteronomy 30:3; 2 Chronicles 28:15; Psalm 78:38; Matthew 15:32; Luke 10:30-37

See **compassionate ministry, justice, love, mercy, ministry, service, suffering**

compassionate ministry (kum-PA-shuh-nut MIN-uh-stree) *noun phrase:*

Compassionate ministry is the service Christians offer because they have compassion. Compassionate ministry can be done in many ways. Some examples are feeding the hungry, helping homeless people, finding housing, giving medical care, and so on. Compassionate ministry is one way the Church expresses the gospel of Christ.

See **compassion, gospel, ministry, service**

conceit (kun-SEET) *noun:*

Conceit is having too high an opinion of oneself. Conceit is sinful pride.

Jeremiah 48:29; Romans 11:20, 25; 12:3, 16; Galatians 6:1-5; Philippians 2:1-4

See **pride, sin, vanity**

concubine (KAHN-kyew-bien) *noun:*

A concubine is a woman married to a man. But she is not a wife in the full sense. She does not have the legal rights of a wife. Concubines were common in Old Testament times. They helped make sure men would have sons.

Genesis 16:1-6; Deuteronomy 21:10-14; 1 Kings 11:1-8

See **marriage, right**

condemn (kun-DEM) *verb:*

Condemn means to judge an act or attitude as wrong. God condemns evil because it is wrong. He is fair and just when He condemns evil and sin.

Sometimes people condemn other people by saying false things about them. This is wrong. The Bible teaches that people should not condemn other people in this way. Only God is able to judge with justice.

Deuteronomy 25:1-3; Job 10:2; Proverbs 12:2; Matthew 12:7, 41-42; Mark 10:33; John 3:17; Romans 8:1-4; 14:1-23; James 5:6; 1 John 3:20-21

See **evil, forgiveness, God, judge, judgment, justice, sin**

condemnation (KAHN-dem-NAY-shun) *noun:*

Condemnation is a kind of judgment on a person who has done wrong. It is also the inner feeling of guilt a sinner has.

John 3:19; 5:24; Romans 8:1; James 5:12

See **condemn, guilt, judgment**

confess (kun-FES) *verb:*

To confess may mean to admit to God that one is a sinner. To confess may mean to agree that Christ is Lord. To confess is also to put into practice what one believes about Christ.

Matthew 10:32-33; John 12:42-43; Romans 10:9-13; Philippians 2:11; James 5:16

See **Christ, confession, Lord, sinful nature, sinner, testimony**

confession (kun-FESH-un) *noun:*

A confession is a statement. A confession states something that has much meaning for one or more persons. There are three important types of Christian confession:

1. A confession is a statement about what a group of people believe about God. This kind of confession is called a confession of faith.

2. People can make a confession of faith by the way they live. Christians confess their faith living right. They put into practice what they say they believe about God.

3. A confession can be a time when a person says "I am sorry." The person has done something that hurts someone else. A person makes a confession to God when he or she sins against Him. People make a confession to other persons when they harm others. Harm can happen through speech and in other ways too.

Psalm 51:1-5; Jonah 3:1-10; Luke 9:18-22; 13:2-5; 15:17-21; 18:9-14

See **Apostles' Creed, attribute, confess, creed, doctrine, forgiveness, God, grace, mercy, right, sin, theology**

confessional (kun-FESH-uh-nul) *noun:*

A confessional is a place where people tell their sins to a priest. The use of the confessional is a practice of the Roman Catholic Church.

See **confess, priest, Roman Catholic, sin**

confirmation (KAHN-fer-MAY-shun) *noun:*

Confirmation is a religious rite practiced in many Christian churches. This ceremony is usually done for older children. They confirm their belief in the Christian faith. Churches that practice confirmation believe that a person receives the Holy Spirit at baptism. But the believer receives the Holy Spirit in a new and greater way at confirmation.

Confirmation is done by the laying on of hands by the priest, bishop, or minister. Confirmation usually follows a time of special teaching in the beliefs of the church. Those who are confirmed may then receive the Lord's Supper for the first time.

Few Evangelical churches practice the rite of confirmation. They have different beliefs about when and how people receive the Holy Spirit.

See **baptism, baptism with the Holy Spirit, bishop, evangelical, Holy Spirit, laying on of hands, Lord's Supper, minister, priest, rite, ritual**

congregation (KAHN-gri-GAY-shun) *noun:*

A congregation is a group of people who meet regularly for worship.

Psalm 22:22; Acts 13:43; Hebrews 10:23-25

See **Body of Christ, church, fellowship, koinonia, worship**

conquest (KAHN-kwest)

1. *noun:* Conquest means winning a war or defeating an enemy.

2. *proper noun:* The Conquest in the Bible is the time when Israel took over Canaan. It was the Promised Land, the land promised to Abraham by God. Israel fought against the people who lived in Canaan. The Conquest happened after the Exodus from Egypt and before the time of the Judges. The story of the Conquest is told in the Book of Joshua.

See **Canaan (map 3), Exodus, Israel, Joshua, Judges, Palestine**

conscience (KAHN-shuns) *noun:*

Conscience is the inner sense of right and wrong. It makes people feel bad when they do wrong. It also approves people when they do right. It helps people to avoid wrong. God usually speaks to people through the conscience.

Romans 2:12-16; 1 Corinthians 4:3-5; 8:7-13; 1 Timothy 1:3-5, 18-19; 2 Timothy 1:3; Titus 1:15; Hebrews 10:22; 1 Peter 2:19

See **conviction, ethics, morality, nature**

consecrate (KAHN-see-krayt) *verb:*

To consecrate means to give oneself or something to be used only by God. God makes holy what is consecrated to Him.

Exodus 28:3; 30:30; Numbers 6:7, 9, 12; Joshua 6:19; Micah 4:13; Hebrews 10:20

See **consecration, holy, sanctify**

consecration (KAHN-see-KRAY-shun) *noun:*

Consecration is the act of giving or presenting something to God. People or things may be consecrated to God. Consecration means giving oneself to God to live a holy life. God sanctifies people who trust Him and consecrate themselves to Him.

Exodus 28:3, 41; Matthew 12:4; Luke 2:23; Romans 6:15-19; 12:1-2

See **consecrate, dedication, holy, purification, sanctification**

conservative (kun-SER-vuh-tiv)

1. *adjective:* Conservative describes persons or beliefs that hold to the basic doctrines of Christianity. Conservative may also describe a person who follows traditional Christian faith and moral ideas.

2. *noun:* A conservative in Christianity is a conservative Christian, a fundamentalist, or an evangelical.

See **conservative Christianity, doctrine, evangelical, fundamentalism**

conservative Christianity (kun-SER-vuh-tiv KRIS-chee-AN-uh-tee) *noun phrase:*

Conservative Christianity is a branch of the Christian Church. It stresses the basic doctrines of the Bible. It also stresses the connection between Christian faith and morality.

Conservative Christianity differs from Fundamentalism in some important ways. Fundamentalism calls the biblical account of creation in Genesis "Creation Science." Conservative Christianity believes that God alone could create the world. It sees the Bible as a book of faith, not a book of science. But what is true in science does not disagree with the Bible. All conservative Christians believe the Bible is true when it says that God created the world. But they accept what science can prove about how God created it.

Conservative Christianity also places a high value on modern forms of biblical scholarship. But it does not believe that the Bible must be proved by reason. It believes in the divine inspiration of the Bible. But it does not say that each and every word was given by God. It believes that God guided the thoughts of the people who wrote the Bible. Thus the Bible can be trusted. The Bible tells of God's plan for the salvation of the world. It shows how God wants people to live. This is the Bible's purpose.

Conservative Christianity differs greatly from liberalism. For example, conservative Christianity holds that Christ was fully God. It also teaches the doctrine of the Virgin Birth and the resurrection of Christ. It also believes in the authority of the Scriptures and the doctrine of the new birth. Liberalism rejects these beliefs.

See **authority of Scripture, Calvinism, creation, divine, evangelical, fundamentalism, inspiration, liberalism, morality, new birth, Protestant, Reformed tradition, salvation, Wesleyanism**

Constantine (KAHN-stun-teen) *proper noun:*

Constantine was a ruler of Rome during the 300s A.D. He made Christianity the main religion of Rome.

See **Christianity, Rome**

contrition (kun-TRI-shun) *noun:*

See **penitence**

conversion (kun-VER-zhun) *noun:*

Conversion is the complete change God makes in people when they become Christians. The grace of God makes sinners new people when they trust Him alone for salvation. God helps them to quit sinning and to obey Him. God forgives those who repent and turn from sin. Conversion is sometimes called being *saved* or *born again*.

Psalm 51:11-14; Matthew 18:1-4; Acts 3:17-21; 1 Thessalonians 1:9-10; James 5:20

See **born again, forgiveness, grace, new birth, repent, salvation, save, sinner**

convert

1. (KAHN-vert) *noun:* A convert is a person who has become a follower of a different religion. A convert is a person who has turned from sin to become a Christian.

2. (kun-VERT) *verb:* To convert means to become a follower of a religion. A person changes to a new way of life when he or she turns to Christ. To convert also means to lead another person to God.

Psalm 19:7; Matthew 13:15; Luke 22:32; Acts 3:19; James 5:19

See **child of God, Christian, conversion, evangelist, new birth, regeneration, religion, salvation, witness**

conviction (kun-VIK-shun) *noun:*

Conviction is knowing that one is guilty before God. Conviction is also a strong belief that something is true.

John 16:5-11; Acts 2:37-38; Romans 8:31-39; 14:1-23; 1 Corinthians 14:20-25; 1 Thessalonians 1:5-6

See **assurance, awakening, belief, conscience, guilt, Holy Spirit**

Corinth (COHR-unth) *proper noun:*

Corinth was a Greek city during Bible times. It was an important city of trade for the Roman Empire. The apostle Paul visited Corinth on his first missionary trip. He started a church there. He wrote two letters to the church.

Acts 18:1-18

See **Corinth (map 11), Corinthians, epistle, Paul, Rome**

Corinthians (kuh-RIN-thee-unz) *proper noun:*

1. The Corinthians were people who lived in the city of Corinth in Greece. The apostle Paul wrote two letters to the Christian converts in that city.

2. First and Second Corinthians are two books in the New Testament. They are two of the epistles. First and Second Corinthians were written by Paul to Christians in the city of Corinth.

First Corinthians tries to help solve problems in the Church. This letter also teaches the meaning of Christian love. It also discusses spiritual gifts. The letter explains the importance of the resurrection of Jesus for Christians.

Second Corinthians describes the Christian ministry. Paul defends his ministry as an apostle of Jesus Christ. Paul also asks for money to help poor Christians in Jerusalem.

Acts 18:1—19:1

See **apostle, convert, Corinth (map 11), epistle, gift, idol, immoral, love, minister, Paul, resurrection, tongue, worship**

cornerstone (KOHR-ner-stohn) *noun:*

A cornerstone is a necessary supporting part of a building. A building will fall down without it.

The New Testament says that Jesus Christ is the Cornerstone of the Church. The Church cannot exist without Him.

Matthew 21:42-43; Ephesians 2:20-22; 1 Peter 2:6-8

See **Christ, church, Jesus, stumbling block**

corruption (kuh-RUP-shun) *noun:*

Corruption is the condition of being very dirty or rotten. Sin causes corruption in the hearts of people. It destroys their minds and bodies.

Romans 5:12-14; 8:20-21; 1 Corinthians 3:16-17; 15:42; Galatians 6:7-8; 2 Peter 1:3-4; 2:4-16

See **death, immoral, impure, wicked**

Counselor (KOUN-suh-ler) *proper noun:*

See **Comforter, Paraclete**

covenant (KUV-uh-nunt) *noun:*

A covenant is an agreement between persons. God also makes covenants with people. He promises to help and be a friend to all those who obey Him.

The most important covenant was made by God with the people of Israel. The original covenant was made with their ancestor Abraham. God brought Israel out of Egypt and into Canaan, the Promised Land. He promised to guide and be with them. He gave them His law to teach them how to live in covenant with Him. But the people of Israel did not obey God. God said that He would make a new covenant with His people. He made this new covenant in Jesus Christ.

Genesis 9:8-17; 17:1-8; Exodus 19:3-6; 24:3-8; 2 Samuel 7:1-17; Jeremiah 31:31-34; Matthew 26:26-29; Luke 22:19-20; 1 Corinthians 11:23-26; 2 Corinthians 3:4-18; Hebrews 8:1-13; 9:15-22

See **Abraham, atonement, blood, cross, forgiveness, Holy Communion, Israel, Jesus, law**

covet (KUV-it) *verb:*

To covet is to desire something very much. To covet usually means to desire something in a way that is wrong. People covet what they do not have but very much want to have. A person can covet the possessions, the husband, or the wife of another. The Ten Commandments say that to covet is a sin. It is a kind of idolatry (Colossians 3:5).

To covet sometimes means to desire something in a good or right way. For example, it is right to covet a person's prayers on our behalf.

Exodus 20:17; Deuteronomy 5:21; Mark 7:20-23; Luke 12:15; Romans 1:29; 7:7-11

See **adultery, covetousness, envy, greed, idolatry, lust, sin, Ten Commandments**

covetousness (KUV-uh-tus) *noun:*

Covetousness is the condition or state of a person who covets. Covetousness is wrong because it is idolatry. It treats as a god what one covets. Covetousness is much the same as greed or sinful lust.

Exodus 20:17; Isaiah 57:17; Mark 7:20-23; Colossians 3:5

See **covet, idolatry, god, greed, lust, sin, Ten Commandments**

creation (kree-AY-shun) *noun:*

Creation is the act of making something. People may create things, but they really only shape material that already exists. Only God can create something out of nothing.

God made the world and all the people and things in the world. New Testament says that God made the world through Christ. God told people to care for what He made. But the creation of God has been harmed by the sin of man.

Creation also describes the act by which God makes sinners into new people. The Church is sometimes called the new creation of God in Christ. God is making the whole world new through Christ. Thus, Christ is the Source of a new creation.

Romans 6:4; 8:18-25; 2 Corinthians 5:16—6:1; Galatians 6:15-16; Ephesians 2:1-22; 4:17-24; 2 Peter 3:1-13; Revelation 21:1-5

See **Christ, church, Creator, God, nature, sin**

Creator (kree-AY-ter) *proper noun:*

Creator is another word for God. God is called Creator because He made the world and all things in it.

Genesis 1:1—2:24

See **creation, God**

creature (KREE-cher) *noun:*

A creature is any living person or animal. These are called creatures because God created them and gave them life.

See **creation, God**

creed (KREED) *noun:*

A creed is a short statement of Christian beliefs. All Christians accept certain basic creeds. These include the Apostles' Creed.

Most Christian groups write statements of their beliefs. They call these statements creeds or agreed statements of belief.

Deuteronomy 6:4; Acts 16:31-32; Romans 10:8-9; Philippians 2:5-11; Colossians 1:15-20; 1 Timothy 3:16

See **Apostles' Creed, Articles of Faith, belief, heresy, manual, orthodox, theology**

Crete (KREET) *proper noun:*

Crete is a large island in the Mediterranean Sea south of Greece. People from Crete were in Jerusalem on the Day of Pentecost (Acts 2:11). A Christian church was started on the island (Titus 1:5-14). The apostle Paul visited Crete on his journey to Rome (Acts 27:7-9).

See **apostle, Crete (map 11), Greece, Mediterranean Sea, Paul, Pentecost, Rome**

crisis (KRIE-sis) *noun:*

A *crisis* is a time when important changes and decisions happen. A crisis is a turning point. A *crisis experience* is a turning point when people make important decisions.

The new birth is the crisis experience when a person becomes a Christian. Entire sanctification is a second crisis experience. Some Pentecostals consider baptism with the Holy Spirit a third crisis experience.

John 3:3; Acts 8:14-17; 9:1-19; Romans 6:1-23; Galatians 3:1-5; 1 Thessalonians 1:2-10; 5:23-24; 2 Thessalonians 2:13-14; 1 Peter 2:9-10

See **baptism with the Holy Spirit, entire sanctification, initial sanctification, new birth, Pentecostal, regeneration, second work of grace**

cross (KRAHS) *noun:*

A cross was made of two pieces of wood. It usually took the shape of the letter *t*. Sometimes it was in the shape of an *x*. The cross was used long ago to kill people guilty of crimes.

Jesus was hung on a cross by His enemies. They wrongly accused Him of blasphemy against God. But Jesus died on the Cross for the sins of the world. This gave the Cross a new meaning for Christians. The Cross became an important Christian symbol for the sacrifice of Jesus for sin.

Matthew 27:35; John 3:16; 19:17-22; 1 Corinthians 1:18; Galatians 2:20; 3:13; Ephesians 2:16; Philippians 2:5-11; Colossians 1:20; 2:14

See **blasphemy, Christian, Christianity, crucifixion, death, God, guilt, Jesus, malefactor, sacrifice, symbol**

crucifixion (KREW-suh-FIK-shun) *noun:*

Crucifixion is one way the ancient Romans killed those guilty of great crimes. Crucifixion means death by hanging on a cross. Jesus died by crucifixion. The crucifixion of Jesus makes salvation possible.

Sometimes the apostle Paul used the word *crucifixion* in a special way. He said that Christians have been crucified with Christ. They have also been crucified to the world. The old sinful life of a person *dies* when he or she becomes a Christian.

Matthew 27:32-37; Luke 14:25-33; John 9:1-18; Romans 6:5-9; 1 Corinthians 1:17—2:5; Galatians 2:14-21; 5:24; 6:14-16; Ephesians 2:13-16; Colossians 2:11-15

See **atonement, cross, crucify, death, Roman, sacrifice, sacrificial death, salvation, world**

crucify (KREW-suh-fie) *verb:*

To crucify means to put to death by hanging on a cross. Most often a person was tied to the cross. Sometimes the hands and feet were nailed to the cross as in the case of Jesus.

Matthew 27:24-38

See **cross, crucifixion, death**

crusade (krew-SAYD) *noun:*

A crusade is an effort to improve or correct a situation. The people conducting a crusade usually possess great zeal and use great energy about their cause.

In the Church, a crusade is usually a large revival or evangelistic effort. For example, the evangelist Billy Graham conducts crusades.

See **Church, Crusades, evangelical, evangelist, Graham, revival**

Crusades (krew-SAYDZ) *proper noun:*

The Crusades were efforts by Christian armies of Europe to take Palestine from the Muslims. These Christians were called the Crusaders. The Crusades took place from the 1000s through the 1200s A.D.

See **Christian, crusade, Islam, Jerusalem, Palestine**

cubit (KYEW-bit) *noun:*

A cubit was a unit of measure used in the Bible. A cubit was about the same as 45 centimeters or 18 inches. It is sometimes thought of as the distance from the elbow to the fingertips.

Genesis 6:15-16; 7:20; Esther 5:14; Revelation 21:17

cult (KULT) *noun:*

A cult is a religious group whose ideas are considered strange. Cults accept some beliefs of Christianity but also reject some important ones. An important difference is their beliefs about Jesus Christ. They do not accept

Him as Savior. They often have their own leader instead. Cults usually claim to be the only true way to God.

See **belief, Christ, Christianity, church, denomination, Jesus, orthodox, sect**

culture (KUL-choor) *noun:*

1. Culture is the ways of living for a group of people. They share these ways of living. Culture includes beliefs and behavior. It shows what the people believe is important. Culture identifies the group of people. It shows some of the differences between one group of people and another. A culture passes its beliefs and values to the children through education.

The Jews in the Old Testament created a culture. Much of the Book of Deuteronomy describes Jewish culture.

2. Culture is improving the mind through education or training. Culture is using beliefs and values to improve our knowledge.

3. Culture is building up what is good. People use music, art, and education to do this.

Exodus 20:1-31; Deuteronomy 5:1-30

See **belief, Deuteronomy, Jew, Jewish, mind, values**

curse (KERS)

1. *noun:* A curse is a spoken wish that evil or harm will come to someone. The judgment of God on a sinner may take the form of a curse. Sometimes people say they wish that God would destroy other people. This is a kind of curse and is wrong (James 3:6-12). A curse sometimes means the use of God's name in a profane way.

2. *verb:* To curse means to wish that evil might happen to someone as in black magic. To curse may also mean to use profane language.

Genesis 27:12; Deuteronomy 11:26; Proverbs 3:33; Acts 23:12; Galatians 3:10; Revelation 22:3

See **accursed, bless, judgment, profane, sin**

Cyprus (SIE-prus) *proper noun:*

Cyprus is a large island in the Mediterranean Sea south of Asia Minor. People took the gospel to Cyprus after Stephen was martyred (Acts 11:19-20). Paul and Barnabas visited Cyprus on the first missionary journey (Acts 13:4-13). Later, Barnabas and Mark returned to Cyprus (Acts 15:36-40).

See **Asia Minor, Barnabas, Cyprus (map 11), martyr, Mediterranean Sea, missionary, Paul, Stephen**

Cyrus (SIE-rus) *proper noun:*

Cyrus was the first king of the great nation of Persia. He allowed the Jews to return to Palestine after their Exile.

2 Chronicles 36:22-23; Ezra 5:6-17; Isaiah 44:27-28; 45:1-5

See **Cyrus (timeline), exile, Jew, Palestine, Persia, Persia (map 1)**

D d

Damascus (duh-MAS-kus) *proper noun:*

Damascus was the capital city of Syria. Paul became a Christian there.

2 Samuel 8:5-6; Acts 9:1-19; Galatians 1:15-17

See **Christian, Paul, Syria (map 9)**

damn (DAM)

1. *verb:* To damn is to condemn a person to punishment. Sinners are damned or condemned to eternal punishment in hell. Sinners are damned because they do not choose Jesus as Savior. God does not want to damn any person. People choose their own damnation by rejecting God. God wants everyone to repent and accept the salvation His Son offers.

2. *noun:* Damn is a curse or swear word. The word *damn* is sometimes used in taking God's name in vain.

Exodus 20:7; Mark 3:29; 16:16; John 5:29; 2 Thessalonians 2:11-12

See **condemn, curse, damnation, hell, eternity, profane, salvation, Savior, sinner, son, Ten Commandments**

damnation (dam-NAY-shun) *noun:*

Damnation is the suffering that results from separation from God. Eternal damnation is separation from God forever. Damnation is the opposite of salvation.

Mark 16:16; John 5:29; Romans 3:8; 14:23; 2 Thessalonians 1:5-12; 2:11-12; 2 Peter 2:3

See **condemnation, death, eternity, hell, judgment, salvation**

Dan (DAN) *proper noun:*

1. Dan was one of the 12 sons of Jacob. His descendants became one of the tribes of the nation of Israel (Genesis 30:5-6; Joshua 19:40-48).

2. Dan was the name of the land occupied by the tribe of Dan.

3. Dan was the most northern city in Palestine. King Jeroboam built a temple to a golden calf there for the people to worship (1 Kings 12:28-30). The saying "from Dan to Beersheba" indicates its importance (Judges 20:1; 1 Samuel 3:20; 2 Samuel 3:10; 17:11; 24:2, 15; 1 Kings 4:25; 1 Chronicles 21:2).

See **Beersheba, Dan (maps 3, 7), Israel, Jacob, Jeroboam, temple, tribes of Israel, worship**

Daniel (DAN-yul) *proper noun:*

1. Daniel was an Old Testament prophet. A Bible book is named for him. As a young man, Daniel was taken with other Jews to Babylon. His name in Babylon was Belteshazzar. Daniel was famous for his wisdom. He is also known for disobeying the king's order against praying to God. For his disobedience, Daniel was put in a den with lions, but God spared his life (Daniel 6:1-24).

2. Daniel is a book in the Old Testament. It is one of the five Major Prophets. The Book of Daniel tells about Daniel and other Jews in exile in Babylon. It also contains visions of the future.

Ezekiel 14:14, 20; 28:3; Daniel 1:6-8

See **apocalyptic, Babylon, Daniel (time line), Darius, exile, Messiah, prophesy, prophet, Son of Man, vision, wisdom**

Darius (duh-RIE-us) *proper noun:*

Darius was probably the last king of Babylon. He was the son of Xerxes (Daniel 9:1). The Book of Daniel says that Darius had Daniel put in a den of lions for praying to God (Daniel 6:1-24).

See **Babylon, Daniel, Xerxes**

darkness (DAHRK-nes) *noun:*

Darkness is the result of no light. Natural darkness is the time without sunshine.

People live in spiritual darkness when they do not know God. They try to hide their sins. Sins are sometimes called works or deeds of darkness.

Matthew 4:16; 10:27; John 1:5; 6:17; 8:12; 12:35; 20:1; Romans 1:21; 2:19; Ephesians 4:18; 5:8

See **deeds of darkness, evil, light, revelation, sin, sorcery**

David (DAY-vid) *proper noun:*

David was the second king of united Israel. He became king after Saul. King Solomon, David's son, and all the kings of Judah were his descendants. He led Israel to become a great nation. Many psalms were written by David. The Jews expected the Messiah to be a descendant of David. Jesus came from the family of David.

As a boy, David was a shepherd. He is famous for killing Goliath, the Philistine giant. He was anointed by Samuel to be king after Saul.

1 Samuel 16:31; 1 Kings 1—2; 2 Kings 22:1-2; Matthew 1:1-17

See **anoint, branch, David (time line), Goliath, Israel, Jesus, Jew, Judah, Messiah, Philistine, Psalms, Samuel, Saul, shepherd, Solomon**

Day of Atonement (DAY uv uh-TOHN-ment) *proper noun phrase:*

See **atonement, festival**

Day of the Lord (DAY uv thuh LOHRD) *proper noun phrase:*

The day of the Lord is the end of history. The people of Israel looked forward to the Day of the Lord. They thought God would give them great blessings then. They thought He would punish their enemies. The true prophets did not agree. They warned that it would be a sad time for evil people. This would be true for all nations, not just Israel. God would bless only the righteous people.

The Day of the Lord in the New Testament refers to the second coming of Jesus. His return will bring history to an end. God will raise the dead.

The judgment will take place. God will separate good and evil people. Sinners will be punished. God will reward believers. Everything will be under the control of God. Evil days will be past. God will rule over all.

The Day of the Lord is not the same as the Lord's Day. The Lord's Day is Sunday, the Christian Sabbath.

Isaiah 13:9-22; Amos 5:1-27; Luke 17:22-37; 1 Corinthians 1:4-9; 3:10-15; 1 Thessalonians 4:13—5:11

See **apocalypse, eschatology, heaven, hell, Israel, judgment, Lord's Day, prophet, resurrection, righteous, Second Coming**

deacon (DEE-kun) *noun:*

A deacon is a person who serves the church. The term in Greek means "servant" or "minister." It includes both men and women. Deacon was a title of certain officers in the Early Church.

Deacon is still the name used for church officers in some denominations. God calls deacons to care for the needs of the church other than preaching.

Some churches use the name *deaconess* for female deacons. These women also serve the needs of people in the church.

Acts 6:1-6; Romans 16:1-16; Philippians 1:1; 4:2-3; 1 Timothy 3:8-13

See **bishop, Body of Christ, church, denomination, elder, Greek, laity, minister, ordain**

deaconness (DEE-kun-nes) *noun:*

See **deacon**

Dead Sea (DED SEE) *proper noun phrase:*

The Dead Sea is a body of water in southern Palestine. Water does not flow out of it. Its water contains so much salt that nothing can live in it. Thus, it is sometimes called the Salt Sea. It is also called by other names in the Old Testament. The Jordan River flows into the Dead Sea.

Genesis 14:3; Deuteronomy 3:17; Ezekiel 47:8, 18

See **Dead Sea (map 8), Jordan River (map 8), Old Testament, Palestine**

Dead Sea Scrolls (DED SEE SKROHLZ) *proper noun phrase:*

The Dead Sea Scrolls are a group of ancient writings. They were found in caves near Qumran (KEWM-rahn) by the Dead Sea in 1947. Some of the writings are books of the Old Testament. Other writings were by the Jews who lived there shortly before the time of Jesus. These Jews probably belonged to the sect called the Essenes.

The Dead Sea Scrolls are important for at least two reasons. First, they include the oldest copies of the Old Testament. Second, they give scholars a better understanding of what the Essenes believed.

See **Dead Sea (map 8), Essenes, Jesus, Jew, Old Testament, Qumran (map 8), scroll**

death (DETH) *noun:*

Death is the end of natural life. The Bible says that death is a result of sin.

Spiritual death separates people from God. Sinners are spiritually dead even though they are alive physically. Spiritual death brings eternal death to sinners who do not repent.

Jesus' death was the result of the sins of all people. His death on the Cross is now the means of atonement.

Deuteronomy 34:5-8; Psalms 23:1-6; 49:1-20; 88:1-18; 115:16-18; Ezekiel 18:1-32; Matthew 4:12-17; Romans 5:12—6:23; 1 John 3:11-18; 5:11-12

See **atonement, eternal death, eternal life, hell, immortality, life, repent, salvation, sin, spiritual, wages of sin**

Deborah (DEB-uh-ruh) *proper noun:*

Deborah was a judge and prophetess during the time of the judges. She is also known as a military leader. She was a poet, who wrote a song after winning a great battle (Judges 5).

Judges 4:4—5:31

See **Gideon, judge, prophet, prophetess**

debt (DET) *noun:*

A debt is something that one person owes another.

People should obey God. They owe God a debt when they sin and do not obey Him. Sins are sometimes called debts in the Bible. Jesus taught His disciples to pray, "Forgive us our debts, as we also have forgiven our debtors" (Matthew 6:12).

1 Samuel 22:1-2; 2 Kings 4:1-7; Matthew 6:12; 18:21-35

See **atonement, disciples, Lord's Prayer, obedience, redemption, sin**

Decapolis (duh-CAP-uh-lus) *proper noun:*

Decapolis was an area in Palestine south and east of the Sea of Galilee. The area had 10 cities settled by Greeks after Alexander the Great conquered Palestine. Many people from the Decapolis followed Jesus in his early ministry (Matthew 4:25).

Mark 5:20; 7:31

See **Alexander the Great, Galilee, Palestine, Ten Towns (map 8)**

deceive (dee-SEEV) *verb:*

To deceive is to cause someone to believe what is not true. A person who deceives often tells a lie.

The Bible condemns deceiving as a serious sin. Jesus said that the devil "is a liar and the father of lies" (John 8:44). Those who deceive others follow the devil.

Exodus 20:16; Proverbs 24:28; Jeremiah 9:1-6; Matthew 24:3-28; John 8:44; Ephesians 4:25; 5:6; 1 Thessalonians 2:3-8; Revelation 19:20; 20:10; 21:8

See **adversary, antichrist, bear false witness, devil, heresy, hypocrisy, lie, responsibility, slander, truth**

decision (dee-SI-zhun) *noun:*

A decision is a choice to act in one way and not another. For example, people choose either to serve God or to reject Him. The grace of God makes people free to decide for Christ. We sometimes call this act of our will a *decision for Christ.*

Joshua 24:14-27; John 1:12; Galatians 3:6-9, 23-29

See **death, grace, responsibility, will, willful**

decree (dee-KREE)

1. *noun:* A decree is an order that must be obeyed. Caesar Augustus once issued a decree that all people had to be counted (Luke 2:1). A decree can also mean a plan of God that will not be changed.

2. *verb:* To decree is to make a command that must be obeyed.

Job 22:28; Psalms 2:7; 148:6, Jonah 3:7-9;

See **Augustus, Caesar, commandment, obedience, Ten Commandments**

dedicate (DED-un-kayt) *verb:*

To dedicate is to set someone or something apart for a special purpose. To dedicate means about the same as to consecrate. The word *dedicate* has a special meaning in the Bible.

Deuteronomy 20:5; Judges 17:3; 1 Kings 7:51; 8:63; 2 Kings 12:4; 2 Chronicles 2:4

See **ceremony, consecrate, dedication**

dedication (DED-uh-KAY-shun) *noun:*

Dedication is the act of setting something or someone apart for a special purpose. Dedication has a special meaning in the Bible. It means giving something to God. Dedication means about the same as consecration. Sometimes new church buildings are dedicated to God in a special dedication ceremony.

Dedication is also the ritual in which parents present their children to God. This shows that their children belong to God and can be used by Him. Parents present their children in dedication as an act of worship.

Deuteronomy 20:5; Judges 17:3; 1 Kings 7:51; 8:63; 2 Chronicles 2:4; Luke 2:21-24

See **consecration, gift, offering, ritual, sacrifice, sanctify**

deeds of darkness (DEEDZ uv DAHRK-nes) *noun phrase:*

Deeds of darkness are sinful acts. They are acts that serve Satan. Darkness is often used in the Bible to speak of sin and all that opposes God. God is truth and light. Darkness is false. It is spiritual death. All who obey the will of God live in light. All who disobey His will live in darkness.

John 1:5; 3:19; 8:12; Romans 2:19; 13:12; Ephesians 5:11

See **darkness, death, holiness, light, Satan, sin, works of the flesh, truth**

Deism (DEE-iz-um) *proper noun:*

Deism is a kind of belief in God or the deity. It believes that God created the world. But Deists believe that God is no longer present in it. Deism believes that people can know all they need to know about God through reason alone. Deism says the belief that God speaks to people causes trouble and confusion.

See **creation, deity, immanence, reason, theism, transcendence**

deity (DEE-uh-tee) *noun:*

Deity means a male or female god. Christians use the word *deity* to refer to the one true God.

See **divine, divinity, God**

deliverance (dee-LIV-er-uns) *noun:*

Deliverance is the act of being freed from something by someone. The Bible uses deliverance in a special way. It refers to the act of God that frees people from oppression. The oppression may have been caused by slavery, sin, or demons. For example, there was the deliverance of the Israelites from Egypt called the Exodus. People have deliverance from sin when they become born-again Christians. Jesus Christ provides this deliverance.

Genesis 45:7; Exodus 3:7-11; Job 10:7; Psalms 32:7; 33:19; 50:15; Proverbs 4:9; Daniel 3:17; Matthew 6:13; Romans 7:6

See **born again, demon, Exodus, freedom, redemption, sin, slave**

deluge (DEL-yewj or DEL-yewzh) *noun:*

A deluge is a flood. The great Flood of the time of Noah is called the Deluge.

Genesis 6:5—8:22

See **ark, flood, Noah**

demon (DEE-mun) *noun:*

A demon is an evil spirit. In the Bible, demons are often called *devils* and sometimes called *unclean spirits*. Demons work for the cause of evil and for Satan. They oppose the good purposes of God. They especially opposed the ministry of Jesus. But Jesus showed that He was the Master over them.

Demons are evil spirits that cannot be seen. So people cannot know for certain what demons cause. Demons try to destroy all that is good. They oppose God and the life He wants people to enjoy. Evil people and events help demons get their way.

Matthew 8:16; 9:33; 10:1; 17:18; Mark 1:23-24, 27; 5:6-8; 9:25; Luke 8:26-36; 10:17, 20; 13:11-17; Ephesians 6:12; 1 Timothy 4:1-5; 2 Timothy 3:1-9; Revelation 9:20-21; 16:14

See **demon possession, demonic, devil, evil, exorcism, Jesus, Satan**

demon possession (DEE-mun puh-ZESH-un) *noun phrase:*

Demon possession is the control of people by demons. Sometimes demon possession in the Bible was a type of sickness. Jesus healed people who suffered from all kinds of sickness (Matthew 4:23-24; 8:16-17). He freed people who were controlled by demons. His power over demons was a sign that the kingdom of God had come. It showed that Satan was a defeated enemy. The Bible sometimes called this devil possession.

Mark 1:32, 34; 5:1-20; 9:17-27; Luke 4:40-41; 8:26-36

See **demon, demonic, devil, evil, exorcism, healing, Jesus, Satan, sign**

demoniac (duh-MOH-nee-ak) *noun:*

A demoniac is a person who is possessed by a demon or evil spirit. Jesus healed a demoniac. This miracle amazed the people.

Mark 5:1-20

See **demon, demon possession, demonic, evil, miracle, spirit**

demonic (duh-MAH-nik)

1. *adjective:* Demonic describes something that is under the power of a demon. Demonic people first allow demons to control their lives. Then they become helpless slaves of demons. Demonic things are totally evil, and all evil results may be called demonic. These things are called demonic because they serve the purposes of Satan.

2. *noun:* The demonic is the power demons use to destroy life. Some things that happen seem to be totally evil. Such things are sometimes called the demonic.

See **demon, evil, Satan**

denarius (duh-NAIR-ee-us) *noun:*

The denarius was a coin used in Palestine during the time of Jesus. A denarius was the usual pay a worker earned in a day.

Matthew 20:1-16

See **Jesus, Palestine**

denomination (dee-NAHM-uh-NAY-shun) *noun:*

A denomination is an organized group of Christians. It is made up of a number of congregations. Each denomination understands the Christian faith in some ways that are different from other denominations. These include different views of doctrine, church government, and forms of worship. All Christian denominations say they believe that Jesus Christ is Lord. They also agree that all Christians are members of the Body of Christ.

See **Body of Christ, Christian, Christianity, church, congregation, doctrine, Jesus, Lord, polity, worship**

depravity (dee-PRAV-uh-tee) *noun:*

Depravity is the sinful condition of the human race that resulted from the Fall. It means that every person from birth has the tendency to sin. This condition makes it easy for people to disobey God.

People cannot win back favor or fellowship with God by their own efforts. This condition can be changed only by the grace of God. Depravity affects the individual and all of society. All of human existence has been damaged by sin.

Mark 7:20-23; Romans 5:12-21; 8:10

See **baptism with the Holy Spirit, circumcision, entire sanctification, Fall, indwelling sin, original sin, sinful nature, total depravity**

Deuteronomy (DEW-ter-AHN-uh-mee) *proper noun:*

Deuteronomy is the fifth book in the Old Testament. It is part of the Pentateuch. The word *deuteronomy* means "second law." The book repeats many of the laws given in the Book of Exodus. It contains the last words of Moses to the people of Israel. He said that God would bless them if they obeyed Him. But God would curse them if they were not faithful to the covenant.

See **Bible, covenant, curse, Exodus, law, Moses, Old Testament, Pentateuch**

devil (DEV-ul) *noun:*

The word *devil* means "one who slanders another." The devil slanders God and His people. Thus, he is the enemy of God. The Bible says that the devil is "like a roaring lion looking for someone to devour" (1 Peter 5:8). The Bible calls Satan the devil.

Matthew 4:1; 7:22; 9:34; 25:41; Mark 1:34; Luke 4:2; John 7:20; 10:21; Acts 13:10; Ephesians 4:27; 6:11; James 2:19; 4:7; Revelation 12:9; 20:10

See **demon, God, Satan, slander**

devotions (dee-VOH-shunz) *noun:*

Devotions are the private, spiritual practices of a Christian. These include prayer, Bible study, and meditation. Devotions may also include fasting and reading Christian books. Devotions are a form of worship and a means of grace.

See **Bible, fast, means of grace, meditation, prayer**

devout (dee-VOUT) *adjective:*

Devout describes a person who loves God and tries to please Him.

Luke 2:25; Acts 10:1-48; 22:12

See **disciple, faithful, piety**

Diaspora (die-AS-puh-ruh) *proper noun:*

See **Dispersion, exile**

dichotomy (die-KAHT-uh-mee) *noun:*

Dichotomy is from a Greek word that means "cut in half." Some people believe that humans have two parts: the physical part and the spiritual part. These parts are also called body and soul.

Other people reject this view. They believe that humans must be seen as whole persons and not divided.

See **body, dualism, man, person, soul, spiritual, trichotomy**

didache (DID-ah-kay) *noun:*

Didache is the Greek word used for *teaching* in the New Testament. It means teaching what the Christian faith means.

The Didache is the so-called Teaching of the Twelve Apostles. It was actually written about A.D. 125 as a summary of Christian doctrine.

Matthew 28:19-20; Acts 2:41-42; 2 Timothy 3:14-17

See **apologetics, apostle, Christian, disciple, doctrine, Greek**

Didymus (DID-uh-mus) *proper noun:*

See **Thomas**

disciple (duh-SIE-pul)

1. *noun:* A disciple is a person who follows the teaching and example of another person. Those who follow Jesus Christ are His disciples. They are sometimes called followers of Christ. They are also called Christians.

Jesus had 12 disciples who were later called apostles.

2. *verb:* To disciple means to teach a new Christian how to be a follower of Christ. Some churches help disciple new Christians in discipleship programs.

Matthew 10:1; 11:1, 28-30; 28:19-20; Mark 2:18; Luke 14:26; John 9:28; Acts 1:15-22; 11:26

See **apostle, Christ, Christian, discipleship, follower, Jesus**

discipleship (duh-SIE-pul-ship) *noun:*

Discipleship is the condition or state of being a disciple. In the Christian faith, discipleship means being a disciple of Jesus Christ. Some churches have discipleship programs to help disciple new Christians.

See **Christian, disciple, faith, Jesus**

Disciples of Christ (duh-SIE-pulz uv KRIEST) *proper noun:*

See **Christian Restorationism**

discipline (DIS-uh-plun)

1. *noun:* Discipline is the control of life by values and rules. A person may accept discipline for himself, or discipline may be forced on him. Christian discipline describes the life of a person under the control of Jesus Christ. Christian disciplines have usually included prayer, fasting, Bible study, and other habits of devotion. The Bible sometimes refers to discipline as *chastening.*

2. *verb:* To discipline means to improve oneself or another person through rules and values.

Job 36:10; Hebrews 12:3-11, Revelation 3:19

See **abstinence, Bible, Christian, devotions, disciple, fast, prayer**

disease (duh-ZEEZ) *noun:*

See **healing, health**

dispensation (DIS-pun-SAY-shun) *noun:*

A dispensation is a plan for doing something. It is also the way the plan is carried out.

Christian doctrine uses the word "dispensation" in a special way. It refers to the ways God has carried out His plan for the world. His purpose to redeem man has been the same in both the old and new covenants. But the way God did this changed when He sent Jesus into the world.

1 Corinthians 9:17; Ephesians 1:10; 3:2; Colossians 1:25

See **covenant, dispensationalism, doctrine, God, redeem, Son of God**

Dispensationalism (DIS-pun-SAY-shun-ul-iz-um) *proper noun:*

Dispensationalism is the teaching that God acts in different ways at different times in history. Dispensationalism is a special way of interpreting the Bible that began during the 1800s. It is one type of premillennialism. It usually divides history into seven periods or dispensations. It is known for its special teaching about the second coming of Christ. Dispensationalism teaches that the Rapture of the Church will be a secret event. Christ will return openly after that.

See **church, dispensation, eschatology, interpretation of the Bible, millennium, rapture, Second Coming**

Dispersion (dis-PER-zhun or dis-PER-shun) *proper noun:*

The Dispersion is a name given to faithful Jews living outside of Palestine. More Jews during the first century lived outside of Palestine than in Palestine. This was partly the result of the Exile. The Dispersion is sometimes called the Diaspora.

The New Testament sometimes uses the term Dispersion to refer to Christians. Their true home is heaven, although they still live in this world.

Deuteronomy 4:27; 28:64-68; Isaiah 11:12; John 7:35; Acts 5:37; James 1:1; 1 Peter 1:1-2

See **Christian, exile, Jew, New Testament, Palestine**

divine (duh-VIEN) *adjective:*

Divine describes someone or something as having the nature of God. The statement "Jesus is divine" means that He is truly God.

Hebrews 9:1; 2 Peter 1:2-3

See **deity, God, Jesus, nature**

divinity (duh-VIN-uh-tee) *noun:*

Divinity is the state or condition of being divine. A divinity is a divine being or deity. According to the Christian faith, God is the only real Divinity.

Divinity also means theology or the study of divine things. A divinity school is a seminary or a school to study religious courses or subjects.

See **deity, divine, God, theology**

divorce (duh-VORS)

1. *verb:* To divorce means to end a marriage by law. To divorce in the Bible also meant for a husband and wife to separate.

2. *noun:* A divorce is the ending of a marriage by means of law. Jesus

taught that divorce was not God's plan for married people. God desires married people to remain so for life. But the New Testament does give some conditions under which divorce is allowed.

Matthew 5:31-32; 19:3-9; 1 Corinthians 7:10-16

See **adultery, fornication, marriage**

Docetism (doh-SEE-tiz-um or DOH-suh-tiz-um) *proper noun:*

See **Gnosticism**

doctrinal (DAHK-truh-nul) *adjective:*

Doctrinal refers to a religious belief or beliefs. Doctrinal means that a statement or belief is theologically important.

1 Timothy 1:3-20; 4:1-16; Titus 2:1-2

See **belief, creed, doctrine, dogma, theology**

doctrine (DAHK-trun) *noun:*

Doctrine is the teaching that is accepted by the members of a religion. Christian doctrine is the set of beliefs about God as accepted by Christians. Christians believe that revelation and tradition are the sources of their doctrines.

Deuteronomy 32:2; Job 11:4; John 7:16-17; Acts 2:42; Romans 6:17

See **belief, didache, dogma, revelation, theology, tradition**

dogma (DAWG-muh) *noun:*

A dogma is the teaching agreed upon by a Christian group. The teaching becomes dogma by church law. Such churches believe that dogma comes from God. Thus, a person who denies a dogma is believed to be guilty of heresy.

See **Christian, church, doctrine, heresy, law, revelation, theology**

dogmatic (dawg-MAT-ik) *adjective:*

Dogmatic describes people who hold so strongly to beliefs that they will not change. For example, Christians are dogmatic in their belief that Jesus is the Christ. Some people are dogmatic about ideas that do not have biblical support. Thus, dogmatic can describe people who will not listen to reason or reality.

See **belief, dogma, law, reason**

dominion of sin (duh-MIN-yun uv SIN) *noun phrase:*

The dominion of sin is the power that sin has over sinners. God frees people from the rule of sin when they become Christians. He also destroys the power of sin in Christians who are entirely sanctified.

Romans 6:1-14

See **Christian, entire sanctification, salvation, sin, sinner**

dove (DUV) *noun:*

A dove is a bird like a pigeon. It was used for sacrifice by poor people in Bible times.

The dove has become a symbol of the Holy Spirit. The Holy Spirit came upon Jesus at His baptism like a dove. The dove is also a symbol of peace.

Leviticus 5:7; Matthew 3:13-17; Mark 1:9-11; Luke 2:24

See **baptism, Holy Spirit, sacrifice, sign, symbol**

dragon (DRAG-un) *noun:*

Dragon is a word sometimes used in the Bible for Satan. He is like a great, evil serpent. The angel Michael is at war in heaven against the dragon.

Genesis 3:1-15; Revelation 12:3-17, 20:2

See **Bible, devil, Satan**

drunkenness (DRUNG-kun-nes) *noun:*

Drunkenness is the condition that comes from drinking too much alcohol. The Bible says this is wrong.

Deuteronomy 21:18-21; Proverbs 23:29-35; Matthew 24:45-51; Romans 13:11-14; 1 Corinthians 5:9-13; 6:9-11; Galatians 5:19-21; Ephesians 5:18

See **abstinence, temperance, wine**

dualism (DEW-ul-iz-um) *noun:*

Dualism is the belief that every living thing is made up of only two substances. One is good and the other is evil. These substances have always existed and will always exist. They are opposite, and they war against each other. These substances are called by different names. They may be called spirit and matter, mind and matter, or mind and body. They may also be called good and evil or God and Satan.

God is the Lord of all creation. He made all of His creation good. He is the only God. He does not share His power with any other. But some of His creatures have turned away from Him. This is the source of evil. The Bible is opposed to dualism.

See **creation, dichotomy, evil, God, Lord, materialism, mind, Satan, spirit**

E e

earnest of the Spirit (ER-nust uv thuh SPIR-it) *noun phrase:*

Earnest means a down payment. It is a pledge to pay the full amount later.

Earnest of the Spirit is the assurance that God will keep His promises about the future. The Holy Spirit himself is His pledge or promise. God has given His Holy Spirit to Christians. He is the reason Christians have hope.

2 Corinthians 1:18-22; 4:16—5:5; Ephesians 1:11-14

See **assurance, Christian, eschatology, God, Holy Spirit, hope, Spirit, witness of the Spirit**

Easter (EE-ster) *proper noun:*

Easter is the special Sunday when Christians celebrate the resurrection of Jesus. Protestants and Roman Catholics celebrate Easter on a Sunday between March 22 and April 25. Eastern Orthodox churches sometimes celebrate it later.

See **Christ, Eastern Orthodoxy, Jesus, Lord's Day, resurrection**

Eastern Orthodoxy (EE-stern OHR-thuh-dahk-see) *proper noun phrase:*

Eastern Orthodoxy is a group of Christian denominations. It came from the Eastern part of the Early Church that spoke Greek. Differences developed between the East and West early in church history. By A.D. 1054, the East and West churches were separated by the year.

There are some important differences between Eastern Orthodoxy and Roman Catholicism. They celebrate Easter and Christmas on different days. Their views on the Trinity differ. Eastern Orthodoxy allows small children to receive Holy Communion, and its priests to marry.

See **Christian, denomination, Holy Communion, priest, Protestant, Roman Catholic, Trinity**

Ebenezer (EB-uh-NEE-zer) *proper noun:*

Ebenezer is a Hebrew name meaning "stone of help." Samuel set up a stone marker to remind Israel that the Lord had helped them. He called it Ebenezer.

1 Samuel 7:5-17

See **Hebrew, Israel, Samuel**

Ecclesiastes (ee-KLEE-zee-AS-teez) *proper noun:*

Ecclesiastes is one of the books of the Old Testament. It is one of the five wisdom or poetry books. The word *Ecclesiastes* comes from a Greek word that means "teacher of a congregation." The writer of Ecclesiastes told about his search for the meaning of life. He found that life without God had no meaning. The reason for many things is known only to God. Therefore people must trust and reverence God.

See **congregation, God, life, Old Testament, wisdom**

ecclesiastical (ee-KLEE-zee-AS-ti-kul) *adjective:*

Ecclesiastical describes something that relates to the church. For example, an ecclesiastical tradition is the tradition of a denomination or group. The term *ecclesiastical* comes from the Greek word that means "church."

See **church, denomination, tradition**

ecumenical (EK-yew-MEN-uh-kul) *adjective:*

Ecumenical describes something that includes the whole world or universe. For example, the ecumenical creeds are those that were accepted by all churches. Today, ecumenical describes the efforts by many Christians to overcome the divisions within Christianity. Some of these efforts seek to replace the many denominations with one unified church.

See **Christian, Christianity, church, creed, denomination**

Eden (EE-dun) *proper noun:*

Eden in Hebrew means "pleasant." Eden was the region in which God made a garden at the time of creation. He placed Adam and Eve there. Every desirable fruit was to be found in the garden. The tree of life was there. The tree of the knowledge of good and evil was also there. Adam and Eve lived in the garden until they sinned. It cannot be known for certain where Eden was located.

Genesis 2:8-17

See **Adam, creation, Eve, Fall, sin, tree of knowledge, tree of life**

edification (ED-uh-fuh-KAY-shun) *noun:*

Edification is an effort by one person to build up another person. An edification is an effort to encourage someone in their walk with Jesus. It is an effort to encourage persons to become more mature Christians. Songs and sermons can be used as an edification. An edification can be directed toward a whole church.

Matthew 6:25-34; Luke 12:35-40; Romans 6:12-14; Galatians 5:16-24; 1 Peter 2:1-5

See **church, edify, koinonia, maturity, sermon, walk**

edify (ED-uh-fie) *verb:*

To edify means to build up, to make stronger, or to instruct. The gifts of the Spirit are given to help Christians edify one another.

Romans 14:19; 1 Corinthians 8:1; 14:5, 26; 12:19; Ephesians 4:11-16; 1 Thessalonians 5:11

See **Christian, gift**

Edom (EE-dum) *proper noun:*

Edom was another name given to Esau. The name *Edom* in Hebrew means "red."

Edom was also the name of the nation made up of the descendants of Esau. The soil in the land of Edom was red in color. Edom is called Idumea (ID-yew-MEE-uh) in the New Testament.

Genesis 25:19-34; 36:1-43

See **Arab, Edom (map 4), Edomites, Esau, Hebrew, Idumea (map 8), New Testament**

Edomites (EE-dum-iets) *proper noun:*

Edomites were persons from the nation of Edom. Edomites were closely related to the people of Israel. But the Edomites were enemies of Israel.

See **Arab, Edom, Edomites (map 4), Israel**

efficacious (EF-uh-KAY-shus) *adjective:*

Efficacious describes something that has the power to produce a desired result. It refers to the grace of God that produces salvation in those who believe. The atonement of Christ makes possible the salvation of everyone. It is efficacious for those who believe. It is also efficacious for those who are unable to believe. Some are unable to believe because they are too young. Others cannot believe because their minds are not normally developed.

See **atonement, grace, prevenient grace, salvation**

Egypt (EE-jipt) *proper noun:*

Egypt was the name of a large and powerful nation southwest of Palestine. Egypt in Bible times was usually not as powerful as the nations of Mesopotamia. Still, Egypt often had an important part in the events of Palestine.

The Nile River usually provided Egypt with the water necessary for growing crops. Palestine sometimes did not have enough rain to grow food. Thus, the people of Palestine often went to Egypt to buy food (Genesis 12:10-20; 41:1—50:26).

Palestine was often caught in battles between Egypt and the nations of Mesopotamia. This caused problems for the people of Israel and Judah (1 Kings 11:40—12:20; 14:25-28; 2 Kings 24:1-7; 25:22-26).

Egypt is best known in the Bible as the land of bondage. It was there that the people of Israel suffered as slaves for 400 years. But God set them free in the Exodus led by Moses (Exodus 1:8—15:21).

See **Assyria, Babylon, Egypt (map 2), Exodus, Israel, Judah, Mesopotamia, Mesopotamia (map 1), Nile River (map 2), Palestine, slave**

Ekron (EK-rahn) *proper noun:*

Ekron was one of five main cities of the Philistines. It was located near the Mediterranean Sea in the southwest part of Israel.

The Philistines captured the ark of the covenant from Israel. It was in Ekron for a short time before it was returned to Israel.

Joshua 15:11, 45-46; 1 Samuel 5:10-12; 7:14; 17:52

See **ark, Ekron (map 4), Israel, Mediterranean Sea, Philistine**

Elah (EE-lah) *proper noun:*

1. Elah was the fourth king of Israel, the Northern Kingdom. He was the son of Baasha. Elah ruled for two years. He was killed by Zimri who then became king (1 Kings 16:8-14).

2. Elah was the name of valley west of Bethlehem. Here the army of Israel fought against the Philistine army. David killed the giant Goliath in this valley (1 Samuel 17:1-11, 48-50; 21:9).

***See* Baasha, Bethlehem, David, Elah (time line), Goliath, Israel, Philistine, Zimri**

elder (EL-der) *noun:*

An elder is a person chosen to lead. Elders in Old Testament times were usually old, wise men. They were leaders of a family, tribe, or city. Elders served as judges. They settled differences among people on the basis of the law.

Elder in the New Testament refers to three different kinds of leaders. Some were simply old people. Some were Jewish religious and political leaders in the Sanhedrin. Some leaders in the Early Christian Church were called elders.

An elder today is usually an ordained minister.

Numbers 11:25; Psalm 107:32; Proverbs 31:32; Luke 7:3; 22:52; Acts 4:4-5; 14:23; 20:17; Titus 1:5; Hebrews 11:2; James 5:14; 1 Peter 5:1

***See* bishop, church, Jew, judge, law, minister, ordain, ordination, Sanhedrin**

elect (ee-LEKT)

1. *verb:* To elect is to choose someone or some group for a special purpose. God elected Israel as a means for making himself known to all nations (Deuteronomy 7:6-11). God chose the Church to be holy and blameless in Christ. God chose Jesus Christ to be the Savior of all who will trust in Him.

2. *adjective:* Elect describes someone God has chosen for His purpose (2 John 13).

3. *noun:* The elect are the chosen people of God. The people of Israel were the elect in the Old Testament. The Church is the elect of God in the New Testament. The Church includes Jews and Gentiles who have accepted the call of God to salvation.

Isaiah 42:1; 45:4; Matthew 24:22; John 6:37-44; Acts 13:48; Romans 8:27-33; 9:11-18; 11:2; 1 Corinthians 1:26-31; Ephesians 1:4-11; 1 Thessalonians 1:2-7; 1 Peter 1:1-2; 5:13

***See* call, decree, freedom, God, grace, Israel, predestination**

election (ee-LEK-shun) *noun:*

Election is the act of choosing. Election is a Christian doctrine that explains how God chooses to save sinners.

All Christians agree that God elected to save sinners through Jesus Christ. But they do not agree about how or whom God elects.

Some Christians believe that God chooses to save only certain people. These people teach that those God chooses will be saved no matter what they do. Some believe that God also elected certain people to be lost. Many in the Reformed tradition accept these views.

Others believe that God through Christ elected to save all sinners. But they also say that each person has the power of choice. He or she can choose to accept or refuse the offer of salvation. Wesleyans hold this last view.

Wesleyans believe that God first elected His Son to be the Savior of the world. They believe that God then elected to create the Church through Christ. The Church is made up of all who accept Christ as Savior. The Church will be saved. Wesleyans also believe that through Christ everyone may become a part of His Church. God wants no one to be lost.

Election can also mean a call to a special task. For example, Israel was elected by God to be a light to the Gentiles. The Church was elected through Christ to proclaim the gospel of grace. The prophets were chosen by God to speak for Him. Today, certain people have been chosen as special ministers of the gospel.

Deuteronomy 4:37; 7:6-7; 1 Kings 3:8; Isaiah 44:12; Mark 13:20, 22, 27; Luke 23:35; John 3:16-17; 6:37, 44; Acts 13:48; Romans 5:11-21; 8:33; Ephesians 1:4; Colossians 3:12; 1 Peter 2:4, 6, 8; 2 Peter 3:9

***See* Apostasy, Arminianism, backslide, call, Christ, elect, freedom, Gentiles, grace, predestination, prophet, Reformed tradition, salvation, Wesleyanism**

Elijah (ee-LIE-juh) *proper noun:*

Elijah was a prophet in the Old Testament. He spoke for God against the worship of the false god Baal. He challenged the prophets of Baal on Mount Carmel (1 Kings 18:16-40). He especially condemned the evil King Ahab of Israel. The life of Elijah on earth ended when he was taken up to heaven. The story of Elijah is told in 1 Kings 17:1—21:28 and 2 Kings 2:1-12.

Some people expected a prophet like Elijah to come before the Messiah would come (Malachi 3:1). Jesus said that John the Baptist was this prophet (Matthew 11:7-15).

***See* Ahab, Baal, Elisha, heaven, Israel, Jesus, John, Messiah, miracle, Old Testament, prophet**

Elisha (ee-LIE-shuh) *proper noun:*

Elisha was a disciple of Elijah. God did many miracles through Elisha even as He had through Elijah. Elisha also continued to condemn the worship of idols in northern Israel. The story of Elisha is told in 2 Kings 2:1—13:21.

***See* disciple, Elijah, idol, Israel, miracle, Old Testament, prophet, worship**

Elohim (el-OH-him) *proper noun:*

Elohim is the most often used name for God in the Old Testament. It is found most frequently in the Pentateuch and in some psalms. Elohim refers to God's fullness or completeness. Many Jews used Elohim instead of using God's personal name, *Yahweh.*

The word *Elohim* also refers to gods in general. The word probably means strength and power.

Exodus 5:1; 12:12; 22:28; Deuteronomy 5:6; 32:17; Joshua 24:4, 19; Judges 5:8; 1 Samuel 5:7-8; 10-11; 2 Kings 1:2-3; Psalm 7:9; Isaiah 65:16; Malachi 2:17

See **Adonai, God, god, Pentateuch, Yahweh**

Emmanuel (ee-MAN-yew-wel) *proper noun:*

See **Immanuel**

En Gedi or Engedi (en-GED-ee) *proper noun:*

En Gedi is an oasis on the western shore of the Dead Sea. Its water comes from a spring. En Gedi is known for its palm trees. Today, it is a resort for tourists.

David lived in a cave at En Gedi when he fled from King Saul (1 Samuel 23:29; 24:1).

See **David, Dead Sea, En Gedi (map 3), Saul**

Enoch (EE-nuk) *proper noun:*

Enoch is the name of a man in the Old Testament. He was the father of Methuselah. Enoch was a man of great faith. The Bible says that Enoch did not die.

Genesis 5:18-24; Hebrews 11:5

See **faith, Methuselah, translate**

entire sanctification (EN-tier SANGK-tuh-fuh-KAY-shun) *noun phrase:*

Entire sanctification is the act of God that makes Christians completely His. God destroys the sinful nature in Christians through the Holy Spirit. He helps them to live in a way that pleases God. He destroys the power of sin in their lives and makes them truly holy.

Entire sanctification is a crisis experience that happens after a person has become a Christian. The Holy Spirit sanctifies Christians when they give themselves fully to God. Entire sanctification happens at once when Christians trust God to purify their hearts.

The Holy Spirit cleanses consecrated Christians from original sin. He helps them to love God completely and to love others as themselves. He gives Christians power to live lives that please God. This is possible because Jesus died on the Cross to give full salvation.

Entire sanctification increases the desire of Christians to grow in grace. Entire sanctification does not do away with the need for self-discipline. Sanctified believers must daily obey the Holy Spirit. He leads the sanctified Christians toward maturity.

Entire sanctification is also known by other terms. Some of them are *Christian perfection, perfect love,* and *heart purity.* Other terms include *baptism of (or with) the Holy Spirit, filled with the Spirit,* and *the fullness of the blessing.*

Entire sanctification is an important doctrine of Wesleyan theology.

John 17:17; Acts 2:1-4; 8:4-8, 14-17; Romans 6:6, 13, 19, 22; 8:1-5; 12:1-2; Galatians 3:14; Ephesians 5:18; 1 Thessalonians 3:9—4:8; 5:22-24

***See* Christian perfection, cleanse, consecrate, consecration, crisis, growth in grace, holiness, Holiness Movement, initial sanctification, original sin, pure, sanctification, theology, Wesleyan, Wesleyanism**

envy (EN-vee)

1. *noun:* Envy is the pain people feel when someone else has something they want. These people are not satisfied when others are happy. The Bible says that envy is a wrong attitude.

2. *verb:* To envy is to be unhappy over the blessings of another person.

Exodus 20:17; 1 Samuel 18:7-9; Matthew 27:18; Romans 1:29; Galatians 5:19-26; Philippians 1:15; 1 Timothy 6:4; Titus 3:3; James 4:5; 1 Peter 2:1-2

***See* covet, greed, lust, sin**

Epaphras (ee-PAF-rus) *proper noun:*

Epaphras was a fellow worker of the apostle Paul. He started a Christian church in Colosse, a town in Asia Minor.

Colossians 1:7; 4:12

***See* apostle, Asia Minor, Colosse, Colosse (map 11), Colossians, Paul**

Ephesians (ee-FEE-zhunz) *proper noun:*

1. The Ephesians were people who lived in the city of Ephesus in Asia Minor. The apostle Paul wrote a letter to the Christian converts in that city.

2. Ephesians is a book in the New Testament. It is one of the epistles. Ephesians was written by Paul to the church he started in Ephesus. Some scholars think the letter was also written for other churches in the area.

Ephesians tells of the concern Paul had for the unity of the Christians. Christ made Jews and Gentiles "one new man . . . through the cross" (Ephesians 2:15-16). The Church is the *body* of Christ, and He is its *head* (1:22-23). He has given the Church gifts to build it up in love (4:11-16). Christ loved the Church as His Bride (5:21-33).

***See* apostle, Body of Christ, bride, church, convert, cross, Ephesus, Ephesus (map 11), epistle, Gentile, gift, head, Jew, New Testament**

Ephesus (EF-uh-sus) *proper noun:*

Ephesus was an important city in Asia Minor during New Testament times. It was well known for its temple to the goddess Diana.

The apostle Paul visited Ephesus on his second missionary journey (Acts 18:19-21). He started a church there. On his third journey, he spent almost three years in Ephesus (Acts 19). Paul later wrote a letter, the Book of Ephesians, to the Christians in this city. Some scholars think that the letter was also written for other churches in the area.

See **apostle, Ephesians, Ephesus (map 11), god, missionary, Paul**

Ephraim (EE-free-um or EF-rum) *proper noun:*

1. Ephraim was the younger son of Joseph. The descendants of Ephraim became one of the 12 tribes of Israel. The tribe of Ephraim became one of the most important in northern Israel. Thus, the prophets sometimes used the word Ephraim to mean the whole nation of Israel.

2. Ephraim was the name of the land occupied by the tribe of Ephraim.

Genesis 41:52; 48:1-22; Joshua 16:5-10; Judges 12:1-6; Isaiah 7:1-2; Jeremiah 31:9; Hosea 4:17; 11:1-12

See **Ephraim (map 3), Israel, Jacob, Joseph, Old Testament, prophet, tribes of Israel**

Epiphany (ee-PIF-uh-nee) *proper noun:*

Epiphany means "appearing." Epiphany is a holy day celebrated by Christians on January 6. It marks the time when Jesus' parents took Him to the Temple as an infant. Simeon saw the Baby Jesus and knew that He was the Messiah (Luke 2:21-40).

Christians also celebrate Epiphany as a time when the wise men came. The wise men presented gifts to the Child Jesus (Matthew 2:1-12).

Epiphany is also called the "Twelfth Night." Epiphany comes 12 days after Christmas.

See **Christmas, gift, Messiah, Simeon, wise men**

episcopal (ee-PIS-kuh-pul) *adjective:*

Episcopal describes something that relates to a bishop. Episcopal comes from a Greek word meaning "bishop."

Episcopal describes a form of church government led by bishops.

The Episcopal church is the name of a denomination in America. It is similar to the Church of England or Anglican Church.

See **Anglican, bishop, church, denomination, Greek, Protestant**

epistle (ee-PIS-ul) *noun:*

An epistle is a letter. The letters of the New Testament are called Epistles. Of the 27 books in the New Testament, 21 are epistles.

The apostle Paul wrote 13 or 14 epistles. They are Romans, 1 and 2 Corinthians, Galatians, Ephesians, Philippians, Colossians, 1 and 2 Thessalonians, 1 and 2 Timothy, Titus, and Philemon. Bible scholars are not certain who wrote Hebrews.

There are 7 other books called General Epistles. These are named for their authors. They are 1 and 2 Peter; 1, 2, and 3 John; and Jude.

See **apostle, Colossians, Corinthians, Ephesians, Galatians, Hebrews, James, John, Jude, New Testament, Paul, Peter, Philemon, Philippians, Romans, Thessalonians, Timothy, Titus**

eradication (ee-RAD-uh-KAY-shun) *noun:*

Eradication is the act of God that cleanses Christians from the carnal nature.

See **carnal, cleanse, entire sanctification, God, heart purity, nature, original sin**

Esau (EE-saw) *proper noun:*

Esau was a son of Isaac and twin brother of Jacob. His name in Hebrew means "one with a lot of hair." He was also called Edom.

Genesis 25:24-25, 30-34; 26:34; 27:32—33:15; Romans 9:10-13; Hebrews 12:16-17

See **Arab, Edom, Hebrew, Isaac, Jacob**

eschatological (ES-kuh-tuh-LAH-juh-kul) *adjective:*

Eschatological describes events related to the end times. For example, the second coming of Christ is an eschatological event. Others things that are expected when Christ returns may be called eschatological.

See **antichrist, eschatology, heaven, hell, millennium, parousia, resurrection, Second Coming, tribulation**

eschatology (ES-kuh-TAH-luh-jee) *noun:*

Eschatology is the doctrine about the end of the world or the last times. *Eschatology* comes from two Greek words that mean "the study of last things."

Many Jews before New Testament times expected an early end of the world. They believed that the Messiah would soon bring the kingdom of God. Then God would destroy all evil. He would bring justice and would end oppression. He would give His Holy Spirit to all people. He would resurrect the dead. He would make Israel great again.

The New Testament teaches that the kingdom of God appeared in Jesus Christ. Christians believe that Jesus is the Messiah. But He is not the kind of Messiah the Jews expected. He preached the good news of salvation for all people. He freed people from the power of evil. He brought the rule of God to earth. His enemies crucified Him, but God raised Him from the dead. Thus, the resurrection of the dead expected in the last days had already begun. The resurrected Christ gave the Holy Spirit to His Church.

Early Christians believed that the end times had already begun. The second coming of Christ would bring the kingdom of God in its fullness.

The Bible does not answer all the questions people ask today about future events. But Christians live in the sure hope that God will complete what He has begun.

Matthew 24:3—25:46; Romans 8:18-25; 1 Corinthians 15:12-58; 2 Corinthians 4:16—5:11

See **Christ, church, crucify, doctrine, earnest of the Spirit, evil, Greek, Holy Spirit, Israel, Jesus, Jew, kingdom of God, Messiah, New Testament, resurrection, revelation, salvation, Second Coming**

Essenes (es-EENZ) *proper noun:*

The Essenes were a sect of Jews who lived in Palestine during the time of Jesus. They are not mentioned in the New Testament. The Essenes lived a simple life and obeyed strict rules of conduct. The Essenes may have written or helped write the Dead Sea Scrolls, which included books of the Old Testament. These scrolls give information about how the Essenes lived.

See **Dead Sea (map 8), Dead Sea Scrolls, Jews, Palestine, Qumran (map 8)**

Esther (ES-ter) *proper noun:*

1. Esther is the name of a Jewish woman in the Old Testament. A book in the Bible is named for her. She lived in Persia during the time of the Exile. The king of Persia took Esther as a wife. Later, she used her position as queen to save the Jews from death.
2. Esther is a book in the Old Testament. It is one of the history books.

See **exile, festival, Jew, Old Testament, Persia (map 6), Xerxes**

eternal (ee-TER-nul) *adjective:*

Eternal describes that which has no beginning or end. God alone is eternal. Eternal also describes things that God says will never end.

Deuteronomy 33:27; Nehemiah 9:5; Daniel 4:34; Habukkuk 3:6; 1 Timothy 1:17

See **eternal death, eternal life, eternal punishment, eternity**

eternal death (ee-TER-nul DETH) *noun phrase:*

Eternal death means separation from God in the life to come. Hell is the place of eternal death.

Matthew 25:41; 2 Thessalonians 1:5-10

See **damnation, eschatology, eternal, eternal punishment, eternity, hell**

eternal life (ee-TER-nul LIEF) *noun phrase:*

Eternal life is the quality of life that God gives. Those who trust in Jesus Christ for salvation receive the gift of eternal life. People begin to enjoy eternal life when they become Christians. Eternal life is life with God, the Eternal One.

Eternal life also means life after death for Christians. They will live forever with the Lord in heaven. Eternal life in heaven is sometimes called *everlasting life.*

Matthew 19:16, 29; Luke 10:25; 18:18, 30; John 3:17; 5:24, 39-40; 6:27-69; 10:27-29; Acts 13:46, 48; Romans 2:7; 5:21; 6:22-23; Galatians 2:20; Titus 3:4-7; 1 John 1:2; 2:25; 3:15; 5:11-12

See **Christ, eternal, eternity, God, heaven, immortality, life, resurrection, salvation**

eternal punishment (ee-TER-nul PUN-ish-munt) *noun phrase:*

Eternal punishment is the separation from God of those who finally refuse His salvation. Hell is the place of eternal punishment.

Matthew 18:8; 25:41-46; Mark 3:29; Luke 3:17; John 5:28-29; 1 Thessalonians 1:8-9; 2 Peter 2:9-10; Revelation 20:14-15; 21:8

See **damnation, eternal, eternal death, eternity, grace, heaven, hell**

eternal security (ee-TER-nul see-KYOOR-uh-tee) *noun phrase:*

Eternal security is a central doctrine of Calvinism. Calvinists believe that God elects certain people to be saved. Those whom God chooses to save are secure in Christ no matter what they do. But John Calvin taught that those who are truly elect will live righteous lives.

Wesleyans believe that a Christian's security depends on obedient faith.

John 10:27-29; Romans 8:35-39; Philippians 1:6; 1 Peter 1:5

See **Calvinism, doctrine, elect, election, faith, righteousness, salvation, sinning religion, Wesleyanism**

eternity (ee-TER-nuh-tee) *noun:*

Eternity is existence that is not limited by time and space. God alone lives in eternity. But He has chosen to make himself known to people in history.

Eternity sometimes means the future life of Christians with God in heaven.

Psalms 41:13; 90:2; 119:142; Isaiah 57:15; Jeremiah 10:10; Revelation 1:4-10

See **eternal, eternal life, future, God, heaven**

ethics (ETH-iks) *noun:*

Ethics is the study of moral conduct. It is a system of beliefs about how people should make moral decisions. Morality is the practice of ethics. Ethics guides moral conduct.

See **Christian, faith, gospel, morals, morality, values**

Eucharist (YEW-kuh-rust) *proper noun:*

Eucharist is the Lord's Supper or Holy Communion. *Eucharist* in Greek means giving thanks.

Luke 22:14-20; 1 Corinthians 11:23-26

See **Holy Communion, Lord's Supper**

eunuch (YEW-nuk) *noun:*

A eunuch is a human male who does not have testicles. He may be a eunuch because he was born with no testicles. He may be a eunuch because an accident caused him to lose them. Or, he may be a eunuch because someone removed them.

Some government officials in ancient Egypt were eunuchs. A Pharaoh wanted to know that he was the father of his many wives' children.

The Old Testament excludes eunuchs from joining God's people (Leviticus 21:20; Deuteronomy 23:1). Prophets believed the future people of God would include eunuchs (Isaiah 56:3).

The New Testament tells about a eunuch who became a Christian. He was an official in the government of Ethiopia. Philip explained the good news about Jesus to him (Act 8:26-39).

Some men make themselves eunuchs for the sake of the kingdom of heaven (Matthew 19:12). This may mean only that they choose not to marry. Some of them may not have been true eunuchs. They do not marry so as to give more time to serving the Lord (Matthew 19:1-12).

See **Egypt, good news, kingdom of heaven, Pharaoh, Philip, prophet**

Euphrates (yew-FRAY-teez) *proper noun:*

Euphrates is the name of a large river in western Asia. It was one of the rivers of the Garden of Eden (Genesis 2:10-14). The ancient nations of Mesopotamia and Babylon were by the Euphrates. Also, the city of Ur was located beside the Euphrates.

Genesis 15:18; Deuteronomy 1:7; Joshua 1:4

See **Abraham, Babylon, Euphrates (maps 1, 6), Garden of Eden, Mesopotamia, Tigris, Ur**

evangelical (EE-van-JEL-uh-kul)

1. *adjective:* Evangelical describes those Christians who stress the message of justification by grace through faith alone. *Evangelical* comes from the Greek word meaning "gospel" or "good news."

The leaders of the Protestant Reformation were among the first Christians called evangelical.

Today, there are a number of Evangelical denominations. They are united in their focus on the need for personal salvation. They stress the doctrine of justification by grace through faith alone. They believe that justified Christians should live holy lives. They also emphasize the deity of Christ and the authority of the Scriptures.

Evangelical Christians differ from one another in some ways. For example, they differ on what the authority and inspiration of the Bible means. They also differ in their views about the second coming of Christ.

2. *noun:* An Evangelical is an evangelical Christian.

See **authority of Scripture, born again, deity, denomination, faith, gospel, grace, inspiration, justification, justification by grace through faith alone, reformation, Second Coming**

evangelism (ee-VAN-juh-liz-um) *noun:*

Evangelism is the work of telling the gospel to people who are not Christians. The purpose of evangelism is to bring these people to faith in Christ. *Evangelism* comes from the Greek word meaning "preaching the gospel."

Personal evangelism means one person telling the gospel to another person who is not a Christian. This usually happens when a Christian witnesses to another about his faith.

Mass evangelism means preaching the gospel where many people have gathered to hear it. The purpose is to win many converts to Christ.

See **Christian, convert, cross, evangelist, faith, gospel, preach, salvation, witness**

evangelist (ee-VAN-juh-list) *noun:*

An evangelist is a person who preaches the gospel to other people. The evangelist tries to win converts to Christ. *Evangelist* comes from a Greek word meaning "a messenger of the good news."

All Christians should help tell the gospel to those who have not heard it. They are evangelists or witnesses when they do this. Some Christians have been called by God to preach the gospel as evangelists (Ephesians 4:11).

Matthew 28:16-20; 2 Timothy 4:5

***See* call, Christ, convert, evangelical, evangelism, gift, gospel, Great Commission, preach, witness**

evangelize (ee-VAN-juh-liez) *verb:*

To evangelize means to announce the gospel of Christ to those who are not Christians. Jesus told His followers to go into all the world to evangelize (Matthew 28:16-20).

***See* convert, evangelical, evangelism, evangelist, Great Commission, Jesus, gospel**

Eve (EEV) *proper noun:*

Eve was the wife of Adam, the first man. The name *Eve* sounds like the Hebrew word for "living." She and Adam had several children, including Cain, Abel, and Seth.

Genesis 2:18—3:21; 4:25-26

***See* Adam, Abel, Cain, Hebrew, Seth**

everlasting life (EV-er-LAST-ing LIEF) *noun phrase:*

***See* eternal life**

evil (EE-vul)

1. *adjective:* Evil describes anything or anyone that opposes God and His plans for the world. For example, evil people are those who do not worship God and serve Him. Evil is the opposite of good.

2. *noun:* Evil is anything that opposes the plans God has for His world. Evil brought pain and unhappiness into the world.

Evil in the Bible usually means "sin." It is sin when people choose to reject the will of God. Murder, hate, and adultery are examples of religious or moral evils.

Evil is not always sinful. For example, disease, death, illness, and storms may destroy the lives of people. These are called natural evils.

Sometimes the laws and customs of a society may harm certain people. People of a certain sex, age, or race may be treated unfairly. This is called a social evil.

Sometimes it is difficult to tell whether something is evil or good. Something that at first seems evil may turn out to be good (Genesis 50:19).

Genesis 3:16-19; Proverbs 8:13; Isaiah 45:7; Romans 8:18-22

***See* law, morality, morals, religious, sin, will, worship**

evolution (EV-uh-LEW-shun) *noun:*

Evolution is one view of how life on earth developed. It teaches that higher forms of life came from lower forms of life. Teachers of science do not agree on how this happened. They also do not agree on what caused this to happen or how it started. Most evolutionists do not believe God created the earth.

See **creation, God, life, nature**

excommunication (EKS-kuh-MYEW-nuh-KAY-shun) *noun:*

Excommunication means forcing a person to leave a religious community. This happens when a person disagrees with the community and will not stop. This individual refuses to obey the leaders who tell him or her to do so.

Excommunication was practiced in both Old and New Testament times. Excommunication has not been practiced often in Protestant churches. But the practice was once common in the Roman Catholic Church. Excommunication meant that people could not receive the sacraments.

Exodus 30:22-38; Matthew 18:17; 1 Corinthians 5:1-8; Galatians 5:2-12

See **church, community, New Testament, Old Testament, Protestant, Roman Catholic, sacrament, salvation**

exegesis (EK-suh-JEE-sis) *noun:*

Exegesis is the process scholars use to discover the meaning of Scripture. The word *exegesis* comes from a Greek word that means "reading out the meaning."

Acts 8:26-35; 2 Timothy 2:15

See **exposition, Greek, Scripture**

exhort (eg-ZOHRT) *verb:*

Exhort means to urge another person to do something. Exhort also means to urge a person not to do something. Exhort means to advise a person or a group. It means to encourage or warn about something a person might say or do.

In the Old Testament, the prophets exhorted the Jews to obey God. In the New Testament, Peter exhorted people to become Christians. The writers of the New Testament epistles often exhorted the readers.

Acts 2:40: 27:22; 2 Corinthians 9:5-7; 1 Thessalonians 4:1; 2 Thessalonians 3:12; 1 Timothy 2:1-2; 5:1 Titus 1:9; 2:6; Hebrews 3:13; 1 Peter 5:1-10

See **epistle, exhortation, Peter, prophet, prophesy**

exhortation (EG-zohr-TAY-shun) *noun:*

An exhortation is the act of exhorting. An exhortation gives urgent advice. Preaching of the Word of God often includes exhortation.

Exhortation or encouragement is listed as one of the gifts in the Body of Christ (Romans 12:8).

The Bible contains many exhortations. For example, the Book of Hebrews is an exhortation to Christians who are being tempted to turn away from Christ.

Acts 13:15; 20:2; 1 Thessalonians 2:3; Hebrews 12:3-11; 13:22-24

See **Body of Christ, church, exhort, gift, Hebrews, preaching, prophecy, tempt**

exile (EG-ziel or EK-siel)

1. *verb:* To exile means to force people to leave their homeland. Assyria exiled the northern tribes of Israel to the land of Assyria. Babylon exiled the tribes of Judah and Benjamin to the land of Babylon.

2. *noun:* An exile is a person who is exiled. Exiles are held as captives in another country or land.

The Exile is the time Israel and Judah spent in Assyria and Babylon. Most of the exiles of Israel never returned to the land of Palestine. Some of the exiles of Judah returned after Persia defeated Babylon. The time of the Exile is also known as the captivity.

The New Testament says that heaven is the true home of Christians. So, their life on earth is called an exile (1 Peter 1:1).

2 Kings 17:1-41; 24:1—25:30; Jeremiah 1:3; 13:19; 46:13-18

See **Assyria (map 6), Babylon, Babylon (map 6), Benjamin, Dispersion, Israel, Judah, Palestine, Persia, tribes of Israel**

Exodus (EK-suh-dus) *proper noun:*

1. The Exodus was when God helped the people of Israel to escape from Egypt. Egypt had made the people of Israel slaves. God called Moses to lead them out of Egypt. The Pharaoh of Egypt would not let them go. So God sent plagues to force Pharaoh to let His people go. The Exodus is the most important event of redemption in the Old Testament.

2. Exodus is the second book in the Old Testament. It is part of the Pentateuch. It tells the story of the events of the Exodus. It also tells about how God led Israel to Mount Sinai. There He gave them the Ten Commandments. He also gave them other laws and made a covenant with them. The book gives the plans for building the Tabernacle where Israel worshiped God.

See **covenant, Egypt (map 2), God, Israel, law, Moses, Mount Sinai (map 2), Old Testament, Pentateuch, Pharaoh, plague, redemption, Sinai, slave, tabernacle, Ten Commandments, worship**

exorcism (EK-sohr-SIZ-um) *noun:*

Exorcism is the act of casting out demons. It also means the ritual used in the process of exorcism. Jesus practiced exorcism when He freed people from the power of demons. His disciples did also.

Mark 6:13; Luke 4:31-37; 10:17-20

See **demon, demon possession, Jesus, ritual**

expiation (EK-spee-AY-shun) *noun:*

Expiation means the covering or washing away of sins through the blood of a sacrifice.

The death of Christ provides expiation for all sin. This expiation is called the Atonement. Expiation sometimes means the same as forgiveness.

Romans 3:21-26; 1 John 2:1-2

See **atonement, blood, Calvary, Christ, forgiveness, meritorious death, propitiation, sacrifice, sin**

exposition (EK-spuh-ZI-shun) *noun:*

An exposition is an explanation of a section of the Bible. An exposition can also be a sermon that explains the meaning of a scripture passage. A sermon that does this is called an expository sermon. A Bible study or Sunday School lesson may also be an exposition.

Exposition reveals the meaning of a scripture passage in some detail. It may explain what the authors of the Bible wanted to tell their first readers. But its main purpose is to help people today. Exposition explains how we may put the scripture into practice. It helps us see how we should behave and what we should believe.

An expository sermon often takes the theme of a single Bible passage. It may briefly refer to other scriptures that help make its meaning clearer. But the biblical text decides what points the preacher will make in an expository sermon.

A topical message is different from an expository message. A topical message is concerned with a theme, such as love or grace. It may refer to many different biblical passages that discuss this theme. But it does not treat any passage in detail. It has little interest in the contexts of these passages. The preacher decides the points he wants to make in the sermon.

See **Bible, biblical, preacher, scripture, sermon, topical**

expository (ek-SPAH-zuh-TOHR-ee) *adjective:*

See **exposition**

Ezekiel (ee-ZEE-kee-ul) *proper noun:*

1. Ezekiel was an Old Testament man who was both a priest and a prophet. His prophecies are found in the Book of Ezekiel.

Ezekiel preached to the exiles of Judah in Babylon. He assured them that God was still with them. He said that God would return the exiles to their homeland. God would do this to show the world that He is God. Ezekiel also stressed that each person would pay for his own sin.

2. Ezekiel is a book in the Old Testament. It is one of the Major Prophets.

See **Babylon (map 6), exile, God, Judah, Old Testament, priest, prophet, sin**

Ezra (EZ-ruh) *proper noun:*

1. Ezra is the name of a Jewish leader and scribe in the Old Testament. A Bible book is named for him.

Ezra (continued)

Ezra helped lead the Jews when they returned to Jerusalem after the Exile. He directed the building again of the Temple. He also taught the people the law of Moses.

2. Ezra is a book in the Old Testament. It is one of the history books.

***See* exile, law, Moses, Old Testament, scribe, temple**

F f

faith (FAYTH) *noun:*

Faith is trust. Faith usually refers to trust in God. It means totally depending on God and His promises.

Faith in God is a way of confessing that He is God alone. Thus, faith is an act of worship.

Faith is also a confession that the whole world was created by God. People who put their faith in Him show that He alone gives true life. There is only death without Him.

Faith shows itself in obedience to God (Romans 1:5; Galatians 5:6). Faith is the right response by people to God's gift of salvation. Salvation by faith alone was the main truth that started the Reformation. Faith is also needed for the working of miracles.

Faith sometimes means to believe that something is true. This is a weak form of faith. Even demons believe that there is a God. But this belief does not save them. Belief must follow worship and lead to obedience (James 2:14-26).

Habakkuk 2:4; Matthew 8:10; 9:22; 21:21; Mark 4:40; Luke 7:50; Acts 3:16; 6:5; 11:24; 14:9; 15:9; 16:5; 26:18; Romans 5:1; 2 Corinthians 1:24; 5:7; 2 Timothy 4:7; Hebrews 11; 12:2; James 5:15; 1 John 5:4

***See* belief, confess, confession, creation, death, demon, gift, God, good works, justification, life, miracle, obedience, reformation, salvation, worship**

faithful (FAYTH-ful) *adjective:*

Faithful describes a person who can be trusted. A faithful person is loyal. Such people keep their promises. They can always be depended upon to do what they say they will do.

The Bible teaches that God is faithful to His people. It also teaches that His people should be faithful to Him and to others.

Deuteronomy 7:9; 1 Thessalonians 5:24; 2 Thessalonians 3:3; 1 Peter 4:19; 1 John 1:9; Revelation 2:10; 7:13-17

***See* faith, God, loyalty, promise**

faithfulness (FAYTH-ful-nus) *noun:*

Faithfulness is the quality of a person who is faithful. God is always faithful. The faithfulness of God is the reason people can trust Him.

Psalm 40:10; 89:1-2; 33; 92:1-2; 119:89-90; Lamentations 3:22-23

***See* faith, faithful, God, trust**

Faith Promise (FAYTH PRAHM-us) *proper noun phrase:*

Faith Promise is a promise people make to support missions and missionaries. They promise to support missionaries through prayers and by giving money. A person promises by faith how much money he or she will give during the year.

Several denominations use the Faith Promise program to raise their mission offerings and funds. These churches usually plan a Faith Promise convention or emphasis once a year.

Acts 13:1-3; 2 Corinthians 8:3-5; 9:6-7

See **church, denomination, faith, missionary, missions, offering**

Fall (FAWL) *proper noun:*

The Fall is the original sin of Adam and Eve and its results. The Fall damaged the image of God in people. But it did not destroy this image. The Fall separated people from a right relationship with God. This brought humans into moral depravity and spiritual death. It was no longer possible for humans to do the will of God.

The Fall harmed all of creation. It destroyed the peace among people and between people and the rest of creation. The evil results of the Fall continue to harm people and the whole creation.

Genesis 3:1-24; Romans 5:12-21; 8:18-25; Ephesians 4:17-24

See **Adam, carnal, creation, death, depravity, Eve, image of God, man, morality, nature, original sin, redemption, regeneration, sin, will**

fallen nature (FAWL-un NAY-cher) *noun phrase:*

See **depravity, Fall, image of God, nature**

false prophet (FAWLS PRAH-fit) *noun phrase:*

A false prophet is one who claims to speak for God but does not. False prophets say those things that please themselves or others but not what pleases God. They speak words of comfort when God has planned judgment. True prophets call sinners to repentance. The Bible says that false prophets deceive and destroy people.

Jeremiah 28; Matthew 7:15-23; 24:24

See **Bible, cult, God, judgment, prophet, repent, repentance**

false witness (FAWLS WIT-nus) *noun phrase:*

See **bear false witness, deceive, lie, witness**

family of God (FAM-uh-lee or FAM-lee uv GAHD) *noun phrase:*

The family of God is composed of all born-again believers. They have been adopted into God's family. They are called the children of God.

Romans 8:16-17

See **adoption, believer, born again, child of God, church, father**

fast (FAST)

1. *verb:* To fast is to do without food for a time as a spiritual discipline. The Old Testament law required fasting only on the Day of Atonement.

Moses, Elijah, and Jesus fasted for 40 days (Exodus 34:27-28; 1 Kings 19:8; Matthew 4:1-2). The Pharisees fasted twice a week (Luke 18:9-14). Fasting became a ritual without meaning for some people.

Jesus taught that people should not fast simply to prove their piety

(Matthew 6:16-18). The prophets taught that true fasting meant more than just doing without food. It also meant doing righteous acts (Isaiah 58:1-12).

2. *noun:* A fast is a time of fasting for a religious purpose. It usually means a time when a person chooses to do without food.

See **abstinence, atonement, discipline, Elijah, forty days, Jesus, justice, law, Moses, Old Testament, Pharisee, piety, prophet, religious, righteous, ritual, spiritual**

fatalism (FAYT-ul-iz-um) *noun:*

Fatalism is the belief that people have no control over what happens to them. Things happen either by accident or because they must happen. People cannot change what will happen. This power that causes things to happen is called fate. Belief in fate is called fatalism.

The Bible teaches that God, not fate, rules the world. God gives freedom to people to make decisions that help control their future.

See **belief, Bible, fate, freedom, future, God**

fate (FAYT) *noun:*

Fate means a power that controls persons, things, and events. Fate is a power that cannot be controlled. Fate is not the same as God, nor does fate depend on God. People who believe in fate do not trust God. They do not believe that God rules the world. Christians do not believe in fate. Christians believe that God is love. They believe that God rules the world through His love.

The Bible does not use the word *fate.* The word *fate* comes from the name of three ancient Greek female gods.

See **Bible, faith, fatalism, God, god, Greek, love, sovereignty, trust**

father (FAH-th̲er):

1. *noun:* A father is a male parent.

2. *proper noun:* The Father is one person of the triune God.

The Bible teaches that God is like a father. But, this does not mean that He is a male in the human sense. He is not the same as an earthly parent. God is the Heavenly Father because He created all people (Acts 17:28-29). But He also acts like a father in His love and care for them. Jesus called God His Father and taught His disciples to do the same. Jesus taught that God loved everyone and wanted all people to become His children.

Sinners can know God as Father only through faith in Christ. They become adopted children of God through receiving Christ as Savior.

Matthew 5:16; 6:8-9; Mark 14:36; Luke 2:49; John 1:14; 3:35; 5:21; 12:27; Romans 8:15-17; 2 Corinthians 1:3; Galatians 4:4-7; 1 John 1:3; 3:1

See **adoption, child of God, Christ, creation, disciple, faith, God, heaven, new birth, regeneration, Savior, sinful nature, son, Trinity, triune**

fear (FEER)

1. *noun:* Fear is an emotion people have when their safety is in danger. Fear sometimes means worry. Fear may also mean great reverence.

The Bible says, "The fear of the Lord is the beginning of wisdom" (Proverbs 9:10; see also Job 28:28; Proverbs 1:7; Ecclesiastes 12:13). This means that people should obey God and have reverence for Him. People learn the true meaning of life in this way. People who fear God need not be afraid of people or evil. Faith in God and His love can free people from fear.

2. *verb:* To fear is to be afraid or to worry. To fear may also mean to have reverence. For example, to fear God is to reverence Him.

Matthew 6:25-34; 10:26-33

See **Bible, evil, faith, freedom, life, Lord, obedience, reverence, slave**

feast (FEEST) *noun:*

See **festival**

fellowship (FEL-oh-ship) *noun:*

Fellowship means sharing or taking part in a common love or friendship.

Fellowship is possible when people have something in common. Christian fellowship is the shared life that Christ gives. This makes it possible for Christians to love one another and to love God. Christians may have fellowship with God as the Father, Son, and Holy Spirit.

A fellowship may be a community of Christians in a local church.

Fellowship sometimes refers to a time when Christians gather as friends.

Acts 2:42; 1 Corinthians 1:9; 2 Corinthians 6:14-18; Galatians 2:9; Philippians 1:5; 2:1; 3:10; 1 John 1:3-6

See **Christian, church, community, koinonia, prayer, witness of the Spirit**

festival (FES-tu-vul) *noun:*

A festival is a period of religious celebrating and rejoicing. The people of Israel offered special sacrifices on their festival days. The Bible refers to eight Jewish festivals.

1. The Festival of Unleavened Bread, or Passover, celebrated the Exodus events. It was celebrated for a week every spring. Jews today sometimes refer to this by its Hebrew name, Pesach (PAY-sahk).

2. The Festival of Weeks, or Pentecost, was another spring celebration. This one-day festival came seven weeks after Passover. It was also called the *festival of harvest* and the *day of firstfruits* (Exodus 23:16; 34:22; Numbers 28:26). It came in New Testament times to celebrate the giving of the law. It was at this festival that the Holy Spirit was given (Acts 2:1-4).

3. The Festival of Tabernacles or Booths lasted for one week. It was also called the *festival of ingathering* (Exodus 23:16; 34:22; Leviticus 23:34;

Deuteronomy 16:13). It celebrated Israel's 40 years of wandering before entering the Promised Land of Canaan. The Festival of Tabernacles is observed every fall.

4. The Sabbath Day was also considered a festival (Leviticus 23:2-3). It was observed every week on the seventh day.

5. The Festival of Trumpets was celebrated every fall. The priests blew trumpets, or special horns, on this day. This marked the beginning of the Jewish year (Leviticus 23:24; Numbers 29:1). Jews today call this festival Rosh Hashanah (RAHSH huh-SHAH-nuh).

6. The Day of Atonement was a day of fasting each year (Leviticus 23:26-31). Jews today call this holy day Yom Kippur (YOHM kuh-POOR). It is celebrated one week after Rosh Hashanah.

7. The Festival of Purim (POOR-um) celebrated the escape of the Jews from total destruction. It is also called the Festival of Lots. Lots had been drawn to set the day on which to destroy the Jews. This yearly feast day began during the time of Esther (Esther 9). It is celebrated in late February or early March.

8. The Festival of Dedication celebrated the dedication of the Temple by the Maccabees (John 10:22). It was also called the *feast of lights*. It was a week-long festival held every December. Jesus declared himself to be the Light of the World during one of these festivals. Jews today call this festival Hanukkah (HAH-nuh-kuh) or Chanukah.

***See* abomination of desolation, atonement, Bible, celebrate, dedication, Esther, Exodus, fast, holy, Israel, Jew, law, Maccabees, New Testament, Palestine, Pentecost, Sabbath, sacrifice, tabernacle, temple, unleavened bread**

filled with the Spirit (FILD with thuh SPIR-ut) *verb phrase:*

***See* baptism with the Holy Spirit, Charismatic Movement, entire sanctification, glossolalia**

Finney, Charles G. (FIN-ee, CHAHRLZ) *proper noun:*

***See* revival**

firmament (FER-muh-munt) *noun:*

Firmament means the sky or the heavens. The sky looks something like a huge bowl covering the earth. But it really is not solid as the word *firmament* seems to suggest. The Hebrew word translated *firmament* may mean simply "empty space."

Genesis 1:6-8; Job 26:7; Isaiah 40:22

***See* Bible, heaven, Hebrew**

firstborn (FERST-BOHRN) *noun:*

The firstborn is the first son born to a husband and wife. He inherits the birthright.

Jesus Christ is the "firstborn over all creation" (Colossians 1:15). This means that the creation belongs to Him. Christ is also "the firstborn from among the dead" (v. 18). This means that He was the first one resurrected from the dead. Believers hope for a resurrection like His. Christ is also "the firstborn among many brothers" (Romans 8:29). This means that God plans for Christians to become like Christ.

See **adoption, birthright, brother, Christ, Christian, God, hope, inheritance, resurrection, Son of God**

first work of grace (FERST WERK uv GRAYS) *noun phrase:*

First work of grace is a term some people use for the new birth. This refers to a person becoming a Christian, being born again, or being saved.

The term is often used by people in the Holiness Movement. Entire sanctification is called the second work of grace. Therefore, the conversion experience is called the first work of grace.

John 3:3-8; 1 John 3:9

See **born again, conversion, entire sanctification, grace, Holiness Movement, new birth, salvation, save, second work of grace**

fleece (FLEES) *noun:*

A fleece is a skin of a sheep. The Bible tells the story of Gideon, who tested God by using a fleece. Gideon wanted to be sure God would help Israel defeat its enemies. So he put a fleece on the ground one night. He asked God to make it wet and the ground around it dry. The next night he asked that the fleece be dry and the ground wet. It happened both times. This proved to him that God would give Israel victory (Judges 6:37-40).

Today, Christians sometimes test God by putting out a *fleece*. This means that they set certain conditions as a way of determining His will.

See **faith, Gideon, will**

flesh (FLESH) *noun:*

Flesh is the body of a living creature. It also means the natural life of a creature. It especially refers to the natural life of humans (Genesis 6:12-13). Flesh also includes all that people depend on for life, other than God. The word *flesh* means much more than the body.

The Bible teaches that God created the flesh and called it good. People simply live as human beings when they "live in the flesh" (Galatians 2:19-20).

Flesh becomes sinful when people turn away from God. They make themselves the center of life rather than God. They worship the creature instead of the Creator (Romans 1:25). The New Testament calls this "life after the flesh" (Romans 8:5, 13; Galatians 5:19-21). Thus, the Greek word for *flesh* is sometimes translated "sinful nature." Life lived after the flesh is life under the power of sin. It is the opposite of life controlled by the Holy Spirit.

Romans 3:20; 7:5; 8:1-17; 1 Corinthians 3:1-3; Galatians 3:5

See **body, carnal, creation, Creator, depravity, faith, life, man, nature, sinful nature, spirit, worship**

flood (FLUD) *noun:*

A flood is a large amount of water that covers the ground. The Bible tells the story of the great Flood during the time of Noah. The people who lived at that time were very sinful. The Flood was a judgment from God. God saved Noah and his family in the ark. God promised that there would never be such a flood again. The rainbow is the sign of this promise.

Genesis 6:5—9:17

See **ark, Bible, deluge, God, judgment, Noah, promise, sin**

follower (FAH-luh-wer) *noun:*

A follower is a person who follows another person. A follower accepts the ideas and teachings of someone else. Followers try to imitate their leaders.

Followers of Christ believe in His teachings. They are Jesus' disciples and strive to follow Him. Jesus said that people were to follow Him (Matthew 4:19-20; 16:24; 19:21). Christians are to imitate Jesus Christ.

Paul told the early Christians to follow his example (1 Corinthians 4:16).

Matthew 8:19; John 12:26; 1 Peter 2:21

See **believer, Christ, Christian, Jesus, disciple, Paul**

fool (FEWL) *noun:*

The Bible says a fool is someone who tries to live as though there is no God. A fool tries to live by his or her own wisdom and power. Fools reject the law of God.

Those who accept Christ as Savior are called fools by those who reject Him. Those who reject Christ think that they are wise. But Paul says that they are fools. The wisdom of this world is not true wisdom. God's wisdom is revealed in the cross of Christ. True wisdom comes through faith in Christ.

Psalms 14:1; 53:1; Proverbs 1:7-9; Luke 12:20; 1 Corinthians 1:18-31; Ephesians 5:15

See **cross, faith, humility, law, salvation, Savior, Torah, wisdom**

forbearance (fohr-BAIR-uns) *noun:*

See **patience**

foreknowledge (fohr-NAH-lij) *noun:*

Foreknowledge is God's knowledge of the future. God knows all that can be known about the past, present, and future. He is omniscient or "all knowing."

No one really knows the full meaning of the foreknowledge of God. God knows that His plans for the world will be completed in the future. Yet people still have freedom of choice. They may choose not to be a part of the plan of God. Human freedom is not limited by the foreknowledge of God.

God knows sinners before they know Him. He calls them to become His children. He makes them able to repent of their sins and obey Him. This is called prevenient grace. Thus, the foreknowledge of God is one part of His prevenient grace.

Acts 2:23; Romans 8:29; 11:2; 1 Peter 1:2

See **child of God, election, freedom, God, grace, obedience, omniscience, prevenient grace, repent, sin**

forgive (fohr-GIV) *verb:*

To forgive is to set a person free from guilt and blame. To forgive is to pardon someone who has wronged you. It means to treat one as though he or she did nothing wrong. To forgive is to stop feeling badly towards the person who did the wrong. You treat the person as a friend.

The Bible teaches that God forgives those who sin against Him. He forgives those who repent of their sins. He forgives because of His love for the sinner. This forgiveness was made possible through the death of Jesus on the cross.

People can also forgive. They can forgive other people who do wrong to them. We should forgive others as God has forgiven us.

Exodus 32:32; Psalm 25:18; Jeremiah 31:34; Matthew 6:12-15; 9:2-6; 18:21; Luke 5:20-24; John 7:16-17; Ephesians 1:7; Colossians 3:13; 4:32; 1 John 1:9

See **atonement, forgiveness, guilt, love, new birth, pardon, repent, sin, sinner**

forgiveness (fohr-GIV-nes) *noun:*

Forgiveness is an act that frees a person from guilt and blame. The person who has done wrong is pardoned. The person who pardons is the one who was wronged.

The Old Testament shows the love of God in His forgiveness of sinners (Exodus 34:6-7; Psalms 78:37-38; 130:3-4; Daniel 9:9). Jesus offered sinners forgiveness from God even before He died on the Cross (Mark 2:3-10). The death of Jesus is the perfect and final revelation of the mercy of God. It reveals His suffering love for sinners. It shows how willing God is to forgive all who trust in Jesus (Romans 3:21-28). This is the Atonement.

God offers His forgiveness to sinners who will accept it. Those who receive His forgiveness by faith are freed from their guilt. God puts them in a right relation with himself (Romans 4:5-8). They are born again by the Spirit of God and become His children.

People who have been truly forgiven by God must forgive others who wrong them (Matthew 6:9-15; 18:21-35; Luke 6:37).

Psalm 130:4; Luke 17:4; Acts 5:31; 13:38; 26:18; Ephesians 1:7-14

See **atonement, born again, child of God, expiation, faith, forgive, guilt, justification, mercy, pardon, propitiation, repent, revelation, sin, sinner**

fornication (FOHR-nuh-KAY-shun) *noun:*

Fornication usually means sex between a man and woman who are not married. The Greek word for *fornication* in the New Testament often means more than this. It may mean adultery, sex with a harlot, or other immoral acts. The Bible teaches that fornication is wrong. Only sex between a husband and wife is approved by God.

Acts 15:20; 1 Corinthians 5:1; 6:13-20; Ephesians 5:3-4; 1 Thessalonians 4:3-8; Revelation 14:8

See **adultery, Bible, Greek, harlot, immoral, marriage**

forty days (FOHR-tee DAYZ) *noun phrase:*

Forty days in the Bible means a period of time, perhaps about a month. People in Bible times were not always interested in being exact as we are today. This explains why so many things in the Bible lasted "for forty days." The word *forty* is used often in the Bible.

Genesis 7:4; 12; 8:6; Exodus 24:18; 34:28; Deuteronomy 9:9; 11, 18, 25; 10:10; Jonah 3:4; Matthew 4:2; Acts 1:3

See **Bible, forty years**

forty years (FOHR-tee YEERZ) *noun phrase:*

Forty years in the Bible means a period of time of about one generation. It does not always refer to an exact number of years. A generation may actually be as few as 25 years.

The use of 40 years can also refer to longer periods of time. For example, 480 years is 12 generations. The word *forty* is often used in the Bible.

Genesis 25:20; Exodus 16:35; Numbers 14:33-34; Deuteronomy 2:7; Joshua 14:7; Judges 3:11; 5:31; 8:28; 1 Samuel 4:18; 2 Samuel 5:4; 11:42; Ezekiel 29:11-13

See **Bible, forty days**

free agency (FREE AY-jun-see) *noun phrase:*

See **freedom**

Free Methodist church (FREE METH-uh-dist) *proper noun phrase:*

See **Holiness Movement, Wesleyanism**

free will (FREE WIL) *noun phrase:*

See **freedom, will**

freedom (FREE-dum) *noun:*

Freedom is the quality of not being limited. People are free to make choices. But they are not completely free of limits. Only God has total freedom. Yet even He has chosen to limit himself in some ways.

Freedom in the Bible is always a gift from God. For example, the people of Israel were once slaves in Egypt. Their masters decided what they could and could not do. But God set them free in the Exodus (Exodus 7:6-11; 19:3-6; 20:2). The people of Israel were free to obey God or to return to slavery in Egypt. They found true freedom in their covenant relation with God.

The Exodus taught Israel to value freedom as a great gift of God. Jesus told His followers to respect the freedom of nations, societies, and people.

Real freedom means to be loosed from all forms of spiritual slavery. It is freedom from the power of sin, legalism, and Satan. True Christian freedom is found in salvation. God alone is the Source of such true freedom.

Freedom is not only freedom from different kinds of slavery. It is freedom to love and serve other people. It is freedom to live by new values and to please God (Galatians 5:1, 13).

The Bible teaches that freedom is a gift. But, it can be lost by failing to keep it safe. Christians should not allow themselves to become slaves to their old master, Satan (Galatians 4:9, 21; 5:1, 13; Ephesians 6:10-17).

Free agency is one kind of freedom. This means that God has given people the power to make moral choices. People are responsible for their choices because they have free agency.

Free will is another kind of freedom that God has given people. Sinners are able to have faith in Christ only because of prevenient grace.

See **Bible, Christ, Christian, convenant, death, Egypt (map 2), Exodus, faith, gift, God, grace, Israel, legalism, love, morality, prevenient grace, responsibility, salvation, Satan, servant, sin, slave, spiritual, values, will**

fruit (FREWT) *noun:*

Fruit is the natural product that results from the growth of a plant. It develops naturally as part of the life of the plant.

The Bible talks about the fruit that comes from spiritual growth. People who have been made right with God live righteous lives. They bear the "fruit of righteousness" (Philippians 1:11). This is a witness to others that they are Christians.

John 4:36; 12:24; 15:2; Romans 6:21-22; 7:4; Hebrews 12:11; James 3:17;

See **disciple, fruit of the Spirit, God, growth in grace, righteousness**

fruit of the Spirit (FREWT uv thuh SPIR-it) *noun phrase:*

The fruit of the Spirit are Christian virtues. The Holy Spirit helps a Christian to develop a character like that of Jesus Christ. Galatians 5:22-23 lists the fruit of the Spirit. The fruit of the Spirit and spiritual gifts are not the same.

See **character, Christ, Christian, fruit, gift, Holy Spirit, Jesus, spirit, virtue**

full salvation (FOOL sal-VAY-shun) *noun phrase:*

Full salvation is a phrase that is sometimes used for entire sanctification.

See **entire sanctification, fullness of the Spirit**

fullness of the Spirit (FOOL-nus uv thuh SPIR-it) *noun phrase:*

Fullness of the Spirit is a phrase sometimes used to mean entire sanctification. It refers to the act of the Holy Spirit that cleanses from all sin. The Christian who has the fullness of the Spirit belongs completely to God.

See **baptism with the Holy Spirit, cleanse, entire sanctification, heart purity, Holy Spirit, initial sanctification, sanctification, spirit**

fundamentalism (FUN-duh-MEN-tul-iz-um) *noun:*

Fundamentalism is one way of understanding the Christian faith and life. It began in the 1800s as a response to liberalism. It is an important part of Christianity today.

Fundamentalism stresses five basic beliefs: (1) Jesus was born of the Virgin Mary. (2) Jesus died to pay the price for the sins of man. He died in the place of sinners. (3) God gave the very words of the Bible to its writers. (4) The resurrection of Jesus means that His dead body received new life from God. (5) The second coming of Christ to earth will be premillennial and physical. These five beliefs are called "the fundamentals."

Fundamentalism is often thought to be the same as evangelicalism and conservative Christianity. But these forms of Christianity differ in some important ways. A person or group that accepts fundamentalism is described as fundamentalist.

See **atonement, Calvinism, conservative Christianity, evangelical, inspiration, inspiration of the Bible, liberalism, propositional truth, reformed tradition, resurrection, Virgin Birth, Wesleyanism**

fundamentalist (FUN-duh-MEN-tuh-list)

1. *adjective:* Fundamentalist describes a person or belief as related to Fundamentalism. For example, a Fundamentalist church is one that accepts the basic beliefs of Fundamentalism.

2. *proper noun:* A Fundamentalist is a person who generally accepts Fundamentalism.

See **Fundamentalism**

future (FYEW-cher) *noun:*

Future is time that follows now. Future is what will happen in time to come. People often view the future as including eternity. The Bible teaches that God works to make the future serve His will. Christians can be sure that God will use the future for their good. The kingdom of God will be completed in the future.

Mark 13:9-23; Romans 8:37-39; Revelation 1:17-19

See **eschatology, eternity, good, kingdom of God, omniscience, patience, Revelation, Second Coming, will**

G g

Gabriel (GAY-bree-ul) *proper noun:*

Gabriel is the name of an angel in the Bible. Gabriel was sent by God to take messages to certain people. He appeared to Daniel and Mary.

Daniel 8:16-27; 9:21; Luke 1:11-22, 26-31

See **angel, Daniel, Mary**

Gad (GAD) *proper noun:*

1. Gad was one of the 12 sons of Jacob. His descendants became one of the tribes of the nation of Israel.

2. Gad was the name of the land occupied by the tribe of Gad.

Genesis 30:10-11; Numbers 26:15-18

See **Gad (map 3), Israel, Jacob, tribes of Israel**

Galatia (guh-LAY-shuh) *proper noun:*

Galatia was a Roman province in Asia during New Testament times. The apostle Paul visited Galatia on his missionary journeys. He started several churches there. He wrote a letter, now known as the Book of Galatians, to churches in this area.

1 Corinthians 16:1; Galatians 1:2; 2 Timothy 4:10; 1 Peter 1:1

See **Asia Minor, Galatia (map 11), Galatians, missionary, Paul, Roman, Rome**

Galatians (guh-LAY-shunz) *proper noun:*

1. The Galatians were people who lived in the area of Galatia in Asia Minor. The apostle Paul wrote a letter to the Christian converts in Galatia.

2. Galatians is a book in the New Testament that is one of the epistles. Galatians was written by the apostle Paul to some Christian churches in Asia Minor. The letter is important for its teaching about justification by grace through faith alone.

The letter answers the question of whether Gentile Christians must accept Jewish laws. Some Jewish Christians in Galatia argued that faith in Christ was not enough for salvation. They believed that these Gentile Christians had to obey the laws of Moses. This meant they should be circumcised. Paul said that these ideas were a "false gospel." The true gospel says that people are justified through faith in Christ alone.

Galatians also teaches that Christ gives freedom from slavery to the Jewish law. Christians are free to be guided by the Holy Spirit. The Spirit helps them to produce the fruit of the Spirit (Galatians 5:22-23). He makes it possible for them to show their faith in love and service (vv. 6, 13-14).

Acts 16:6-10; 18:23; 1 Corinthians 16:1; Galatians

See **Asia Minor (map 11), convert, epistle, faith, flesh, freedom, fruit of the Spirit, Galatia (map 11), Gentile, Holy Spirit, justification, justification by**

grace through faith alone, law, legalism, New Testament, Paul, works of the flesh

Galilean (GAL-uh-LEE-un)

1. *proper adjective:* Galilean describes someone or something from the region of Galilee in northern Palestine.

2. *proper noun:* A Galilean was a person from Galilee. Galileans spoke Aramaic in a different way than other people in Palestine. Thus, people in Jerusalem could tell Galileans by their speech.

Matthew 26:73; Luke 13:2; John 4:45

See **Aramaic, Galilee, Palestine**

Galilee (GAL-uh-lee) *proper noun:*

1. Galilee was a region in northern Palestine. Many Gentiles lived there. Jesus spent most of His life in Galilee.

2. The Sea of Galilee was a large lake in the eastern part of Galilee. The lake was also called Chinnereth, Gennesaret, and Tiberias.

Numbers 34:11; Isaiah 9:1; Matthew 2:22; 21:11; Mark 7:31; Luke 5:1; John 6:1

See **Galilee (map 8), Gentile, Jesus, Palestine**

Gamaliel (guh-MAY-lee-el) *proper noun:*

Gamaliel was a Pharisee and teacher. The apostle Paul was one of his students.

Acts 5:34-35; 22:3

See **apostle, Pharisee, Paul**

Garden of Eden (GAHR-dun uv EE-dun) *proper noun:*

See **Eden**

Garden of Gethsemane (GAHR-dun uv geth-SEM-uh-nee) *proper noun:*

See **Gethsemane**

Gath (GATH) *proper noun:*

Gath was one of five main cities of the Philistines. It was located near the Mediterranean Sea in the southwest part of Israel. Goliath, the Philistine giant, was from Gath.

1 Samuel 5:8-9; 6:17; 17:4; 21:10; 2 Samuel 21:19-22

See **Gath (map 4), Goliath, Israel, Mediterranean Sea, Philistine**

Gaza (GAH-zuh) *proper noun:*

Gaza was one of five main cities of the Philistines. It was located near the Mediterranean Sea in the southwest part of Israel. Samson was captured by the Philistines and put in prison in Gaza. Samson died in Gaza.

Genesis 10:19; Joshua 15:47; 1 Samuel 16:1, 21, 30-31; 2 Kings 18:8

See **Gaza (map 4), Israel, Mediterranean Sea, Philistine, Samson**

Gehenna (guh-HEN-uh) *proper noun:*

See **hell**

genealogy (JEE-nee-AHL-uh-jee) *noun:*

A genealogy is a list of the important ancestors of a person, family, or nation. Genealogies were very important to the Jews. Genealogies showed how they were related to Abraham. The Gospels of Matthew and Luke give the genealogy of Jesus. Matthew shows the relation of Jesus to Abraham and David. Luke shows the relation of Jesus to Adam.

Matthew 1:2-26; Luke 3:23-38

See **Abraham, David, generation, Jesus, Jew, Luke, Matthew**

generation (JEN-uh-RAY-shun) *noun:*

A generation is the time period between the age of parents and their children. A generation is about 25 years.

A generation is all the people living at about the same period of time (Matthew 11:16-19; 24:34; Philippians 2:15).

Generation may also mean giving birth to or producing a person or thing (Genesis 2:4; 5:1).

See **forty years, genealogy**

Genesis (JEN-uh-sis) *proper noun:*

Genesis is the first book in the Old Testament. It is a part of the Pentateuch or Torah, the Law of Moses. It tells about the creation of the world and of the human race. Genesis mainly tells about the beginnings of the Hebrew people. It tells stories about the great patriarchs: Abraham, Isaac, Jacob, and Joseph. It tells how God called Abraham from Mesopotamia to live in Canaan. God promised the land of Canaan to his descendants. But the book ends with the descendants of Abraham living in Egypt.

See **Abraham, Canaan (map 1), creation, Egypt (map 2), Hebrew, Isaac, Jacob, Joseph, law, Mesopotamia (map 1), Old Testament, patriarch, Pentateuch, Torah**

Gennesaret (guh-NES-uh-rut) *proper noun:*

See **Galilee**

Gentile (JEN-tiel) *proper noun:*

A Gentile is a person who is not a Jew. The Hebrew and Greek words for Gentile mean "people" or "nations." The Jews called all nations other than their own *Gentile.*

The gospel of Jesus teaches that there is no real difference between Jews and Gentiles. Everyone may be a part of the family of God through Jesus Christ.

Isaiah 49:6; Matthew 4:15-16; Romans 2:14; 3:29; 4:9-12; Galatians 2:14-16; 3:14, 23-29

See **church, family of God, gospel, Jew**

Gethsemane (geth-SEM-uh-nee) *proper noun:*

Gethsemane was the name of a garden at the foot of the Mount of Olives. Jesus prayed there the night of His betrayal.

Matthew 26:36-56; John 18:1-12

See **betrayal, Gethsemane (map 10), Jesus, Mount of Olives (map 10)**

Gideon (GID-ee-un) *proper noun:*

Gideon was one of the leaders of Israel during the period of the judges. He was a great warrior. He is also known for using a fleece to determine God's will.

Judges 6:1—8:33

See **fleece, Israel, judge, Judges, will**

gift (GIFT) *noun:*

A gift is something given by one person to another. A gift is given without charge. People give gifts because they want to, not because they have to. Salvation is a gift from God (Ephesians 2:8-10).

The wise men presented gifts to the child Jesus (Matthew 2:1-12).

The gift of the Spirit is the Holy Spirit, who is given to Christians (Acts 2:38; Galatians 3:1-14; 4:6). The Holy Spirit makes them new people. He works in Christians to make them like Christ.

The gifts of the Spirit are the helps the Holy Spirit gives to Christians. These spiritual gifts help them to do the work of Christ on earth. They show that God is working in the Church. All Christians receive at least one of the gifts to use in God's work.

Some examples of the gifts of the Spirit are teaching, prophecy, and healing. The New Testament lists some of the gifts of the Spirit in four places: Romans 12:6-8; 1 Corinthians 12:4-10, 28; Ephesians 4:11-14; Hebrews 2:4.

See **charismatic, Christ, church, fruit of the Spirit, grace, healing, Holy Spirit, Pentecostal, prophecy, spiritual, talent, tongue**

gifts of the Spirit (GIFTS uv thuh SPIR-it) *noun phrase:*

See **gift**

Gilead (GIL-ee-ud) *proper noun:*

Gilead was a part of Palestine on the east side of the Jordan River. Its boundaries went from the Sea of Galilee to the Dead Sea. Gilead was known for its healing balm.

Genesis 37:25; Numbers 32:1, 26, 29; Jeremiah 8:22, 46:11

See **balm, Dead Sea, Gad, Gilead (map 7), healing, Jordan, Palestine**

Gloria Patri (GLOH-ree-uh PAH-tree) *proper noun:*

The Gloria Patri is a short Christian hymn to the Father, the Son, and the Holy Spirit. Gloria Patri means "Glory to the Father." The Gloria Patri is sometimes called the lesser doxology.

See **doxology, father, glorify, glory, God, hymn, Son, spirit, Trinity, worship**

glorification (GLOH-ruh-fuh-KAY-shun) *noun:*

Glorification is the time when believers will be given a resurrected body. This will happen at the second coming of Christ. It will be the final and full redemption of the body (Romans 8:23). It is the time when believers are finally prepared for heaven. Christians will receive immortality at the time of glorification (1 Corinthians 15:33).

Romans 8:18-24; 1 Corinthians 15:12-58; Philippians 3:10-12, 20-21; 1 John 3:2-3

See **heaven, immortality, parousia, perfection, redemption, resurrection, Second Coming**

glorify (GLOH-ruh-fie) *verb:*

To glorify means to give praise to someone. People who glorify God show that they reverence Him as Lord. To glorify God is to worship Him.

Psalm 86:9; John 12:28; 17:1: 1 Corinthians 6:20

See **glory, God, praise, worship**

glorious (GLOH-ree-us) *adjective:*

Glorious describes a person or event that shows the glory of God. One example in the Bible is the glorious name of the Lord (Nehemiah 9:5). Two other examples are the glorious grace of Christ (Ephesians 1:6) and the glorious gospel (1 Timothy 1:11).

Psalm 87:3; 111:3; 145:5; Isaiah 42:21; 63:15; Luke 9:30-31; Acts 2:20; Romans 8:21; Titus 2:13; 1 Peter 1:8-9

See **glorify, glory, God, gospel, grace, Lord, name**

glory (GLOH-ree) *noun:*

Glory is the quality of being very great and important. Sometimes the Bible speaks of people who have glory. Such people may be rich or powerful.

But the Bible usually reserves the word *glory* for God. He alone is truly great. The glory of God is His holiness as it is revealed to people. Sometimes the glory of God is described in the Bible as "bright" and "shining." People who give glory to God praise Him for his greatness.

Jesus Christ is the perfect revelation of the glory of God. He shows people what God is really like. People who come to know God in Christ share His glory. This means that God changes them so they become more and more like Christ (John 1:1-18; 2 Corinthians 3:17-18; 4:6).

Sometimes the glory of God means the future hope of Christians (Romans 5:2; Colossians 1:27; 3:4; 1 Thessalonians 2:12; 1 Timothy 3:16; Hebrews 2:10; 1 Peter 5:1, 4, 10). Thus, the glory of God may mean heaven.

See **Christ, Christian, glorification, glorify, God, heaven, holiness, hope, perfect, praise, revelation, worship**

glossolalia (GLAHS-uh-LAY-lee-uh) *noun:*

Glossolalia comes from two Greek words meaning "speaking in tongues." Usually glossolalia refers to speaking in a language that people cannot understand. The words do not seem to make any sense.

People who use glossolalia believe that the Holy Spirit is speaking through them. They believe that glossolalia is the spiritual gift of tongues described in 1 Corinthians 12—14. People who believe this way are called charismatic Christians. Pentecostal churches stress this belief.

Some charismatics claim that glossolalia proves that a Christian is filled with the Spirit.

Acts 2:1-4; 10:44-46

See **belief, charismatic, Christian, 1 and 2 Corinthians, entire sanctification, Greek, Pentecostal, spirit, tongue**

gnostic (NAHS-tik)

1. *adjective:* Gnostic describes someone or something related to Gnosticism.

2. *noun:* A gnostic is a person who accepts the beliefs of Gnosticism.

See **Gnosticism**

Gnosticism (NAHS-tuh-SIZ-um) *proper noun:*

Gnosticism was a belief that stressed secret knowledge as the way to salvation. The term comes from a Greek word meaning "knowledge." Gnosticism began about the same time as Christianity.

The beliefs of Gnosticism were difficult to understand. Its most important beliefs were these: The true God is pure spirit. Spirit alone is good. The world of matter was created by a lower god. All that is made of matter is evil. This includes the human body. Thus, creation was a serious mistake. Salvation comes by learning that a person has the Spirit of God in him.

Gnostics did not agree among themselves in their views on morality. They agreed that their bodies were evil. But they disagreed in their beliefs about how they should behave. Some types of Gnosticism encouraged their followers to use their bodies to do evil. This would show their dislike for the body. Others taught their followers to avoid all pleasures. This also would show their dislike for the body.

Some early Christians seem to have been influenced by Gnosticism. These gnostic Christians believed that Christ was the Redeemer. But they denied that He was a real human being. This belief was called Docetism. They also denied that He was truly God. He was only a good, lower god. Gnostic Christians denied that God the Father was the Creator. They worshiped angels as gods.

See **angel, belief, body, Christ, Christian, Christianity, church, creation, evil, God, god, heresy, immoral, morality, redeemer, salvation, spirit, spiritual, worship**

God (GAHD or GAWD) *proper noun:*

God is the one Being who is the only Source of His own Being. He gives existence to the world. All life and being come from Him. And there is no life or being apart from Him. He alone is the Eternal One. All else is made by Him. He is Lord over all.

People know God by the ways in which He reveals himself to people. He reveals himself through what He does and says. The Bible records the ways in which God has made himself known.

He has made himself known as Creator and Redeemer. God created the world out of nothing and called it "good." The whole world depends on Him for existence. No other powers are equal to His power.

God acted to redeem His creation after the Fall. He showed by this that He is love. His love shows His concern for the world He created.

God shows who He is by the way He acts in history. He showed His power and love when He set Israel free from slavery in Egypt. He showed His love when He made a covenant of friendship with them. He showed His power by bringing them into the land He had promised them. He showed His love by forgiving them when they had sinned against Him.

The greatest example of His power and love was shown in Jesus Christ. God was fully present in His Son, Jesus Christ. All that Christ did showed what God is like. Jesus showed the power and love of God by defeating Satan and forgiving sinners. The death of Jesus on the Cross showed how much God loves the world.

The resurrection of Jesus showed the power of God over death. It showed His power over all that opposes the kingdom of God on earth.

All the deeds of God show His holiness and love. The Second Coming will show the final victory of His holiness and love.

God is omnipotent. He is all-powerful. No one can stop Him from doing what He plans to do. He is also omniscient. He knows all that can be known. He is also omnipresent. He is present now in all creation. And He is eternal. He always has been and always will be.

God is sovereign. He is not limited in power. He is always in control of all things and all people. God showed His sovereignty in creation. He also showed His sovereignty in the life, death, and resurrection of Jesus.

God is Spirit. He is not limited by time and space. People do not see Him with their eyes as they see other persons. But God completely relates to people as a person.

God is One. But He is also Triune. He reveals that He is at once Father, Son, and Holy Spirit.

***See* Allah, attribute, Bible, Christ, covenant, creation, cross, deism, deity, Egypt, eternal, Fall, glory, holiness, Immanuel, Incarnation, Israel, Jesus, kingdom of God, love, omnipotent, omnipresent, omniscient, pantheism, polytheism, redemption, resurrection, revelation, salvation, Satan, Second Coming, sovereign, spirit, theism, Trinity, Yahweh**

god (GAHD or GAWD) *noun:*

A god is anyone or anything a person worships. People may worship idols, which are images made by other persons. These are false gods. False gods, such as Baal, are mentioned in the Bible.

People may also worship the things they own. They may worship their family, race, nation, or place in society. Anyone or anything a person loves more than God is a false god. The Bible says that worshiping false gods is a sin (Exodus 20:1-6).

Judges 6:31; 1 Kings 18:22-29, 36-39; 1 Corinthians 8:4-6

See **Asherah, Ashtaroth, Baal, God, idol, idolatry, Ten Commandments, worship**

God-fearer (GAHD-FEER-er) *proper noun:*

God-fearer was a term used to refer to Gentile converts to Judaism. These proselytes accepted basic Jewish beliefs but were not circumcised.

Acts 10:1-2

See **circumcise, convert, Gentile, Jew, Judaism, proselyte**

Godhead (GAHD-HED) *proper noun:*

Godhead is a word sometimes used in the King James Version of the Bible. It means Deity, the Triune God.

Acts 17:29; Romans 1:20; Colossians 2:9

See **deity, God, Trinity, version**

godliness (GAHD-lee-nus) *noun:*

Godliness is a way of life for people who believe in God. It shows that they worship and obey God. The Greek word for godliness means piety or reverence.

1 Timothy 2:2; 3:16; 4:7-8; 6:3, 5-6, 11; 2 Timothy 3:5; Titus 1:1; 2 Peter 1:3, 6-7; 3:11

See **Christian perfection, Greek, piety, reverence, worship**

godly walk (GAHD-lee WAWK) *noun phrase:*

The Bible sometimes uses the word *walk* to mean how a person lives. A godly walk is a life that shows proper reverence for God and love for one's neighbor. Christians should try to please God in their spiritual walk. They should try to obey God and His laws. They should do justice, love mercy, and walk humbly with God (Micah 6:8).

Genesis 17:1; Luke 1:6; Acts 9:31; 1 John 1:7; 2 John 4

See **disciple, discipline, godliness, holiness, justice, law, light, reverence, spiritual, walk**

God's will (GAHDZ WIL) *noun phrase:*

See **God, will**

God's Word (GAHDZ WERD) *proper noun phrase:*

See **Bible, Jesus, word**

Golden Rule (GOHL-dun REWL) *proper noun:*

The Golden Rule is a teaching of Jesus. He said His followers should act toward others as they would want others to act toward them. The Golden

Rule is a part of the Sermon on the Mount (Matthew 7:12). It also appears in the Book of Luke (6:31). There Jesus tells His followers how to respond to those who abuse them.

See **followers, Jesus, Luke, Matthew, Sermon on the Mount**

Golgotha (GAHL-guh-thuh) *proper noun:*

Golgotha is the Hebrew and Aramaic name of the place where Jesus was crucified. The word means "skull" or "the place of a skull." It was a hill near the city of Jerusalem. The Latin word for it is *Calvary*.

Matthew 27:33; Mark 15:22-25: John 19:17

See **Calvary, crucifixion, crucify, Hebrew, Jerusalem, Jesus**

Goliath (guh-LIE-uth) *proper noun:*

Goliath was a giant who fought for the Philistines against the army of Israel. David killed him. Goliath was from Gath.

1 Samuel 17:4-54

See **David, Gath, Israel, Philistine**

Gomorrah (guh-MAWR-uh) *proper noun:*

See **Sodom and Gomorrah**

good news (GOOD NEWZ) *noun phrase:*

See **gospel**

Good News Bible (GOOD NEWZ BIE-bul) *proper noun phrase:*

The *Good News Bible* is a modern-day translation of the Bible.

See **Bible, version**

good works (GOOD WERKS) *noun phrase:*

Good works are the kind of acts that result when a person becomes a Christian. Good works are called *good* because they show love for God and all people. Some people try to win salvation by doing good works. But salvation comes through grace and faith in Jesus Christ only. Good works are natural for Christians, because God works through them.

Ephesians 2:10; Philippians 2:12-13

See **Christian, ethics, faith, grace, justification, love, morality, salvation**

Goshen (GOH-shun) *proper noun:*

Goshen was a part of Egypt where the children of Israel lived for many years. It was called "the best of the land" (Genesis 47:6). Jacob had sent his sons to Egypt to buy food during a famine. There they found Joseph, their brother, whom they thought was dead. Joseph had his entire family move to Egypt to live in the land of Goshen. The Hebrews lived in Goshen until Moses led them out of Egypt.

Genesis 45:10; 46:28-29; 34; 47:1, 4, 27; Exodus 9:26

See **children of Israel, Egypt (map 2), Exodus, Goshen (map 2), Jacob, Joseph, Passover, plague**

gospel (GAHS-pul):

1. *noun:* The gospel is the good news about Jesus Christ. Gospel is from the Greek word *evangel,* which means "the good news of victory." The victory of Jesus over sin has made salvation possible for all people. This is the message of the gospel. It is the message that God loves sinners and wants to forgive them. He wants them to be free from sin and spiritual death.

Jesus preached that the kingdom of God had come near in Him. This is good news. The kingdom of God breaks the rule of Satan. People know that they cannot be free themselves. But Jesus sets them free from the power of evil and guilt. He makes them new people. They become citizens of the kingdom of God.

2. *proper noun:* The first four books of the New Testament are called Gospels. These books are Matthew, Mark, Luke, and John. They are called Gospels because they tell the good news of salvation through Christ. They tell the story of the life and ministry of Jesus. The Gospels tell how the kingdom of God came near in Jesus Christ. The writers of the Gospels are called evangelists. The word *evangelist* in Greek means "one who preaches good news."

Matthew 4:23; 26:13; Mark 1:1, 14-15; Luke 4:18; 9:6; 20:1; Acts 5:17; Romans 1:16; 1 Corinthians 4:15; Galatians 1:8-9

See **Christ, death, evangelist, God, good news, grace, guilt, Incarnation, Jesus, justification, kingdom of God, love, ministry, mission, salvation, sin**

gospel song (GAHS-pul SAHNG) *noun phrase:*

A gospel song is a song in which a testimony to salvation is given. It gives praise to God for His gift of salvation. It tells of the joyful good news experienced in salvation through Jesus Christ.

Psalm 28:8; 40:3; 96:1; Ephesians 5:19; James 5:13

See **God, good news, gospel, hymn, new birth, praise, Psalms, salvation, testimony**

gossip (GAHS-up)

1. *verb:* To gossip is to speak carelessly of another person. To gossip is to say things about others that are meant to hurt them. It means to tell what may be true but should not be told. It is to slander the name of another.

2. *noun:* Gossip is careless speech about another person. It is usually speech that tries to make one person think less of another person. Gossip is also a person who does this.

Psalms 15:3; 31:13; 101:5; Proverbs 10:18; Jeremiah 6:28; Romans 1:30; 2 Corinthians 12:20

See **blasphemy, envy, hate, inveigh, judge, slander, temperance**

grace (GRAYS) *noun:*

Grace means favor shown or received. Grace in the Bible refers to the favor that God shows to sinful people. It is the love He shows them. God does this even though sinful people do not deserve His favor. So grace is not earned.

Grace is also the help God gives those who cannot help themselves. He gives this help through the Holy Spirit.

The whole Bible tells how God gives His grace to all people. He showed His grace to Adam and Eve, Noah, Abraham, Moses, and David. But the highest and most complete revelation of God's grace was in Jesus Christ. The New Testament tells of the grace of God revealed in Christ. Sinners can experience the love and forgiveness of God through Christ. Thus, salvation is called a work of grace.

Genesis 6:8; 19:19; 33:10; Exodus 33:12-17; Proverbs 3:34; Jeremiah 31:2; John 1:14-17; Acts 14:3, 26; 15:11; Romans 1:5, 7; 3:24; 5:2, 15, 17, 20; Galatians 1:3, 6, 15; 6:18

See **Christ, cross, first work of grace, forgiveness, justification, love, mercy, prevenient grace, repent, revelation, salvation, second work of grace, sin**

gracious (GRAY-shus) *adjective:*

Gracious describes someone who is kind and pleasant to others. The word *gracious* is most properly applied to God. But people may also be called gracious. Such persons are thoughtful of others. They are willing to share what they have to help others.

Genesis 43:29; Exodus 33:19; Amos 5:15; 1 Peter 2:3

See **God, grace, humility**

Graham, Billy (GRAY-um, BIL-ee) *proper noun:*

Billy Graham is a Christian evangelist. He is the best-known evangelist of the 20th century. Billy Graham is a member of the Southern Baptist Convention. He was born in Charlotte, North Carolina, in 1918.

Graham has conducted evangelistic crusades in major cities all over the world. He started these major crusades in 1949. He is the founder of the Billy Graham Evangelistic Association (BGEA). "The Hour of Decision" is a weekly radio program on which Graham or one of his helpers preach. *Decision* is the name of the magazine that the Billy Graham Evangelistic Association prints each month.

Billy Graham has retired as the head of the BGEA. Franklin Graham, a son of Billy Graham, is now the president of BGEA. He conducts crusades, now called *festivals,* in much the way his father did.

See **Baptist, crusade, evangelical, evangelist, revival**

Great Commandment (GRAYT kuh-MAND-munt) *proper noun phrase:*

The Great Commandment is what Jesus said was the most important commandment. Jesus summed it up in the command to love God and to love one's neighbor (Matthew 22:36-40; Mark 12:28-34; John 13:34). This command quotes the Shema of Deuteronomy 6:4-5 and Leviticus 19:18.

See **commandment, Deuteronomy, God, Jesus, law, Leviticus, love, neighbor, Shema**

Great Commission (GRAYT kuh-MISH-un) *proper noun phrase:*

The Great Commission is the mission that the risen Christ gave to His disciples. Their mission included several parts. They were to be witnesses to Jesus Christ. They were to preach the good news about Him to everyone. They were to teach people to obey all that Jesus taught. They were to baptize everyone who accepted their preaching and teaching. Christ promised that He would be with them as they carried out their mission.

Matthew 28:18-20; Mark 16:15-18; Luke 24:46-49; Acts 1:8

See **baptism, Christ, disciple, evangelism, good news, gospel, Jesus, Lord, mission, preach, promise, testimony, witness**

Greece (GREES) *proper noun:*

Greece was an important world power during the 300s B.C. Its leader, Alexander the Great, ruled most of the nations around the Mediterranean Sea. He defeated nations as far east as India. Greek philosophy, culture, and language became known everywhere Greece ruled.

See **Alexander the Great, Greece (map 11, time line), Greek, Israel (map 8), Mediterranean Sea (map 11), philosophy**

greed (GREED) *noun:*

Greed is a great desire to have much more than a person needs. It is a powerful desire to own much more than a person can use.

Proverbs 1:19; 15:27; 21:26; Isaiah 56:11; Ephesians 5:3-5; 1 Timothy 3:3

See **covet, envy, lust, sin**

Greek (GREEK) *proper adjective:*

Greek is the language of Greece. It was spoken everywhere around the Mediterranean Sea during New Testament times. The New Testament was written in Greek.

Greek describes persons or things from Greece. Greece often refers to the culture of Greece.

See **Greece, Greek (time line), Mediterranean Sea (map 11), New Testament, Septuagint**

grove (GROHV) *noun:*

See **Asherah**

growth in grace (GROHTH in GRAYS) *noun phrase:*

Growth in grace is the spiritual growth the grace of God makes possible for Christians. The Holy Spirit helps Christians develop and increase in their knowledge of God. He helps them become more like Christ.

Romans 8:28-30; Ephesians 2:19-22; 4:15-16; 1 Thessalonians 4:1, 9-12; 1 Peter 2:1-3; 2 Peter 3:18

See **Christ, Christian, edify, God, grace, knowledge, means of grace, process in sanctification, spiritual, will**

guilt (GILT) *noun:*

Guilt is the blame people bear for doing wrong. Guilt results from disobeying God. Guilt is the pain that people feel when they have sinned. People cannot always depend on feelings of guilt. The conscience may be mistaken. Sometimes people may feel guilty when they are not. At other times, they may not feel guilty when they really are. God alone decides who is guilty and who is innocent.

Romans 2:1-16; 8:1-17; 1 Corinthians 4:3-5; Ephesians 2:1-10; 1 John 3:19-24

***See* condemnation, conscience, forgiveness, guiltless, guilty, innocent, judgment, justification, responsibility, sin**

guiltless (GILT-lus) *adjective:*

Guiltless describes persons or actions that are free from guilt. People who have not done wrong are guiltless. People whom God has forgiven for doing wrong are guiltless.

Exodus 20:7; 1 Kings 2:9; Romans 4:7-8

***See* forgiveness, freedom, guilt, guilty, innocent**

guilty (GILT-ee) *adjective:*

Guilty describes someone who has done something wrong. The person is guilty even if he or she does not feel guilty for doing wrong. Guilty people will be punished for their sins unless they repent and ask God for forgiveness.

Matthew 23:18; James 2:10

***See* forgiveness, guilt, guiltless, repent, sin**

H h

Habakkuk (huh-BAK-uk or HAB-uh-kuk) *proper noun:*

1. Habakkuk was one of the prophets in the Old Testament. A Bible book is named for him. Habakkuk spoke against the evils of his nation, Judah, and its enemy Babylon. He told the people of Judah that Babylon would come to punish them. But he said the faithful people of Judah would be kept from harm.

2. Habakkuk is a book in the Old Testament. It is one of the Minor Prophets.

See **Babylon, Bible, evil, faith, faithful, Judah, Old Testament, prophet**

habit (HAB-ut) *noun:*

A habit is a behavior or action that is done almost without thinking. People develop habits from doing the same thing over and over again for a long time.

Some habits are good, and some habits are bad. Bad habits make it hard for people to do what is right. This may be true even after a person becomes a Christian. A new Christian must guard against returning to the bad habits of his past. God can set people free from their bad habits. But people must also discipline themselves. They should develop good habits to take the place of bad habits.

Luke 4:16; 1 Corinthians 6:9-20; Colossians 3:1-17; 2 Peter 2:20-22

See **backslide, deliverance, discipline, forgiveness, freedom, good works, right**

Hades (HAY-deez) *proper noun:*

Hades is the place the New Testament says people go after death. *Hades* is the Greek word for "grave." The Hebrew word *Sheol* means the same. Sometimes Hades may mean "hell."

Psalm 16:10; Matthew 11:20-24; 16:13-20; Luke 16:19-31; Acts 2:22-36; Revelation 20:11-15

See **abyss, death, hell, purgatory, Sheol**

Hagar (HAY-gahr or HAY-ger) *proper noun:*

Hagar was a concubine of Abraham. She gave birth to a son whose father was Abraham. The name of the son was Ishmael.

Genesis 16:1-15; 21:8-21; Galatians 4:24-25

See **Abraham, Arab, concubine, Ishmael**

Haggai (HAG-ee-ie or HAG-ie) *proper noun:*

1. Haggai was one of the prophets in the Old Testament. A Bible book is named for him. Haggai preached to the Jews who returned to Palestine from their Exile in Babylon. He encouraged them to build again the Temple in Jerusalem. The prophet Zechariah worked with Haggai.

2. Haggai is a book in the Old Testament. It is one of the Minor Prophets.

See **Bible, exile, Jew, Judah, Old Testament, prophet, temple, Zechariah**

hallelujah (HAL-uh-LEW-yuh) *interjection:*

Hallelujah means "praise the Lord." It is a Hebrew word used in the Old Testament. Alleluia is the Greek form of the same word. *Hallelujah* and *alleluia* are still used to praise God and call others to worship Him.

Psalms 106:1; 111:1; 112:1; 113:1, 9; 135:1-21; 146:1-10; 148:1-14; 150:1-6; Revelation 19:1-6

See **amen, glorify, God, Lord, praise, Psalms, worship, Yahweh**

hallow (HAL-oh) *verb:*

To hallow is to make holy or to honor as holy. "Hallowed be thy name" is a phrase from the Lord's Prayer. This phrase is used to give praise to God as the Holy One.

Matthew 6:9-13; Luke 11:2-4

See **Bible, holiness, holy, Lord's Prayer, praise, sanctification**

hamartiology (hah-MAHR-tee-AHL-oh-jee) *noun:*

Hamartiology is the doctrine of sin. The word *hamartiology* comes from two Greek words meaning "sin" and "study."

See **doctrine, sin**

Hanukkah (HAH-nuh-kuh) *proper noun:*

Hanukkah is Jewish festival held in December. It is also called the Festival of Dedication. Hanukkah is also known by Chanukah.

See **festival**

Haran (HAYR-un) *proper noun:*

Haran was a city in Mesopotamia in Old Testament times. It was an important city of trade. Abraham and his family lived in Haran for a time (Genesis 11:31-32).

Genesis 12:4-5; 27:41-45; 28:10; 29:4

See **Abraham, Chaldea, Haran (map 1), Mesopotamia**

harlot (HAHR-lut) *noun:*

A harlot is a woman who has sex with another person for money. Another word for harlot is *prostitute.* The Bible says this is wrong.

The Bible sometimes uses the word *harlot* in a special way. Harlot may mean the people of God who are not faithful to Him. A harlot may be a person who does the serious sins of idolatry or apostasy.

Genesis 34:31; Exodus 20:14; Joshua 2:1; 6:17; Isaiah 1:21; Jeremiah 3:1; 1 Corinthians 6:15

See **adultery, apostasy, faithful, fornication, idolatry, sin, unclean**

harvest (HAHR-vust)

1. *verb:* To harvest means to gather a crop.

2. *noun:* Harvest means the crop that is gathered. This is usually fruit or grain that has been grown on the land. Harvest also means the season when the crops are gathered. A harvest may mean any result of something that is done.

The New Testament uses the word *harvest* in a special way. A harvest there means people ready to hear the gospel. Harvest means the people God gathers into His kingdom. Harvest may also mean the time of final judgment.

Leviticus 19:9-10; Ruth 2:7; Matthew 9:35-38; 12:1-8; 13:24-30, 36-43; John 4:31-38; 1 Corinthians 3:5-9; Galatians 6:7-10

See **convert, evangelism, fruit, gospel, inheritance, judgment, kingdom of God, reward**

Hasmoneans (HAZ-muh-NEE-unz) *proper noun:*

The Hasmoneans were a family of priests in Israel. They were also known as the Maccabees. They were Jewish rulers and leaders in the first and second centuries B.C.

See **Maccabees, priest**

hate (HAYT)

1. *verb:* To hate means to dislike someone or something very much. It also means to oppose someone or something as an enemy.

The Bible says that God hates sin. This means that He is against evil. He hates evil actions and evil things. For example, He hates idols. But He loves all people, both sinners and righteous people.

The Bible also says that He wants people to hate evil. But they should not hate other people. They should love even their enemies.

Sometimes the Bible says that one person should hate another person. In this case it means that people should not let their love for others replace their love for God (Luke 14:25-27).

2. *noun:* Hate is a strong feeling or dislike. Hate is usually the opposite of love.

Psalm 97:10; Proverbs 8:13; Hosea 11:1-12; Amos 5:14-15; Matthew 5:43-48; Luke 14:25-33; Romans 12:9-21

See **enemy, evil, God, idol, love, righteous, sin, sinner**

head (HED) *noun:*

A head is the upper part of the body. It contains the eyes, ears, nose, mouth, and brain.

The head of a river is the place where it begins. It is the river's source.

The Bible writers did not speak of the head as the thinking part of a person. They viewed the head as the source of life itself. They knew that the body could not live without the head.

The New Testament says that the Church is like a body. Christ is the

Head of that Body. He is its Source of life, power, and unity. He is also the Lord of the Church.

The New Testament also says that a married couple is one body. The husband is the head of the wife. He is to protect and care for her. But he is not her lord. Christ is the Lord of both the husband and wife.

Ephesians 5:21—6:9; Colossians 1:15-29; 3:18—4:1

See **Body of Christ, Christ, church, ecumenical, life, marriage, obedience, unity**

heal (HEEL) *verb:*

To heal means to give healing.

See **healing, health**

healing (HEEL-ing) *noun:*

Healing is the act or process of returning people to health. Healing makes better the bodies, minds, or spirits of people who are ill. Thus they become well and normal again.

The Bible says that all healing comes from God. This is true whether the healing is natural or is a miracle. The Bible gives many examples of both kinds of healing.

The Bible considers death and illness to be enemies. Life and health are the good gifts of God. Thus, the Bible urges sick people to seek medical help and to pray for healing. But it does not promise that all illnesses will be healed in this life. Perfect health should be expected only in heaven.

Salvation in the Bible means the healing of a person from the disease of sin. People are made spiritually well when they are saved from sin.

Exodus 15:22-27; Deuteronomy 32:39; Psalm 6:1-10; Isaiah 57:14-21; Jeremiah 33:1-9; Hosea 5:13—6:3; Malachi 4:1-3; Luke 4:16-30; 13:10-17; 2 Corinthians 12:7-10; Revelation 22:1-5

See **affliction, anoint, body, death, evil, health, heaven, laying on of hands, life, mind, miracle, salvation, save, spirit, spiritual, suffering, tree of life**

health (HELTH) *noun:*

Health is the normal condition of a living being. Health means that sickness or disease is absent from the body. A person who has health is well in his or her whole person: body, mind, and spirit. Spiritual health means to be well morally and spiritually.

See **affliction, anoint, body, death, evil, healing, laying on of hands, morals, spirit, spiritual, tree of life**

heart (HAHRT) *noun:*

The heart is the part of the body that pumps blood. But in the Bible the heart means the center of a person or thing. The heart means the inner person. It is the person as he or she really is. It includes the mind, will, emotions, desires, and plans.

God knows the heart of every person (1 Samuel 16:7). He knows who a person really is on the inside. People know each other only on the outside.

People should love God with all their hearts (Mark 12:28-34). Their hearts are right with God when they love Him completely (Acts 13:22).

Sinners do not love and obey God as they should. They need a changed heart. This change begins with repentance. Then God gives them a new heart. God changes sinners on the inside so that they can love and obey Him. Christ lives in changed hearts. He is at the center of everything a Christian is, says, and does.

Deuteronomy 6:4-15; 1 Kings 15:14; 2 Chronicles 16:9; Psalm 51:10, 17; Ezekiel 18:31; 36:22-32; Matthew 6:21; 12:33-37; 15:1-20; John 14:18-24; Acts 8:21-22; Romans 2:25-29; 5:1-11; Galatians 4:4-6; Ephesians 3:14-21; 1 Thessalonians 3:11-13; 2 Thessalonians 2:16-17; 1 Timothy 1:5; 2 Timothy 2:20-26; Hebrews 3:7—4:13; 10:19-25; Revelation 2:23

See **body, born again, circumcision, conversion, holiness, love, mind, new birth, perfect, repent, repentance, sinner, spirit, trichotomy**

heart purity (HAHRT PYOOR-uh-tee) *noun phrase:*

Heart purity in a person means that he or she is pure or clean in his or her inner life. This is the result of the cleansing of the heart by the Holy Spirit. He frees Christians from the nature that makes it easy for them to disobey God. Thus people are free to love and obey God completely. They want to do what pleases Him. Their motives are pure and right before God. Heart purity makes a person all that God wants him or her to be.

Heart purity in churches of the Holiness Movement means the same thing as entire sanctification.

Psalms 24:4; 51:10; Matthew 5:8; Acts 15:9; 2 Timothy 2:22; Titus 2:11-14; James 4:8; 1 Peter 1:22

See **cleanse, entire sanctification, heart, Holiness Movement, perfect, pure**

heathen (HEE-thun) *noun:*

A heathen is a person who does not worship the true God. A heathen usually worships false gods. The word *heathen* usually refers to all who are not Jews or Christians. The words *heathen* and *pagan* usually have the same meaning.

Psalm 2:1-11; Romans 1:20-23

See **belief, conversion, convert, Gentile, God, god, pagan, worship**

heaven (HEV-un) *noun:*

Heaven is the home of God and His angels. Heaven is a term that means that God is beyond human and earthly limits.

The Bible sometimes uses the word *heaven* to mean simply the sky. Heaven is the part of creation that is not earth (Genesis 1:1).

The Jews were careful about the use of God's name. They avoided using His name if possible. They sometimes used the word *heaven* when they meant God.

The kingdom of God is the same thing as the kingdom of heaven. People sin against heaven when they sin against God. Christians live on earth, but they are really citizens of heaven. This means that their final loyalty is to God, not to any human ruler.

Believers will go to heaven after the second coming of Jesus Christ. They will always be with the Lord. They will live together in a new heaven and a new earth (Revelation 21:1-4). Heaven and earth will no longer be divided. The rule of God will be complete. Heaven is that place where the will of God is done completely.

Deuteronomy 26:15; Isaiah 65:17; 66:22; Matthew 5:45; 6:10; Mark 13:32; Luke 15:18; 2 Corinthians 4:15—5:10; Philippians 3:20; Colossians 1:5; 1 Peter 1:4; 2 Peter 3:10-13; Revelation 21:1-27

See **Abraham's bosom, angel, believers, creation, Day of the Lord, eschatology, eternal life, eternity, firmament, hell, hope, immortality, inheritance, judgment, kingdom of heaven, loyalty, paradise, Second Coming, transcendence**

heavenly (HEV-un-lee) *adjective:*

Heavenly describes something that is related to God or heaven. For example, the Heavenly Father is God. A heavenly gift is one that God gives.

Matthew 5:48; 6:14, 26, 32; John 3:12; Hebrews 6:4; 11:16

See **father, gift, God, heaven**

Hebrew (HEE-brew) *proper noun:*

Hebrew is the language in which the Old Testament was first written. It was spoken by the ancient people of Israel and Judah. Hebrew is the language spoken in Israel today.

Genesis 14:13; John 19:17

See **Israel, Judah, Old Testament**

Hebrews (HEE-brewz) *proper noun:*

1. The people of Israel and Judah were called Hebrews. The name *Hebrews* was used to separate the Israelites from other nations. Abraham was called a Hebrew (Genesis 14:13). The Bible says that Yahweh was God of the Hebrews (Exodus 3:18; 5:3; 7:16; 9:1, 13; 10:13).

2. Hebrews is a book in the New Testament. It is one of the epistles. No one knows for certain who wrote the book or to whom it was written. Some Bible scholars think the apostle Paul wrote this letter. It probably was a sermon that was then sent to a church as a letter.

The Book of Hebrews shows how Christ is greater than anything in Judaism. Christianity is better than the religion of the Hebrew people. It warns Christians of the dangers of rejecting Christ.

Genesis 39:14, 17; 40:15; 41:12; 43:32; Exodus 1:15-19; 2:6-7, 11-13; 21:2; Deuteronomy 15:12; 1 Samuel 4:6, 9; 13:3, 7, 19; 14:11, 21; Jonah 1:9

See **Abraham, Christ, Christianity, epistle, Hebrew, Israelites, Judaism, New Testament, Yahweh**

Hebron (HEE-brun) *proper noun:*

Hebron was one of the most ancient cities of Palestine. It was located south of Jerusalem. Abraham built an altar there (Genesis 13:18). David lived there for a time (2 Samuel 2:1-3). Later, David reigned as king of Judah in Hebron for seven years (2 Samuel 5:5).

See **Abraham, David, Hebron (maps 3, 4, 7, and 8), Judah**

hell (HEL) *noun:*

Hell is a place of separation from God that lasts forever. The Hebrew word for hell is *Sheol.* The dead exist in Sheol. The Greek word for Sheol is *Hades.* The New Testament also uses the Greek word *Gehenna* for hell. Gehenna was the name of the place where trash from Jerusalem was burned. Jesus used this word to refer to hell.

Deuteronomy 32:22; Psalm 139:8; Matthew 5:22; 10:28; 11:23; 16:18; Luke 16:23; James 3:6; 2 Peter 2:4; Revelation 20:14

See **damn, damnation, eternal death, Hades, New Testament, Sheol**

henotheism (HEN-uh-thee-IZ-um) *noun:*

Henotheism is the worship of one god by people who believe that other gods exist.

See **God, god, monotheism, theism, worship**

heresy (HAIR-uh-see) *noun:*

A heresy is a false belief or practice that departs from Christian truth. Heresy harms the unity of the Church. The Greek word for heresy means sect or division.

Acts 24:14; 1 Corinthians 11:19; Galatians 5:19-21; 2 Peter 2:1

See **belief, Christian, church, creed, doctrine, dogma, truth**

heretic (HAIR-uh-tik) *noun:*

A heretic is a person whose beliefs and practices are false.

See **heresy**

Herod (HEHR-ud) *proper noun:*

Herod was the name of several rulers in Palestine who served Rome.

1. Herod the Great was king of the Jews when Jesus was born (Matthew 2:1-23). He had the Temple in Jerusalem built again the way it used to be.

2. Herod Antipas (AN-tuh-puhs) was the son of Herod the Great. He had John the Baptist killed (Matthew 14:1-12).

3. Herod Agrippa I was a grandson of Herod the Great. He had the disciple James killed (Acts 12:1-23). He was the ruler Paul had to face (Acts 25:13—26:32).

See **Agrippa, Jesus, John, Palestine (map 8), Rome (map 11), temple**

Hezekiah (HEZ-uh-KIE-uh) *proper noun:*

Hezekiah was a king of Judah, the Southern Kingdom. He was the son of

Ahaz. Hezekiah was king for 29 years. He lived at the same time as the prophet Isaiah. Hezekiah was one of the few kings of Judah who was righteous. He brought religious reform to the nation.

2 Kings 18:1—20:21; 2 Chronicles 29:1—32:33

See **Ahaz, Hezekiah (time line), Isaiah, Judah, prophet, righteous**

high priest (HIE PREEST) *noun phrase:*

The high priest in Israel was the leader of the priests. The high priest was also called the chief priest. His most important task was done in the Temple on the Day of Atonement. He offered sacrifice for his sins and the sins of the people on this day. The high priest in the days of Jesus led the Sanhedrin.

The Book of Hebrews says that Jesus is a better High Priest. Jesus was without sin. He offered himself as the perfect sacrifice for the sins of the world.

Exodus 28—29; Leviticus 8; John 11:45-53; Acts 23:1-5; Hebrews 4:14—5:10; 6:13—10:25

See **atonement, Hebrews, Israel, mercy seat, priest, sacrifice, Sanhedrin, sin**

Hinduism (HIN-dew-iz-um) *proper noun:*

Hinduism is a religion that began in India. No one person started Hinduism. It began almost 3,500 years ago. There are so many forms of Hinduism that it is really a family of religions. People who follow Hinduism are called Hindus. Hindus believe that the world does not have lasting value. They also believe that there are many ways to find salvation.

See **religion, salvation, values**

Hinnom (HIN-um) *proper noun:*

Hinnom is a valley on the west side of Jerusalem. It joins the Kidron Valley. Human sacrifices were made in the Hinnom Valley in Old Testament times (2 Kings 23:10; Jeremiah 32:35). It was also called the "Valley of Slaughter" (Jeremiah 7:30-34; 19:6).

Joshua 15:8; 18:16; 2 Chronicles 28:3; 33:6

See **Baal, Jerusalem, Kidron, sacrifice**

Hittites (HIT-iets) *proper noun:*

Hittites were people who lived Canaan in Old Testament times. They were one of the Canaanite tribes. The Hittite kingdom was quite large, which included Syria and Asia Minor. Joshua did not conquer all the Hittites. The Israelites and Hittites lived together for many years.

Genesis 10:15; Exodus 3:8, 17; 13:5

See **Asia Minor, Canaanites, Hittites (map 3), Israelites, Joshua, Syria**

Hivites (HIV-iets) *proper noun:*

Hivites were people who lived in Canaan in Old Testament times. They were one of the Canaanite tribes.

Genesis 10:17; 36:2; Exodus 3:8, 17; 13:5

See **Canaan, Canaanites**

holiness (HOH-lee-nus)

1. *noun:* Holiness is the quality of God that makes Him completely different from His creation. He is the Creator. Everything else is His creation. No created being is His equal. The correct relation of a created being to God is one of worship. He alone is worthy of worship. He alone is holy.

Jesus Christ is the perfect revelation of the holiness of God. He shows what God is like. His life also shows how God wants people to live.

The holiness of God does not simply mean moral perfection. He is holy not just because He is morally perfect. He is holy because He alone is God. God's will is right because He wills it. Thus, He is the Judge of what is morally right. Morality is human behavior that agrees with the will of God.

God desires to make himself known as the holy God. He shows His holiness in His redeeming acts. He shows himself to be a God of justice and mercy. This shows His righteousness. He wants His people also to show His righteousness in all they do. They, too, should act justly and love mercy (Micah 6:8).

Christian holiness is the sanctification of believers through Jesus Christ. This comes when Christians give themselves fully to God. They receive the cleansing by faith. This makes them holy before God. God is the source of all holiness.

2. *proper adjective:* Holiness sometimes describes denominations that teach the doctrine of entire sanctification.

Deuteronomy 7:6-11; 1 Samuel 2:2; 1 Chronicles 16:8-34; Isaiah 5:16; 6:1-9; 40:25; 45:20-25; Luke 1:68-79; Romans 1:1-6, 19-32; 6:15-22; 12:1-2; 2 Corinthians 6:14—7:1; Ephesians 4:22-24; 1 Thessalonians 3:11—4:7; 5:23-24; Hebrews 12:10-14

See **consecrate, consecration, creation, death, doctrine, entire sanctification, holy, justice, mercy, obedience, original sin, revelation, righteousness, sanctification, sanctify, worship**

Holiness Movement (HOH-lee-nus MEWV-munt) *proper noun phrase:*

The Holiness Movement is a term that refers to churches that stress entire sanctification. These churches understand entire sanctification as a second work of grace. They generally have viewed entire sanctification and the baptism with the Holy Spirit as the same.

The Holiness Movement began after 1850 in a revival of interest in entire sanctification. This was a central doctrine of the early Methodists. But many leaders of the Holiness Movement came from churches of the Reformed tradition. Most churches of the Holiness Movement consider themselves Wesleyan in their beliefs.

A number of denominations came into existence as a result of the Holiness Movement. They include, among others, the Church of the Nazarene and the Pilgrim Holiness church.

Some Holiness churches began before the Holiness Movement started. These include the Free Methodist Church, the Wesleyan Methodist Church, and the Salvation Army. The Wesleyan Methodist and Pilgrim Holiness churches later united to form The Wesleyan Church. These denominations are a part of the Holiness Movement today. Many in the Holiness Movement still belong to the United Methodist church and other denominations.

Most denominations of the Holiness Movement are members of the Christian Holiness Partnership.

See **baptism with the Holy Spirit, Church of the Nazarene, denomination, doctrine, entire sanctification, Methodist, Reformed tradition, second work of grace, Wesleyan, Wesleyanism**

holy (HOH-lee) *adjective:*

Holy describes the perfection and purity of God that is His alone. Holy also describes that which is set apart for God's use. People, days, places, and things become holy when they are set apart for God's service. These are called holy because the presence of God sanctifies them.

The Holy Spirit is the Spirit of God. Jesus Christ is "the Holy One" and "the Holy One of God" (Mark 1:24; Acts 3:14). He is called this because He is the incarnation of God. The Holy Spirit came on Him when He was baptized. He is holy also because He gave himself to do His Father's will perfectly. He obeyed His Father and gave His life on the Cross for people's sins. He makes it possible for all people to be holy through His full salvation.

Leviticus 19:1; 20:7, 26; Numbers 5:17; 6:5-8; Deuteronomy 7:6; 14:2; Colossians 1:22; 1 Peter 1:15-16

See **Christ, dedication, God, holiness, Holy Spirit, incarnation, new birth, perfection, pure, righteousness, salvation, sanctification, sanctify, service, will**

Holy Communion (HOH-lee kuh-MYEWN-yun) *proper noun phrase:*

Holy Communion means the Lord's Supper. The bread and wine (juice) are used to represent the body and blood of Christ. Christ is present with His people in Holy Communion. It reminds Christians of the death and second coming of Jesus Christ.

Holy Communion celebrates the unity of the Church. Christians give thanksgiving to God for their salvation. This is why Holy Communion is also called the Eucharist. Holy Communion is one of the ways God gives His grace to Christians.

Luke 22:14-20; 1 Corinthians 11:23-26

See **bread, celebrate, crucifixion, Eucharist, grace, koinonia, Lord's Supper, means of grace, sacrament, salvation, unity, wine**

Holy Ghost (HOH-lee GOHST) *proper noun:*

Holy Ghost is a name that is sometimes used for the Holy Spirit. The term *Holy Ghost* is used in the King James Version of the Bible.

Luke 1:15; 3:22; 12:12; John 7:39; Acts 1:8; 2:4; 6:3; 1 Corinthians 2:13; 1 Peter 1:12

See **Holy Spirit, spirit, Trinity, version**

holy of holies (HOH-lee uv HOH-leez) *noun phrase:*

The holy of holies was the central part of the Jewish Temple. It was also called the most holy place. The whole Temple was called the holy place. This was because it was God's home on earth. God is the Holy One. In the inner part of the Temple was a small, special room. The ark of the covenant was kept in this room. This box was the symbol of the presence of God who could not be seen. Only the High Priest could enter the holy of holies. He did this only once each year on the Day of Atonement.

Exodus 26:33; Hebrews 9:1-3

See **ark of the covenant, atonement, festival, God, high priest, holy, symbol, tabernacle, temple, veil**

holy place (HOH-lee PLAYS) *noun phrase:*

The holy place was the outer part of the Tabernacle and Temple. The holy place was separated from the holy of holies by a curtain.

Exodus 26:31-35

See **holy of holies, tabernacle, veil**

Holy Spirit (HOH-lee SPIR-ut) *proper noun:*

The Holy Spirit is the Third Person of the Trinity (see Spirit).

See **Comforter, God, holy, Paraclete, Trinity**

hope (HOHP)

1. *verb:* To hope is to wish for and fully expect to receive something in the future. To hope is to accept a promise as true.

2. *noun:* Hope is faith that God will do in the future what He has promised. Hope is trusting God. The glorious hope of Christians is the return of Jesus Christ and the resurrection. He is the basis of the Christian's hope. Hope makes Christians able to live joyfully in the present, even when they suffer.

Psalm 38:15; 39:7; 146:5; Jeremiah 14:8; 17:13; Acts 28:20; Romans 4:18; 5:1-11; 8:18-39; 12:12; 15:4, 13; 1 Corinthians 13:7; 15:19; Galatians 5:5; Colossians 1:27; 1 Thessalonians 1:3; 4:13—5:11; Titus 2:11-14; Hebrews 6:11, 18; 7:19; 11:1; 1 Peter 1:3; 3:15

See **earnest of the Spirit, faith, joy, life, promise, resurrection, Second Coming, spirit, suffering, trust**

hosanna (hoh-ZAN-uh or hoh-ZAHN-uh)) *noun:*

See **Triumphal Entry**

Hosea (hoh-ZAY-uh) *proper noun:*

1. Hosea was a prophet from the Northern Kingdom of Israel. He lived during the 700s B.C. A Bible book is named for him.

Hosea's wife, Gomer, was not faithful to him. But Hosea still loved her and returned her to his home.

Hosea knew that Israel was like Gomer. Israel was not faithful to her "husband," God. Like Hosea, God begged for His people to return to Him.

This story is told in the Book of Hosea. The book especially stresses God's covenant love for Israel even though it worshiped idols.

Hosea predicted that Israel's sins would cause the people to become exiles in Assyria. But he also reminded them that the love of God was their only hope. He begged them to repent and return to God.

2. Hosea is a book in the Old Testament. It is one of the Minor Prophets.

See **Assyria, Baal, bless, covenant, exile, faithful, harlot, hope, idol, Israel, love, Old Testament, prophesy, prophet, repent, slave, worship**

Hoshea (hoh-SHEE-uh) *proper noun:*

1. Hoshea was the last king of Israel, the Northern Kingdom. He became king by killing Pekah. "He did evil in the eyes of the Lord" (2 Kings 15:30; 17:1-6).

2. Hoshea was the name of Joshua. Moses gave him the new name (Numbers 13:8, 16).

See **Hoshea (time line), Israel, Joshua, Moses, Pekah**

hospitality (HAHS-puh-TAL-uh-tee) *noun:*

Hospitality means taking care of someone who is not of one's own home. This could be a traveler, a friend, or a foreign person. Hospitality means welcoming with kindness a person who is in need.

Jesus says that showing hospitality to the needy is one form of receiving Him (Matthew 25:34-35). Paul says that Christians should show hospitality, especially to other Christians (Romans 12:13).

1 Kings 17:10-24; 1 Timothy 3:2; Titus 1:8; 1 Peter 4:9

See **alien, compassion, gracious, koinonia, minister, responsibility**

house of the Lord (HOUS uv thuh LOHRD) *noun phrase:*

House of the Lord probably meant the Tabernacle and later the Temple in the Bible. It also referred to synagogues.

Today Christians use the phrase to mean a church building in which God is worshiped.

Exodus 25:9—27:19; 1 Kings 6:1; 9:1; Ezra 1:2-5; Psalms 23:6; 27:4

See **church, synagogue, tabernacle, temple, worship**

human (HYEW-mun)

1. *adjective:* Human is a term that describes people. It describes that which has the character, form, and attributes of a person.

2. *noun:* A human is a man, woman, youth, or child. Humanity is a word that means all humans on earth.

The Bible says that God created humans in His own image. This makes humans different from the rest of God's creation.

Genesis 1:26-28

See **attribute, character, creation, image of God, man, nature, person**

humanism (HYEW-mun-iz-um) *noun:*

See **secular humanism, secularism**

humble (HUM-bul)

1. *verb:* To humble means to produce the quality of humility. A person can humble himself or herself. Or one person may humble another. Thus it means to force someone to accept a lower view of himself or herself. But it can also mean to hurt someone.

The Bible often speaks of God humbling people or nations. This means that He did something to break their sinful pride. He made them see that they were His creatures. They were not that great in themselves.

2. *adjective:* Humble describes a person who has the character of humility. Sometimes it describes a thing that is simple or has little value.

Deuteronomy 8:2-3; Psalms 10:12; 34:2; Proverbs 16:19; Daniel 5:22; 2 Corinthians 12:21; Philippians 2:8; James 4:6

See **affliction, Beatitudes, conceit, envy, gracious, humility, love, mercy, modesty, piety, pride, suffering, vain, vanity, virtue, wisdom**

humility (hyew-MIL-uh-tee) *noun:*

Humility is an attitude of modesty. It sometimes means the quality of being gentle, meek, and full of mercy. Humility is being not too proud of successes. It means freedom from conceit.

Humility is an important Christian virtue. It is a condition for receiving the grace of God. It is the attitude of people who depend on God. It is knowing that one is not worthy of the grace and presence of God. Humility includes respect for the worth of other people.

The Bible also speaks of humility as part of the character of God. This means that He shows loving care for His creation. He is gentle toward those who serve Him.

The New Testament speaks of the humility of Christ. He freely left heaven to live among people and reveal the love of God. Christ became a servant to others. He commanded His followers to do the same.

Proverbs 15:33; 18:12; 22:4; Acts 20:19; Colossians 2:18, 23; 1 Peter 5:5

See **affliction, conceit, envy, gracious, humble, justice, kenosis, love, mercy, modesty, piety, pride, suffering, vain, vanity, virtue, wisdom**

hymn (HIM) *noun:*

A hymn is a song written in praise and worship of a god. Hymn is used by Christians to refer to songs praising the Triune God.

Many of the Old Testament psalms could be called hymns. The New

Testament includes some poetry that may have been early Christian hymns.

Luke 1:46-55, 68-79; 1 Corinthians 13; Philippians 2:6-11; Colossians 1:15-20

See **gospel song, praise, Psalms, worship**

hymnal (HIM-nul) *noun:*

A hymnal is a book of hymns and similar songs. Hymnals often have gospel songs and choruses. Many hymnals have Scripture readings, the Apostles' Creed, and the Lord's Prayer. Hymnals are used in church services to worship and praise God.

See **Apostles' Creed, gospel song, hymn, Lord's Prayer, praise, worship**

hypocrisy (hi-PAHK-ruh-see) *noun:*

Hypocrisy is the act of claiming to be something that one is not. It is the attempt to live in such a way as to deceive people. Hypocrisy is the act of claiming to believe what a person really does not believe. It is living a lie. The Bible says that God hates hypocrisy.

Isaiah 32:6; Matthew 23:28; 1 Timothy 4:2; 1 Peter 2:1

See **belief, deceive, hyprocrite, lie, truth**

hypocrite (HIP-uh-krit) *noun:*

A hypocrite is a person who practices hypocrisy. A hypocrite says one thing and does another. Jesus said that the Pharisees were hypocrites.

Job 8:13; 13:16; Proverbs 11:9; Matthew 6:2, 5, 16; 23:28; Mark 12:15; Luke 11:44; 12:1; Galatians 2:10-21; James 3:17

See **hypocrisy**

hyssop (HIS-up) *noun:*

Hyssop is a plant referred to in the Bible. A number of plants have been suggested as the hyssop of the Bible. It is a kind of tall grass.

Hyssop was used in the Passover ritual (Exodus 12:22). It was used to sprinkle the blood onto the doorposts. It was used at the Crucifixion to put vinegar onto Jesus' lips (John 19:29). Hyssop mixed with cedar and red wool was also used to purify lepers (Leviticus 14:4). The same mixture was used to treat plagues (Leviticus 4, 6, 49-52). It was also used in the red heifer sacrifice (Numbers 19:2-6).

Numbers 19:18-19; 1 Kings 4:33; Psalm 51:7; Hebrews 9:19

See **Bible, blood, crucifixion, leper, Passover, plague, purification, ritual, sacrifice**

I i

idol (IE-dul) *noun:*

An idol is anything that is worshiped instead of God. An idol is a false god. The term *idol* most often refers to an image made by people. But people make idols of other things. For example, they make an idol of their race, nation, or place in society. Anything that a person loves more than God is an idol.

The Bible says that the worship of idols is wrong. God alone should be worshiped.

Deuteronomy 16:22; 29:17; 2 Kings 17:12; Ezekiel 14:3-7; 1 Corinthians 8:7-10

See **Asherah, Baal, deity, God, idolatry, Rimmon, worship**

idolatry (ie-DAHL-uh-tree) *noun:*

Idolatry is the practice of worshiping idols. Most of the nations around Israel worshiped images of false gods. God told Israel that they should worship Him alone.

God is the Creator. Everything else is His creation. It is wrong for people to worship what God made or what they have made. The worship of idols usually included practices that Jews and Christians considered immoral.

Exodus 20:1-6; 32:1-29; Isaiah 44:1-20; 45:20-23; Romans 1:18-32; 1 Corinthians 10:1-22; 1 Thessalonians 1:9

See **Asherah, Baal, creation, Creator, God, idol, immoral, Israel, Rimmon, Savior, worship**

Idumea (ID-yew-MEE-uh) *proper noun:*

See **Edom, Idumea (map 8)**

image of God (IM-ij uv GAHD) *noun phrase:*

Image of God is a phrase used in the Bible story of creation (Genesis 1:26-28). Human beings were created in the image of God. This means that people were similar to God in certain ways. Only humans were created in the image of God. Only humans were enough like God to enjoy fellowship with Him. The image of God is what makes people different from other creatures.

People were separated from fellowship with God because of the Fall. They continued to be human beings. But they did not live up to the purposes of God for them.

Christian doctrine teaches that the natural image and the moral image of a person are different. The fall of men and women did not change their natural image. People continued to be different from the other animals. But humans lost the moral image of God. They no longer enjoyed the fellowship they once had with God. Instead, Adam and all his descendants were separated from God and His holiness. It became easier for people to do wrong than to do good.

Jesus Christ was the "new Adam." He was the kind of person God intended humans to be. He made it possible for people to enjoy close fellowship with God once again. He did this by giving His life for the sins of the world. Now it is possible for all people to live once more in the image of God.

Genesis 5:1; 9:6; Romans 5:12-21; 1 Corinthians 15:45-49; Ephesians 4:22-24; James 3:9

***See* Adam, Christ, creation, doctrine, Fall, fellowship, gift, God, holiness, Jesus, morality, nature, original sin, person, personality**

immanence (IM-uh-nuns) *noun:*

Immanence means that God is present in the world. God is related to the world in a close way. The world exists because God exists in it. Immanence is not the same as imminence.

Exodus 3:1-22; Psalms 8:1-9; 139:1-12; Matthew 1:23; 18:20; John 1:1-5; Colossians 1:15-20; Revelation 21:1-4

***See* creation, God, imminence, Incarnation, transcendence**

Immanuel (i-MAN-yuh-wul) *proper noun:*

Immanuel is a Hebrew name that means "God is with us." The Gospel of Matthew gives this name to Jesus. God is with us in Jesus Christ. Immanuel is sometimes spelled Emmanuel.

Isaiah 7:14; Matthew 1:23; John 1:1-5, 14-18; Philippians 2:5-11; Hebrews 1:1-4

***See* Hebrew, immanence, Incarnation, Jesus, Matthew**

immersion (i-MER-shun) *noun:*

Immersion is one of the ways used in baptizing Christian believers. The person who is baptized is placed under water by the minister. Then he or she is quickly brought out of the water.

Mark 1:9-11; Luke 3:16, 21; Acts 8:37-39; Romans 6:3-4

***See* baptism, Christian, minister, pouring, sprinkling**

imminence (IM-uh-nuns) *noun:*

Imminence means that an event is about to happen. The time of the return of Christ is imminent, or near. Imminence is not the same as immanence.

Matthew 24:36-44; Revelation 22:12

***See* immanence, parousia, rapture, Second Coming**

immoral (im-MOHR-ul) *adjective:*

Immoral describes wrong behavior. People are immoral when they break moral laws. For example, the Bible strongly condemns sex sins as immoral.

1 Corinthians 5:9-11; 6:9-11; Ephesians 5:5; Hebrews 13:4

***See* adultery, condemn, fornication, immorality, morals, Ten Commandments**

immorality (IM-mohr-RAL-uh-tee) *noun:*

Immorality is the result of doing immoral deeds.

***See* adultery, fornication, immoral, morals**

immortality (IM-mohr-TAL-uh-tee) *noun:*

Immortality is life that does not end. God alone has immortality. He will give immortality to Christians at the time of the resurrection.

Eternal life is not the same as immortality. Eternal life is the new life God gives by His Spirit to believers. This means that Christians can enjoy eternal life now (John 20:31; 1 John 5:11-12).

Matthew 25:31-46; 1 Corinthians 15:12-57; 1 Thessalonians 4:13-18; 5:9-10

See **death, eternal, eternal death, eternal life, heaven, resurrection**

imparted righteousness (im-PAHR-tid RIE-chus-nus) *noun phrase:*

Imparted righteousness is the gift of God that makes believers truly righteous. Wesleyans stress this part of the new birth. They stress that God not only forgives sinners, but He also changes them. Christians can live lives that please God.

Romans 5:19-21; 1 Corinthians 6:9-11; 2 Corinthians 5:17; Galatians 5:6, 13-14, 22-25; Ephesians 2:8-10; Philippians 2:12-13; 3:7-11; Titus 2:11-14

See **Christian, gift, imputed righteousness, initial sanctification, justification, new birth, regeneration, righteousness, Wesleyanism**

impenitent (im-PEN-uh-tunt)

1. *adjective:* Impenitent describes a person who has not repented of his or her sins. Impenitent persons are not sorry for their sins. They do not let God forgive them.

2. *noun:* People in hell are sometimes called the impenitent.

Romans 2:5-8; Hebrews 2:1-4; Revelation 9:20-21; 16:10-11

See **damnation, forgive, hell, judgment, repent, sin**

impure (im-PYOOR) *adjective:*

Impure describes someone or something that is not clean. Acts, thoughts, and purposes can also be impure. Impure acts, thoughts, and purposes are sinful. God can make impure people clean.

Leviticus 10:10-11; Isaiah 35:8-10; Luke 11:24-26; 2 Corinthians 6:14—7:1

See **cleanse, holiness, immoral, pure, sin**

imputed righteousness (im-PYEW-tud RIE-chus-nus) *noun phrase:*

Imputed righteousness is the acceptance by God of sinners who repent and receive Christ. They are then considered to be righteous. They are accepted by God as having no guilt. Those of the Reformed tradition stress this side of the new birth. Some people teach that the righteousness of Christ hides a believer's sins from God.

Wesleyans also say that converted sinners are accepted by God. They are justified in the sight of God. But Wesleyans believe that much more happens when people are converted. A real change takes place in them. They are cleansed from their sins. God's righteousness is given or imparted to them. This is called regeneration. It is the beginning of sanctification.

Luke 18:9-14; Romans 3:21-28; 4:3-8; 5:19-21; 1 Corinthians 1:30; 6:9-11; 2 Corinthians 5:16-21; Galatians 2:15-21; 3:6-9; Ephesians 2:8-10

See **atonement, Calvinism, conversion, forgiveness, imparted righteousness, initial sanctification, justification, new birth, reconciliation, Reformed tradition, regeneration, repent, righteousness, sacrificial death, sinner, substitutionary theory of the Atonement, Wesleyan**

inbred sin (IN-bred SIN) *noun phrase:*

See **carnal, depravity, Fall, flesh, nature, original sin**

Incarnation (IN-kahr-NAY-shun) *proper noun:*

Incarnation is the event of God becoming man. The eternal Son of God entered into history in the person of Jesus. Still, He continued to be God. Jesus Christ is fully God and fully human.

John 1:1-18; Romans 1:3-4; 2 Corinthians 5:18-19; Philippians 2:5-11; Colossians 1:15-20; Hebrews 1:1-4

See **Christ, eternal, flesh, God, Immanuel, man, revelation, Son of God, Son of Man, Trinity, Virgin Birth**

incense (IN-sens) *noun:*

Incense was a substance burned as a part of worship in the Temple of Israel. Its smoke and smell rose upward. The burning of incense was thus a symbol for the prayers that rose to God. Some churches today burn incense as part of their worship.

Exodus 30:1, 7-9; 31:11; Luke 1:8-11; Revelation 5:8

See **prayer, ritual, symbol, temple, worship**

inclined to evil (in-KLIEND tew EE-vul) *adjective phrase:*

Inclined to evil means the tendency to do what is sinful. People find it easier to do evil than to do good. The tendency of people to do evil resulted from the Fall. This tendency is also called original sin.

Genesis 6:5; Jeremiah 17:9; Romans 1:18-32; 3:9-20; 7:7-25

See **carnal, evil, Fall, fallen nature, indwelling sin, original sin, sin**

indulgence (in-DUL-juns) *noun:*

An indulgence is a belief of the Roman Catholic church. An indulgence is an excuse that frees a person from punishment for small sins. Indulgences free people from the need of penance. Indulgences also lessen their time in purgatory. The saints have done more good deeds than are necessary for salvation. This makes indulgences for people today possible. Indulgences can help the living and the dead.

Protestants reject the idea of indulgences. They believe people are saved by the grace of God through faith in Jesus Christ alone.

See **belief, faith, forgiveness, good works, grace, merit, penalty, penance, Protestant, purgatory, reformation, Roman Catholic, saint, sin**

indwelling sin (in-DWEL-ing SIN) *noun phrase:*

Indwelling sin is the sinful nature that rules people because of the Fall. Wesleyanism believes that a person may be freed from indwelling sin. This is known as entire sanctification.

Psalm 51:5-12; Romans 7:13-25; 8:1-9

See **carnal, cleanse, entire sanctification, eradication, inclined to evil, nature, original righteousness, original sin, sin, Wesleyanism**

inerrant (in-AIR-unt) *adjective:*

Inerrant describes someone or something that is free from error. Only God is completely free from error. The Bible inerrantly reveals the will of God in all things necessary to salvation. It can be fully trusted as revealing the will of God.

See **authority of Scripture, Bible, inspiration, plenary, revelation, salvation, Scripture, will**

infinite (IN-fuh-nut) *adjective:*

Infinite describes someone or something without limits of any kind. God is the only being who is infinite. This is one of His attributes. The love, power, and knowledge of God are not limited. No one can measure the greatness of God.

Psalm 147:5; Romans 11:33-36; Ephesians 3:14-21; Jude 24-25

See **attribute, God, omnipotence, omnipresence, omniscience**

inheritance (in-HAIR-uh-tuns) *noun:*

Inheritance is what a person receives because he or she is an heir. Heirs receive the property and goods of their families. For example, God promised Abraham and his family the land of Canaan as an inheritance.

The death and resurrection of Jesus provided the gift of eternal life. It made it possible for people to become members of the family of God. They became heirs of God by faith in His Son, Jesus Christ. Inheritance in the New Testament includes the gift of the Holy Spirit. It also includes eternal life and the blessings of heaven.

Genesis 12:1-3; 13:14-17; Romans 8:12-17; 2 Corinthians 1:19-22; Galatians 3:6—4:7; Hebrews 1:1-2; 9:15; 1 Peter 1:4-5

See **adoption, Canaan, child of God, earnest of the Spirit, eternal life, family of God, resurrection, Son of God, spirit**

inherited depravity (in-HAIR-uh-tud dee-PRAV-uh-tee) *noun phrase:*

See **carnal nature, depravity, fallen nature, flesh, inclined to evil, indwelling sin, original sin**

initial sanctification (i-NISH-ul SANGK-tuh-fuh-KAY-shun) *noun phrase:*

Initial sanctification is the beginning of the work of sanctification. Initial sanctification happens at the time of justification and regeneration. It marks the beginning of the real change the Holy Spirit makes in believers. They are born anew by the Spirit and cleansed from the guilt of sin. Initial sanctification is not the same as entire sanctification. But it leads toward it.

Romans 6:12-13; 19-22; 1 Corinthians 1:2; 6:9-11; 2 Corinthians 7:1; Ephesians 4:13

***See* entire sanctification, imparted righteousness, justification, new birth, regeneration, salvation, sanctification, spirit**

innocent (IN-uh-sunt) *adjective:*

Innocent describes a person who is free from guilt or blame. Innocent people may be accused of doing wrong. But that does not mean they are guilty. They are still innocent.

Psalm 19:12-14; Jeremiah 2:34; Matthew 27:19; Luke 23:1-5, 47; Acts 20:26; James 5:6

***See* forgiveness, guilt, justification**

inspiration (IN-spuh-RAY-shun) *noun:*

Inspiration is the special direct influence of God's Spirit on human speech or writing. Inspiration in Greek means "God-breathed." Prophets in the Old Testament spoke the messages that God gave to them. Their messages were "breathed into them" by God.

Job 32:8; Psalm 33:6; 2 Timothy 3:16-17; 2 Peter 1:19-21

***See* anoint, authority of Scripture, Bible, inspiration of the Bible, prophesy, prophet, spirit**

inspiration of the Bible (IN-spuh-RAY-shun uv thuh BIE-bul) *noun phrase:*

Inspiration of the Bible means that God's Spirit helped certain people to write the Bible. He guided them to know what to say. Thus, their writings became the means by which God made His saving message known. Christ is the living Word of God. The Scriptures are the written Word of God. They give true witness to Him. Christians believe that the Bible tells people all they need to know to be saved. No other book is inspired in the way the Bible is inspired.

2 Timothy 3:14-17; 2 Peter 1:19-21

***See* authority of Scripture, Bible, canon, inerrant, inspiration, plenary, Scripture, spirit, witness, word**

instantaneous (IN-stun-TAY-nee-us) *adjective:*

Instantaneous means happening suddenly or in a moment of time. Justification and entire sanctification are instantaneous. They happen in a moment of faith. This changed relation with God makes possible continued growth in grace and faith.

Luke 18:9-14; 19:1-10; Acts 9:1-9; Romans 5:1-6; Ephesians 3:14-21; 1 Thessalonians 3:13; 5:23-24

See **crisis, entire sanctification, faith, grace, growth in grace, justification, new birth, salvation, sanctification, second work of grace**

intercede (IN-ter-seed) *verb:*

See **intercession, intercessory, mediator, pray, prayer**

intercession (IN-ter-SESH-un) *noun:*

Intercession is what a person does to present the needs of one person to another. Intercession is the work of a mediator. Intercession is prayer.

For example, Moses prayed that God would not destroy Israel. God answered the prayer of Moses and spared the sinful people of Israel.

Jesus is the great Mediator between God and people. He calls people to become followers of God. He also asks God to hear those who pray to Him.

The Holy Spirit intercedes for believers. He prays for Christians when they do not know what to say (Romans 8:26-27).

Christians can pray to God to ask Him to help other people. These are called intercessory prayers.

Exodus 32:1-29; Isaiah 53:12; John 17:1-26; Hebrews 7:23-25; 8:1-2; 1 John 5:13-17

See **atonement, Israel, mediator, Moses, pray, prayer, spirit**

intercessory (IN-ter-SES-uh-ree) *adjective:*

Intercessory describes something as it relates to intercession. Prayer for another person's needs is called intercessory prayer.

See **intercession, mediator, pray, prayer**

interpretation of the Bible (in-TER-pruh-TAY-shun uv thuh BIE-bul) *noun phrase:*

Interpretation of the Bible is an attempt of people to understand what the Bible means. People try to see how the message of the Bible fits into their daily lives.

The Bible speaks of interpretation of dreams. For example, Joseph and Daniel interpreted dreams for their kings (see Genesis 40:1-23 and Daniel 2:1-49).

Daniel 2:1-49; Romans 15:4; 1 Corinthians 10:6-11; 2 Timothy 3:14-17; 2 Peter 1:20-21

See **Bible, exegesis, message, Scripture**

inveigh (in-VAY) *verb:*

To inveigh is to speak or act against something or someone. A person can inveigh against the doctrines of the Church and thus try to destroy it.

1 Corinthians 15:12-19; Philippians 3:17-21; 2 Timothy 2:14-19

See **deceive, doctrine, heresy, orthodox**

invitation (IN-vuh-TAY-shun) *noun:*

An invitation is the act of inviting. In evangelical churches, ministers sometimes invite people after the sermon to accept Jesus Christ as Savior. This event is called the invitation. It is also referred to as an altar call.

The minister invites people to come forward to the front of the sanctuary. Sometimes people kneel at an altar to pray. At other times the people remain standing while the minister prays with them. In some churches, the people go to another room, where they meet with counselors.

Ministers may give invitations for other reasons. For example, they may invite people to pray for sanctification, healing, or intercession for others.

See **altar, evangelical, healing, intercession, minister, salvation, sanctification, Savior, sermon**

Isaac (IE-zik) *proper noun:*

Isaac was the son of Abraham and Sarah. He was the father of Jacob and Esau. Isaac in Hebrew means "laugh." Isaac was one of the patriarchs of the Hebrew people.

Genesis 15:1-21; 35:27-29

See **Abraham, Esau, Hebrew, Isaac (time line), Jacob, patriarch, Sarah**

Isaiah (ie-ZAY-uh or ie-ZIE-uh) *proper noun:*

1. Isaiah is the name of a prophet in the Old Testament who wrote a book of the Bible. The book has three main messages: (1) Judah will be destroyed by Babylon. The people of Judah will be taken from their homeland. (2) God will be with the people and will help them return to their country. They should put their trust in God alone (30:15). (3) The coming kingdom of God will be greater than any earthly kingdom. Isaiah is best known for what the book says about the Suffering Servant (42:1-4; 49:1-6; 50:4-9; 52:13—53:12; 61:1-3).

2. Isaiah is the name of a book in the Old Testament. It is one of the Major Prophets.

See **Babylon, Bible, exile, Isaiah (time line), Judah, kingdom of God, Palestine, prophet, servant, suffering**

Iscariot (is-KAIR-i-ut) *proper noun:*

See **Judas**

Ishmael (ISH-may-ul) *proper noun:*

Ishmael was the son of Abraham by his concubine, Hagar. The descendants of Ishmael are the people now called Arabs.

Genesis 16:1-16; 17:18-20; 25:12-18

See **Abraham, Arab, concubine, Hagar, Palestine**

Islam (IS-lahm) *proper noun:*

Islam is the name of a religion that arose in the 600s A.D. Those who practice Islam are called Muslims or Moslems. The words *Islam* and *Muslim* mean "one who submits to God." Islam was begun in Arabia by its founder, Muhammad, also spelled Mohammed. Islam believes in one

God, whom it calls Allah. Thus Islam is a monotheistic faith. Islam teaches that Muhammad was the greatest of all prophets. But Muslims do not worship him. The scriptures of Islam are called the Koran.

***See* Allah, God, Koran, monotheism, prophet, religion, Scripture**

Israel (IZ-ree-ul or IZ-rul) *proper noun:*

Israel usually means the special people of God. Israel has six different meanings in the Bible.

1. Israel is another name for Jacob, the second son of Isaac (Genesis 32:28). God gave Jacob this new name. It means "he who struggles with God."

2. The descendants of Jacob are called the people of Israel or Israelites.

3. Israel was the name of the united kingdom ruled by Saul, David, and Solomon.

4. The united kingdom divided after the death of Solomon. The northern part took the name Israel. The southern part took the name Judah (1 Kings 11:31). The people of Judah came to be called Jews.

5. Israel is the name of a modern nation in this same part of the world.

6. The Church is sometimes called "the true Israel" or "the new Israel." Israel here means the faithful people of God.

1 Samuel 15:17; Romans 9:6-7, 27—10:4; 11:1-6, 25-26; Galatians 6:16; Philippians 3:2-7

***See* Canaan (map 3), church, David, Isaac, Israel (time line), Jacob, Jew, Judah, Palestine, Saul, Solomon**

Israelite (IZ-ree-uh-liet or IZ-ruh-liet) *proper noun:*

An Israelite is one of the people of Israel. Israelites are also known as the children of Israel. The term *Israelites* is used for the members of the 12 tribes of Israel. Jacob, who later became Israel, was the father of the Israelites.

Genesis 32:32; 49:16, 28; Exodus 32:4; Deuteronomy 4:1; 27:9; 1 Samuel 17:52-53; 1 Kings 8:1; 9:7; 12:16; 14:7

***See* children of Israel, Israel, Jacob, tribes of Israel**

Issachar (IS-uh-kahr) *proper noun:*

1. Issachar was one of the 12 sons of Jacob. His descendants were known as the tribe of Issachar.

2. Issachar was the name of the land occupied by the tribe of Issachar.

Genesis 30:17-18; 35:23; Joshua 19:17-23; 1 Chronicles 7:1

***See* Israel, Issachar (map 3), Jacob, tribes of Israel**

Italy (IT-uh-lee) *proper noun:*

Italy is a country in southern Europe. Most of it is a peninsula in the Mediterranean Sea. During New Testament times, Italy was the center of the Roman Empire.

Acts 10:1; 18:2; 27:1, 6

***See* Italy (map 11), Mediterranean Sea, Rome**

J j

Jacob (JAY-kub) *proper noun:*

Jacob was the son of Isaac and the twin brother of Esau. His name in Hebrew meant "the cheat." God changed Jacob's name to Israel. He was the father of the 12 tribes of Israel. He was one of the patriarchs.

The names of Jacob's sons were Reuben, Simeon, Levi, Judah, Dan, Naphtali, Gad, Asher, Issachar, Zebulun, Joseph, and Benjamin.

Genesis 25:19; 29:30—30:24; 35:16-26; 50:12-14

See **Ephraim, Esau, Hebrew, Isaac, Israel, Jacob (time line), Manasseh, patriarch, tribes of Israel**

James (JAYMZ) *proper noun:*

1. Four men in the New Testament have the name James.

a. James, the brother of John, was a disciple of Jesus. He was killed by Herod Agrippa I (Matthew 4:18-22; 17:1-8; Acts 12:1-2).

b. James was the name of another disciple of Jesus (Matthew 10:3).

c. James, a brother of Jesus, became a leader of the Early Church in Jerusalem. He is that man who, according to Christian tradition, wrote the Book of James (Acts 15:12-21; 21:17-26; Galatians 1:19; 2:9).

d. James was the father of a disciple named Judas (Luke 6:16).

2. James is the name of a book in the New Testament. It is one of the epistles. James stresses the importance of good works. Good works should result from faith. The book also teaches the importance of Christian wisdom. Some believe that the writer was James, a brother of Jesus.

See **Bible, church, disciple, epistle, good works, Herod, Jerusalem (map 10), Jesus, John, Judas, New Testament, tradition**

Jebus (JEE-bus) *proper noun:*

See **Jebusites, Jerusalem**

Jebusites (JEB-yew-siets) *proper noun:*

Jebusites were people who lived in Jerusalem in Old Testament times. They named the city Jebus (Judges 19:10-11). They were one of the Canaanite tribes (Genesis 10:16). Joshua was not able to conquer the Jebusites. David finally conquered the city.

Exodus 3:8, 17; 13:5

See **Canaanites, David, Jerusalem, Joshua**

Jehoahaz (juh-HOH-uh-haz) *proper noun:*

1. Jehoahaz was a king of Israel, the Northern Kingdom. He was the son of Jehu. He ruled for 17 years. He did evil in the eyes of the Lord. He was an idol worshiper (2 Kings 13:1-9).

2. Jehoahaz was a king of Judah, the Southern Kingdom. He was the son

of Josiah. Jehoahaz ruled for only three months. Then he was taken to Egypt as a prisoner by the Pharaoh (2 Kings 23:31-34).

See **Egypt, idol, Israel, Jehoahaz (time line), Jehu, Josiah, Judah, Pharaoh**

Jehoash (juh-HOH-ash) *proper noun:*

Jehoash was a king of Israel, the Northern Kingdom. He was the son of Jehoahaz. He ruled for 16 years. He did "evil in the eyes of the Lord."

2 Kings 13:10-13

See **Israel, Jehoahaz, Jehoash (time line)**

Jehoiachin (juh-HOY-uh-kin) *proper noun:*

Jehoiachin was the next to the last king of Judah, the Southern Kingdom. He was the son of Jehoiakim. Jehoiachin was also known as Jeconinah (1 Chronicles 3:16). He ruled for only three months. Nebuchadnezzar took him to Babylon as an exile.

2 Kings 24:8-15; 25:27-30

See **Babylon, exile, Jehoiachin (time line), Jehoiakim, Judah, Nebuchadnezzar**

Jehoiakim (juh-HOY-uh-kim) *proper noun:*

Jehoiakim was one of the last kings of Judah, the Southern Kingdom. He was the son of Josiah. He became king when his brother Jehoahaz was taken to Egypt by the Pharaoh. He ruled for 11 years. He was known as an evil king. Later he was taken to Babylon as an exile by Nebuchadnezzar.

2 Kings 23:36—24:6; 2 Chronicles 36:5-8

See **Babylon, Egypt, exile, Jehoahaz, Jehoiakim (time line), Josiah, Judah, Nebuchadnezzar, Pharaoh**

Jehoram (juh-HOH-rum) *proper noun:*

Jehoram was the fifth king of Judah, the Southern Kingdom. He was the son of Jehoshaphat. He married Athaliah, daughter of Ahab and Jezebel. Jehoram ruled for eight years. He did evil in the eyes of the Lord. He started the worship of idols again in Judah.

2 Kings 8:16-24; 2 Chronicles 21:1-20

See **Ahab, Athaliah, Jehoram (time line), Jehoshaphat, Jezebel, Judah, idol, Israel**

Jehoshaphat (juh-HAHSH-uh-fat) *proper noun:*

Jehoshaphat was the fourth king of Judah, the Southern Kingdom. He ruled for 25 years. His father was Asa. Jeshoshaphat was a righteous king like his father. He destroyed idols and pagan worship in Judah. He sent priests and teachers throughout the country to teach the law of God. He made a treaty with Ahab, king of Israel. His son Jehoram married Ahab's daughter Athaliah. This brought peace and wealth to Judah.

1 Kings 22:41-50; 2 Chronicles 17:1-9; 18:1; 19:1-10; 20:31-34

See **Ahab, Asa, Athaliah, idol, Israel, Jehoshaphat (time line), Jehoram, Judah, king, law, priest, pagan, righteous, worship**

Jehovah (juh-HOH-vuh) *proper noun:*

See **God, Lord, Yahweh**

Jehu (JEE-hew) *proper noun:*

Jehu was a king of Israel, the Northern Kingdom. He ruled for 28 years. The prophet Elisha anointed him as king. He killed Joram, the king before him. He killed Ahaziah, the king of Judah. He also had Jezebel and all the family of Ahab killed. He destroyed Baal worship in Israel, yet he did not completely obey God.

2 Kings 9:1—10:35

See **Ahab, Ahaziah, Baal, Elisha, Israel, Jehu (time line), Joram, Judah, worship**

Jeremiah (JAIR-uh-MIE-uh) *proper noun:*

1. Jeremiah is the name of a prophet. A book in the Bible is named for him. Jeremiah is known as "the weeping prophet." He preached and prophesied during the last years of the kingdom of Judah.

2. Jeremiah is a book in the Old Testament. It is one of the Major Prophets. Jeremiah tells of the sins of Jerusalem. Its king and people did not trust or obey God for protection. Jeremiah lived to see Jerusalem destroyed.

See **Bible, exile, Israel, Jeremiah (time line), Jerusalem, Judah, Lamentations, Old Testament, prophesy, prophet, Yahweh**

Jericho (JAIR-uh-koh) *proper noun:*

Jericho is probably the oldest known city in the world. It is located a few miles from the Jordan River and the Dead Sea.

Jericho was destroyed when Joshua and the Israelites came into Canaan (Joshua 6:1-25). It was rebuilt during King Ahab's reign (1 Kings 16:34). Jesus healed two blind men at Jericho (Matthew 20:29-34). It was the home of Zaccheus (Luke 19:1-10).

See **Ahab, Canaan, Dead Sea, Israelites, Jericho (map 3, 4, 7), Jesus, Jordan River, Joshua, Zacchaeus**

Jeroboam (JAIR-uh-BOH-um) *proper noun:*

1. Jeroboam I was the first king of Israel, the Northern Kingdom. He ruled for more than 20 years. He built his first capital city at Shechem. Jeroboam was an evil king. He led the people to worship idols. He built shrines of golden calves at Dan and Bethel.

1 Kings 11:26-40; 12:1-19, 12-33; 14:1-19

2. Jeroboam II was one of the last kings of Israel, the Northern Kingdom. He was the son of Jehoash. He ruled for 41 years. He did evil in the eyes of the Lord (2 Kings 14:23-29).

See **Bethel, Dan, idol, Israel, Jehoash, Jeroboam (time line), Shechem, shrine**

Jerusalem (juh-REW-suh-lum) *proper noun:*

Jerusalem is the most important city of Palestine. Its history has made it important for at least 4,000 years. The name Jerusalem means "peace," but there have been many wars in its history.

Jerusalem was called Salem or Shalem during the time of Abraham (Genesis 14:18). It was a Canaanite city called Jebus during the Conquest (Judges 1:8, 21). David captured the city and again named it Jerusalem. He made it the capital of united Israel (2 Samuel 5:6-8). Solomon had the Temple built there. Jerusalem remained the capital of Judah after the division into two kingdoms.

Jerusalem was destroyed in 586 B.C. by the armies of Babylon (2 Kings 25:8-12). The Jews who returned after the Exile rebuilt the city and made it larger (Ezra 1). The city was destroyed again in A.D. 70 by the Roman army (Luke 19:41-44). The city was built again after A.D. 132 as a pagan city, Aelia Capitolina.

Jerusalem is considered a holy city by the three major monotheistic religions of the world. Jews consider it important as the capital of Israel. Christians view the city with reverence because Jesus was crucified and resurrected there. Muslims consider it one of their three holy cities. They believe that their prophet Muhammad went to heaven from Jerusalem.

See **Arab, Babylon, Canaanite, conquest, Constantine, crucify, David, heaven, holy, Islam, Israel, Jerusalem (maps 1-11), Jesus, Jew, Judah, monotheism, Palestine, religion, Roman, Solomon, temple**

Jerusalem Bible (juh-REW-suh-lum) *proper noun phrase:*

The *Jerusalem Bible* is a modern translation of the Scriptures. Its abbreviation is JB.

See **Bible, Scriptures, version**

Jesse (JES-ee) *proper noun:*

Jesse was the father of King David. He was an ancestor of Jesus.

Ruth 4:13-22; 1 Samuel 16:1-23; Matthew 1:5-6; Luke 3:32

See **Branch, David**

Jesus (JEE-zus) *proper noun:*

Jesus was the name given to the Son of the Virgin Mary. The name means Savior. Jesus is also known as the Christ, the One whom God promised. Jesus Christ is the Son of God who came to earth. Christians worship Him as Lord.

The story of the earthly life of Jesus is told in the four Gospels. Little is known about Him beyond the stories and sayings they report. But the goal of the Gospels is to proclaim the good news about Jesus. It is not simply to provide interesting facts about Him. For example, Mark's Gospel tells nothing about the life of Jesus before His baptism.

Only the Gospels of Matthew and Luke report the birth of Jesus. They stress that God was fulfilling His promise in this special birth. The same God who acted in the Old Testament was at work in Jesus. Matthew refers to Jesus as the true descendant of Abraham and of David. He is the King of the Jews, the Messiah of Israel. Luke refers to Jesus as the Second Adam, the Son of God.

The Gospel of John does not tell the story of Jesus' birth. Instead, John pushes the story out of time backward into eternity. John begins his Gospel by referring to the eternal Word of God. The Word became incarnate as the Man, Jesus of Nazareth. God was fully revealed in Jesus.

The basic facts of the life of Jesus are as follows: He was born in Bethlehem. He lived a normal life as a child and young man in Nazareth. He learned the trade of a carpenter from His earthly father. He was neither a priest nor a rabbi.

Jesus was baptized by John the Baptist in the Jordan River. The Gospels report that this event marked an important change in Jesus' life. The Holy Spirit, who had long been absent in Israel, came upon Him. The voice of the Father confirmed that Jesus was His chosen and much-loved Son. Jesus was the Suffering Servant Messiah prophesied in the Old Testament. The Temptation tested Jesus' faithfulness to this mission.

Jesus returned from the time of temptation preaching the good news of God's love. His usual message included the news that God, not Satan, ruled. It also included a call to repent and believe the Good News.

Jesus was a great teacher. He often used parables to help His hearers understand His message. Jesus invited all who would listen to accept God's grace. He taught that being a follower of God demanded total obedience.

Jesus gained a great following as a healer. He also cast out demons from people who were possessed by them. His healings were signs that the kingdom of God was near. God was defeating Satan's power.

Jesus called people to become His followers. Those who believed that He was the Messiah became His disciples. But Jesus usually did not refer to himself as the Messiah. He most often spoke of himself as the Son of Man. The Gospel of John refers to Jesus as the Son of God.

Jesus was opposed by many leaders of the Pharisees. They said He did not take the law seriously enough. He did not treat the Sabbath the way they thought He should. He shared meals with sinners. The Pharisees envied the following He had from the crowds.

Once Jesus forced the money changers to leave the Temple. This led the Sadducees to join the Pharisees in opposing Him. His enemies handed Jesus over to the Romans, who had Him crucified. He died on the Cross and was buried in a tomb. His enemies thought that was the end of Him.

Jesus rose from the dead on the morning of the third day. The enemies of Jesus were wrong. The Resurrection proved that Jesus was both Lord and Savior. Jesus fulfilled all the promises of God.

***See* baptism, Bethlehem, Branch, Christ, cross, disciple, eternity, exorcism,**

gospel, Immanuel, Incarnation, Jesus (time line), Jerusalem, John, kingdom of God, logos, Lord, Luke, Mark, Matthew, Messiah, miracle, Nazarene, parable, Pharisee, resurrection, Sadducee, Satan, Savior, Second Coming, Son of God, Son of Man, stumbling block, temptation, Transfiguration, Triumphal Entry, Virgin Birth, worship

Jesus Christ (JEE-zus KRIEST) *proper noun:*

Jesus Christ means Jesus who is the Christ. *Christ* is the Greek word for *Messiah.* The name *Jesus Christ* is a confession of faith that Jesus is the Christ of God.

The term *Jesus Christ* is found throughout the New Testament (Acts 2:38; Romans 1:6; Ephesians 1:5; 1 John 2:1). Sometimes the phrase *Christ Jesus* is used (Galatians 3:26; Ephesians 2:6-7; 3:20-21; Colossians 2:6-7). Both terms refer to Jesus as the Messiah.

See **Christ, Jesus, Messiah**

Jew (JEW) *proper noun:*

Jew is the name given to a descendant of Abraham and Jacob. The name comes from Judah, one of the 12 tribes of Israel. The people of Israel were first called Jews during the Exile. It became their common name.

Nehemiah 1:2; Esther 3:4; 7:1-4; 8:7-12; Matthew 2:2; John 19:21-22; Romans 1:16; 2:25-29

See **exile, Gentile, Israel, Judah, Tribes of Israel**

Jewish (JEW-ish) *proper adjective:*

Jewish describes someone or something as related to the Jews. For example, a Jewish synagogue is a place where Jews worship.

See **Jew, synagogue**

Jezebel (JEZ-uh-bel) *proper noun:*

Jezebel was the evil wife of King Ahab. She was the daughter of a king of Phoenicia. Jezebel encouraged the worship of the false god Baal in Israel. The prophet Elijah strongly opposed her.

1 Kings 16:29-33; 19:1-3; 21:1-26; 2 Kings 9:4-7, 30-37

See **Ahab, Baal, Elijah, god, Israel, Jezebel, Phoenicia (map 9)**

Jezreel (JEZ-ree-el or JEZ-reel) *proper noun:*

1. Jezreel was a town in Israel near Mount Gilboa. It was located in the Valley of Jezreel. It was on an important trade route. King Ahab had a palace in Jezreel (1 Kings 21:1). Queen Jezebel was killed in this city (2 Kings 9:30-35).

2. Jezreel is the name of a large valley in Israel (Joshua 17:16). The valley was also called the Plain of Esdraelon and Armageddon. The valley extended from Mount Carmel to Mount Gilboa. It was important for trade routes in Bible times. It was also the site of several great battles.

Judges 6:33; 1 Samuel 29:1; 1 Kings 18:45; 2 Kings 9:10, 15, 17, 30, 36-37; 10:1, 6-7, 11

See **Ahab, Armeggedon, Israel, Jezebel, Jezreel (map 4)**

Joash (JOH-ash) *proper noun:*

Joash was a king of Judah, the Southern Kingdom. He is also known as Jehoash. He was the son of Ahaziah. When Athaliah became queen, Joash was hidden for six years by an aunt. At age seven, Joash became the king, and he ruled for 40 years. He was a righteous king for most of his reign. Joash was killed by two of his own servants.

2 Kings 11:1—12-21

See **Ahaziah, Athaliah, Joash (time line), Judah, righteous**

Job (JOHB) *proper noun:*

1. Job is the name of a righteous man in the Old Testament. A book in the Bible tells his story.

2. Job is a book in the Old Testament. It is one of the five books of poetry. The Book of Job tells of the suffering of Job and of his faith in God. The book teaches that suffering is not always the result of sin.

See **Bible, faith, Old Testament, righteous, suffering**

Joel (JOH-ul) *proper noun:*

1. Joel was one of the prophets in the Old Testament. A book in the Bible is named for him. Joel told about the troubles that would come upon Judah because of their sins. Joel told the people to repent. He predicted the coming of the Holy Spirit (2:28). The Holy Spirit came to the Church on the Day of Pentecost.

2. Joel is a book in the Old Testament. It is one of the Minor Prophets.

Acts 2:16-21

See **Bible, Holy Spirit, Joel (time line), Judah, Old Testament, Pentecost, prophet, repent**

John (JAHN) *proper noun:*

1. There are several men in the Bible by the name of John. Two of them were very important in the New Testament.

a. John the Baptist was the son of Zechariah and Elizabeth. He was a cousin of Jesus. God chose John to prepare the way for the coming of Jesus. John preached a message of coming judgment and repentance. He baptized those who accepted his message. This is why he was called *the Baptist*. John baptized Jesus. John was put in prison by Herod Antipas and then was killed (Mark 6:14-29; Luke 1:5-25, 57-80; 3:1-22).

b. John the apostle was a disciple of Jesus. He and his brother James were fishermen when Jesus chose them as disciples. John was very close to Jesus (Matthew 4:21-22; Mark 9:2; John 13:23). It is believed that John wrote five of the books of the New Testament. They are the Gospel of John, three letters with John's name, and the Revelation.

2. There are four books in the New Testament with the name of John.

a. John is the name of the fourth Gospel. Most people believe that

John the apostle wrote this book. It tells the story of Jesus, the Son of God. It stresses that Jesus is the Revelation of God in human flesh. He reveals who He is through the miracles He does. This Gospel calls miracles *signs*. The Gospel of John is different from the Synoptic Gospels (Matthew, Mark, and Luke). For example, it does not tell any of Jesus' parables. It does not tell of His casting out demons. It stresses the teaching of Jesus on the Holy Spirit.

b. John is also the name of three letters in the New Testament. They are three of the epistles. They are First John, Second John, and Third John. They stress that Jesus was the true Revelation of God. He was truly human as well as divine. They also stress the importance of putting love into practice. The Church has generally believed that the apostle John also wrote all these books.

See **apostle, baptism, Bible, disciple, epistle, gospel, Herod, Jesus, John the Baptist (time line), judgment, message, miracle, New Testament, parable, prophet, repentance, revelation, sign, Synoptic Gospels, Zechariah**

John the Baptist (JAHN thuh BAP-tist) *proper noun phrase:*

See **Baptist, John, John the Baptist (time line)**

Jonah (JOH-nuh) *proper noun:*

1. Jonah is the name of a prophet in the Old Testament. A book in the Bible is named for him. God called Jonah to preach in Nineveh. Nineveh was the wicked capital city of Assyria, a powerful enemy of Israel. Jonah tried to go someplace else. But in three days a huge fish changed his mind. The people of Nineveh repented, so God did not destroy the city.

2. Jonah is a book in the Old Testament. It is one of the Minor Prophets.

2 Kings 14:25; Matthew 12:38-41; Luke 11:29-30

See **Assyria, Bible, Israel, Jonah (time line), Nahum, Old Testament, prophet, repent**

Jonathan (JAHN-uh-thun) *proper noun:*

Jonathan was one of the sons of King Saul. He was a close friend of David.

1 Samuel 13:16; 14:1-45; 19:1-7; 20:5-42; 31:2; 2 Samuel 1:1-27; 9:1-13

See **David, Saul**

Joppa (JAHP-uh) *proper noun:*

Joppa was an important city on the coast of the Mediterranean Sea. It is mentioned several times in the Bible, both in the Old and New Testaments. For example, the prophet Jonah took a boat from Joppa when he ran from the Lord (Jonah 1:3). The apostle Peter saw his vision of the beasts in Joppa (Acts 10:1-23).

2 Chronicles 2:16; Ezra 3:7; Acts 9:36-43

See **Jonah, Joppa (maps 3, 4, 7, 8, 9), Mediterranean Sea, Peter**

Joram (JOH-rum) *proper noun:*

Joram was a king of Israel, the Northern Kingdom. He is also known as Jehoram. He was the son of Ahab and Jezebel. He became king after his brother Ahaziah was killed in battle. Joram ruled for 12 years. He did "evil in the eyes of the Lord." He was killed by Jehu.

2 Kings 3:1-3; 9:14-24

***See* Ahab, Ahaziah, Israel, Jehu, Jezebel, Joram (time line)**

Jordan River (JOHR-dun RIV-er) *proper noun:*

The Jordan River flowed from north to south in Palestine. It ran from north of the Sea of Galilee to the Dead Sea.

The people of Israel crossed the Jordan River to enter the land of Canaan (Joshua 3:1-17).

Jesus was baptized by John the Baptist in the Jordan River (Matthew 3:1-17).

***See* Canaan, Dead Sea, Galilee, Israel, Jesus, John, Jordan River (map 3), Palestine**

Joseph (JOH-suf) *proper noun:*

Joseph is a common name in the Bible. Four men by that name are important.

1. Joseph was a man in the Old Testament who was one of the 12 sons of Jacob. Joseph had two sons named Manasseh and Ephraim (Genesis 41:51-52). They became two the 12 tribes of Israel (see map 3).

Joseph's brothers sold him into slavery in Egypt. He later became an important leader there (Genesis 35:24; 37:3; 39—50; Exodus 13:19). He was one of the patriarchs.

2. Joseph was the man engaged to Mary when Jesus was born. He was a carpenter in the town of Nazareth. An angel told him that Mary would give birth to Jesus (Matthew 1:18-25; 2:13-23; Luke 2:1-5, 41-51).

3. Joseph was a wealthy, secret disciple of Jesus. He was also a member of the Sanhedrin. He was called Joseph of Arimathea (AIR-uh-muh-THEE-uh), because he was from a town by that name. He buried Jesus in his own new tomb (Matthew 27:57-66; Mark 15:43-46).

4. Joseph was the lesser-known name of the early Christian disciple called Barnabas (Acts 4:36-37).

***See* angel, Barnabas, bondage, cross, crucifixion, disciple, Egypt, Ephraim, Exodus, Israel, Jacob, Joseph (time line), Manasseh, Mary, Nazareth (map 8), patriarch, Sanhedrin, tribes of Israel, Virgin Birth**

Josephus, Flavius (FLAY-vee-us joh-SEE-fus) *proper noun:*

Flavius Josephus was an important Jewish historian and military leader. He was born in about A.D. 37 or 38. He died in the second century. Josephus wrote books that told part of the Jewish history. He also wrote books that dealt with other topics. Two important books are *Jewish War* and *Antiquities of the Jews*. These books help us understand the times in which Jesus lived. They also help us understand the early years of the Church.

See **church, Essenes, Jewish**

Joshua (JAHSH-yew-uh) *proper noun:*

1. Joshua was a leader of the Israelites. A book in the Bible is named for him.

Joshua was one of the 12 spies who were sent to explore Canaan. Joshua and Caleb believed that God would help the Israelites to capture the land. The other spies feared the giants there.

Joshua became the leader of Israel after the death of Moses. Joshua led the Israelites into the Promised Land. He led them in the battles to conquer the enemies there.

2. Joshua is a book in the Old Testament. It is one of the history books.
3. Joshua is the Hebrew form of the Greek name Jesus.

Exodus 17:9; Numbers 13:16-17; 14:6; 27:18-23

See **Bible, Canaan, Caleb, conquest, Israel, Israelites, Joshua (time line), Moses, Old Testament, Promised Land**

Josiah (joh-SIE-uh) *proper noun:*

Josiah was a king of Judah, the Southern Kingdom. He was the son of Amon. Josiah became king at age eight, when his father was killed. Josiah ruled for 31 years. He was a righteous ruler. He led Judah in a revival of the worship of God. He destroyed idols and wicked places. He repaired the Temple and once again made it a center of worship.

2 Kings 22—23; 2 Chronicles 34—35

See **Amon, God, idol, Josiah (time line), Judah, revival, righteous, temple, worship**

Jotham (JOH-thum) *proper noun:*

Jotham was a king of Judah, the Southern Kingdom. He was the son of Uzziah. He was king for 16 years. He was a righteous king, like his father.

2 Kings 15:32-38; 2 Chronicles 27:1-9

See **Jotham (time line), Judah, righteous, Uzziah**

joy (JOY) *noun:*

Joy is the emotion of one who is pleased and happy. A person may have joy even though conditions are not desirable.

Joy is the result of salvation. Joy is a fruit of the Spirit. God gives inner joy that nothing can take away.

1 Kings 8:66; Psalm 66:1-4; 100:1-5; Habakkuk 3:17-19; Matthew 5:2-12; Luke 15:7, 10; Acts 13:52; Romans 14:17; 2 Corinthians 7:4; Galatians 5:22; Philippians 1:15-26; 3:1; 4:1, 4, 10-13

See **Beatitudes, fruit of the Spirit, grace, hope, salvation, suffering**

jubilee (JEW-buh-lee) *noun:*

A jubilee is a time of celebration.

The year of jubilee was a special year of celebration for the Israelites. It happened every 50 years. It followed the seventh Sabbath Year. During the year of jubilee, people returned to their homes. Also, all land was returned to its original owner. This year was also a time of rest from growing crops for the land. God declared that this was to be a holy year (Leviticus 25:12).

Leviticus 24:8-54; 27:17-24; Numbers 36:4

See **holy, Israelites, Sabbath**

Judah (JEW-duh) *noun:*

1. Judah was one of the sons of Jacob (Genesis 35:22-26). The descendants of Judah became one of the 12 tribes of Israel.

2. Judah was the land occupied by the tribe of Judah.

3. Judah was the Southern Kingdom in the Old Testament. Its name came from Judah, one of the sons of Jacob. The nation of Israel was divided after the death of King Solomon. The Northern Kingdom kept the name Israel. The Southern Kingdom took the name Judah.

1 Kings 11—12; 2 Kings 24—25

See **Israel, Israel (map 7), Jacob, Jew, Judah (maps 3, 7, time line), tribes of Israel**

Judaism (JEW-duh-iz-um) *proper noun:*

Judaism is the religion of the Jewish people. Worship of one God is its central belief. The Old Testament is its Bible. Christianity arose out of Judaism. There are three major groups in Judaism today. They are Orthodox, Reform, and conservative Judaism.

Acts 2:11; 13:43; Galatians 1:13-14

See **Bible, God, Jew, monotheism, Torah, worship**

Judaizer (JEW-duh-ie-zer) *proper noun:*

A Judaizer was a person who tried to force Gentile Christians to become Jews.

Judaizers were a serious problem in the Early Church. They urged Gentiles to practice Jewish rituals and customs. They expected all men to be circumcised. They stressed food laws that required Jews not to eat with Gentiles.

Some Judaizers were Jews who did not accept Jesus. Others were Christians who held to Jewish customs. Judaizers of both kinds opposed the apostle Paul. The Book of Acts often mentions Paul's opponents. See Acts 13:43—14:5; 17:1-9; 18:5-16.

Christian Judaizers believed that Gentile converts had to become Jews to become true Christians. Paul said that such ideas were false. He believed that Gentiles should not be required to observe Jewish laws. Paul taught that faith in Christ alone was necessary to become a Christian. Paul rejected the views of the Judaizers. He even opposed the apostle Peter on this issue. Peter's bad example in Antioch seemed to support the views of the Judaizers. See Galatians 2:1-21; Acts 10.

See **Acts, Antioch, Christian, circumcision, faith, Galatians, Gentile, Jew, Jewish, justification, law, Paul, Peter, ritual**

Judas (JEW-dus) *proper noun:*

Judas was a common name in New Testament times. It is the Greek form of Judah.

1. Judas was one of the 12 apostles, who was also called Thaddaeus (Matthew 10:3; Luke 6:16; Acts 1:13). This Judas was not the same as Judas Iscariot.

2. Judas Iscariot was a disciple of Jesus Christ. He betrayed Jesus with a kiss (Matthew 10:4; 26:25; Mark 3:19).

3. Judas was a brother of Jesus (Matthew 13:55; Mark 6:3). The New Testament book named for him is called Jude.

4. Judas was a man from Galilee who rebelled against Rome and was killed (Acts 5:37).

5. Judas was a man in Damascus with whom Paul stayed for a short time (Acts 9:11).

6. Judas was also a man who once traveled with Barnabas and Paul (Acts 15:22, 27, 32).

See **betrayal, disciple, Jude, kiss, New Testament, Paul, Rome**

Jude (JEWD) *proper noun:*

1. Jude was the writer of a book in the New Testament. A brother of Jesus was named Jude (Judas). An apostle of Jesus was also called Jude (Judas), or Thaddaeus. The writer of the book was probably the brother of Jesus.

2. Jude is a book in the New Testament. It is one of the epistles. Jude was written to encourage persecuted Christians. It warns Christians that they can lose their salvation. But it says that God can keep them from sinning.

Matthew 10:3; 13:55; John 14:22

See **apostle, Bible, epistle, Judas, New Testament, persecution**

Judea (jew-DEE-uh) *proper noun:*

Judea is the name for the land of the Old Testament kingdom of Judah. Judea was the name used in the New Testament. Later, it was used to refer to all of Palestine.

Matthew 2:1, 5, 22; 3:1, 5; 4:25; 19:1; Mark 1:4-5; 3:7; 10:1; Luke 1:5; 2:4; 3:1; 5:17; 6:17; John 3:22; 4:3; 7:1-3; 11:7; Acts 1:8; 2:8-11, 14; 8:1; 9:31; 12:19; 2 Corinthians 1:16; Galatians 1:22; 1 Thessalonians 2:14

See **Judah, Judea (maps 8, 11), Palestine**

Judeo-Christian (jew-DAY-oh KRIS-chun) *proper adjective:*

Judeo-Christian describes the faith and practices shared by Jews and Christians. The Judeo-Christian tradition has had a strong influence on the Western world.

See **Christian, Christianity, faith, Judaism, tradition**

judge (JUJ)

1. *verb:* To judge is to give an opinion about right or wrong. It is also to settle differences among people.

To judge can also mean to decide who should be forgiven by God. In this sense it means to deny God's forgiveness or love to someone. People are not to judge in this way.

2. *noun:* A judge is one who judges. A judge is to make certain that justice is done. The Bible teaches that God is the final Judge (Genesis 18:25). But people may also serve as judges. God told Israel to choose officers who could settle differences among the people.

The time of the Judges was a period of Old Testament history. They were leaders of the Israelites until Saul became king. Some of the Judges were Deborah, Gideon, Samson, and Samuel.

Genesis 16:5; Leviticus 19:15; Deuteronomy 16:18-20; Judges 3:10; Luke 6:37; Romans 2:15-16; 14:3-4, 10-13; 1 Corinthians 4:3-5; Philippians 1:9-10; Hebrews 4:12-13; 12:23; James 4:12; Revelation 20:12

See **Bible, Deborah, forgiveness, Gideon, God, Joshua, judges (time line), judgment, justice, Samson, Samuel**

Judges (JUJ-uz) *proper noun:*

Judges is a book in the Old Testament. It is one of the history books. The leaders of Israel were called judges after the time of Joshua. The need for judges ended when Saul became king. God chose them to lead Israel in difficult times. They did not judge in the sense of settling differences among people. They helped free the Israelites from their enemies. They also turned the Israelites back to God.

See **Bible, Israel, Israelites, Joshua, judge, Judges (time line), Old Testament, Saul**

judgment (JUJ-munt)

1. *noun:* Judgment is the decision someone makes about another person's actions and deeds. A judgment may result in punishing evil. It may also result in rewarding good. Or it may result in forgiveness for someone who has done wrong.

2. *proper noun:* The Last Judgment is the time when God separates righteous people from evil people. The righteous will be rewarded, and the evil will be punished. Justice will be done.

Psalm 1:5; Ecclesiastes 12:14; Matthew 5:21-26; 25:31-46; John 16:7-11; 2 Corinthians 5:10; Hebrews 9:27-28; Revelation 20:4-15

See **damnation, eschatology, evil, forgiveness, heaven, hell, judge, justice, reconciliation, reward, righteous**

judicial (jew-DISH-ul) *adjective:*

Judicial describes things that are related to judgment. A judicial decision is one made by a judge.

In the church, judicial decisions are sometimes made about the actions of its members. These decisions may be made by a committee or a person with authority. These people are acting as judges.

See **church, judge, judgment, justice**

Jupiter (JEW-puh-ter) *proper noun:*

See **Zeus**

just (JUST)

1. *adjective:* Just describes someone or something that is fair and right. The Hebrew and Greek words for *just* in the Bible mean "right" or "righteous." A just person, a just act, or a just thing is faithful to what is right.

2. *noun:* The just are just people. People who are right with God and do right are called the just. God is called the Just One.

Leviticus 19:36; Deuteronomy 16:18-20; Proverbs 16:8-13; Isaiah 45:21; Ezekiel 18:5-9; Habakkuk 2:4; Zephaniah 3:5; Matthew 1:19; 5:45; Acts 3:14; 10:22; 22:14; Philippians 4:8; 1 John 1:9; Revelation 15:3

See **faithful, God, justice, right, righteous**

justice (JUS-tus) *noun:*

Justice is the result of doing what is fair and right. Justice brings comfort to people who suffer wrong. God is against those who do not do justice. God defends those who cannot defend themselves. This is what He wants His people to do. He acts on the basis of love and justice.

Job 37:23-24; Psalms 9:8, 16; 11:7; Amos 5:15, 21-24; Micah 6:6-16; 7:8-9; Matthew 5:6; 6:33; Romans 2:1-16; 3:1-6, 21-26

See **evil, forgiveness, judge, judgment, justification, law, love, retribution, righteousness**

justification (JUS-tuh-fuh-KAY-shun) *noun:*

Justification is the act of God by which He makes people right with Him. God forgives their sins. Justification is the free gift of God to those who trust in Jesus Christ. Justification creates a new relation between God and the sinner. Justification reconciles the sinner to God. The death and resurrection of Christ makes justification possible.

Justification by grace through faith alone is the way people become Christians. The grace of God makes faith in Christ possible. Salvation is completely the work of God. Even faith is a gift (Romans 10:17). But people must exercise faith to be justified. Good works add nothing to justification. But those who have been justified will do good works.

Luke 18:9-14; Romans 3:21-28; 4:4-8, 16-25; 5:1-11; 11:6; Galatians 2:15-21; 3:14-21; 5:6; Ephesians 2:8-10; Philippians 3:3-11; Titus 3:3-7

See **born again, Christian, conversion, faith, forgiveness, good works, grace, imparted righteousness, imputed righteousness, justification by grace through faith alone, justify, new birth, new man, reconciliation, redemption, regeneration, righteousness, salvation, save**

justification by grace through faith alone (JUS-tuh-fuh-KAY-shun bie GRAYS threw FAYTH uh-LOHN) *noun phrase:*

Justification by grace through faith alone means that only God's grace can save us. This is a doctrine that many Christian denominations accept and believe.

God alone can forgive sins and give peace. Human efforts cannot win God's favor. Salvation is completely the work of God. Jesus Christ made salvation possible. God makes people new creatures through Jesus Christ. We must express faith in Christ as Savior to be saved. But faith is also a gift from God. Faith is a gift of God's grace. The Holy Spirit makes it possible to have faith in Christ.

The Holy Spirit sets a person free to become a Christian. Faith is the work of God. But God helps us express our desire for forgiveness and peace with God. Salvation is the work of God alone.

Romans 3:19-26; 5:1-11; 6:1-11; 1 Corinthians 1:26-31; 2 Corinthians 4:5-6; 5:14-15; Colossians 2:13-15; 1 Peter 1:18-21; 2 Peter 1:3-4

See **atonement, denominations, doctrine, gift, grace, faith, forgiveness, freedom, justification, new birth, peace, regeneration, repentance, righteousness, salvation, save**

justify (JUS-tuh-fie) *verb:*

To justify means to forgive and make right. God justifies people when they repent of their sins. Christians are justified by grace through faith alone.

See **forgiveness, justification, justification by grace through faith alone, reconciliation, repent**

K k

Kadesh Barnea (KAY-desh bahr-NEE-uh) *proper noun:*

Kadesh Barnea was a place located in the desert south of Canaan. It was often called just Kadesh.

The Israelites visited Kadesh Barnea several times when wandering in the wilderness for 40 years. Moses sent the 12 spies to Canaan from Kadesh Barnea (Numbers 13:1-2, 26; 32:8). Miriam, Moses' sister, died at Kadesh (Numbers 20:1). Moses disobeyed God here by hitting a rock instead of speaking to it to get water (Numbers 20:1-13).

Numbers 20:14-22; 27:14; 33:36-37; Deuteronomy 1:19, 46; 2:14; 9:23; Joshua 10:41; 14:6-7; 15:3; Judges 11:16-17

See **Canaan, forty years, Israelites, Kadesh Barnea (maps 2, 4), Moses,**

kenosis (kuh-NOH-sus) *noun:*

Kenosis is the act of the Son of God humbling himself to become human. He accepted all that was necessary to become truly human. The word *kenosis* in Greek means "emptying."

2 Corinthians 8:9; Philippians 2:5-11

See **Christ, Greek, humility, Immanuel, incarnation, Son of God**

kerygma (kuh-RIG-muh) *noun:*

Kerygma is the gospel message that is preached. The word *kerygma* in Greek means "preaching."

Romans 10:14-17; 1 Corinthians 1:18-25; 2:1-5; 1 Thessalonians 2:13; 1 Peter 1:12; 4:6

See **didache, evangelism, gospel, Greek, preach, proclamation**

Keswick (KEZ-ik) *proper noun:*

Keswick is the name of a Christian group concerned for holy living. These people stress the importance of the Spirit-filled life. They believe the Holy Spirit gives Christians power over sin. But they do not believe that the Spirit cleanses Christians from original sin.

The name Keswick comes from the town in England where the group began. Those who believe this way are sometimes called Keswickians (kes-WIK-ee-unz).

See **eradication, heart purity, holiness, Holy Spirit, original sin, Wesleyan**

Keturah (kuh-TOOR-uh) *proper noun:*

Keturah was the second wife of Abraham. She and Abraham had six sons.

Genesis 25:1-2

See **Abraham, concubine, Sarah**

Kidron (KID-run) *proper noun:*

Kidron is a valley on the east side of Jerusalem. It separated the hill on which the Temple was built and the Mount of Olives. A small brook ran through the valley. It joined the Valley of Hinnom.

2 Samuel 15:23; 1 Kings 2:37; 15:13; 23:6, 12; 2 Chronicles 30:14; John 18:1

See Hinnom, Jerusalem, Kidron Valley (maps 5, 10), Mount of Olives, Temple

king (KING) *noun:*

A king is a male ruler of a city, tribe, or nation. He usually inherits his office and reigns for life.

Saul became the first king of Israel after the time of the judges. David and his son Solomon were also kings over united Israel. The descendants of David continued to rule in Judah. Northern Israel was led by kings from many different families. Enemy nations destroyed both the northern and southern kingdoms.

The Jews hoped for the coming of a future king, the Messiah. They thought that the Messiah would make Israel great again. Christians believe that Jesus is the Messiah. But His kingdom includes every nation. The Bible sometimes calls Him the "King of kings" (1 Timothy 6:15; Revelation 17:14; 19:16).

1 Samuel 8:1-22; 12:12; Psalms 5:2; 10:16; 24:7-10; 44:4; 47:2, 6-7; Isaiah 6:5; 43:15; 44:6; Matthew 2:2; 27:29, 42

See **Caesar, David, Israel, Judah, kingdom of God, Lord, Messiah, omnipotence, Saul, Solomon, sovereign**

King James Version (KING JAYMZ VER-zhun) *proper noun phrase:*

The King James Version is an early English translation of the Bible. It was first printed in 1611 in England. KJV is the abbreviation used for it. The KJV has been the most widely used English version. The KJV in use today was revised in the 19th century.

See Bible, translate, version

kingdom of God (KING-dum uv GAHD) *noun phrase:*

The kingdom of God is the power God has over all the world. God is the Creator of everything. But only those who obey God are part of His kingdom.

The world has refused to obey God. God sent His Son to bring the world back under His rule. Jesus preached, "The kingdom of God is near. Repent and believe the good news!" (Mark 1:15).

Jesus taught His disciples to pray, "Your kingdom come, your will be done on earth as it is in heaven" (Matthew 6:10).

The kingdom of God is both present and future. God rules now through Jesus Christ. But God's rule will be complete only when all powers are under His control. This will happen when Jesus comes again.

The Church includes all who are in the kingdom of God through Jesus Christ. But the Church is not the same as the kingdom of God.

Psalms 22:28; 103:19; 145:8-13; Matthew 4:12-17; John 3:3-5; Romans 14:17; 1 Corinthians 15:20-28

See **Christ, church, Creator, eschatology, gospel, Jesus, repent, Second Coming, will**

kingdom of heaven (KING-dum uv HEV-un) *noun phrase:*

The kingdom of heaven is the kingdom of God. This term is used many times in Matthew's Gospel. It does not mean the same as heaven.

Matthew 4:17; Mark 1:15

See **gospel, heaven, kingdom of God, Matthew**

Kings (KINGZ) *proper noun:*

First and Second Kings are books in the Old Testament. They are two of the history books. These books tell the story of the kings of Israel and Judah. The history begins with the reign of Solomon. It ends with the destruction of the kingdoms of Israel and Judah. The author says that they were destroyed because the people did not obey God. Most of the kings were bad examples for their people.

See **Babylon, exile, Israel, Judah, king, Solomon**

KJV, *abbreviation:*

KJV is an abbreviation for the King James Version of the Bible.

See **Bible, translate, version**

kiss (KIS)

1. *verb:* To kiss is to show love by touching another person with one's lips.

2. *noun:* A kiss is the act of kissing. A kiss may show sexual love. But it may show only friendship or family love, as a handshake does today. Early Christians greeted one another with a kiss.

Proverbs 24:26; Song of Solomon 1:2; Luke 7:36-50; Romans 16:16; 1 Corinthians 16:20; 1 Thessalonians 5:26; 1 Peter 5:14

See **fellowship, koinonia, love**

koinonia (KOYN-oh-NEE-uh) *noun:*

Koinonia means "fellowship" or "community." It is a Greek word used in the New Testament to describe the Church. Koinonia exists where love unites people in Christ. Believers often have koinonia when they take Communion together. The Holy Spirit makes koinonia possible.

Acts 2:41-47; 1 Corinthians 1:9; Philippians 2:1-4; 3:10-11

See **church, Communion, community, fellowship, holy, Lord's Supper, spirit**

Koran (kuh-RAN, kuh-RAHN, or KOH-run) *proper noun:*

The Koran is the book of sacred writings of the Muslims and Islam religion. The Koran is also spelled Qur'an.

See **Allah, Islam, religion, sacred**

kosher (KOH-sher) *adjective:*

Kosher describes food that rabbis approve for Jews to eat. Kosher food satisfies the rules about diet and ritual. To be kosher means to live by the Jewish rules about food. The rules come from the Old Testament and Jewish tradition. Not all Jews live by kosher rules.

Leviticus 11:1-11; Deuteronomy 12:18-19

See **Jew, Leviticus, rabbi, ritual, Seder, tradition**

kurios (KEW-ree-ahs) *noun:*

Kurios is a Greek word used in the New Testament. Kurios has the following meanings:

1. Lord and master (Matthew 12:8)
2. Owner (Matthew 20:8)
3. King (Acts 25:6)
4. Deity (1 Corinthians 8:5)
5. The Lord Jehovah (Matthew 1:22)
6. The Lord Jesus Christ (Matthew 24:42; Mark 6:19; Luke 10:1; John 4:1; 1 Corinthians 4:5)
7. A term of respect for a person in authority (Matthew 13:27; Acts 9:6)

See **Christ, deity, Jesus, king, lord, master**

Kyrios (KEW-ree-ahs)

See **kurios**

L l

laity (LAY-uh-tee) *noun:*

Laity means all the people of God. It usually means Christians who are not preachers or priests. The New Testament does not make this difference. All the people of God have a special place of service in the Church. Laity is from a word in Greek that means "people."

Ephesians 4:7-16; 1 Peter 2:4-10

See **Christian, church, clergy, layman, minister, pastor, preach, priest**

Lamb of God (LAM uv GAHD) *proper noun phrase:*

The Lamb of God is a name given Jesus by John the Baptist (John 1:36). Lambs were used as a sacrifice for sins in the Old Testament. Jesus Christ is the final sacrifice for the sins of all people.

Genesis 22:1-14; Exodus 12:1-7; Isaiah 53:1-9; John 1:36; 1 Corinthians 5:7; 1 Peter 1:18-20; Revelation 5:1-14; 13:7-8

See **Christ, cross, expiation, Jesus, John, mercy seat, Passover, propitiation, sacrifice, sacrificial death**

Lamb's Book of Life (LAMZ BOOK uv LIEF) *proper noun phrase:*

See **Book of Life**

lament (luh-MENT)

1. *verb:* To lament is to show deep sorrow and grief. The prophet Jeremiah lamented the sins of his people. He lamented the destruction of Jerusalem. Jesus lamented when the people rejected Him.

2. *noun:* A lament is the cry of one who is in deep sorrow or grief.

2 Samuel 1:17; Isaiah 3:26; Jeremiah 4:5-8; 7:29; Matthew 23:37-39

See **Jeremiah, Jerusalem, Jesus, Lamentations, suffering**

Lamentations (LAM-un-TAY-shunz) *proper noun:*

Lamentations is a book in the Old Testament. It is one of the five Major Prophets. The book tells how the people of Jerusalem suffered when Babylon destroyed the city. Many people used to think Jeremiah wrote these poems of lament.

See **Bible, exile, Jeremiah, Judah, lament, Old Testament**

Last Days (LAST DAYZ) *proper noun phrase:*

See **eschatology**

Last Judgment (LAST JUJ-munt) *proper noun phrase:*

See **judgment**

Last Supper (LAST SUP-er) *proper noun phrase:*

The Last Supper was the meal Jesus ate with His disciples just before His crucifixion. This may have been a Passover meal. Jesus gave His disciples bread and wine at the Last Supper. He said that these represented His body and blood. He told them to eat meals like this often to remind them of Him. Such meals would help them understand the meaning of the Lord's death. It would also remind them of His second coming.

Luke 22:14-23; 1 Corinthians 11:20-32

See **covenant, crucifixion, Eucharist, Holy Communion, Jesus, Lord's Supper, Passover, sacrament, Second Coming, wine**

Latin (LAT-un) *proper noun:*

Latin is the language that was spoken by the Romans in the time of Jesus. It later became the most important language in the western part of the Roman world. It is no longer spoken.

See **Roman Catholic, Rome (map 11), translate**

law (LAW) *noun:*

Law means guidance or direction. The Hebrew word for Law is "Torah." Torah means "the way of the Lord." God showed himself and His will for His people through the Law. The Law told the people how to be faithful to their covenant with God. The Law told Israel how to worship God and how to live with one another. Torah is the name given to the first five books of the Old Testament.

By the time of Jesus, many Jews began to view the Law in a wrong way. Religious leaders had added many laws or traditions of their own. Many Jews saw the Law only as a list of rules. They thought God loved only people who kept the Law perfectly. Jesus rejected this view. He said that the Law is kept when people love God and other people.

Paul said that keeping the Law does not make a person right with God. Only faith in Christ makes people right with God. People who are right with God are able to do what the Law really demands. People who have faith in Christ can truly love God and their neighbors. They give the true worship that the Law demands.

Law may also mean the rules of a king or country. Citizens should obey these rules unless the laws go against the laws of God.

Law sometimes describes the sure results that follow from certain actions (Romans 7:23; 8:2).

Exodus 19:3-6; 20:1-20; Deuteronomy 4:44; 6:1-9, 20-25; 8:11-20; Joshua 23:6-13; Nehemiah 8:8; Psalms 19:7-11; 119:44-45, 136, 162-168; Mark 12:28-31; Romans 7:23; 8:1-4; 13:8-10; Galatians 5:13-14; James 1:25; 2:8-13

See **canon, commandment, covenant, decree, Great Commandment, legalism, morality, Pharisee, right, Sinai, Ten Commandments, Torah**

laying on of hands (LAY-ing ahn uv HANZ) *noun phrase:*

The laying on of hands is a religious act. One person places hands on the head of another person. This shows that he or she wants to give another person the blessing of God. Sometimes the blessing is the gift of the Holy

Spirit. Sometimes it is the healing of the body. Sometimes it is the right to do a special work for God.

Genesis 48:14-18; Mark 6:5; 10:13-16; Acts 6:1-6; 8:17-18; 19:6; 1 Timothy 4:11-16

See **anoint, confirmation, healing, ordination**

layman (LAY-mun) *noun:*

A layman is a Christian male who is not an ordained minister. Today the term *layperson* is often used.

See **laity, laywoman, minister, ordain**

laywoman (LAY-WOO-mun) *noun:*

A laywoman is a Christian female who is not an ordained minister. Today the term *layperson* is often used.

See **laity, layman, minister, ordain**

Lazarus (LAZ-uh-rus) *proper noun:*

Lazarus was the name of two men in the New Testament. Lazarus is the Greek form of the Hebrew name Eleazar that means "God helps."

1. Lazarus was the name of a poor, sick beggar in a parable Jesus told. Lazarus went to Abraham's bosom when he died (Luke 16:19-31).

2. Lazarus was a close friend of Jesus. He was the brother of Mary and Martha of Bethany. Jesus raised Lazarus from the dead (John 11:1—12:11).

See **Abraham's bosom, Bethany (map 8), Greek, Hebrew, Jesus, Martha, Mary, New Testament, parable**

Leah (LEE-uh) *proper noun:*

Leah was the first wife of Jacob. She was the mother of six sons who became tribes of Israel. Her sons were Reuben, Simeon, Levi, Judah, Issachar, and Zebulun.

Genesis 29:16—30:21

See **Israel, Issachar, Jacob, Judah, Levi, Reuben, Simeon, tribes of Israel, Zebulun**

leaven (LEV-un) *noun:*

Leaven was a small piece of old dough used to make bread rise. It was used in Bible times. Yeast is a kind of leaven. Only a small amount of leaven will go through the entire loaf.

The New Testament uses leaven to represent the great influence that small things can have. A few Christians can change the world. But a little sin may destroy a church.

Matthew 13:33; 16:5-12; 1 Corinthians 5:6-8; Galatians 2:15-21; 3:6-9; 5:1-12

See **unleavened bread**

Lebanon (LEB-uh-nun) *proper noun:*

1. Lebanon is the name of a mountain range in the country of Lebanon. During Bible times, the Lebanon mountains were famous for cedar trees.

King Solomon used "cedars from Lebanon" in building the Temple in Jerusalem.

2. Lebanon is a country in western Asia today. It is a part of the Middle East. It is located north of Israel on the Mediterranean Sea coast.

1 Kings 5:6; 7:1-3

See **Israel, Jerusalem, Lebanon Mountains (maps 7-8), Mediterranean Sea, Middle East, Solomon, temple**

legalism (LEE-gul-iz-um) *noun:*

Legalism is the belief that a person may earn salvation by keeping the rules of the Law. Legalism puts more emphasis upon rules of behavior than on the grace of God.

Matthew 23:23-28; Romans 3:19-20; 4:6; 9:30—10:4; Ephesians 2:8-10; Philippians 3:3-11

See **grace, justification, law, merit, Pharisee**

legalistic (LEE-gul-IS-tik) *adjective:*

Legalistic describes an action, attitude, or habit that depends on works instead of grace. Legalistic describes a person who tries to gain salvation by works instead of grace. A legalistic attitude judges a person's relationship with God by the rules that he or she keeps. A legalistic attitude toward discipleship puts rules in place of grace. Many Pharisees in the Bible are examples of legalistic persons.

Matthew 15:1-14; Luke 6:1-11; 7:36-50; 10:25-28; 14:1-6; 15:25-32; Romans 7:13-25; Galatians 5:1-18

See **discipleship, grace, law, legalism, merit, Pharisee, salvation, works**

Lent (LENT) *proper noun:*

Lent is the period of 40 days before Easter. Roman Catholicism and many Protestant denominations observe this sacred time. It is usually observed by denying oneself in some way.

See **denomination, discipline, Easter, Protestant, Roman Catholic, self-control**

leper (LEP-er) *noun:*

A leper is a person with a serious skin disease. The disease is called leprosy. Lepers were required to stay away from people who did not have the disease. A person was considered "unclean" if he or she touched a leper.

Leviticus 13—14; Luke 17:11-19

See **leprosy, unclean**

leprosy (LEP-ruh-see) *noun:*

Leprosy was a name given to several kinds of skin diseases in Bible times. Leprosy in the Bible was not the same as the leprosy of today.

See **leper**

Levi (LEE-vie) *proper noun:*

1. Levi is the name of one of the 12 sons of Jacob (Genesis 35:23-26).

The descendants of Levi became the tribe of Levi. The priests of Israel came from among the tribe of Levi (Numbers 1:47-53).

2. Levi, a tax collector, may have been one of the 12 disciples of Jesus. Some Bible scholars think Levi and Matthew were the same man. (See Matthew 10:3; Mark 2:14; 3:16-19; Luke 5:27.)

***See* disciple, Israel, Jacob, Levite, priest, tribes of Israel**

Levite (LEE-viet) *proper noun:*

A Levite was a descendant of the family of priests in Israel. The Levites helped the priests in the Temple.

Numbers 3—4; Deuteronomy 10:8-9; Luke 1:5

***See* Israel, Levi, Leviticus, priest, tabernacle, temple**

Leviticus (luh-VIT-uh-kus) *proper noun:*

Leviticus is the third book in the Old Testament. It is part of the Pentateuch or Books of the Law. It tells how the priests and Levites were to lead the worship of Israel. It stressed ritual holiness.

***See* atonement, Bible, holiness, Levite, Old Testament, Pentateuch, priest, ritual, worship**

liberal (LIB-er-ul)

1. *adjective:* Liberal in Christian doctrine describes persons or beliefs that do not follow traditional ideas.

2. *noun:* A liberal in Christianity is a person who accepts the ideas of liberalism. Liberals are not bound by traditional doctrines.

***See* doctrine, liberalism, tradition**

liberalism (LIB-er-ul-IZ-um) *noun:*

Liberalism is a view that tries to explain Christian beliefs in new ways. It is sometimes called modernism. Liberalism often disagrees with many basic Christian doctrines. The deity of Christ is one example. Liberalism admits that the Bible is important for Christian faith. But it denies that the Bible is divinely inspired. It says that the Bible must often be judged by reason and science.

***See* authority of Scripture, belief, conservative Christianity, deity, doctrine, dogma, evangelical, evolution, fundamentalism, inspiration, modernism, orthodox, reason, theology, tradition**

libertine (LIB-er-teen) *noun:*

A libertine is a person who claims liberty and freedom. The word is used in two special ways in the Bible and Christian doctrine.

1. The libertines were Jews who had been slaves. These freed slaves formed a special group in Jerusalem. They had their own synagogue there (Acts 6:9).

2. Libertines are people who oppose the law of God by living immorally. They use their freedom wrongly (1 Corinthians 6:12-20; 10:23-33; Galatians 5:13).

***See* freedom, immoral, law, slave**

lie (LIE)

1. *verb:* To lie means to say what is not true. A person who lies tries to deceive someone who should be told the truth. The Bible teaches that lying is wrong. To lie is sometimes called to bear false witness.

2. *noun:* A lie is a false statement meant to deceive someone. A person who tells lies is called a liar or a false witness.

Exodus 20:16; Numbers 23:19; Habakkuk 2:3; Acts 5:4; Colossians 3:9; Titus 1:2; James 3:14

See **bear false witness, deceive, Ten Commandments, truth**

life (LIEF) *noun:*

Life is what makes plants and animals different from rocks. It is the state of being alive and the opposite of being dead. The Bible says that God created life. God still makes all life possible.

Life also refers to the activity of people on earth. The Bible teaches that humans may enjoy a special kind of life. This life is salvation. Jesus Christ made salvation possible by giving His life for the sins of the world. This is also called spiritual life. The gift of eternal life is given to those who receive His forgiveness. Eternal life gives Christians hope.

John 1:1-5; 3:14-17; 10:14-18; 11:25; 14:6; Romans 1:16-17; 5:6—6:23; 8:1-11; 14:7-9; 1 Corinthians 15:12-57; 2 Corinthians 5:15; 1 John 1:1-2; 3:15-16; 5:11-20

See **crucifixion, death, eternal life, hope, image of God, light, new birth, resurrection, salvation**

light (LIET) *noun:*

Light is what helps make it possible for a person to see. The Bible says that God created light. Light is necessary for life.

The Bible also uses light in a special way. God's light means revelation. God gives His light to help people understand themselves and Him. People live in spiritual darkness if they do not have the light of God. God's light lets people see what is true. It teaches them how they should live. Many people choose darkness because they do not want to know the truth.

The light of God is the life of people. Only those who know God can have spiritual life. Jesus is the Light of the World because He shows people what God is like.

Christians who live in God's light enjoy friendship with Him and with one another. Christians are lights in the world because they show how God changes people.

Genesis 1:3-18; Psalm 118:27; Matthew 5:14-16; John 1:1-18; Romans 13:11-14; 2 Corinthians 3:17—4:6; 1 Peter 2:9-10; 1 John 1:5-7

See **Bible, creation, darkness, deeds of darkness, God, life, revelation, salvation, spiritual**

liturgical (luh-TER-ji-kul) *adjective:*

See **liturgy**

liturgy (LIT-er-gee) *noun:*

Liturgy is an order of things said and done when people come together for worship. The leader of worship serves God and the people through the liturgy. The Greek word for liturgy means "service." The liturgy includes the words spoken and things done during the Lord's Supper. A church service or ceremony may be described as liturgical.

See **church, Eucharist, Greek, Lord's Supper, ritual, sacrament, sanctuary, servant, service, worship**

Living Bible (LIV-ing BIE-bul) *proper noun phrase:*

The Living Bible is a modern version of the Bible. It translates the ideas, not the exact words.

See **Bible, translate, version**

logos (LOH-gahs or LOH-gohs) *noun:*

Logos is a Greek word that means "word." Greeks thought that the Logos was the Power that created order in the world. The Old Testament uses "word" to refer to the revelation of the will of God. "Wisdom" often means the same as "word." The New Testament says that the eternal Son of God is the Logos. The Gospel of John says that the Logos became incarnate in Jesus of Nazareth. Sometimes Logos means the gospel. Also, it may mean simply a word that is spoken.

Psalms 33:6; 119:11; Amos 8:11; John 1:1-5, 14; 1 Thessalonians 1:5-6; 2:13; 1 John 1:1-2

See **eternal, gospel, Incarnation, Jesus, oracle, reason, revelation, Scripture, Trinity, wisdom, word**

Lord (LOHRD) *proper noun:*

Lord means "one who rules." The word *lord* in the Bible sometimes means a human person who deserves respect. But the name *Lord* is usually the title for God. The Jews used the word *Lord* for Yahweh, the name of the God of Israel. They did this because they thought Yahweh was too holy to say.

The disciples of Jesus called Him Lord. They first meant only that they had great respect for Him. Later they understood that He was one with God. So the earliest Christian creed was "Jesus is Lord." The phrase *Lord Jesus Christ* is sometimes used in the New Testament (Ephesians 1:2, 17; Philippians 4:23; Colossians 1:3; 2 Thessalonians 1:12).

Genesis 23:2-16; Exodus 3:1—4:17; Isaiah 40:3; Matthew 3:1-3; 18:21; Acts 2:32-36; Romans 10:5-13; 1 Corinthians 12:3; Philippians 2:5-11; Revelation 4:8; 6:10

See **Christ, creed, God, Incarnation, Jesus, Jesus Christ, king, rabbi, Son of God, worship, Yahweh**

Lord's Day (LOHRDZ DAY) *proper noun phrase:*

The Lord's Day is Sunday. This is the day of worship for most Christians. It is sometimes called the Christians' Sabbath.

Jesus was resurrected on Sunday. He appeared to His disciples on Sunday, the first day of the week. Paul referred to the Lord's Day as "the first day of the week" (1 Corinthians 16:2). The Early Church celebrated the Lord's Supper on the Lord's Day. Christian worship on the Lord's Day began in the Early Church.

The Lord's Day is not the same as the Day of the Lord.

John 20:1, 19, 26; Acts 2:46; 20:7; Revelation 1:10

See **Lord's Supper, rest of faith, Sabbath, worship**

Lord's Prayer (LOHRDZ PRAYR) *proper noun phrase:*

The Lord's Prayer is a model prayer that Jesus taught His disciples to pray. Christians often unite in praying the Lord's Prayer when they worship.

Matthew 6:9-13; Luke 11:2-4

See **disciple, Jesus, Lord, prayer, worship**

Lord's Supper (LOHRDZ SUP-er) *proper noun phrase:*

The Lord's Supper is a special way Christians remember the death of Christ. The Lord's Supper repeats the last meal that Jesus ate with His disciples before His death. He shared bread and wine with them during that meal. Jesus told His disciples that the bread and wine represented His body and His blood.

Christ is present with His Church in a special way at the Lord's Supper. It is a time for giving thanks to Christ for His gift of salvation. Other names for the Lord's Supper are Holy Communion and Eucharist.

Matthew 26:20-29; Mark 14:17-21; Luke 22:14-23; John 13:1-11

See **blood, church, Eucharist, Holy Communion, Jesus, Last Supper, ritual, sacrament, salvation, wine, worship**

lost (LAWST):

1. *adjective:* Lost describes someone or something that is missing. Someone who has lost something does not know where it is. People who are lost do not know where they are. Something or someone that is lost may be in great danger.

Christian doctrine teaches that those who do not know Christ are lost. They are in great danger of eternal damnation if they do not return to God. God shows sinners that they are lost. Jesus came to find and save lost sinners. He said that God rejoices when lost people repent.

2. *noun:* The lost are people who do not know where they are. In Christianity, the lost usually refers to people who do not know Jesus Christ as Savior.

Jeremiah 50:6; Ezekiel 37:11-14; Matthew 10:6; 18:10-14; Luke 15:3-32; 19:1-10; John 18:9; 1 Corinthians 5:10-15; Philippians 3:7-8

See **damnation, death, doctrine, eternal death, new birth, repent, salvation, sinners**

Lot (LAHT) *proper noun:*

Lot was the nephew of Abraham. He became a citizen in the city of Sodom. Angels told Lot to leave wicked Sodom because God was going to destroy it.

Lot was the father of Moab and Ammon. Their descendants are included among the Arabs.

Genesis 11:31; 13:5-13; 14:12-16; 19:1-28

See **Abraham, Arab, Moab, Sodom and Gomorrah**

love (LUV)

1. *verb:* To love is to act in the best interest of another person. It is to act in a way that seeks to create fellowship with another. To love an object is to want to possess it.

2. *noun:* Love is the action of one who seeks fellowship with another person. Love tries to create a bond of loyal friendship.

There are different kinds of human love. Friendship is a kind of love. The care members of a family have for each other is another form of love. The desire of man and woman for each other is another kind of love.

The love God gives is a special kind of love. He loves the world. He cares for His whole creation. But His special concern is for people. He loves them even when they do not accept His love. Sinful people reject the love of God. Instead, they love things that will destroy them. But God is not satisfied to let them be lost in sin. He sent His Son to save them because of His eternal love. This is why Christians say God is love.

Christians know that God loves and accepts them through Christ. God gives them His spirit as proof of His love. The Holy Spirit helps them love God and other people. Christian faith also shows love for God through good works.

Leviticus 19:18; Deuteronomy 6:5; Proverbs 3:3; Matthew 5:44; Mark 12:30-33; John 3:16; 13:34; 15:12; Romans 5:1-11; 13:8-10; 1 Corinthians 13; 1 Peter 4:8; 2 Peter 1:7; 1 John 2:15; 4:8; 3 John 1

See **agape, Christ, creation, eternal, forgiveness, God, good works, grace, Great Commandment, Jesus, loving-kindness, loyalty, new birth, perfect love, sacrifice, sinful nature, spirit**

love feast (LUV FEEST) *noun phrase:*

The love feast was a meal shared by early Christians. The meal showed their unity and love for one another. The love feast and the Lord's Supper are not the same. But the two meals may have been eaten at the same worship service.

Acts 2:41-47; 20:7; 1 Corinthians 11:17-34; Jude 12

See **Body of Christ, bread, fellowship, Holy Communion, koinonia, Lord's Supper, service, unity, worship**

loving-kindness (LUV-ing-KIEND-nes) *noun:*

Loving-kindness is the mercy and faithfulness of God. Loving-kindness shows how God is true to His covenant promises. The Hebrew word for loving-kindness also means steadfast love, mercy, and pity.

Genesis 32:9-12; Exodus 34:6-8; Psalms 57:3; 63:1-8; 89:14; Isaiah 63:7; Jeremiah 9:23-24; Luke 1:50, 78; James 2:13; Jude 21

See **covenant, faithful, love, loyalty, mercy, promise**

loyalty (LOY-ul-tee) *noun:*

Loyalty is a strong devotion to someone or something. Loyalty lasts even through bad experiences. Loyalty to God is the right human response to the loving-kindness of God.

1 Samuel 18:1-4; 19:1-7; Philippians 4:3

See **covenant, faith, faithful, loving-kindness**

Lucifer (LEW-suh-fer) *proper noun:*

Lucifer is the Latin name for Venus, the morning star. The name means "light-bearer."

Lucifer began to be used as a name for Satan during the A.D. 200s. This happened because of a mistaken understanding of Isaiah 14:12 and Luke 10:18. These texts are not about the fall of Satan from heaven.

The morning star in Isaiah 14:12 is a symbol for the king of Babylon (verse 4). The morning star appeared to be bright in the darkness of night. But the sun would soon rise and show how dim the star really was. The king of Babylon claimed to be a god. But the one true God would soon prove that he was nothing.

Isaiah 14:3-23

See **Babylon, Satan**

Luke (LEWK) *proper noun:*

1. Luke is the name of the third Gospel in the New Testament. The Gospel of Luke tells the story of Jesus. It stresses the concern of Jesus for lost people.

2. Luke is also the name of a man who worked with Paul. The Church has generally believed that he wrote the Gospel of Luke. The Book of Acts was probably written by Luke also.

Colossians 4:14; 2 Timothy 4:11; Philemon 24

See **Acts, Bible, gospel, New Testament, Paul**

lust (LUST)

1. *verb:* To lust is to desire in a sinful way to have someone or something.

2. *noun:* Lust is selfish, sinful desire. It is usually related to a wrong desire for sex.

Psalm 106:14; Proverbs 6:23-35; Romans 1:27; 1 Corinthians 10:6-13; Galatians 5:17-21; Colossians 3:5

See **love, passion, sin, temptation**

Luther, Martin (LEW-ther, MAHR-tun) *proper noun phrase:*
Martin Luther was the major leader of the Protestant Reformation during the 1500s. He was once a Roman Catholic priest and teacher in Germany. But he learned that a person is justified by grace through faith alone. He began to preach this in his church. He also taught that doctrines that do not agree with the New Testament are wrong. Luther was excommunicated from the church for doing this. He also translated the Bible into the German language.

See **doctrine, excommunication, faith, justification, Lutheran, Protestant, reformation, Roman Catholic**

Lutheran (LEW-ther-un)

1. *proper adjective:* Lutheran describes a group of Protestant denominations that developed from the teachings of Martin Luther. There are nine Lutheran denominations that developed in the United States.

Lutherans stress the doctrine of justification by grace through faith alone. They celebrate two sacraments: baptism and the Lord's Supper. They believe that sacraments are ways through which God gives His grace to people. Lutherans baptize infants.

2. *proper noun:* A Lutheran is a person who is a member of a Lutheran church.

See **baptism, denomination, God, grace, justification, Lord's Supper, Martin Luther, Protestant, reformation, Roman Catholic, sacrament**

M m

Maccabees (MAK-uh-beez) *proper noun:*

The Maccabees were a family of priests in Israel. The Maccabees were also known as the Hasmoneans. They freed the people of Israel from the Greek ruler Antiochus Epiphanes. They ruled over Palestine during the second and first centuries B.C. Their story is told in two books of the Apocrypha called Maccabees.

See **abomination of desolation, Alexander the Great, Apocrypha, Greek, Hasmoneans, Israel, Maccabees (time line), Palestine, priest**

Macedonia (MAS-uh-DOH-nee-uh) *proper noun:*

Macedonia was a Roman province north of Greece in New Testament times. The apostle Paul went to Macedonia on his second missionary journey. Paul had a vision in which a Macedonian man asked him to come there (Acts 16:6-10). The cities of Berea, Philippi, and Thessalonica were located in Macedonia.

See **apostle, Greece, Macedonia (map 11), missionary, Paul, Philippi, Roman, Rome, Thessalonica, vision**

Magdala (MAG-duh-luh) *proper noun:*

Magdala was a small town on the west shore of the Sea of Galilee. It was the home of Mary Magdalene (Matthew 27:56, 61; Luke 8:2). It is also known as Magadan (Matthew 15:39).

See **Galilee, Magadan (map 8), Mary**

magi (MAY-jie) *noun:*

The magi were wise men who studied the stars. Some magi came to worship Jesus when He was a young child. They gave Him gifts. This is one reason why people give gifts to others at Christmas.

Matthew 2:1-12

See **Christmas, Virgin Birth, wise men**

magic (MAJ-ik) *noun:*

Magic is trying to use evil spirits to get power. People try to use magic to control other people or events. The Bible opposes this. Magic is also called sorcery.

Another kind of magic is the use of tricks to amuse or fool people.

Exodus 7:8-13; 22:18; Daniel 1:20; Acts 13:8-11; Galatians 5:19-21; Revelation 9:21; 18:23; 21:8

See **condemn, demon, evil, fool, occult, sorcery, supernatural, witchcraft**

Malachi (MAL-uh-kie) *proper noun:*

1. Malachi was a prophet in the Old Testament. His prophecies are in the last book of the Old Testament. Malachi preached after the Jews returned

from the Exile. He stressed pure worship in the Temple. He called on the people of Jerusalem to keep the covenant.

2. Malachi is the last book in the Old Testament. It is one of the Minor Prophets.

See **Bible, covenant, exile, Jerusalem (map 7), Jew, Malachi (time line), Old Testament, preach, prophet, temple, worship**

malefactor (MAL-uh-FAK-ter) *noun:*

A malefactor is one who breaks the laws of a government. He or she is one who does evil and is guilty of serious crime. A malefactor is also called a criminal. Jesus was crucified with two malefactors.

Luke 23:32-43

See **crucifixion, evil, guilty, law**

mammon (MAM-un) *noun:*

Mammon means wealth or what people own. Jesus said that people cannot love both God and their possessions. He told His disciples to use their possessions to serve God.

Matthew 6:24; Luke 14:33; 16:1-14; 18:18-30; 1 Timothy 3:1-3; 6:10; Hebrews 13:5; 1 Peter 5:1-3

See **idolatry, materialism, secularism**

man (MAN) *noun:*

Man means a human being. God made man as male and female. Together He called them "man" (Genesis 5:2). Both were created in the image of God. The New Testament says that men and women are equal in Christ.

Genesis 1:26-31; 2:7-8, 18-23; Psalm 139:13-16; Galatians 3:27-29; Ephesians 2:14-16; 4:22-24

See **creation, human, image of God, new man**

Manasseh (muh-NAS-uh) *proper noun:*

1. Manasseh is a name of two important men in the Old Testament.

   a. Manasseh was one of the two sons of Joseph. His descendants became one of the 12 tribes of Israel (Genesis 41:51; 48:8-20; Joshua 12:4-6; 17:5-10).

   b. Manasseh was the most wicked of the kings of Judah. He was a son of the good King Hezekiah (2 Kings 21; 2 Chronicles 33).

2. Manasseh was the land occupied by the tribe of Manasseh.

See **Hezekiah, Israel, Jacob, Joseph, Judah, Manasseh (map 3, time line), Tribes of Israel**

manger (MAYN-jer) *noun:*

A manger is a large box often made of wood or stone. It holds food for animals to eat. Jesus was put into a manger when He was born.

Isaiah 1:3; Luke 2:1-7

See **Jesus**

manna (MAN-uh) *noun:*

Manna was the food eaten by the Israelites during their 40 years in the desert. The people gathered it daily, except for the Sabbath. The supply lasted until the people entered Canaan (Exodus 16:1-35).

Jesus referred to manna as the "bread of heaven." He said that He was the bread of God who came down from heaven (John 6:30-33).

See **bread, Canaan, forty years, heaven, Israelites, Sabbath**

manual (MAN-yew-wul or MAN-yul) *noun:*

A manual is a book that tells how something works. A church manual explains what a denomination believes and how it is governed.

See **denomination, doctrine, polity**

Mark (MAHRK) *proper noun:*

1. Mark is the name of the second Gospel in the New Testament. The Gospel of Mark tells the story of Jesus. It was probably the first of the Synoptic Gospels to be written. It tells of the mighty works of Jesus. It also stresses that Jesus was the suffering Son of God.

2. Mark is also the name of a man in the New Testament. His full name was John Mark. The Gospel of Mark was probably written by him. John Mark traveled with the apostles Paul and Peter. He probably got most of his facts about Jesus from Peter's preaching.

Acts 12:12, 25; 15:36-39; 2 Timothy 4:11; 1 Peter 5:13

See **Bible, gospel, New Testament, Paul, Peter, Synoptic Gospels**

marriage (MAIR-ij) *noun:*

Marriage is the relationship of a man and woman as husband and wife. They vow to be faithful to each other for life. The church and the state publicly approve a marriage.

The New Testament compares the relationship of Christ and the Church to a marriage.

Genesis 2:24; John 2:1-2; Romans 7:2-6; 1 Corinthians 7:3-5, 10-11; Ephesians 5:22-23

See **bride, bridegroom, church, divorce, marriage supper of the Lamb**

Marriage Supper of the Lamb (MAIR-ij SUP-er uv thuh LAM) *proper noun phrase:*

The Marriage Supper of the Lamb is one way Christ's second coming will be celebrated.

The Church is sometimes called the Bride of Christ. Christ is sometimes called the Lamb. This is because He gave himself as a sacrifice for the sins of the world. Christ is also the Bridegroom of the Church. Marriages in Bible times were celebrated with special meals. The Marriage Supper of the Lamb celebrates the "marriage" of Christ to the Church. The unity of Christ and His Church will be complete at the Second Coming.

Revelation 19:1-8

See **bride, bridegroom, church, eschatology, Lamb of God, sacrifice, Second Coming, unity**

Mars Hill (MAHRZ HILL) *proper noun phrase:*

See **Areopagus**

Martha (MAHR-thuh) *proper noun:*

Martha is the name of a woman in the New Testament. She was the sister of Mary and Lazarus of Bethany. She and her family were close friends of Jesus.

Luke 10:38-42; John 11:1-5

See **Bethany (map 10), Jesus, Lazarus, Mary, New Testament**

martyr (MAHR-ter) *noun:*

A martyr is one who gives his or her life for a cause. There have been many martyrs in the history of the Christian Church. They were killed because they would not give up their faith. Stephen is known as the first Christian martyr.

Acts 7:54—8:2

See **faith, Stephen, testimony, witness**

Mary (MAIR-ee) *proper noun:*

Mary was the name of several women in the New Testament.

1. Mary was the mother of Jesus (Matthew 1:16; 13:55; Luke 1:26-56).
2. Mary of Bethany was a friend of Jesus (Luke 10:39; John 11:1—12:8).
3. Mary Magdalene was a disciple of Jesus. He had freed her from the power of demons (Luke 8:2; John 20:1-18).
4. Other Marys are also named in the New Testament (Matthew 27:56, 61; John 19:25; Acts 12:12; Romans 16:6).

See **Bethany (map 10), demon, Jesus, Lazarus, Martha, virgin, Virgin Birth**

Masada (muh-SAH-duh) *proper noun:*

Masada is the name of a small flat mountain on the west side of the Dead Sea. Herod the Great had a fort and castle built on it. Masada became a small town. Herod planned to go there if he needed to escape his enemies. The word *Masada* probably means "mountain castle."

Masada was the location of a famous struggle between the Jews and the Romans. About 70 years after Herod died, some Zealots revolted against Roman rule of Israel. But the Romans destroyed most of the rebels. The survivors escaped by hiding on Masada. The Roman army fought a group of 960 Jewish rebels for three years. When the Roman army was about to capture Masada, most of the Jews killed themselves. They preferred to die rather than become slaves of Rome.

Masada is not mentioned in the Bible. Jewish historian Josephus tell about it. A few of the Dead Sea Scrolls came from Masada.

See **Dead Sea (map 3), Dead Sea Scrolls, Herod, Josephus, Rome, Roman, slave, zealot**

Mass (MAS) *proper noun:*

The Mass is the main and highest act of worship in the Roman Catholic Church. It is the celebration of the sacrifice of Christ. It is sometimes called the Eucharist. It gives thanks to Christ for His gift of salvation. Catholics believe the bread and wine used actually become the body and blood of Christ.

See **blood, body, Christ, Eucharist, Holy Communion, Lord's Supper, Roman Catholic, sacrifice, salvation**

mass evangelism (MAS ee-VAN-juh-LIZ-um) *noun phrase:*

Mass evangelism means preaching the gospel to large groups of people. The purpose of mass evangelism is to win converts to Christ.

Acts 2:14-41; 8:4-8

See **Christ, convert, evangelism, gospel, Billy Graham, preach, salvation**

materialism (muh-TIR-ee-ul-IZ-um) *noun:*

Materialism is the belief that possessions are more important than anything else. For example, materialism gives highest value to money and property. Materialism places higher value on material things than on the kingdom of God. Jesus spoke strongly against materialism.

Matthew 6:19-34; Romans 1:24-32; Philippians 3:18-21; Colossians 2:16—3:2

See **carnal, kingdom of God, lust, mammon, pride, values**

Matthew (MATH-yew) *proper noun:*

1. Matthew is the first book in the New Testament. The Gospel of Matthew is one of the three Synoptic Gospels. It tells the story of Jesus as the promised Messiah of the Jews. It stresses His teaching ministry.

2. Matthew is also a man in the New Testament. Matthew was one of the apostles or 12 disciples of Jesus. It is believed that he wrote the first book in the New Testament. Matthew may also be Levi mentioned in Mark 2:14 and Luke 5:27.

See **apostle, Bible, disciple, gospel, Levi, Messiah, New Testament, Synoptic Gospels**

Matthias (muh-THIE-us) *proper noun:*

Matthias was the disciple chosen to take the place of Judas Iscariot. He became one of the 12 apostles (Acts 1:15-26).

See **apostle, disciple, Judas, New Testament**

maturity (muh-CHOOR-uh-tee) *noun:*

Maturity means being fully developed. For example, an adult has reached physical maturity. He will not grow taller. A mature person is one who is fully developed.

Christians should move toward spiritual maturity. Christian maturity is a high level of growth in grace.

Ephesians 4:11-13; Hebrews 6:1-2

See **Christian perfection, entire sanctification, growth in grace, spiritual**

means of grace (MEENZ uv GRAYS) *noun phrase:*

The means of grace are the ways God helps people grow as Christians. The means of grace include private and group worship. Worship includes prayer, Bible study, fellowship, preaching, the sacraments, and other spiritual disciplines.

See **baptism, church, devotions, discipline, fellowship, grace, Holy Communion, prayer, sacrament, spiritual, worship**

Medes (MEEDZ) *proper noun:*

Medes are the people who live in Media.

See **Media**

Media (MEE-dee-uh) *proper noun:*

Media was an ancient kingdom during Old Testament times. It was located east of Mesopotamia. In the Bible, Media is connected with Persia. The phrases "Medes and Persians" or "Media and Persia" are mentioned several times (Esther 1:3, 14, 18-19; 10:2; Daniel 5:28; 6:8, 12, 15; 8:20).

See **Media (map 6), Mesopotamia, Persia**

mediator (MEE-dee-AY-ter) *noun:*

A mediator is one who represents the interests of one person to another person. Mediators help to settle problems between people. Moses is the greatest mediator in the Old Testament. Prophets, priests, and kings were also mediators.

Jesus Christ is the perfect Mediator between God and man. He died to show people how much God loves them. He alone is truly God and truly man. Only Jesus Christ truly brings people and God together.

Romans 5:1-11; 2 Corinthians 5:11-21; 1 Timothy 2:5-6; Hebrews 8:6; 9:11-15

See **covenant, intercession, law, Moses, reconciliation, redemption**

meditation (MED-uh-TAY-shun) *noun:*

Meditation is the spiritual discipline of thinking about God and His will for people. It usually takes place in prayer.

See **devotions, discipline, means of grace, prayer, spiritual**

Mediterranean Sea (MED-uh-tuh-RAY-nee-un SEE) *proper noun phrase:*

The Mediterranean Sea is a large body of salt water west of Palestine. Mediterranean comes from the Latin words meaning "between the lands." It separates the three continents of Europe, Asia, and Africa. The apostle Paul started churches in many major cities along its northern shores. Many of his missionary journeys took him by boat on its waters.

The Mediterranean Sea is known by other names in the Bible. It is called "the Sea" (2 Chronicles 20:2) and the "Western Sea" (Deuteronomy 11:24). It is also known as the "Great Sea" (Joshua 1:4; 23:4) and the "Sea of the Philistines" (Exodus 23:31).

See **Mediterranean Sea (maps 2, 3, 4, 6, 7, 8, 9, and 11), Paul**

meek (MEEK) *adjective:*

See **humility**

Megiddo (muh-GID-oh) *proper noun:*

Megiddo was an important city in Old Testament times. It was located on the southwestern side of the Valley of Jezreel. It protected a pass across the Carmel mountain range. Several kings used Meggido as a home, including Solomon, Ahab, and Josiah.

1 Kings 9:15; 2 Kings 9:27; 23:29-30

See **Ahab, Carmel, Jezreel, Josiah, Meggido (maps 3, 4, 7), Solomon**

Melchizedek (mel-KIZ-uh-dek) *proper noun:*

Melchizedek was a Gentile king of Salem during the time of Abraham. Melchizedek was called "priest of God Most High" (Genesis 14:18).

Genesis 14:18-22; Psalm 110:4; Hebrews 5:5-10; 6:20: 7:1-17

See **Abraham, Gentile, priest, Salem**

Menahem (MEN-uh-hem) *proper noun:*

Menahem was a king of Israel, the Northern Kingdom. He became king by killing Shallum. He ruled for 10 years. He was an evil king.

2 Kings 15:14-23

See **Israel, Menahem (time line), Shallum**

Mennonite (MEN-uh-niet) *proper noun:*

A Mennonite is a person who follows the teachings of Menno Simons. The Mennonites began in the 16th century A.D. in Europe. Menno Simons became the most important leader. Mennonites make up one part of the Christians called Anabaptists.

The early Mennonite leaders thought that Martin Luther did not make enough changes. They thought he still accepted too many Roman Catholic beliefs. Mennonites thought the New Testament should be the rule for all beliefs and practices. They believed that Christians should not fight in wars. They would not swear to obey a government. Mennonites were often persecuted for their beliefs. Thousands of Mennonites were killed. Many Mennonites sought religious freedom. They moved from Europe to the United States and Canada.

Mennonites believe that the Bible is the main authority for faith and doctrine. They baptize only adults who are Christians. Mennonites believe that community is very important for Christians. They must help each other when a person needs money, food, or housing. Mennonites believe that Jesus is the Prince of Peace. Therefore, usually they will not fight in war or in self-defense. Mennonites are pacifists, which means they will not use violence. They also believe that guidance by the Holy Spirit is important.

See **Anabaptist, baptism, community, faith, Holy Spirit, Martin Luther, pacifism, persecution, Protestant, reformation, Roman Catholic**

mercy (MER-see) *noun:*

Mercy is the help given those who cannot help themselves. God and people may show mercy. They may seek justice for those who suffer persecution. They may forgive those who have done wrong. God shows mercy when He forgives sinners, for they really deserve punishment. Jesus said that those who show mercy will receive mercy from God.

Exodus 20:6; 1 Chronicles 16:34; Psalms 103:8-18, 136; Hosea 6:6; Micah 6:8; Matthew 5:7; Romans 9:15-18; 12:1; 2 Corinthians 1:3; Ephesians 2:4-5; Titus 3:4-7; 1 Peter 1:3

See **Beautitudes, faithful, forgiveness, God, grace, gracious, justice, love, loving-kindness, patience, persecution**

mercy seat (MER-see SEET) *noun phrase:*

The mercy seat was the lid of the ark of the covenant. It was the most important part of the Temple furniture. The high priest sprinkled blood from a sacrificed bull there once each year. This was the Day of Atonement when God forgave the sins of the people.

The New Testament says that Jesus Christ has become the Mercy Seat. The Greek word for mercy seat means the way God chooses to forgive sins. Jesus Christ made final atonement for the sins of the world.

Exodus 25:17-20; 26:34; 30:6; 37:6-9; Leviticus 16:1-15; Romans 3:20-25; Hebrews 9:5

See **ark, atonement, covenant, expiation, forgiveness, mercy, propitiation, sacrifice, sin, temple**

merit (MAIR-it) *noun:*

Merit is the reward given to a person for something good he or she has done. It may also mean something that is of high quality or value.

See **good works, grace, meritorious death, reward**

meritorious death (MAIR-uh-TOR-ee-us DETH) *noun phrase:*

The meritorious death is the death of Christ on the Cross. He has done all that is necessary for the salvation of the whole world. Nothing that people do themselves can earn salvation. Sinners are saved by the merits of Christ.

Romans 5:15-21

See **Christ, cross, forgiveness, good works, grace, justification, love, merit, salvation, sinner**

Mesopotamia (MES-uh-puh-TAY-mee-uh) *proper noun:*

Mesopotamia was the land between the Tigris and Euphrates rivers east of Palestine. Mesopotamia in Greek means "between the rivers." Several great nations in Bible times were located in or near Mesopotamia. They included Assyria, Babylon, and Persia.

See **Assyria, Assyria (maps 1, 6), Babylon, Babylon (maps 1, 6), Chaldea, Euphrates River (maps 1, 6), Greece, Persia, Persia (map 6), Tigris River (maps 1, 6)**

message (MES-ij) *noun:*

A message is a written or spoken way to share news. God made His will known through the messages of His prophets or angels. A sermon may also be called a message. Sermons tell the good news of salvation.

1 Samuel 9:8; 2 Kings 3:7; Daniel 10:1; Matthew 10:7; Acts 2:41; Hebrews 2:2; 1 John 1:5; 2:7

See **angel, gospel, kerygma, preach, prophet, salvation, sermon, will**

messenger (MES-in-jer) *noun:*

A messenger is a person who delivers news. The message may be written or spoken. It may be from God or from another person. The messenger may be an angel, or the messenger may be a person, such as a preacher.

1 Samuel 23:27; Job 1:14; Isaiah 41:27; 42:19; Mark 1:1-3; Luke 1:26-28; 7:27; 2 Corinthians 12:7; Philippians 2:25

See **angel, God, Gospel, message, Messiah, prophet**

Messiah (muh-SIE-uh) *proper noun:*

Messiah means a person chosen by God to do His will. The word *Messiah* in Hebrew means "the anointed one." Men were anointed when they became kings. The Jews hoped for a future king from the family of David. He would be their Messiah. He would free them from their enemies. He would make Israel a great nation again. They thought their Messiah would be like an earthly king.

"Christ" is the Greek word for Messiah. The disciples believed that Jesus was the Messiah. He had been anointed by the Holy Spirit. God had chosen Him to bring salvation. The enemy He came to destroy was sin. He brought the kingdom of God. Christians believe that He is the King of Kings.

Psalm 2:2; Daniel 9:26; Matthew 1:17; John 1:41; 4:25; Acts 4:26-27; 10:38; Revelation 11:15

See **anoint, Christ, David, Israel, Jesus, Jew, king, kingdom of God, Lord, prophesy, salvation, sin, will**

messianic (MES-ee-AN-ik) *adjective:*

Messianic describes a person or thing that is related to the promised Messiah. For example, a messianic prophecy was one that predicted the coming of the Messiah.

See **Jew, Messiah, prophesy**

Methodist (METH-uh-dist) *proper noun:*

Methodist is the name of several denominations that developed from the teachings of John Wesley. About 20 different denominations use Methodist as part of their name. Members of these churches are called Methodists. The United Methodist church is the largest of these denominations.

The first Methodists were a group of students at Oxford University in England. They met regularly to follow a strict discipline of Bible study and prayer. John Wesley and his brother Charles were leaders of these "Methodists."

A great revival in England came through the ministry of John and Charles Wesley. Their converts formed a large group known as Methodists. The Methodists in England became a separate denomination from the Anglican Church. This happened only after John Wesley's death. But the Methodist denomination in America was formed in 1784. This was seven years before Wesley's death.

See **Anglican, convert, discipline, Holiness Movement, Protestant, reformation, revival, Charles Wesley, John Wesley, Wesleyanism**

Methuselah (muh-THEW-zuh-luh) *proper noun:*

Methuselah was the son of Enoch and the grandfather of Noah. Methuselah lived to be 969 years old. He was the oldest person who ever lived. He was an ancestor of Jesus.

Genesis 5:21-27; Luke 3:37

See **Enoch, Jesus, Noah**

Micah (MIE-kuh) *proper noun:*

1. Micah was a prophet in the Old Testament. His messages are found in the book that carries his name. Micah stressed justice, mercy, and being humble. He warned the people of Judah to repent of their sins. Micah said that God would forgive the people if they would repent.
2. Micah is a book in the Old Testament. It is one of the Minor Prophets.

See **Bible, humble, Judah, justice, mercy, Old Testament, prophet, repent**

Michael (MIE-kul) *proper noun:*

Michael is the name of an angel in the Bible. In Revelation Michael fought against the dragon.

Jude 9; Revelation 12:7

See **angel, dragon, Revelation**

Middle East (MID-ul EEST) *proper noun:*

The Middle East is the area where most of the Bible events happened. It includes the regions of Asia Minor, Mesopotamia, Palestine, the Sinai, and Egypt.

See **Arabia (map 6), Asia Minor (map 11), Bible, Egypt (map 2), Mesopotamia, Palestine, Sinai**

millenium (muh-LEN-ee-um) *noun:*

The millennium is the 1,000-year reign of Christ. It will be a time of peace on earth. The millennium is spoken of in the Bible in Revelation 20:1-10.

Scholars do not agree about what the millennium means. Some think that Christ will come again before the millennium. They believe that He will reign in Jerusalem for 1,000 years. This view is called premillennialism. Dispensationalism is one form of premillennialism.

Some believe that Christ will return after the millennium. This view is called postmillennialism.

Others believe that the millennium is the present reign of Christ in the Church. The 1,000 years is a sign that Christ is already reigning. He is already bringing peace on earth through the Church. This view is called amillennialism.

Some say that the millennium stands for only a long period of time.

1 Corinthians 15:20-28; Revelation 20:1-10

See **apocalyptic, church, dispensationalism, eschatology, kingdom of God, prophesy, Second Coming**

mind (MIEND) *noun:*

The mind is what makes it possible for people to think and reason. It helps them know themselves and their world. A person's mind is his or her ability to think, to choose, and to have feelings.

The Bible uses the word *mind* in a special way. The mind is the center of who a person is. It shows what he or she loves and wants. A person who chooses evil things has a sinful or carnal mind. He or she is controlled by sin. A person who chooses what God wants has a spiritual mind. He or she is controlled by the Holy Spirit (Romans 8:5-17).

Sometimes, mind means the attitude or character of a person. The New Testament says Christians may have the mind of Christ. This means they may have an attitude like His. They can choose to do the will of God.

Mark 5:15; 12:30; Romans 1:28; 7:25; 1 Corinthians 1:10; 2:14-16; Philippians 1:27; 2:1-13; 3:15-21; Colossians 2:18-19; 1 Peter 1:13-16

See **attitude, carnal, disciple, entire sanctification, ethics, fullness of the Spirit, humility, perfect love, piety, regeneration, spiritual, virtue, will**

minister (MIN-is-ter)

1. *verb:* To minister is to serve God or people. All Christians are called to minister.

2. *noun:* A minister is a person who serves God and people. Today a minister is usually a pastor or priest. He has been ordained as a spiritual leader. But a person can minister and not be ordained.

Exodus 28:1; Joshua 1:1; Romans 15:7-9; 2 Corinthians 3:4-6; 4:1-3; 11:8, 15, 23; Ephesians 4:11-16; 2 Timothy 4:5

See **Christian, laity, ordain, ordination, pastor, priest, servant, service, spiritual**

ministry (MIN-is-tree) *noun:*

Ministry is the act of service by one person to others. It is the act of doing something to help or honor another person or persons.

Ministry in the Bible usually means service to God. Worship of God is ministry to Him. Doing His will is ministry to God. Ministry to God in the Old Testament was usually done by priests. They led the people in worshiping God. This was their special job.

Angels also minister to God.

People may minister to other persons by serving them. Servants may minister to their masters. Friends may minister to friends by serving their needs.

Christ ministered to His disciples through His service to them. Christians minister to God through their service to Him. They are to be His ministers.

Ministry sometimes describes persons who are ministers. They may be preachers, missionaries, or teachers.

Exodus 24:13; Joshua 1:1; Matthew 20:26; Luke 10:40; 12:37; 22:27; Romans 1:10; 12:1; 2 Corinthians 6:4; 11:23; Ephesians 3:7; Philippians 1:1; 1 Timothy 3:6-11; Hebrews 8:2; 2 Peter 1:1

See **angel, apostle, intercession, laity, minister, missionary, mediator, pastor, preacher, priest, servant, service, will, worship**

miracle (MIR-uh-kul) *noun:*

A miracle is an event that cannot be explained naturally. It shows the power of God. People in the Old Testament believed that all of life was a miracle.

Jesus showed the power of God in special ways. Some of the deeds He did on earth were miracles. He healed the sick. He helped blind people to see. He fed hungry people. He set people free from the power of demons. Yet the enemies of Jesus refused to see what God was doing through Jesus.

Miracles are accepted only by believers. They worship God because of what they have seen of His power. Those who will not believe try to explain miracles in some other way.

Deuteronomy 11:1-7; 29:2-5; Matthew 4:23-25; 12:22-28; John 2:1-11; 20:30-31; Acts 2:22

See **demon, exorcism, God, healing, Jesus, Old Testament, omnipotence, sign, worship**

Miriam (MIR-ee-um) *proper noun:*

Miriam was a sister of Moses and Aaron. She was a prophet. She helped Moses lead the Israelites from Egypt to Canaan.

Exodus 15:19-21; Number 12:1-15

See **Aaron, Canaan, Egypt, Israelite, Moses, prophet, prophetess**

mission (MISH-un) *noun:*

A mission is a special task to be done. The mission of the Church is to take the good news of salvation to the world. It is to make disciples of all people. It is to baptize and teach those who believe the gospel. It is also to continue the ministry of Jesus.

Most Christian denominations have mission organizations to fulfill Christ's Great Commission (Matthew 28:19-20). Missionaries are sent to carry out the church's mission plans.

John 17:17-20; 20:19-23; Acts 1:1-8; 10:34-43; Romans 11:13; 15:14-29; 2 Corinthians 5:11—6:10; 1 Peter 2:9-10

***See* baptism, disciple, evangelism, good news, gospel, Great Commission, ministry, missionary, preach**

missionary (MISH-uh-NAIR-ee) *noun:*

A missionary is a person who takes the story of salvation to another. A missionary is called by God and sent by the church. This person usually takes the gospel to people of another culture. A missionary tells others about Jesus Christ.

The Early Christian Church had several missionaries. The apostle Paul was the great missionary of Christianity during this time. He made three missionary journeys to western Asia and southern Europe. See Acts 13—21.

Matthew 28:19-20; Acts 13:1-5

***See* apostle, call, church, evangelist, gospel, mission, Paul, Paul's missionary journeys (map 11), preach, salvation**

Moab (MOH-ab) *proper noun:*

Moab was the name of a nation related to the people of Israel. Moab was a son of Abraham's nephew Lot. The people of Moab were bitter enemies of Israel. A person from Moab was called a Moabite. The land of Moab was east of the Dead Sea.

Ruth was from the land of Moab.

Genesis 11:31; 19:30-38; Deuteronomy 23:3-6; Ruth 1:4

***See* Abraham, Arab, Dead Sea (map 3), Israel, Lot, Moab (map 7), Moabites (map 3), Ruth**

Moabite (MOH-uh-biet) *proper noun:*

***See* Moab**

modernism (MAHD-ern-IZ-um) *noun:*

Modernism was one way that some Christians responded to modern science. Modernism taught that Christian faith should yield to science whenever these two beliefs disagree. Modernism began in the late 1800s. It denied the central doctrines of the Christian faith. Fundamentalism arose partly as an attack on modernism. Modernism began to give way to postmodernism during the 1970s.

***See* authority of Scripture, conservative Christianity, doctrine, evangelical, fundamentalism, liberalism, Protestant**

modesty (MAHD-us-tee) *noun:*

Modesty is using proper care in dressing, speaking, and acting. Standards of modesty are influenced by culture. Therefore, modesty may differ from country to country. Christian modesty is based on the Scriptures and on what the church considers proper. Modesty means being neither too proud nor too humble.

Romans 12:3; 1 Corinthians 12:14-26; 1 Timothy 2:9-10; 1 Peter 3:3-4

See **ethics, humility, morality, piety, pride, profane, vanity**

Mohammed (moh-HAM-ud) *proper noun:*

See **Islam**

money changers (MUN-ee CHAYN-jerz) *noun phrase:*

Money changers were people in the Temple who exchanged regular money for Temple money. Temple worshipers could not give their offerings in coins with images on them. Jesus said that the money changers were cheating the people. He forced the evil money changers to leave the Temple.

Mark 11:15-18; John 2:13-17

See **evil, offering, temple, worship, wrath, zeal**

monk (MUNK) *noun:*

A monk is a man who is a member of a religious group. This group lives in a community separated from other people. A monk gives much of his time to prayer and other spiritual activities.

The religious community of which a monk is a part is a religious order. A monk lives in a place called a monastery. A monk makes a vow to own nothing and to obey his leaders. He vows not to be married and lives by the rules of his religious order. Monks are found in the Roman Catholic Church and Greek Orthodox Church.

See **community, discipline, Eastern Orthodoxy, marriage, nun, Roman Catholic, vow**

monotheism (MAHN-uh-thee-IZ-um) *noun:*

Monotheism is the belief that there is only one God. All other powers in the world are subject to Him.

Three of the great world religions accept monotheism. They are Judaism, Christianity, and Islam.

Exodus 3; Deuteronomy 6:4-5; Isaiah 44:1-20; Romans 1:20-23; 1 Corinthians 8:4-6; Ephesians 4:6; 1 Thessalonians 1:9

See **belief, Christianity, confess, creed, God, Islam, Judaism, religion, Ten Commandments, Trinity, unity**

monotheistic (MAHN-uh-thee-IS-tik) *adjective:*

Monotheistic describes a religious belief, practice, or a religion that relates to a belief in only one God. For example, a monotheistic practice is not worshiping idols.

See **Christianity, God, idols, monotheism, worship**

Moody, Dwight L. (MEW-dee DWIET) *proper noun:*

See **revival**

moral (MOHR-ul) *adjective:*

Moral describes what agrees with morality. The moral values of a person are what he or she believes to be right and wrong.

See **morality, morals, right, values**

moral nature (MOHR-ul NAY-cher) *noun phrase:*

See **ethics, morality, nature**

morality (muh-RAL-uh-tee) *noun:*

Morality is the practice of what is ethically correct. Morality is the practice of ethics. The Bible helps Christians know what is right or wrong. God gives Christians power to do the right.

See **Bible, Christian, ethics, nature, right, values**

morals (MOHR-ulz) *plural noun:*

Morals are values that a person lives by. Rules of moral conduct are based on those values.

See **ethics, morality, values**

Moriah (muh-RIE-uh) *proper noun:*

Moriah is a hill in Jerusalem where Solomon built the Temple (2 Chronicles 3:1). Moriah is also the place where Abraham went to sacrifice his son, Isaac (Genesis 22:2). Mount Moriah is a sacred place for three religions: Christianity, Judaism, and Islam.

See **Abraham, Christianity, Isaac, Islam, Judaism, sacrifice, Solomon, temple**

Mormon (MOHR-mun) *proper noun:*

Mormon is the name of a religious group that follows the teachings of Joseph Smith. The correct name for this group is the Church of Jesus Christ of Latter-day Saints.

Other denominations are related to the Mormons. The largest of these is the Community of Christ (formerly the Reorganized Church of Jesus Christ of Latter-day Saints). This denomination is more like Evangelical Christianity than is the Mormon church.

Mormons differ from Christianity in several important ways. They believe that Jesus Christ was created by God as Adam was. They say that He is not truly God. Mormons consider the Book of Mormon to be holy Scripture along with the Bible. The word *Mormon* comes from the name of a prophet and historian named Mormon. According to Mormon history, he wrote the Book of Mormon from the writings of many ancient prophets.

See **Bible, Christ, Christianity, creation, God, gospel, Incarnation, Jesus, prophet, saint, Scripture, Son of God**

mortal sin (MOHR-tul SIN) *noun phrase:*

Mortal sin is the name Roman Catholics give to one type of sin. A mortal sin is a very serious one. It is serious because it is done with full knowledge and on purpose. It is the result of sinful desire and sinful attitude.

Roman Catholicism makes a difference between mortal and venial sins. This difference is not stressed today as it once was.

A venial sin is a sin done with less than full knowledge and desire. It does not come from a desire of the heart to disobey God. Thus, venial sins can be forgiven without the sacrament of penance. However, mortal sins can be forgiven only through the sacrament of penance.

See **penance, Roman Catholic, sacrament, sin, venial sin, Wesleyanism**

Moses (MOH-zis) *proper noun:*

Moses was a great leader and prophet of the Hebrew people. God called him to lead the people of Israel out of slavery in Egypt. Moses led the people first to Mount Sinai. God made a covenant with them there through Moses. God gave His law to Moses, and Moses gave it to Israel. Thus, the books of the law, the Torah, are called the law of Moses. An important part of the law is the Ten Commandments.

Exodus 2:1—34:35; Numbers 10:35—14:45; Deuteronomy 1:1—34:12

See **Aaron, covenant, Egypt (map 2), God, Hebrew, Israel, law, Moses (time line), Miriam, Mount Sinai (map 2), prophet, Sinai (map 2), slavery, Ten Commandments, Torah**

Moslem (MAHZ-lum) *proper noun:*

See **Islam**

motive (MOH-tiv) *noun:*

A motive is an emotion or desire that causes a person to do something. The motives of people are also their reasons or purposes for acting.

People with good motives want to do what is right. But what they do may not turn out to be right. For example, a person who tries to help others may sometimes harm them by mistake. It is important that one's motives are right.

A person may do something that seems right but with an evil motive. For example, he or she may be nice to others because he or she wants to cheat them.

See **affection, ethics, evil, forgiveness, good works, guilt, innocent, responsibility, right, willful**

Mount of Olives (MOUNT uv AH-luvz) *proper noun phrase:*

The Mount of Olives is a long ridge of hills just east of Jerusalem. Jesus made His triumphal entry into Jerusalem from there on the first Palm Sunday (Matthew 21:1-11). He predicted the second destruction of Jerusalem from there (24:1-3). The Garden of Gethsemane was located on the lower part of the Mount of Olives. The disciples of Jesus witnessed His ascension on the Mount of Olives (Luke 24:50; Acts 1:6-12).

Olivet was another name for the Mount of Olives.

See **Ascension, disciple, Gethsemane, Jerusalem, Jerusalem (map 10), Mount of Olives (map 10), olive, Palm Sunday, Triumphal Entry**

movement (MEWV-munt) *noun:*

A movement is a number of related events done by a group of people. These related events have a goal or purpose. These events usually unite large numbers of people. The related events and the people who take part in them are called a movement.

The people in a movement usually try to get others to join them. A movement usually has strong leaders. A movement is usually marked by fast growth. Methodism is the result of a religious movement called the Evangelical Revival.

See **Christian Restorationism, evangelical, Holiness Movement, Methodist**

Muhammad (moh-HAM-ud) *proper noun:*

See **Islam**

Muslim (MUZ-lum) *proper noun:*

See **Islam**

mystery (MIS-tuh-ree) *noun:*

Mystery is the truth of God that was once not known. Jesus Christ made this mystery known. He revealed the way by which the world would be brought back to God. This mystery includes the Church uniting people of all types into one body.

Mark 4:10-20; Romans 11:25-32; 16:25-27; Ephesians 1:9-14; 3:7-13; Colossians 1:24—2:5; 2 Thessalonians 2:7; 1 Timothy 3:16

See **Body of Christ, church, kingdom of God, reconciliation, revelation**

mystic (MIS-tik) *noun:*

See **mysticism**

mysticism (MIS-tuh-SIZ-um) *noun:*

Mysticism is the belief that a person may be directly united with God. A person who practices mysticism is called a mystic. Pure mystics would say that they do not need the ordinary means of grace. Such persons believe that they have direct knowledge of God.

See **God, means of grace, unity**

N n

NAB, *abbreviation:*

NAB is an abbreviation for the *New American Bible.*

See **Bible, New American Bible, translate, version**

Nadab (NAY-dab) *proper noun:*

Nadab was the second king of Israel, the Northern Kingdom. He was the son of Jeroboam. Nadab ruled for only a short time. He was killed by Baasha, who then became king.

1 Kings 14:20; 15:25-28, 31

See **Baasha, Israel, Jeroboam, Nadab (time line)**

Nahum (NAY-um) *proper noun:*

1. Nahum was a prophet in the Old Testament. A Bible book is named for him. Nahum said the city of Nineveh would be destroyed. Nineveh was the capital of the evil nation of Assyria. This happened in 612 B.C. as Nahum predicted.

2. Nahum is the name of a book in the Old Testament. It is one of the Minor Prophets.

See **Assyria, Jonah, judgment, Nineveh (map 6), Old Testament, prophet, sin**

name (NAYM) *noun:*

A name is a word or title used to identify someone or something.

Names were very important in the Bible. A name usually showed what a person was like. Sometimes God gave names to people to show their special relation to Him. God often used a name to send a message to His people. He changed the names of persons when He made a covenant with them.

The personal name of the God of Israel is Yahweh. His name means that He is always present with His people to help them. He alone is God of all the earth.

God warns people not to use His name carelessly. They are to use it with reverence. The name of God represents Him. People show their faith in God's power when they use His name in worship.

God shows who He is in Jesus Christ. God told Mary to name her Son Jesus. *Jesus* means "Savior." God sent His only Son to be the Savior of the world. The name *Christ* means "Chosen One of God." It is the Greek word for Messiah.

Genesis 4:26; Exodus 20:7; Psalm 8:1; 96:8; Matthew 1:21

See **anoint, Christ, covenant, faith, God, Jesus, message, Messiah, Moses, Savior, Son of God, worship, Yahweh**

Naphtali (NAF-tuh-lie) *proper noun:*

1. Naphtali was one of the 12 sons of Jacob. His descendants became one of the tribes of the nation of Israel.

2. Naphtali was the name of the land occupied by the tribe of Naphtali.

Genesis 30:8; 35:25; Joshua 19:23-39

***See* Canaan, Israel, Jacob, Naphtali (map 3), tribes of Israel**

NASB, *abbreviation:*

NASB is an abbreviation for the *New American Standard Bible.*

***See* Bible, New American Standard Bible, translate, version**

Nathan (NAY-thun) *proper noun:*

Nathan was a prophet during the time of David and Solomon. He did not write an Old Testament book.

2 Samuel 7:1-29; 12:1-15; 1 Kings 1:1-40

***See* David, prophet, Solomon**

Nathanael (nuh-THAN-yul) *proper noun:*

Nathanael was one of the 12 disciples of Jesus. John's Gospel calls him by this name. He may be the same person called Bartholomew in the Synoptic Gospels.

John 1:45-51; 21:1-14

***See* apostle, Bartholomew, disciple**

nativity (nuh-TIV-uh-tee) *noun:*

Nativity means "birth." The Nativity usually refers to the birth of Jesus Christ.

Matthew 1:18—2:23; Luke 2:1-20

***See* Christ, Christmas, Immanuel, Incarnation, Jesus, Virgin Birth**

nature (NAY-cher) *noun:*

Nature is the basic character of a person or thing. The divine nature is what is true about God. Human nature means who man or woman is as a creature made in the image of God. The moral nature of people makes it possible for them to know right from wrong. The sinful or carnal nature of people makes it easy for them to disobey God. This is because of the fall of humanity.

Nature also means the world that God created. It also means the way God planned His creation should be.

Romans 1:3, 20, 26; 2:14; 8:3-13; 1 Corinthians 11:14; Ephesians 2:3

***See* carnal, creation, entire sanctification, Fall, human, image of God, morality**

Nazarene (NAZ-uh-REEN) *proper noun:*

1. Nazarene means a person from the village of Nazareth in Galilee. Jesus was given the name Nazarene because He grew up there. Early Jewish Christians were sometimes called Nazarenes because they followed Jesus.

2. Nazarene is the name of a denomination called Church of the Nazarene. People of this denomination are called Nazarenes.

Matthew 2:23; Mark 14:67; 16:6; Acts 24:5

See **branch, Church of the Nazarene, Galilee (map 8), Jesus, Nazareth (map 8), Nazirite**

Nazarene Church (NAZ-uh-reen CHERCH) *proper noun:*

See **Church of the Nazarene**

Nazareth (NAZ-uh-ruhth) *proper noun:*

Nazareth is a town in the region of Galilee. It was the home of Joseph and Mary. Jesus grew up in this town. He probably lived here until He was 30 years old.

Luke 1:26, 27; 2:39-52; 3:23; 4:16

See **Galilee, Joseph, Mary, Palestine (map 8)**

Nazirite (NAZ-uh-riet) *proper noun:*

A Nazirite was a person who made a special promise to God. He promised not to cut his hair, drink wine, or touch dead bodies. The Hebrew word *Nazirite* means "dedicated" or "holy."

Numbers 6:1-21; Judges 13:5-7; Isaiah 4:3; Amos 2:11-12; Matthew 2:23

See **dedicate, holy, promise, vow**

NEB, *abbreviation:*

The NEB is an abbreviation for *New English Bible.*

See **Bible, New English Bible, translate, version**

Nebo (NEE-boh) *proper noun:*

Nebo is the name of a mountain in Moab. Moses looked into Canaan from Mt. Nebo. But Moses died on the mountain. He never entered the Promised Land.

Deuteronomy 34:1-6

See **Canaan, Moab, Moses, Mt. Nebo (map 2), Promised Land**

Nebuchadnezzar (NEB-yew-kud-NEZ-er) *proper noun:*

Nebuchadnezzar was a king of Babylon. He fought against the Jews and took many of them as captives. Daniel served in his court and interpreted Nebuchadnezzar's dreams. Nebuchadnezzar is known for putting three Hebrew young men into a furnace of fire.

2 Kings 24:1-2, 10-17; Daniel 1–4

See **Babylon, Babylonia (map 6), Belshazar, Daniel, exile, Jew**

Negev (NEG-uv) or **Negeb** (NEG-ub) *proper noun:*

The Negev is a large desert in the southern part of Israel. The Hebrew word for *Negev* means "dryness." The area of Negev is called "the south" in several Bible verses (Numbers 13:29; Deuteronomy 1:7).

Genesis 13:1-3; 20:1; Joshua 10:40

See **Israel, Negev (maps 3, 4)**

Nehemiah (NEE-uh-MIE-uh) *proper noun:*

1. Nehemiah was a leader of the Jews after the Exile. The Book of Nehemiah in the Old Testament tells the story of his work. He helped the people rebuild the city of Jerusalem.

2. Nehemiah is a book in the Old Testament. It is one of the history books.

Ezra 2:1-2

See **Bible, exile, Ezra, Israel, Jerusalem (map 10), Old Testament**

neighbor (NAY-ber) *noun:*

A neighbor is someone who lives close to another person. A neighbor in the Old Testament was a member of the same tribe or nation. Jews did not consider Gentiles who lived near them their neighbors.

Jesus did not use the word "neighbor" in this limited way. He said a neighbor includes everyone. People should love everyone as they love themselves.

Exodus 20:16-17; Leviticus 19:15; Proverbs 3:29; Luke 10:25-37; Romans 13:8-10; 15:1-6; Galatians 5:14; James 4:11-12

See **Gentile, Golden Rule, Great Commandment, Jesus, love, Old Testament**

Neo-Pentecostalism (NEE-oh-PEN-tuh-KAWST-ul-iz-um) *proper noun:*

See **Charismatic Movement**

New Age (NEW AYJ) *proper noun phrase:*

New Age is a group of beliefs about the world and people that are not well-defined. It is the belief that the world is moving to a new period of peace and perfection. New Age puts emphasis on the goodness of the earth.

New Age beliefs have many parts. Not all people in the New Age movement agree with all the parts. The parts don't always agree with each other. New Age places emphasis on what people can do if they will work together.

People who adopt New Age beliefs want to protect the earth. Some treat the earth like a god. Those who hold New Age beliefs stress what people can do to help the world. They can make the world peaceful if they will work together. They also believe that the mind can be trained to reach higher levels of thought than normal. They believe that there are many kinds of spiritual powers. These powers can help people rise to higher levels of thought.

New Age does not accept the God of the Bible as the only God. There are many powers above humans. People can make use of these powers for good. New Age does not depend on the Bible for its beliefs. It believes that Christ is just one source of power.

See **belief, creation, cult, earth, God, god, kingdom of God, mind, monotheism, omnipotence, perfection, power, spiritual**

New American Bible (NEW uh-MAIR-uh-kun BIE-bul) *proper noun phrase:*

The *New American Bible* is a modern version of the Bible. It was translated by the Roman Catholic Church in the 1950s and 1960s. Its abbreviation is NAB.

See **Bible, translate, version**

New American Standard Bible (NEW uh-MAIR-uh-kun STAN-derd BIE-bul) *proper noun phrase:*

The *New American Standard Bible* is a modern version of the Bible. It was an attempt to improve the *American Standard Version.* Its abbreviation is NASB.

See **American Standard Version, Bible, translate, version**

new birth (NEW BERTH) *noun phrase:*

The new birth is the complete change that happens when people become Christians. God gives them a new start. He forgives them of their past sins. Jesus Christ makes the new birth possible. Those who trust in Jesus Christ are born again. This is also called rebirth.

John 1:10-13; 3:1-21; 1 Peter 1:22-23; 2:2-3; 2 Peter 1:3-4, 9-10; 1 John 3:9; 5:4-5

See **born again, child of God, Christian, conversion, forgiveness, Holy Spirit, initial sanctification, justification, regeneration, save**

new creation (NEW kree-AY-shun) *noun phrase:*

See **creation, new birth, regeneration**

new earth (NEW ERTH) *noun phrase:*

The new earth is the visible part of the changed universe at the end of time. God created the world as a good place for people to live. But sin has harmed it. Righteousness does not seem to be at home here. So God will renew the creation.

God still loves His creation. He will again make the world what He intended in the beginning. God will live close to His people.

Isaiah 65:17; 66:22; Romans 8:21; 2 Peter 3:13; Revelation 21:1

See **creation, eschatology, Garden of Eden, heaven, new heaven, redemption, righteousness, sin, world**

New English Bible (NEW ING-glish BIE-bul) *proper noun phrase:*

The *New English Bible* is a modern version of the Bible. It was translated by British scholars. Its abbreviation is NEB.

See **Bible, translation, version**

new heaven (NEW HEV-un) *noun phrase:*

The new heaven is the invisible part of the changed universe at the end of time. Satan has tried to harm the invisible world where God lives. He leads evil spirits to resist God. He has tried to make the visible world an enemy of God.

One day God will stop Satan and all who help him. He will make everything as He intended it to be in the beginning. God will make a new heaven. Heaven and earth will no longer be divided.

Isaiah 65:17; 66:22; 2 Peter 3:13; Revelation 21:1

See **eschatology, heaven, new earth, principalities and powers, redemption, Satan.**

New International Version (NEW IN-ter-NASH-uh-nul VER-zhun) *proper noun phrase:*

The *New International Version* is a modern translation of the Bible. Its abbreviation is NIV.

See **Bible, translation, version**

New King James Version (NEW KING JAYMZ VER-zhun) *proper noun phrase:*

The *New King James Version* is a modern translation of the Bible. Its abbreviation is NKJV. Its purpose is to use 20th-century English for the King James Version.

See **Bible, King James Version, translation, version**

New Life Version (NEW LIEF VER-zhun) *proper noun phrase:*

The *New Life Version* is a modern translation of the Bible. It was written for people who are learning English as a second language. Its abbreviation is NLV.

See **Bible, translation, version**

new man (NEW MAN) *noun phrase:*

The new man is the person who has become a Christian. Sin separates people from God and from one another. This is the way people are before Christ changes them. Christ brings the separation of God and people to an end. He brings a new start in life.

Romans 5:12-21; 2 Corinthians 5:17-21; Galatians 6:15-16; Ephesians 4:22-24; Colossians 3:9-17

See **Adam, Christ, fall, image of God, justification, new birth, old man, reconciliation, redemption, regeneration, salvation, save**

New Revised Standard Version (NEW ruh-VIEZD STAN-derd VER-ZHUN) *proper noun phrase:*

The *New Revised Standard Version* is a modern translation of the Bible. It was translated in the 1980s. The translators wanted to improve the *Revised Standard Version*, which was translated in the 1950s. Its abbreviation is NRSV.

See **Bible, Revised Standard Version, translation, version**

New Testament (NEW TES-tuh-munt) *proper noun phrase:*

The New Testament is the name given to the second part of the Bible. The first part is the Old Testament. The Bible contains 66 books. There are 27 books in the New Testament. It tells of the new covenant God made with people through Jesus Christ.

The New Testament contains the four Gospels. They tell the story of Jesus and His first disciples. The New Testament also contains the Book of Acts, which tells how the Church began. This is followed by the letters, which told early Christians how to live for Christ. The New Testament closes with the Book of Revelation. It gave Christians hope for the future.

Mark 14:24; 1 Corinthians 11:25; 2 Corinthians 3:4-18; Hebrews 9:1-22

See **Acts, Bible, Christ, Christian, church, covenant, gospel, Jesus, Old Testament, revelation, Scripture**

Nicene Creed (NIE-seen KREED) *proper noun phrase:*

The Nicene Creed is a very important statement of what Christians believe. The Nicene Creed is a Christian confession of faith. It is longer than the Apostles' Creed. The Nicene Creed is accepted by Protestant, Roman Catholic, and Eastern Orthodox churches.

The Nicene Creed says that Jesus Christ is the Son of God. The creed says that the Son is as much God as His Father is. It says that Christians believe in the Holy Spirit.

The Nicene Creed was written by church leaders in A.D. 325. It was written in a town named Nicea, which is now in northwest Turkey.

See **Apostles' Creed, confession, creed, Christ, church, Eastern Orthodoxy, doctrine, faith, God, Holy Spirit, Protestant, Roman Catholic, Son of God, Trinity**

Nicodemus (NIK-uh-DEE-mus) *proper noun:*

Nicodemus was a Jewish leader who became a secret disciple of Jesus. Nicodemus was a Pharisee. Jesus told Nicodemus that it was necessary for people to be born again.

John 3:1-21; 7:50-51; 19:39

See **born again, disciple, Jew, Pharisee**

Nile (NIEL) *proper noun:*

The Nile is a river in Egypt in northern Africa. It is the longest river in the world. For many years, the Israelites lived in bondage near the Nile River in Goshen.

Genesis 41:1-3, 17; Exodus 2:3-5; 7:20-24;

See **bondage, Egypt, Goshen, Moses, Nile (maps 1, 2)**

Nineveh (NIN-uh-vuh) *proper noun:*

Nineveh was the capital of the ancient nation of Assyria. It was located in Mesopotamia on the Tigris River. The prophet Jonah went to Nineveh to preach.

Jonah 1:1-2; 3:1-10

See **Assyria, Jonah, Mesopotamia, Nahum, Nineveh (maps 1, 6)**

NIV, *abbreviation:*

NIV is an abbreviation for the *New International Version* of the Bible.

See **Bible, New International Version, translate, version**

NKJV, *abbreviation:*

NKJV is an abbreviation for the *New King James Version* of the Bible.

See **Bible, New King James Version, translate, version**

NLV, *abbreviation:*

NLV is an abbreviation for the *New Life Version* of the Bible.

See **Bible, New Life Version, translate, version**

Noah (NOH-uh) *proper noun:*

Noah is the name of a man in the Old Testament. He and his family were saved from the Great Flood by building an ark. This boat also carried pairs of animals.

Genesis 6—9

See **ark, deluge, flood**

NRSV, *abbreviation:*

NRSV is an abbrevation for the *New Revised Standard Version* of the Bible.

See **Bible, New Revised Standard Version, translate, version**

Numbers (NUM-berz) *proper noun:*

Numbers is the fourth book in the Old Testament. It is part of the Pentateuch, or Books of the Law. It tells about the counting of the people of Israel by Moses. It tells of their life after they left Egypt and before they entered Canaan.

See **Bible, law, Moses, Old Testament, Pentateuch, Torah**

nun (NUN) *noun:*

A nun is a woman who is devoted to religious life. She is a member of a religious community. A nun makes a vow to own nothing and to obey her leaders. She also vows not to be married. Nuns are found in the Roman Catholic Church and the Eastern Orthodox Church.

See **community, Eastern Orthodoxy, marriage, monk, religious, Roman Catholic, vow**

O o

oath (OHTH) *noun:*

An oath is a strong promise. God can make an oath. People can make oaths to God and to each other. An oath can be a strong promise to do good or harm to someone or a group. An oath can also mean a sworn covenant between two people. An oath can mean a strong statement of what is true.

In the Bible, oaths have two parts. The first part is the promise. The second part is a request to God to hear the oath.

Genesis 15:18; 26:2-4; Exodus 22:11; Numbers 5:21; 2 Samuel 21:7; Nehemiah 10:29; Ecclesiastes 8:2; 9:2; Matthew 5:33-37; 23:16-22; 26:69-70

***See* covenant, God, promise, truth**

Obadiah (OH-buh-DIE-uh) *proper noun:*

1. Obadiah was a prophet in the Old Testament. An Old Testament book is named for him. Obadiah preached in Judah in the sixth century B.C. He said that the nation of Edom would be destroyed. Many other men in the Old Testament were called Obadiah.

2. Obadiah is a book in the Old Testament. It is one of the Minor Prophets.

***See* Bible, Edom (map 6), Judah, Old Testament**

obedience (oh-BEE-dee-uns) *noun:*

Obedience is obeying directions given to one person by another. The Hebrew and Greek words for obedience refer to hearing. People who hear and do what someone commands them to do give obedience. People who have faith in God prove it by obeying Him and His law.

Obedience to God shows that people accept His right to command them. Jesus Christ was obedient to His Father.

Exodus 19:3-6; Deuteronomy 5:1; 6:4-9; 1 Samuel 15:22; Psalm 119:8, 17, 44-45; John 4:34; 14:23-24; Acts 5:29; Romans 1:5; Philippians 2:8; Hebrews 5:8; 1 Peter 1:2

***See* authority of Scripture, Christ, commandment, faith, father, God, law, Lord, reverence, slave, worship**

obeisance (oh-BEE-suns) *noun:*

Obeisance is showing high respect for someone by bowing. It may mean worshiping that person. For example, a person may show obeisance to a king. People who worship idols show obeisance to a false god. People may show honor to another person, but they should worship only God.

***See* idol, idolatry, king, reverence, worship**

occult (uh-KULT) *adjective:*

Occult describes what is secret and full of mystery. It usually describes strange practices that depend on evil, supernatural powers. It describes knowledge and use of these powers by people.

Acts 19:11-20

See **demon, evil, mystery, occultism, Satan, supernatural**

occultism (uh-KUL-tiz-um) *noun:*

Occultism is the belief in supernatural powers that are hidden and full of mystery. It is the attempt to bring these spiritual powers under human control. Occultism is the practice of knowing and using evil spiritual powers. The Bible opposes occultism. Witchcraft and sorcery are kinds of occultism.

Deuteronomy 18:9-13; 1 Samuel 15:23; 2 Chronicles 33:1-6; Isaiah 8:19; Micah 5:12; Acts 19:17-20; Galatians 5:20

See **demon, evil, mystery, occult, Satan, sorcery, supernatural, witchcraft**

offering (AWF-er-ing or AHF-er-ing) *noun:*

An offering is a gift given as an act of worship to God. Offerings in the Old Testament were sacrifices given to the priests in the Temple. These could be animals, doves, grain, or other gifts.

There were many kinds of offerings in the worship of Israel. Some offerings were to show that the givers were sorry for their transgressions. Other offerings were to show that they had given themselves to God completely. Others were to give thanks for all that God had done for His people.

The prophets warned the people of Israel that God did not want only offerings. He wanted His people truly to love, obey, and serve Him.

Jesus Christ gave himself as an offering to God to provide salvation for everyone (Romans 3:21-26; Galatians 2:19-20; Philippians 2:5-11; Hebrews 10:5-18). Believers should offer themselves as "living sacrifices" to God (Romans 12:1-2). They do this by giving themselves completely to Him and living for Him.

Obedience to God in daily living is the offering that pleases Him most (Romans 15:15-19). This obedience includes giving money to help support the preaching of the gospel (Philippians 4:14-18). Offerings today usually refer to such gifts of money.

Genesis 4:3-5; Exodus 24:5; 25:2; 35:22; Leviticus 1:2-14; Nehemiah 10:37; 13:5; Malachi 3:8

See **gift, Israel, obedience, Old Testament, priest, prophet, sacrifice, stewardship, temple, tithe, transgress, worship**

offertory (AWF-er-TOH-ree) *noun:*

An offertory is the part of a worship service when an offering is received. Usually some form of music is played or sung during the offertory in most churches.

See **offering, service, tithe, worship**

oil (OYL) *noun:*

Oil from olives was the most common oil used in Bible times. Other oils were rare. Oil, along with wine and grain, was a symbol of an abundant harvest. Olive oil was used in many ways by the people.

Oil was used for lighting homes and synagogues. It was used to anoint kings, priest, and prophets. Oil was used in making sacrifices. And oil was used for healing purposes.

Exodus 25:6; Leviticus 2:4; 8:30; 1 Samuel 6:1; 10:1, 13; Isaiah 61:1; James 5:14-15

See **anoint, harvest, king, priest, olive, prophet, sacrifice, synagogue**

old man (OHLD MAN) *noun phrase:*

The *old man* is a name for the sinful condition of people after the Fall. It is the sinful condition of all people before they become believers in Christ. It is the old self that fights against the will of God. All people are born in the sinful condition of Adam. All people who are not in Christ are in Adam.

But the old man can be put to an end through Christ. The salvation that the risen Christ gives makes the believer a new person. All who receive Him are a new creation in Christ. The new man is created by God in righteousness and true holiness (Ephesians 4:22-24).

The new person must, by faith, view himself or herself in Christ as dead to sin. He or she is now alive to God in Christ. Then the person must give himself or herself completely to God for entire sanctification. This is done by consecration of the self to God (Romans 6:11-13, 19).

The new person in Christ must also get rid of his or her old habits and must form new ones. He or she must become like Christ in his or her daily life. He or she must live a new and holy life.

Romans 5:12-21; 6:6, 11-14, 19; 2 Corinthians 5:17; Ephesians 4:17—5:20; Colossians 3:1-17

See **carnal, Christian perfection, creation, entire sanctification, Fall, forgiveness, habit, imparted righteousness, initial sanctification, justification, nature, new birth, new man, regeneration, righteousness, sin, will**

Old Testament (OHLD TES-tuh-munt) *proper noun phrase:*

The Old Testament is the name given to the first part of the Bible. The second part is the New Testament. The Bible contains 66 books. The Old Testament consists of 39 books. The Old Testament tells of the covenant God made with the people of Israel. A covenant is also called a testament. The Old Testament includes the promises God made to His people Israel. The New Testament tells how God fulfilled this covenant in Jesus Christ.

The Old Testament contains 5 books of the Pentateuch and 12 books of history. It contains 5 books of poetry writings. It also has 5 books called the Major Prophets and 12 books called the Minor Prophets.

Matthew 26:28; 2 Corinthians 3:6, 14; Hebrews 9:15

See **Bible, Christ, Christian, covenant, God, Jesus, Judaism, New Testament, Pentateuch, promise, prophet, Scripture**

olive (AH-luv) *noun:*

Olive is the fruit of the olive tree. It is one of the most important plants in Israel today.

The olive was probably the most important plant during Bible days. The oil from the olive was used in several ways. Olive oil was used for light (Exodus 27:20) and for anointing (Exodus 30:22-25). Olive oil was also use for food (Numbers 25:4-5), and for offerings (Leviticus 2:1-7).

The word *olive* was used in various ways in the Bible. For example, the nation of Israel was called an "olive tree" (Jeremiah 11:16). The children of the Hebrews were called "olive shoots" (Psalm 128:3). Paul compared the Gentiles to "wild olive branches" (Romans 11:13, 24).

The olive branch is a symbol of peace. This is based on the dove bringing the olive leaf to Noah's ark after the flood (Genesis 8:11).

See **anoint, ark, flood, Gentile, Hebrews, Israel, Noah, offering, oil**

Olivet (AH-luh-vet) *proper noun:*

See **Mount of Olives**

omega (oh-MAY-guh) *noun:*

See **alpha and omega**

omnipotence (ahm-NIP-uh-tuns) *noun:*

Omnipotence is the quality of God that means He has all power. He is omnipotent. He can fulfill His will for the world. But God may choose to limit himself. The Bible calls God the Almighty and All-powerful One.

Genesis 17:1; Exodus 6:3; Psalm 91:1; Revelation 4:8; 11:17

See **attribute, God, omnipotent, power, sovereignty, will**

omnipotent (ahm-NIP-uh-tunt) *adjective:*

Omnipotent means all-powerful. Only God is omnipotent. Omnipotent means that no one may force God to do anything. Omnipotent means that God is free to be God. No one can limit Him. God can do all that is faithful to His nature.

Genesis 17:1; 18:14; Exodus 3:13-15; Job 42:2; Isaiah 26:4; Matthew 19:26; Luke 1:37; Acts 26:8; Revelation 19:6; 21:22

See **attribute, God, faithful, omnipotence, power, sovereignty**

omnipresence (ahm-ni-PREZ-uns) *noun:*

Omnipresence is the quality of God that means He is everywhere. He is omnipresent. God is always and everywhere present in His world. God is a Spirit. His presence with humanity is limited by neither time nor space.

Exodus 3:11-17; 1 Kings 8:27; 2 Chronicles 2:6; 16:9; Job 34:21-23; Isaiah 66:1; Acts 17:24-28; Ephesians 1:23

See **attribute, God, omnipresent, sovereignty**

omnipresent (ahm-ni-PREZ-unt) *adjective:*

Omnipresent means that God is present everywhere. No place, time, person, or event can leave Him out.

1 Kings 8:27; Psalm 139:3-10; Jeremiah 23:23-24; Acts 17:24-28

See **attribute, God, omnipresence, sovereignty**

omniscience (ahm-NISH-uns) *noun:*

Omniscience is an attribute of God that means He has complete knowledge. Only God is omniscient. God knows all that can be known. The omniscience of God is cause for fear to evil people. The omniscience of God is cause for great comfort to those who love Him.

Exodus 3:11; Deuteronomy 2:7; 1 Chronicles 28:9; Psalm 139:14; Isaiah 42:9; Jeremiah 17:10

See **attribute, God, omniscient, wisdom**

omniscient (ahm-NISH-unt) *adjective:*

Omniscient means all-knowing. It means that God knows all that can be known. The most important thing about omniscience is that God completely knows humans. No human is omniscient. Only God is omniscient. But God makes us safe in His knowledge.

Exodus 37:7-20; Deuteronomy 2:7; 1 Samuel 16:7; 1 Chronicles 28:9; Job 28:10; Romans 8:27; 11:33

See **attribute, God, omniscience, wisdom**

Omri (AHM-ree) *proper noun:*

Omri was the sixth king of Israel, the Northern Kingdom. He was the father of Ahab. He was also the grandfather of Queen Athaliah of Judah. Omri was an evil king. He ruled for about 10 years. He built the city of Samaria.

1 Kings 16:16-28; 2 Chronicles 22:2

See **Ahab, Athaliah, Judah, Israel, Omri (time line)**

Onesimus (oh-NES-uh-mus) *proper noun:*

See **Philemon**

only begotten Son (OHN-lee bee-GAH-tun SUN) *noun phrase:*

Only begotten Son is a phrase used for Jesus in the King James Version. The phrase in Greek means that Jesus Christ is the only Son of God. There is no one else who reveals God as Jesus does. The phrase means that God and Christ are related as Father to Son. But it does not mean that God gave birth to Christ as a child. The relation between God and Christ as Father and Son is eternal.

John 1:14, 18; 3:16, 18; Romans 8:3, 29, 32; 1 Corinthians 15:20-28; Galatians 4:4-6; 1 John 4:9

See **beget, Christ, eternal, father, Jesus, King James Version, Son of God, Trinity**

oppression (uh-PRESH-un) *noun:*

Oppression is making people do what they don't want to do and what is bad for them. Oppression can happen to a person or to a group of people. Oppression is the harm one suffers because of another who hurts him or her. Oppression usually means very serious harm.

The Jews suffered oppression in Egypt because of Pharaoh. The Jews suffered oppression from the Babylonians. They became prisoners in Babylon. Many of the early Christians suffered oppression from Jews and Romans.

The Bible says that Satan and demons oppress people.

Exodus 1:8-14; 2 Kings 25:1-25; Psalm 79; Acts 27:1; Colossians 4:10; Revelation 2:8-11

***See* Babylon, exile, devil, demon, demoniac, oppression, persecution, Pharaoh, Satan, suffering**

oracle (OHR-uh-kul) *noun:*

An oracle is the word of God that He has made known. Oracles in the Old Testament were usually given to priests or prophets. These people told others what God wanted them to know.

Bible scholars use the word *oracle* to refer to a brief sermon by a prophet. For example, Isaiah 13—23 contains a number of oracles about certain nations. The Old Testament prophetic books contain oracles spoken by different prophets at different times.

The *oracles of God* is a phrase used in the King James Version. It means the "Old Testament" in Romans 3:2 and 1 Peter 4:11. It means basic Christian doctrines in Hebrews 5:12.

***See* doctrine, Hebrews, message, mystery, Old Testament, 1 and 2 Peter, priest, prophet, Romans, sermon, word**

ordain (ohr-DAYN) *verb:*

To ordain means to select someone or something for a special ministry. It means to plan or organize events so that the purpose can be fulfilled.

To ordain usually means that God calls a person to become a Christian minister. The church supports that call by ordaining the person. This takes place in a special service with other ordained ministers. They put their hands on the person as a sign that God is ordaining him or her.

God plans how a person can fulfill his or her call to ministry. He ordains or arranges the events that will let this happen.

2 Chronicles 11:15; Psalm 132:17; Jeremiah 1:5; Acts 14:23; 1 Timothy 2:7; 4:14; 2 Timothy 1:6

***See* call, God, laying on of hands, minister, ordination, vocation**

ordination (OHR-duh-NAY-shun) *noun:*

Ordination is the act of ordaining a person as a minister. Christian ordination is the act of ordaining a person as a Christian minister. Other religions also ordain people as special religious leaders. For example, a Jew may be ordained as a rabbi.

***See* call, God, laying on of hands, minister, ordain, rabbi, vocation**

original righteousness (uh-RIJ-uh-nul RIE-chus-nus) *noun phrase:*

Original righteousness is the righteousness that Adam and Eve enjoyed before they sinned. They enjoyed perfect fellowship with God. They did not know the meaning of guilt. They also did not know the meaning of good and evil. The whole human race lost original righteousness because of the sin of Adam and Eve.

The righteousness that comes through Christ is not a return to original righteousness. It is the new righteousness that comes through forgiveness and the new birth. It is a righteousness that knows the difference between good and evil. It rejects evil and loves God. Christ is the Source and Example of the new righteousness.

Genesis 1:26-31; 2:4—3:24; Romans 5:12-21

***See* Christ, Christian, perfection, creation, evil, Fall, forgiveness, God, guilt, image of God, imparted righteousness, new birth, original sin, righteousness, sin**

original sin (uh-RIJ-uh-nul SIN) *noun phrase:*

Original sin is the first human sin, which has affected all people since then. Adam and Eve chose not to obey God. They thought that life would be better if they had their own way. But their sin did not lead to a better life as they expected. It led instead to spiritual death. This was the fall of humanity.

All people are born in sin. They are by nature self-centered. They find it easy to disobey God. This is because they inherited a share in Adam's first sin. They are under the power of a sinful nature.

Jesus Christ came to destroy original sin. "As in Adam all die, so in Christ all will be made alive" (1 Corinthians 15:22). This new life is given in regeneration. It is perfected in entire sanctification. The Holy Spirit cleanses Christians from original sin. However, many of the physical results of original sin remain. Sickness, disease, errors in judgment, and other human failings continue. These will not be destroyed until redemption is finally completed at the resurrection.

Genesis 3:1-19; Romans 1:18-32; 3:23; 5:12-21; 7:7—8:25; 1 Corinthians 15:20-57

***See* Adam, carnal, Christ, cleanse, depravity, entire sanctification, Eve, Fall, flesh, holiness, inclined to evil, indwelling sin, nature, new birth, original righteousness, reconciliation, redemption, regeneration, resurrection, sin**

orthodox (OHR-thuh-dahks) *adjective:*

Orthodox means right teaching. It describes someone or something that supports correct beliefs. An orthodox person is the opposite of a heretic.

Orthodox Christians accept all the basic creeds or beliefs of Christianity. An orthodox Jew accepts all the major beliefs and practices of Judaism.

***See* belief, Christian, Christianity, creed, Eastern Orthodoxy, faith, heresy, Jew, Judaism, right**

orthodoxy (OHR-thuh-DAHK-see) *noun:*

Orthodoxy is an orthodox belief or practice. Christian orthodoxy is faithfulness to the orthodox doctrines and creeds of the Christian faith. One form of Christianity is called Eastern Orthodoxy.

See **Christian, Christianity, creed, doctrine, Eastern Orthodox, orthodox, tradition**

outreach (OUT-REECH) *noun:*

Outreach is an attempt by churches to win people to Christ. Outreach is evangelism.

See **Christian, church, convert, evangelism, faith, witness**

P p

pacifism (PAS-uh-fiz-um) *noun:*

Pacifism is the belief that war must not be used to settle arguments among countries. Pacifism is the belief that war always does more harm than good. A person who believes in pacifism is a pacifist. Pacifists believe that peace will come if an enemy is not opposed. They believe that war makes people become more violent.

Pacifists believe that Jesus taught pacifism to His disciples. In the first 300 years of the Church, Christians refused to be soldiers. Early Christians believed that one could not be a Christian and fight in a war.

Matthew 5:21-22, 38-48

See **Beatitudes, forgiveness, peace**

pacifist (PAS-uh-fust) *noun:*

See **pacifism**

pagan (PAY-gun)

1. *noun:* A pagan is a person who does not worship the one true God. The word *pagan* also refers to people who reject all religion.

2. *adjective:* Pagan describes someone or something opposed to religious values. Thus, a pagan custom is against what religious people consider correct.

1 Corthinians 10:20; 12:2; 1 Peter 4: 3-5

See **Gentile, God, heathen, religion, values, worship**

Palestine (PAL-us-tien) *proper noun:*

Palestine is a later name for the land of Canaan. The name *Palestine* came from the Hebrew word for Philistine. The Philistines lived in the southwest part of Canaan.

The united kingdom of Israel was in the area that became known as Palestine. During the time of Jesus, the country was called Palestine.

In 1948 the country of Palestine was divided into Israel and Jordan. Today there is no country of Palestine.

See **Canaan, Israel (map 3), Judea, Palestine (map 8), Philistine**

Palm Sunday (PAHM or PAHLM SUN-dee) *proper noun phrase:*

Palm Sunday is the day on the Christian calendar one Sunday before Easter. It celebrates the triumphal entry of Jesus into Jerusalem. He rode on a donkey as the King of Peace prophesied in Zechariah 9:9. The people welcomed Him to the city by placing palm branches in His path.

Matthew 21:1-11; Mark 11:1-11; Luke 19:28-44; John 12:12-19

See **celebrate, Christian, Easter, Jerusalem (map 10), Jesus, king, peace, Triumphal Entry, Zechariah**

pantheism (PAN-thee-iz-um) *noun:*

Pantheism is the belief that the world and nature are only the attributes of God. God is different from the forces and laws of the world. But He has no existence apart from the world. The world is to God what a body is to a human being.

Pantheism does not agree with what the Bible says about God. The Bible says that God existed before the world was created. God is near to His creation. He keeps it going. But He does not depend on the world for His existence.

See **attribute, deism, God, theism, world**

papacy (PAY-puh-see) *noun:*

The papacy is the office or rule of the Roman Catholic pope.

See **pope, Roman Catholic**

parable (PAIR-uh-bul) *noun:*

A parable is a short story from everyday life used to teach a lesson. Jesus often used parables in His teaching. He usually used them to explain the meaning of the kingdom of God. Several examples of Jesus' parables may be found in Matthew 13 and Luke 15. The Old Testament also contains some parables. (See 2 Samuel 12:1-14.)

Psalm 78:2; Matthew 13:33-35; Mark 4:33-34; Luke 8:10

See **Jesus, kingdom of God**

Paraclete (PAIR-uh-kleet) *proper noun:*

Paraclete is a Greek term used for the Holy Spirit in the Gospel of John. Paraclete means "helper" and "comforter." The Holy Spirit is the One who teaches, encourages, helps, and comforts Christians. Paraclete also means "advocate." Jesus Christ speaks as an advocate to the Father for Christians who have sinned.

John 14:6, 16-17, 26; 15:26; 16:7-11; 1 John 2:1-2

See **advocate, Comforter, Father, Greek, Holy Spirit, intercession, John, spirit**

paradise (PAIR-uh-dies) *noun:*

Paradise comes from a word that means "garden" or "park." The word "paradise" usually means a beautiful place where there is nothing evil or bad.

The Old Testament does not use paradise to refer to heaven (Nehemiah 2:8; Ecclesiastes 2:5; Song of Solomon 4:13). Ezekiel calls Eden "the garden of God" (Ezekiel 28:13). Many Jews believed that the Messiah would bring paradise back to earth. Life under His rule would be like life in the Garden of Eden.

Other Jews believed that paradise existed in heaven. They believed that the patriarchs now lived in this hidden paradise. People went to paradise after death. Luke 23:43 refers to paradise as the place where righteous people go after death.

Paul said that he was taken up into paradise in a vision. Here, paradise means heaven in all its glory. Christ promises paradise to Christians who overcome temptations and persecutions (Revelation 2:7). Revelation says that paradise will be part of life in the world to come (chapter 22).

See **Bible, Christian, Eden, Ezekiel, heaven, Jew, Messiah, patriarch, Paul, persecution, revelation, temptation**

pardon (PAHR-dun) *noun:*

See **forgiveness**

parousia (PAHR-ew-SEE-uh) *noun:*

The parousia is the second coming of Jesus Christ. *Parousia* in Greek means "coming" or "present." But the term usually refers to the future return of Christ.

Matthew 24:3, 27, 37, 39; 1 Corinthians 15:23; Philippians 2:12; 1 Thessalonians 2:19; 3:13; 4:15; 5:23, 2 Thessalonians 2:1; 1 Peter 5:4; 1 John 2:28

See **Bible, Christ, eschatology, Greek, Jesus, rapture, revelation, Second Coming**

paschal (PAS-kul) *adjective:*

See **Passover**

passion (PASH-un) *noun:*

The English word *passion* translates several different Greek words.

1. A passion may be an emotion or feeling. This feeling may be one of anger or love (Acts 14:15; James 5:17).

Christians sometimes speak of their "passion" to win people to Christ. They mean that they evangelize because they love God and sinners very much.

2. Passion may mean "sinful desire" or "lust" (Romans 7:5; Galatians 5:24; Titus 2:11-14; 1 John 2:15-17).

3. Passion also means "suffering." This is the meaning in the phrase "after his passion" (Acts 1:3, KJV). The passion of Jesus includes the events between the Last Supper and His death. Passion Week is the week of the Christian calendar between Palm Sunday and Easter (Matthew 26:20—27:50). This week reminds Christians of the suffering that Jesus endured to provide salvation.

See **Christian, Easter, evangelism, Greek, Jesus, Last Supper, lust, New Testament, Palm Sunday, salvation, suffering, version**

Passover (PAS-OH-ver) *proper noun:*

Passover is the Jewish feast that celebrates the Exodus from Egypt. The people of Israel were slaves in Egypt, but God set them free. The Hebrew word for the Passover is Pesach.

God brought judgment on Egypt, who had oppressed the people of Israel. Egypt suffered from 10 plagues before the Pharaoh finally let the people go. The last plague was when an angel brought death to the oldest sons in Egypt. But the angel did "pass over" the families of Israel (Exodus 12:23). The people of Israel were told to leave quickly. They did not have time to put leaven in their bread. So the Bible sometimes calls the Passover celebration the Festival of Unleavened Bread.

The word *passover* also refers to the lamb, also known as the paschal lamb, sacrificed on the eve of Passover. The people of Israel marked their houses by sprinkling the blood on their doors. The death angel passed over the houses marked this way. Then they roasted the lamb and ate it with unleavened bread.

Jews still celebrate the Passover during the month of March or April. The Passover meal is called a seder. The date is different each year. The Jewish calendar is set by the moon rather than by the sun. Passover begins on the 15th day of Nisan. Nisan is the first month of the Jewish year. Passover lasts for eight days. The date of Easter is always the Sunday following Passover Week.

The last supper Jesus ate with His disciples was a Passover meal. The sacrament of the Lord's Supper is for Christians what the Passover is for Jews. It celebrates the central event in the history of salvation. Christ is like the Passover lamb. He was sacrificed to free people from slavery to sin (1 Corinthians 5:7-8).

Exodus 1:8—13:22; 34:18-26; Numbers 9:1-14; Matthew 26:17-29; Mark 14:12-25; Luke 22:7-23; John 19:12-22

***See* angel, blood, Christian, Easter, Egypt (map 2), Exodus, festival, freedom, Israel, Jew, judgment, Lamb of God, Last Supper, leaven, Lord's Supper, Pharaoh, plague, sacrament, sacrifice, salvation, seder, slave, unleavened bread**

pastor (PAS-ter) *noun:*

A pastor is a Christian minister who leads a congregation. The word comes from the Greek word that means "shepherd" or "one who leads sheep." A pastor leads a congregation in worship, evangelism, service, and spiritual growth. A pastor acts as a shepherd by counseling, comforting, and caring for the people. Pastors in the New Testament Church were also called bishops.

Jeremiah 3:15; John 21:15-17; Ephesians 4:11; 1 Timothy 3:1-2; 1 Peter 5:4

***See* bishop, church, congregation, evangelism, shepherd, worship**

Pastoral Epistles (PAS-ter-ul ee-PIS-ulz) *proper noun phrase:*

The Pastoral Epistles are three New Testament books: 1 and 2 Timothy and Titus. Paul is the author of these letters. The letters instruct Timothy and Titus in how to lead churches under their care. The Pastoral Epistles give advice to pastors from a pastor.

***See* epistle, pastor, Paul, 1 and 2 Timothy, Titus**

patience (PAY-shuns) *noun:*

Patience means the ability to wait when it would be easier to act. The New Testament names patience among the fruit of the Spirit. It says that Christians should have patience even when they suffer. This shows their faith in God and hope for the future. One meaning of patience is forbearance.

Romans 5:1-5; Galatians 5:22-24

See **character, faith, fruit of the Spirit, hope, peace, perseverance, suffering**

patriarch (PAY-tree-ahrk) *noun:*

Patriarch means "father." A patriarch is someone who begins a group of people or a nation. Abraham, Isaac, Jacob, and his 12 sons are called the patriarchs of Israel. They were the first ancestors of the Hebrew people. The patriarchs lived sometime between 2000 and 1500 B.C. The story of the patriarchs is told in Genesis, chapters 12 through 50.

See **Abraham, Hebrew, Isaac, Israel, Jacob, Joseph, Jew**

See **also time line**

Patmos (PAT-mus) *proper noun:*

Patmos is a small island in the Mediterranean Sea near the coast of Turkey. The apostle John was sent to Patmos for punishment. On Patmos he wrote the Book of Revelation.

Revelation 1:9

See **John, Mediterranean Sea, New Testament, revelation**

Paul (PAWL) *proper noun:*

Paul was the great missionary of the Early Christian Church. Thirteen letters in the New Testament identify him as their author.

Paul was a Jew of the Dispersion whose name in Hebrew was Saul. He was born in Tarsus of Cilicia. Paul was a member of the Jewish sect of the Pharisees. He persecuted Christians before his conversion to Christianity.

Paul's conversion happened when Christ appeared to him on the road to Damascus. Christ called him to become an apostle to the Gentiles.

Paul obeyed his call by preaching the gospel and starting churches. He did this in many of the major cities of the Mediterranean world. Paul wrote letters to guide his churches when he could not visit them personally. Some of these letters were saved and became a part of the New Testament.

The story of Paul's conversion and missionary work is told in Acts, chapters 9—28.

2 Corinthians 11:30—12:10; Galatians 1:13—2:14; Philippians 3:4-11

See **apostle, call, conversion, Damascus (map 9), Dispersion, epistle, Gentile, Mediterranean Sea (map 11), missionary, persecution, Pharisee, Saul**

peace (PEES) *noun:*

Peace in the Bible means life that God has made whole and complete. It is a rest that a person has within. It does not mean that everything in life is pleasant. Peace can exist even when things are not pleasant. Peace often means the absence of war. But people may have peace with God even when war exists all around them. Peace may include material success and physical safety. But peace may exist when these are absent.

Christians try to make the peace of God known among all people. They urge people to be reconciled to God and to one another. They try to stop the things that destroy peace on earth.

Genesis 43:27; Joshua 9:15; Psalms 4:8; 73:3; 85:10; Isaiah 48:18, 22; Jeremiah 29:7; Luke 2:14, 29; 10:5; John 20:19, 21, 26; Romans 1:7; 5:1; 8:6; 14:17; Ephesians 2:13-16; 4:3; Philippians 4:7; Hebrews 12:14

See **Christ, eternal life, forgiveness, God, grace, hope, joy, justice, love, neighbor, reconcile, reconciliation, righteousness**

pearl of great price (PERL uv GRAYT PRIES) *noun phrase:*

The pearl of great price is a valuable pearl of very high quality. The phrase is found in a parable Jesus told. (See Matthew 13:45-46, KJV.) A man searching for fine pearls sold everything he owned to buy the very best pearl. The kingdom of God is like that. People give up everything to enjoy the salvation that the rule of God brings them.

See **God, Jesus, kingdom of God, parable, salvation, version**

Pekah (PEE-kuh) *proper noun:*

Pekah was the next to the last king of Israel, the Northern Kingdom. He became king by killing Pekahiah. He was an evil king in the eyes of the Lord (2 Kings 15:28). He ruled for 20 years according to 2 Kings 15:27.

2 Kings 15:27-31

See **Israel, Pekahiah, Pekah (time line)**

Pekahiah (PEK-uh-HIE-uh) *proper noun:*

Pekahiah was a king of Israel, the Northern Kingdom. He was the son of Menahem. He was an evil king. He had ruled for only two years when he was killed by Pekah.

2 Kings 15:23-26

See **Israel, Menahem, Pekah, Pekahiah (time line)**

penal satisfaction theory of the Atonement (PEE-nul SAT-is-FAK-shun THEER-ee uv thee uh-TOHN-munt) *noun phrase:*

See **atonement, penalty**

penalty (PEN-ul-tee) *noun:*

A penalty is the punishment a person receives for doing wrong. The word does not appear in the Bible, but the idea does. People who disobey God suffer for it. Sometimes this suffering is the judgment of God upon them. Spiritual death is the greatest penalty of all for sin (Romans 5:12, 18-21; 6:23).

Some Christians believe the death of Christ paid in full the punishment for sin. They understand the Atonement as satisfying God's demand for justice. Jesus Christ satisfied the demands of God's law. The law demanded the death of sinners. But Christ became a substitute for the ones chosen to be saved. Thus they did not have to die. (See Isaiah 53:4-5, 10; 1 Peter 2:24.)

Wesleyanism also says that sin brings penalty and causes harm to people. It also agrees that the death of Christ happened because of the sin of man. But it does not accept the Reformed view of election and the Atonement. It believes that Jesus died for all sinners, not just the elect. Prevenient grace makes it possible for sinners to accept or reject His gift of salvation.

Wesleyanism does not believe that God punished Christ as a substitute for punishing humanity. God did not punish Christ. Rather, God himself suffered in Christ for the sin of humanity. God acted through Christ to defeat the power of sin. God's suffering showed how costly forgiveness is and how terrible sin is. The death of Christ showed the love of God and the holiness of God. It showed His victory over sin. Christ's victory through His death makes salvation possible for everyone.

Romans 3:20-26; 5:6-11, 15-18; 8:31-39; 1 Timothy 2:3-6; 1 John 2:1-2

See **atonement, Christ, death, election, forgiveness, God, grace, holiness, Jesus, judgment, law, love, obedience, prevenient grace, propitiation, Reformed tradition, salvation, sin, suffering, Wesleyanism**

penance (PEN-uns) *noun:*

Penance is an act done to show sorrow for sin. Penance is one of the seven sacraments of the Roman Catholic Church. Acts of penance are done under directions from a priest after confession. Catholics believe that doing acts of penance gains the favor of God.

Protestants do not believe in penance. They believe that God through Christ forgives and restores those who confess their sins. This full and free forgiveness makes penance not necessary. Protestants believe in repentance for sin, not penance. They also believe that forgiven people will live in a new way. They will show by obeying God that they are forgiven.

See **confess, forgiveness, grace, justification, merit, penitence, Protestant, reconciliation, repent, restitution, Roman Catholic, sacrament**

Peniel (puh-NIE-ul) *proper noun:*

Peniel was an important place in the life of Jacob. There he met God, and his name was changed to Israel. The name Peniel in Hebrew means "face of God." It is not known for certain where Peniel was located. It was near the place where the Jabbok River joined the Jordan River. This was somewhere between the Sea of Galilee and the Dead Sea.

Genesis 32:24-32

See **Dead Sea, Galilee, Israel, Jacob, Jordan River (map 3)**

penitence (PEN-uh-tuns) *noun:*

Penitence is an attitude of sorrow or regret for sin or doing wrong. Penitence is the way sinners show humility before a holy God. They show that they know their sins have wronged Him.

Penitence is also called sorrow for sins or contrition. Penitence may lead to repentance or a complete turning toward God and away from sin.

2 Corinthians 7:10

See **conversion, holiness, holy, humility, penance, repent, sin**

penitential (PEN-uh-TEN-shul) *adjective:*

Penitential describes something as related to penitence. For example, some of the psalms are called penitential psalms, such as Psalm 51.

See **penance, penitence, psalm**

Pentateuch (PEN-tuh-tewk) *proper noun:*

Pentateuch is the name of the first five books of the Old Testament. These books are Genesis, Exodus, Leviticus, Numbers, and Deuteronomy. The Latin name *Pentateuch* means "five books." These books are also called the Torah and the law of Moses.

See **Bible, Deuteronomy, Exodus, Genesis, Law, Leviticus, Moses, Numbers, Old Testament, Torah**

Pentecost (PEN-tuh-kawst) *proper noun:*

Pentecost is the name of a Jewish festival day also celebrated by Christians. The word *Pentecost* in Greek means 50. The Jewish festival was celebrated on the day following seven weeks after Passover. Thus the Old Testament called Pentecost the Festival of Weeks (Exodus 34:22; Deuteronomy 16:9-10, 16). It was also called the Festival of Harvest or Firstfruits (Exodus 23:16; Deuteronomy 16:16). Later the Jews believed that Pentecost celebrated the giving of the law at Sinai.

Christians celebrate Pentecost as the day the Holy Spirit was given to the Church (Acts 2:1-42). The Christian Pentecost was an important event in the beginning of the new covenant. The Church was born on that day. The new age of the Spirit came in its fullness at Pentecost. The followers of Jesus were filled with the Spirit on that day. The Holiness Movement believes that these people were entirely sanctified because of this filling.

Jeremiah 31:31-34; Ezekiel 36:25-27; Acts 15:8-9; Ephesians 1:22-23; 4:4-16; Hebrews 8:6-13; 10:14-18

See **Christian, church, entire sanctification, festival, Holiness Movement, Jew, law, Old Testament, Sinai (map 2), spirit**

Pentecostal (PEN-tuh-KAW-stul)

1. *proper adjective:* Pentecostal describes someone or something as related to Pentecostalism. The word comes from the Day of Pentecost on which the Holy Spirit was given.

2. *proper noun:* A Pentecostal is someone who is part of Pentecostalism.
See **Pentecost, Pentecostalism, spirit**

Pentecostalism (PEN-tuh-KAW-stul-iz-um) *proper noun:*
Pentecostalism is the name of a religious movement that stresses baptism with the Holy Spirit. Most Pentecostals believe that speaking in tongues is the first sign of this baptism. Pentecostalism stresses the gifts of the Spirit.

Pentecostalism began in the early 1900s as a revival of speaking in tongues. A large number of denominations form Pentecostalism today. Scholars disagree about how Pentecostalism started.

Some Pentecostals teach that the baptism in the Holy Spirit is a third work of grace. They teach that it follows entire sanctification, which is a second work of grace. Others teach that sanctification is a process that follows conversion. They teach that the baptism in the Holy Spirit is the second work of grace. But they do not believe that the baptism in the Holy Spirit purifies the believer's heart.

See **baptism with the Holy Spirit, Charismatic Movement, conversion, gift, Pentecost, Pentecostal, revival, second work of grace, tongue**

perdition (per-DISH-un) *noun:*
Perdition means "endless destruction." It is the condition of the wicked, who reject eternal life. Perdition is another word for what hell is. Perdition is the final condition of those who reject salvation.

Judas Iscariot is called "the son of perdition" (John 17:12, KJV). This means "the son of perishing." His character is that of a lost sinner. Judas chose to betray Jesus and so made destruction his fate.

Antichrist is also called "the son of perdition" (2 Thessalonians 2:3, KJV). He opposes God and will be destroyed when Jesus comes again.

Philippians 1:28; 1 Timothy 6:9; Hebrews 10:39; 2 Peter 3:7; Revelation 17:8, 11

See **antichrist, betrayal, God, hell, Jesus, Judas, King James Version, lost, salvation, Second Coming, sin**

perfect

1. (per-FEKT) *verb:* To perfect means to fulfill the purpose for which a person or thing was made. To perfect means to make complete and whole. To perfect something may mean to remove all its faults. But something that has been perfected may still have certain faults. Such faults do not keep it from fulfilling its purpose. God's central purpose for people is that they should love him completely. He also wills that people should love their neighbors as they love themselves.

2. (PER-fikt) *adjective:* Perfect describes something that has been made complete. It describes that which fulfills its purpose or design. It may describe something that is completely free of error. Only God is completely free of error. Animals that were used for sacrifice in the Old Testament

were to have no serious faults (Exodus 12:5). People who lived in obedience to the law of God were described as perfect. Their character was shaped by the will of God (Genesis 6:9; 17:1; Psalm 119:1).

Christians are perfect when they fulfill the purpose that God has for them. They are not as perfect as God is perfect. But they are perfect because they complete what it means to be God's child. The work of God in them makes them the people He wants them to be. His grace helps them fulfill His plan and become mature Christians.

Matthew 5:48; Romans 8:3-4; 13:8-10; 2 Corinthians 6:14—7:1; Philippians 1:6; 2:12-13; 3:12, 15; 1 Timothy 1:5; James 3:2; 1 John 1:7-9

***See* child of God, Christian, Christian perfection, disciple, entire sanctification, grace, holiness, maturity, obedience, perfect love, perfection, sacrifice**

perfect love (PER-fikt LUV) *noun phrase:*

Perfect love is the condition of complete love for God and people. The Bible tells of the perfect love that God has for the world. It says that God loves His creation completely. The New Testament says that God shows His love through Jesus Christ.

The Holy Spirit helps Christians love God and others. He gives them a love for the law of God. He puts the law of God in their hearts. Thus, they fulfill the purpose for which they were created.

Wesleyans use the phrase "perfect love" to refer to entire sanctification, or Christian perfection. Entire sanctification makes perfect love possible.

Matthew 5:43-48; 19:19; 22:37-40; Luke 6:26, 35; John 3:16-19; 14:15—15:17; Romans 13:8-9; Ephesians 2:4; Hebrews 10:14-18; 1 John 2:10-15; 3:10-23; 4:7—5:2; Revelation 1:5

***See* Christian perfection, creation, disciple, entire sanctification, holiness, Holy Spirit, law, love, perfection, Wesleyanism**

perfection (per-FEK-shun) *noun:*

Perfection is the condition of being complete and whole. It may mean being totally without error or fault. Only God has perfection in this sense.

Christian perfection is the work of God in Christians. It makes it possible for them to fulfill His will. Christians can have perfection because God cleanses them from what opposes His will. They are free to grow in His love. But this does not mean they are free from error or fault. They do not have perfect knowledge of God. They have perfection in that they want to obey God in all things. Also, their perfection does not mean there is no room for spiritual growth. They do not have perfection of character. But they do have perfection in that they want God to shape their character.

Psalm 50:2; Luke 8:14; 2 Corinthians 13:9; Colossians 3:14; Hebrews 6:1

***See* character, Christian perfection, disciple, entire sanctification, growth in grace, holiness, initial sanctification, love, perfect, perfect love, process in sanctification, spiritual, will**

Perizzites (PAIR-uh-ziets) *proper noun:*

Perizzites were people who lived in Canaan in Old Testament times. They were one of the Canaanite tribes. They are mentioned in the Old Testament many times, but not much is known about them.

Genesis 15:20; 34:30; Exodus 3:8, 17; 23:23; Joshua 3:10; 9:1

See **Canaan, Canaanites, Joshua**

persecution (PER-suh-KYEW-shun) *noun:*

Persecution is harm that is done to a person because of hate. This harm is usually cruel and repeated. It is usually done to injure people of other religions, races, or cultures.

Early Christians received persecution from those who opposed Jesus and His teachings. This persecution included being mocked, beaten, put in prison, and even killed. Christians are still persecuted in some parts of the world today.

Early Christians came to expect persecution and to accept it (John 16:33; 1 Thessalonians 3:1-5; 2 Timothy 3:12). They were followers of Jesus Christ, who was himself persecuted (John 15:20).

The Bible encourages believers to remain faithful to Christ when they experience persecution. Even severe persecution cannot separate Christians from their Lord (Romans 8:35-39; 2 Corinthians 4:9). Those who persecute others will be punished by God (2 Thessalonians 1:4-10). Christians should forgive and pray for those who persecute them (Matthew 5:44; Romans 12:14-21).

Some who have called themselves "Christians" have persecuted people who did not agree with them. There have been many examples of this in church history.

Matthew 5:10-12; 10:23; 13:21; 23:24; 1 Corinthians 4:12; 1 Thessalonians 2:15

See **affliction, cross, disciple, faithful, followers, forgiveness, suffering, tribulation**

perseverance (PER-suh-VIR-uns) *noun:*

Perseverance is continuing to do something even when it would be easier to quit. Christian perseverance is continuing faithfulness to Christ. Christians can be faithful even when they are persecuted and tempted. They need not backslide or commit apostasy.

The "perseverance of the saints" has a special meaning for most Calvinists. They hold that all those whom God calls to salvation will finally be saved. This belief is related to the doctrine of eternal security. Arminianism rejects this belief. It believes that final salvation depends on the perseverance of the believer. God will keep believers secure only so long as they remain faithful to Him.

Matthew 24:13; John 15:5-6; Romans 5:3-4; 11:21-22; 1 Corinthians 10:1-13; Galatians 5:4; Ephesians 6:18; Philippians 1:6; Colossians 1:21-23; 1 Thessalonians

1:2-7; 2:13-16; 3:1-13; Hebrews 6:1-12; 2 Peter 1:5-11; 2:20-22; Jude 24-25

See **apostasy, Arminianism, backslide, Calvinism, election, eternal security, faith, faithful, freedom, patience, persecution, Reformed tradition, salvation, temptation**

Persia (PER-zhuh) *proper noun:*

Persia is the name of a country located to the east of Mesopotamia. It is in the area of Media and Elam. The kingdom of Persia ruled most of the Middle East from about 550 to 330 B.C. Persia replaced Babylon as the leading power of that part of the world. Persia was later defeated by Greece.

King Cyrus of Persia allowed the Jewish exiles in Babylon to return to Palestine. They were allowed to live in Judah under the control of the government of Persia.

See **Babylon, Cyrus, exile, Greece, Media and Elam (map 6), Mesopotamia, Middle East, Palestine**

person (PER-sun) *noun:*

Person usually means a human being. A person can think, choose, love, and know right from wrong. Persons are able to love and hate and to develop friendships.

The word *person* is also used to refer to God. He relates to people as a person. This does not mean that God exists as a human being. God does not have a physical body. But He does think, act with purpose, love, and have knowledge. He can have fellowship with people, His creation. The person of God is similar to humans in some ways.

The doctrine of the Trinity teaches that the Father, Son, and Holy Spirit are all Persons. God is fully present in His love and power in each of them (John 14:8-23).

Genesis 1:26-31; Isaiah 44:8; Jeremiah 29:4, 8, 21; Amos 4:11

See **covenant, creation, doctrine, fellowship, God, human, personality, Trinity**

personal evangelism (PER-sun-ul ee-VAN-jul-iz-um) *noun phrase:*

Personal evangelism means one person telling the gospel to another person.

See **evangelism, gospel, witness**

personality (PER-sun-NAL-uh-tee) *noun:*

Personality is all the qualities that identify a person. These qualities include the person's behavior and habits and how the person looks and thinks.

God also has personality. The personality of God includes those qualities that identify Him. His personality includes His attributes. No one can be compared to Him, for He is above all.

Isaiah 40:28; 41:10; 45:18, 25

See **attribute, God, human, person**

Pesach (PAY-sahk) *proper noun:*

See **festival, Passover**

Peshitta (puh-SHEE-tuh) *proper noun:*

See **version**

Peter (PEET-er) *proper noun:*

1. Peter was one of the most important disciples of Jesus. He and his brother, Andrew, had been fishermen. He was leader in the Early Jewish Christian Church. His name had been Simon, but Jesus gave him the new name Cephas. This name meant "rock" in Aramaic. Peter in Greek also means "rock."

2. First and Second Peter are two books in the New Testament. They are two of the epistles. They are letters probably written by the apostle Peter. First Peter was written to encourage Christians in Asia Minor who were being persecuted. Second Peter warns against false teachers, especially those who deny the Second Coming.

Matthew 16:13-23; Mark 3:16; Luke 5:1-11; Acts 1:13-15; 2:14; Galatians 2:1-10

See **Andrew, apostle, Aramaic, Asia Minor (map 11), Cephas, church, disciple, epistle, Greek, Jesus, name, New Testament, Second Coming, Simon**

Pharaoh (FAIR-oh) *proper noun:*

Pharaoh is the title used for the kings of Egypt during Old Testament times. The Old Testament gives the names of few of these Pharaohs (2 Kings 23:29; Jeremiah 44:30).

Genesis 12:15-20; 41:1-55; Exodus 1:11; 2:15, 23

See **Egypt, king, Old Testament**

Pharisee (FAIR-uh-see) *proper noun:*

A Pharisee was a member of a special Jewish religious group. The Pharisees stressed the keeping of the law. The name Pharisee probably meant "a separated person."

The Pharisees tried to apply the law to every detail of life. They stressed the importance of both the written Scriptures and the spoken traditions. One of their main beliefs was in the resurrection of the dead.

Many of the Pharisees were sincere and holy men. But some of their members were guilty of hypocrisy. Jesus attacked such Pharisees as even worse than those they considered sinners. The apostle Paul was once a Pharisee.

The destruction of Jerusalem by Rome in A.D. 70 ended most Jewish religious groups. But the rabbis continued to teach the views of the Pharisees. Modern Judaism developed from this.

Matthew 5:20; 23:1-36; John 3:1-15; Acts 23:6-8; Philippians 3:5

See **apostle, Christian, Gentile, holy, hypocrisy, Jerusalem (map 10), Jew, Judaism, law, legalism, legalistic, New Testament, Paul, rabbi, resurrection, Scripture, tradition**

Philemon (fuh-LEE-mun) *proper noun:*

1. Philemon is the name of a convert of the apostle Paul. A letter Paul wrote to him is in the New Testament. Onesimus was a slave belonging to Philemon. He had run away from his master. But Onesimus had become a Christian after he met Paul in prison.

2. Philemon is the name of a book in the New Testament. It is one of the epistles. The apostle Paul wrote a letter to Philemon about Onesimus. The letter urges Philemon to treat his returned slave, Onesimus, as a Christian brother.

See **apostle, brother, Christian, convert, epistle, New Testament, Paul, slave**

Philip (FIL-up) *proper noun:*

Philip was the name of two men in the New Testament.

1. Philip was one of the 12 disciples of Jesus (Matthew 10:3; John 1:43-45; 6:5-6; 12:20-23; 14:8-14; Acts 1:13).

2. Philip was a Greek-speaking Jew of the Early Jerusalem Church. He was chosen to serve as a deacon. He evangelized with great success in Samaria and later in Caesarea. Thus, he is called Philip the Evangelist (Acts 6:1-7; 8:4-40; 21:8-9).

See **apostle, deacon, disciple, evangelist**

Philippi (FIL-uh-pie or fuh-LIP-ie) *proper noun:*

Philippi was a city in Macedonia, which today is in Greece. Philippi was a city Paul and Silas visited on Paul's second missionary journey. The church at Philippi was the first Christian church in Europe.

Acts 16:6-40; 20:1, 6; 1 Thessalonians 2:2

See **Greece, Macedonia, missionary, Paul, Philippi (map 11), Philippians, Silas**

Philippians (fuh-LIP-ee-unz) *proper noun:*

1. The Philippians were people who lived in the Greek city of Philippi. The apostle Paul wrote a letter to his Christian converts in that city. See Acts 16:11-40.

2. Philippians is the name of a book in the New Testament. It is one of the epistles. The apostle Paul wrote this letter. He wrote from prison where he faced possible death. But joy is the central message of the letter (Philippians 1:4, 19; 2:2; 3:1; 4:1, 10). Paul thanks his converts for their gift to support him (4:18). He reminds them of the example of Jesus Christ and urges humility and unity (2:1-11).

See **apostle, Christ, Christian, convert, epistle, Greek, humility, Jesus, joy, Paul, Philippi (map 11), unity**

Philistia (fuh-LIS-tee-uh) *proper noun:*

Philistia is the land of the Philistines. It was located on the plain of Canaan by the Mediterranean Sea. Palestine derived its name from Philistia.

See **Canaan, Palestine, Philistia (map 7), Philistine, Philistines (map 3)**

Philistine (FIL-us-teen)

1. *proper noun:* Philistine is the name of the people who once lived in southwestern Palestine. They moved there from the islands off the coast of Greece. This happened about the same time as Israel entered the land under Joshua. The Philistines made Israel's efforts to possess the land difficult until the time of David.

Five important city-states of the Philistines are mentioned in the Old Testament. They are Ashdod, Ashkelon, Ekron, Gath, and Gaza.

2. *proper adjective:* Philistine describes someone or something related to the Philistines. For example, Goliath was a Philistine soldier.

Joshua 13:3; Judges 13—16; 1 Samuel 4—6; 2 Samuel 5:17-25

See **Canaan (map 3), Goliath, Israel, Palestine, Philistines (maps 3, 4)**

philosophy (fuh-LAHS-uh-fee) *noun:*

Philosophy is the attempt to discover, understand, and state what is most real. The term comes from two Greek words that together mean "love of wisdom." Philosophy uses reason to understand what is most real and true and to understand life. Philosophy does not make use of revelation as does theology. There are many types of philosophy and many ways to study philosophy.

See **knowledge, reason, revelation, theology, truth, wisdom**

Phoenicia (fuh-NISH-ee-uh) *proper noun:*

Phoenicia was a country in Bible times. It was north of Palestine along the Mediterranean Sea. Its most important cities were Tyre and Sidon.

Matthew 15:21; Mark 7:24-26; 31; Acts 21:1-3

See **Mediterranean Sea, Palestine, Phoenicia (maps 1, 7, 8), Sidon, Tyre**

phylactery (fuh-LAK-ter-ee) *noun:*

A phylactery was a small leather case containing papers with scripture verses on them. The verses were Exodus 13:1-16, Deuteronomy 6:4-9, and 11:13-22. Jewish men wore the phylacteries tied to their heads or arms.

Matthew 23:5

See **Jew, Scripture**

piety (PIE-uh-tee) *noun:*

Piety means sincere devotion to God. It also means the way of life that shows this devotion. Piety is the practice of worshiping God and serving people in love.

1 Timothy 2:2; 3:16; 4:7-8; 6:6, 11; Titus 1:1; 2 Peter 1:3, 7

See **devout, disciple, discipline, ethics, godliness, religious, service, worship**

Pilate (PIE-lut) *proper noun:*

Pilate was a Roman governor of Judea for about 10 years. He was also known as Pontius Pilate. Pilate was governor when Jesus was arrested and put on trial in Jerusalem. Jesus was brought to Pilate by the Jews. But it was Pilate who sentenced Jesus to die by crucifixion. All four of the gospels state that Pilate did not think Jesus was guilty.

Matthew 27:1-26; Mark 15:1-20; Luke 3:1; 23:1-25; John 18:28—19:16

See **crucifixion, Jerusalem, Jesus, Jew, Judea, Rome**

pilgrim (PIL-grum) *noun:*

A pilgrim is someone who travels a distance to a holy place. A pilgrim usually goes to a holy place to worship. He or she may go to a place because a holy person is buried there. This journey is called a pilgrimage.

In the Old Testament, pilgrims went to Jerusalem to worship in the Temple. Some of the psalms are songs of pilgrims going to Jerusalem.

Christians are often called pilgrims. We are on a journey to heaven.

Psalms 132; 133; 134; Luke 2:41-42; Hebrews 11:13-16; 1 Peter 2:11-12

See **heaven, holy, Jerusalem, pilgrimage, Psalms, temple, worship**

Pilgrim Holiness church (PIL-grum HOH-li-nes CHERCH) *proper noun phrase:*

See **Holiness Movement**

pilgrimage (PIL-gruh-mij) *noun:*

A pilgrimage is a journey to a holy or sacred place. A pilgrimage is made by a pilgrim.

Pilgrimage can refer to a person's life or walk with God.

Exodus 6:3; Psalm 119:54

See **holy, pilgrim, sacred, walk**

pious (PIE-us) *adjective:*

Pious describes a person or behavior as related to piety. For example, a pious person is one who practices the disciplines of piety.

See **discipline, godly walk, piety**

plague (PLAYG) *noun:*

A plague is a disease or other event that brings great suffering to people. Plagues may include disease, long periods of darkness, and war.

Plagues in the Bible were seen as the judgment of God on evil people. God sent 10 plagues on the Egyptians as a way to free the Hebrews (Exodus 7—12).

Samuel 5:1-12; Numbers 16:46-50; 21:4-9

See **Ashdod, Egypt, God, Hebrew, judgment, Passover, Pharaoh, suffering**

pledge (PLEJ)

1. *verb:* To pledge means to make a promise to someone. Sometimes it means a promise to give money.

2. *noun:* A pledge is the property of someone who owes a debt. The property is given to the one who makes the loan. The pledge assures pay-

ment of the loan. Sometimes the property of a third person becomes a pledge for another.

The law of Moses would not allow some things to become a pledge. For example, the clothing of a widow could not be taken as a pledge. Another word for *pledge* used in the Bible is "surety."

Pledges are sometimes made in churches today. For example, someone may pledge to give money to a building fund.

Genesis 38:17-26; 43:9; 44:32; Exodus 22:25-27; Deuteronomy 24:10-18; 1 Samuel 17:18; Job 17:3; Proverbs 6:1-5; 11:15; 1 Timothy 5:12; Hebrews 7:22

See **debt, law, Moses, promise**

plenary (PLEN-uh-ree) *adjective:*

Plenary describes something that is complete or full. The word is used to describe the inspiration of the Bible. Plenary inspiration means that the whole Bible was inspired by God. The 66 books contain all that people need to know for their salvation. The Bible is complete in what it says about God, humanity, and salvation. This is what it means to call the Bible the inspired Word of God.

2 Timothy 3:16-17

See **authority of Scripture, Bible, inspiration of the Bible, salvation, word**

pneumatology (NEW-muh-TAHL-uh-jee) *noun:*

Pneumatology is the doctrine of the Holy Spirit. Pneumatology comes from two Greek words meaning "spirit" and "study."

See **doctrine, spirit**

polity (PAHL-uh-tee) *noun:*

Polity is the government of a church or denomination. Polity includes the rules of membership and the way a church is governed.

See **church, denomination, manual**

polytheism (PAH-lee-thee-IZ-um) *noun:*

Polytheism is the belief that there are many gods.

Acts 14:8-18; 17:22-31

See **God, henotheism, idol, idolatry, monotheism, pantheism**

Pontius Pilate (PAHN-chus or PAHN-tee-us PIE-lut) *proper noun:*

See **Pilate**

pope (POHP) *noun:*

The pope is the leader of the Roman Catholic Church. He is called the bishop of Rome. The term *pope* comes from the Greek and Latin words meaning "father." Roman Catholics believe that he is in direct line from Peter, the apostle.

See **apostle, bishop, Peter, Protestant, Roman Catholic**

postmillennialism (POHST-muh-LEN-ee-ul-iz-um) *noun:*

See **millennium**

postmodern (POHST MAHD-ern)

1. *noun:* Postmodern is the period of history that follows the modern period. It started sometime in the 20th century. Different dates are given for the beginning of the postmodern period. There are many different ideas about what postmodern means. The modern period placed great trust in human reason for organizing all life. The postmodern period places less trust in human reason.

A person who holds postmodern beliefs is called a postmodern.

2. *adjective:* Postmodern describes any person, event, or belief of the postmodern period.

See **life, modernism, reason**

pouring (POHR-ing) *noun:*

Pouring is one way Christians are baptized. The minister pours a small amount of water onto the head of the person.

See **baptism, Christian, immersion, minister, sprinkling**

praise (PRAYZ)

1. *verb:* To praise is to approve and honor someone or something. Several different Hebrew and Greek words in the Bible are translated "praise." These words also mean to thank, bless, and tell how great someone or something is.

2. *noun:* Praise is the act of praising someone or something. The Bible usually refers to the praise of God. Such praise is rejoicing in who God is and what He has done. People give praise to God by what they say and do. They show their praise by obeying and serving Him. They tell their praise by thanking Him and speaking to others about His grace. People can praise God by speaking, praying, singing, and playing music. True praise to God is the worship of God alone.

Psalms 135:1-4; 138:1-3; 146:1-2; 150; Luke 1:46-55, 67-69

See **gospel songs, hymn, Psalms, thanksgiving, worship**

pray (PRAY) *verb:*

To pray is to talk to God or a god. A pagan or heathen prays to a god or idol. A Christian prays to the only true God.

Deuteronomy 4:7; 2 Chronicles 7:14; Jeremiah 42:1-4; Matthew 6:5-13, Romans 8:26-27; 1 Thessalonians 5:17; James 5:13-18

See **Christian, God, god, heathen, idol, intercede, pagan, prayer, worship**

prayer (PRAYR) *noun:*

Prayer is talking with God. Prayer includes worship of God and meditation on God. Some hymns that are used in worship are prayers. Prayer often includes a request that God will help someone who is in need. This is called intercession. Christians pray in the name of Christ. They pray with the aid of the Holy Spirit. Prayer is a Christian right and duty.

1 Kings 8:28-54; Psalm 64:1; Proverbs 15:29; Isaiah 38:5; Matthew 6:5-13; John 17; Romans 8:26-27; Philippians 4:6; Colossians 4:2, 12; James 5:13-18; Revelation 5:8

See **God, hymn, intercession, Lord's Prayer, meditation, praise, right, spirit, worship**

preach (PREECH) *verb:*

To preach means to tell the message of God to people. It means to speak out as a messenger of the Lord.

Prophets in the Old Testament spoke for God to the people. They urged their hearers to repent and obey God. Jesus preached the gospel and invited people to enter the kingdom of God. Peter preached the gospel of Christ on the Day of Pentecost. He urged his listeners to believe on Christ and be saved. Paul preached the gospel to the Gentiles.

Ministers who preach the gospel today urge people to obey God. This is sometimes called exhortation. They deliver the message of God to all who will hear.

Nehemiah 6:7; Isaiah 61:1; Luke 3:18; 4:43; 9:60; 16:16; Acts 5:42; 8:4-40; 10:36; 20:7, 9; Ephesians 2:17; Hebrews 4:2

See **apostle, Christ, exhort, exhortation, Gentile, gospel, kerygma, message, messenger, minister, obedience, Paul, Pentecost, preacher, prophet, repent**

preacher (PREECH-er) *noun:*

A preacher is person who preaches. Preachers tell the message of God to people. They are messengers of the Lord.

A preacher may be a person who serves in one of various roles. A preacher may be a pastor, minister, priest, prophet, or evangelist. Some missionaries are preachers. Also, certain laity preach. Most preachers are ordained by their denominations. However, some preachers are not ordained.

Isaiah 61:1; Matthew 10:7; Mark 16:5; Luke 4:18; Acts 16:10; Romans 1:15; 10:14-15; 1 Corinthians 9:14, 16; 2 Timothy 4:1-2

See **denomination, evangelist, message, laity, messenger, minister, missionary, ordain, ordination, pastor, preach, priest, prophet**

predestination (pree-DES-tuh-NAY-shun) *noun:*

Predestination is a doctrine that says God decides ahead of time who will be saved. Calvinism and Arminianism do not agree on this.

Calvinism stresses the sovereignty of God. His will decides everything that will happen. Most Calvinists believe God decides which persons will be saved. He also decides how they will be saved. Some even believe He also decides who will not be saved. Calvinism claims that Scripture supports this view (Romans 9:11-15; 2 Timothy 1:9; 1 Peter 2:8).

Arminianism stresses the freedom of people and the saving purposes of

God. The grace of God is given for all people. But salvation is possible only for those who accept this grace. God decides the conditions, means, and purpose of salvation. He also provides the power for all to be saved. But He does not decide which persons will receive salvation or who will reject it. Arminianism stresses that salvation is for all who have faith in Christ.

John 3:16; Acts 16:30-31; Romans 3:21-26; 5:15-18; 10:9-13; 11:17-24; Galatians 2:14-16; 3:6-14; Ephesians 2:8-10; 1 Timothy 2:3-6; Titus 2:11-14; 2 Peter 3:9; 1 John 1:5—2:2

See **Arminianism, Calvinism, damnation, doctrine, faith, freedom, grace, predestine, Reformed tradition, salvation, save, Scripture, sovereign, will**

predestine (pree-DES-tun) *verb:*

To predestine is to decide ahead of time what events must happen in the future.

The Bible says that God has predestined certain future events. He set up the way of salvation long before the world began (1 Corinthians 2:8). He decided that believers in Jesus Christ will be the children of God. He also decided that believers should become like Christ in character and conduct (Romans 8:28-30).

The Bible teaches that God predestined certain people to serve him in special ways. He chose Israel to make Him known to all people of the earth. He chose Moses to lead Israel and give them His laws. He chose David and his descendants to rule in Jerusalem. He chose Paul to be the apostle to the Gentiles. But those God predestined still had to choose to accept His call (1 Corinthians 9:24-27; 15:7-10; Galatians 1:11-17). The grace of God that allows people to serve Him can rejected.

Romans 8:28—11:36; 2 Corinthians 6:1; Galatians 2:21; 5:1-4

See **believer, Bible, call, character, child of God, damnation, David, election, Gentile, grace, Israel, Jesus, lost, Moses, Paul, praise, predestination, salvation, save, service**

preexistence of Christ (PREE-ig-ZIS-tuns uv KRIEST) *noun phrase:*

The preexistence of Christ means that He existed before He was born in Bethlehem. He was the eternal Son of God before He became the Son of Mary. There never was a time when the Son of God did not exist. The eternal Word of God became a human being in history. He came to be the Messiah of the Jews. He came to make the God of eternity known to people in history. Belief in the preexistence of Christ is necessary for the doctrine of the Incarnation.

John 1:1-15; Romans 8:3; 2 Corinthians 8:9; Galatians 4:4; Philippians 2:5-11; Colossians 1:15-20; Hebrews 1:1-14

See **Bethlehem (maps 7, 8), Christ, Christianity, doctrine, eternal, God, Incarnation, Jesus, Mary, Messiah, Nazareth (map 8), logos, Son of God, word**

premillennialism (PREE-muh-LEN-ee-ul-iz-um) *noun:*

See **millennium**

presbyter (PREZ-buh-ter or PRES-buh-ter) *noun:*

See **elder, Presbyterian**

Presbyterian (PREZ-buh-TIR-ee-un or PRES-buh-TIR-en-un) *proper adjective:*

Presbyterian describes a group of Protestant denominations led by elders. The Greek word for elder is *presbyter.* Many Presbyterian churches accept the Westminster Confession of Faith. This is one of the most important creeds of Calvinism. It was written in England in 1645.

Presbyterian churches are especially known for their form of government. The members of the congregation are represented by elders. Ruling elders are elected from the congregation to govern the church. The pastor is the teaching elder. He is an ordained minister. Presbyterian churches also have deacons who serve the poor.

There are at least 10 Presbyterian denominations in the United States.

See **Calvinism, congregation, creed, deacon, denomination, minister, ordain, pastor, polity, Protestant, reformation, Reformed tradition**

prevenient grace (pree-VEEN-yunt GRAYS) *noun phrase:*

Prevenient grace is the grace of God that is given to all people from birth. It is the grace that comes before a person is converted. God wants to save everyone. So prevenient grace is given to all people to draw them to God. It is the love of God reaching out to everyone. God makes the first move toward people. He makes it possible for them to respond to Him. God places within people the desire for what is good and true. No one can turn to God in his or her own strength. God awakens people to a knowledge of their need for redemption.

This doctrine is stressed by Wesleyans and other churches. It is not taught by Calvinists. Calvinists teach the doctrine of special grace. This means that the call to salvation goes only to the elect, not to everyone. The gift of grace for salvation is given only to the elect. It cannot be resisted. But Wesleyans believe that prevenient grace is given to all. The offer of salvation can be rejected.

John 1:9; 15:5; Romans 1:18-23; 2:14-15; 3:21-26; 5:6-8, 15-16; Ephesians 2:8-10; Titus 2:11-14

See **Calvinism, conversion, convert, doctrine, elect, election, God, grace, love, mercy, salvation, sinful nature, total depravity, Wesleyanism**

Priscilla (pruh-SIL-uh) *proper noun:*

Priscilla was the wife of Aquila. She is always mentioned with her husband in the Bible. Priscilla and her husband were tentmakers. They helped the apostle Paul in his ministry in Europe and Asia Minor.

Acts 18:1-3, 18-19, 24-26; Romans 16:3; 1 Corinthians 16:19; 2 Timothy 4:19

See **apostle, Aquila, Asia Minor, Europe, ministry, Paul**

pride (PRIED) *noun:*

Pride is the claim that someone or something is of value. Pride may be either good or evil.

Pride is good when it gives proper respect to someone or something. People should have a proper respect for themselves. They are created in the image of God. They have worth and should think well of themselves. But they should also respect others and the property of other people. Paul took pride in the spiritual progress his converts made (2 Corinthians 9:2; Galatians 6:4). Pride is also good when it shows a proper respect for God.

Pride is evil when it places too high a value on oneself (Romans 12:3). People who have such pride are vain. They boast about who they are and what they have. They say they do not need to depend on God and others.

Sinful pride worships self instead of God. It forgets that all good things come as gifts from God. This kind of pride can be shown in many ways. Jesus said that some people show evil pride even when they pray.

Christians should live in humility before God and others. All Christians are important. But they are not as important as God. And they are not more important than other people.

Psalms 10:2-11; 73:6-11; Proverbs 16:18; 29:23; Isaiah 10:12-13; 14:11-15; Jeremiah 48:29; Daniel 4:37; Obadiah 3-4; Matthew 6:1-8, 16-18; Mark 7:21-22; 1 Corinthians 4:7; James 4:16

See **Christian, convert, evil, gift, glory, humility, image of God, prayer, self, worship**

priest (PREEST) *noun:*

A priest is a person who represents people to God and God to people. Thus, a priest is a part of the plan of God for redemption. Priests are mediators between God and the people who worship God. They make the will of God known to people. They help others find God's grace and forgiveness. They lead the people in the rituals and ceremonies of worship.

People in the time of the patriarchs served as their own priests. They offered sacrifices for their own sins and the sins of their families. God told Moses that Israel was to be a nation of priests. They were to make God known to all the people of the world (Exodus 19:3-6; Isaiah 61:6). God also told Moses that special priests should come from the descendants of Aaron (Exodus 19:22-24; Numbers 3:1-10). The Pentateuch tells of the many sacrifices and other rituals the priests were to perform (see the Book of Leviticus).

The Book of Hebrews teaches that Jesus is the great High Priest. Priests from the family of Aaron are no longer necessary. Christ made the perfect and final atonement for sin (Hebrews 8:6—10:25). All believers are called by God to be priests. That is, they are to make Christ known to those who do not know Him. They do not offer sacrifices as did the priests in Israel. The sacrifices Christians offer are their lives in the service and praise of God.

Today some denominations still call their ministers priests. They include the Roman Catholic, Anglican, and Eastern Orthodox churches.

See **Aaron, Anglican, atonement, believer, blood, ceremony, Christian, Eastern Orthodoxy, forgiveness, God, grace, high priest, Israel, Jesus, Levite, Leviticus, mediator, minister, patriarch, Pentateuch, perfect, priesthood, redemption, ritual, Roman Catholic, sacrifice, service, sin, will, worship**

priesthood (PREEST-hood) *noun:*

The priesthood is the office or work of priests. The Old Testament priesthood included the high priest, ordinary priests, and Levites. The high priest was the leader of the priests and Levites. He was the only one allowed in the most holy place in the Temple. All priests were Levites, because they belonged to the tribe of Levi. Only Levites who were also descendants of Aaron were priests.

The Levites did a number of different tasks in the Temple. They guarded the Temple gates and kept things clean. They taught people the law. They also provided music for Temple worship gatherings. They led the people in singing praises to God. Only priests served at the altar and in the holy places in the Temple.

Exodus 28:1; 29:9; Numbers 3:10, 38; 4:15, 19-20; 18:1-7; 25:10-13; 1 Chronicles 6:39-43; 15:16-28; 16:4-6; 23:2-6, 24-32: 25:1-9

See **Aaron, altar, high priest, holy of holies, law, Levi, Levite, minister, Old Testament, praise, priest, temple, worship**

principalities and powers (PRIN-suh-PAL-uh-teez and POU-erz) *noun phrase:*

Principalities and powers are human and demonic rulers. Scholars do not completely agree about what the phrase means. Some people think that the principalities and powers are demons who try to rule the earth. Others say that the principalities and powers are government officers.

Some say that principalities and powers are the organized evil in society. Principalities and powers are the evil way society works.

Some say that principalities and powers stand for all that harms people in the world. Principalities and powers are blind forces of nature, such as famines, storms, and diseases. Principalities and powers refer to all types of oppression and the struggles between humans and beasts. The principalities and powers are the evil in society that cannot be explained.

The principalities and powers Paul wrote about claim to be gods. They try to keep God from ruling His world. They want to rule in His place. They are enemies of God and humanity. Paul says that Christ put principalities and powers under His rule through the Resurrection. Christ has defeated all the powers that oppose the rule of God. Paul says that no powers can separate Christians from the love of God.

Romans 8:38-39; 1 Corinthians 2:8; Ephesians 1:21; 3:10; 6:12; Colossians 1:16; 2:10, 15; Titus 3:1

See **Christ, demon, evil, God, god, human, love, Paul, plague, sin**

principles of the world (PRIN-suh-pulz uv thuh WERLD) *noun phrase:*

The principles of the world are probably the false gods of the Gentiles. The worship of such false gods brings their worshipers under the power of demons. Worshipers become slaves of these principles of the world. But Christ sets them free.

Galatians 4:3-9; Colossians 2:8-10, 20-23

See **demon, exorcism, freedom, Gentile, God, god, idol, principalities and powers, slave, worship**

process in sanctification (PRAH-ses in SANGK-tuh-fuh-KAY-shun) *noun phrase:*

Process in sanctification is growth in becoming like Christ. This begins at conversion and continues until glorification. A person who has become a Christian does not become like Christ in a moment.

Wesleyans do not understand this process to be a gradual cleansing from inherited sinfulness. The carnal nature within a person opposes Christian growth. But when a person is entirely sanctified, the carnal nature is cleansed. Then growth in becoming like Christ becomes more natural.

It is not enough for the Holy Spirit to cleanse and fill believers. They must also continue to grow more like Christ. The Holy Spirit will lead them into fuller service and obedience to God. Thus, process in sanctification is growth in grace. Christian salvation is a process of sanctification that begins with the new birth. This process is completed in glorification.

Romans 6:15-22; 8:18-24; 2 Corinthians 3:18; Galatians 5:16-26; Ephesians 4:11-16; Philippians 1:9-11; 1 Thessalonians 3:11-13; 4:9-10; Hebrews 12:12-14; 1 Peter 1:13—2:10; 2 Peter 1:3-11; 1 John 1:7

See **believer, carnal, character, Christ, Christian, cleanse, conversion, disciple, discipline, entire sanctification, glorification, God, grace, growth in grace, holiness, holy, maturity, nature, new birth, obedience, perfect, salvation, sanctification, sanctify, service, spirit, Wesleyanism**

proclamation (PRAHK-luh-MAY-shun) *noun:*

A proclamation is a message given to people by an important person in government. In the church it is the act of preaching the message of the Lord. One who preaches proclaims the Word of God.

Ezra 1:1; Isaiah 61:1-2; Jeremiah 3:12; Daniel 5:29

See **gospel, kerygma, message, messenger, minister, missionary, preach, preacher, prophet, word**

profane (pro-FAYN)

1. *verb:* To profane is to treat as common something that is sacred. It

means to treat the sacred without respect. To profane is to use the sacred in a way that cheapens it. To profane the name of God means to treat His name without reverence. It means to treat Him carelessly.

2. *adjective:* Profane describes something that is not sacred or not concerned with religious matters. It describes someone or something that is not holy or is not given to God. It can also describe someone or something that is ritually unclean.

Exodus 20:7; Leviticus 18:21; 21:14; Ezekiel 44:23; Matthew 12:5; Acts 24:6; 1 Timothy 1:9; Hebrews 12:16

See **curse, God, holy, name, religion, reverence, sacred, temple, unclean, worship**

progressive revelation (pruh-GRES-iv REV-uh-LAY-shun) *noun phrase:*

Progressive revelation is the ways God has added to the knowledge of himself. God has revealed himself in the events of history. For example, He acted in the call of Abraham and in the Exodus events. His perfect revelation came in Jesus Christ.

God revealed himself to people where they were. His purpose was to move them to where He wanted them to be. People understood God better as they continued to follow His leading. This is progressive revelation.

People came to understand God more completely as He revealed himself more fully. Earlier understandings of God were not as complete as later ones. Thus, the Old Testament must be understood as pointing toward the New Testament. For example, the Old Testament priesthood was fulfilled by the atonement of Jesus Christ.

Jesus completed the meaning of the Old Testament (Matthew 5:17-48). For example, Jesus taught people not to take revenge, although the Old Testament permits it (Exodus 21:24; Leviticus 24:20; Deuteronomy 19:21; Matthew 5:38-42). The teaching of Jesus should be accepted over earlier revelation. God has spoken His final word to us in His Son, Jesus (Hebrews 1:1-3).

See **Abraham, atonement, Christ, Exodus, God, Jesus, New Testament, Old Testament, priesthood, revelation, revenge**

promise (PRAHM-is)

1. *verb:* To promise is to give assurance to another person that one will or will not do something.

2. *noun:* A promise is an agreement to do or not do something in the future.

The New Testament often refers to the promises God made in the Old Testament. The covenants God made in the Old Testament were a kind of promise (Ephesians 2:12). God made promises to His people in these covenant agreements. The people were expected to be faithful to their part of their agreement. Yet God was faithful even when His people were not faithful to Him.

Early Christians believed that God had kept all His promises in Jesus Christ (Romans 15:8; 2 Corinthians 1:18-22). The promises God made to Abraham are kept in Christ, his great Descendant (Galatians 3:6-29).

The Holy Spirit is called "the promise of the Father." The Spirit is a gift that Jesus said would come after His ascension (Luke 24:49; Acts 1:4; 2:33, 39; Galatians 3:14; 4:6; Ephesians 1:13).

All of the promises of God will have been completed when Jesus comes again (Acts 26:6; 2 Timothy 1:1; Hebrews 11:1-40; 2 Peter 3:3-13). This is why early Christians believed they were living in the age of promise.

In some Christian churches, "faith promise" means a commitment to give money to support missions.

***See* ascension, assurance, Christ, covenant, faithful, Faith Promise, father, Hebrew, Holy Spirit, Jesus, New Testament, Old Testament, Second Coming, spirit**

Promised Land (PRAHM-ist LAND) *proper noun phrase:*

The Promised Land was the country that God promised to Abraham and his descendants. It was a part of the covenant between God and Abraham. The Promised Land was known as Canaan.

The Israelites occupied the Promised Land after they returned from Egypt. Joshua led the people to conquer the land.

Many Jews returned to the Promised Land after exile in Babylon.

Today many Jews view the nation of Israel as the Promised Land.

Genesis 12:1-3; 13:14-17; 15:18-21; 17:3-8; Joshua 1:1-6

***See* Abraham, Babylon, Canaan (map 3), conquest, covenant, Egypt, exile, Israel, Jew, Joshua, promise**

prophecy (PRAHF-uh-see) *noun:*

A prophecy is a kind of sermon in the Bible. In prophecy a prophet tells his hearers what God is about to do. But a biblical prophecy was not intended to predict the future. Its real purpose was to help the people who heard it to understand the present. God's future plans depended in part on them. What they did when they heard the prophecy decided what God would do.

The books of prophecy in the Old Testament include the 17 books from Isaiah to Malachi. Each of these books contains many different prophecies. Each prophecy is a sermon given by a prophet at different times to the people.

Prophecies of salvation gave people hope that God was about to help them. Prophets in the fifth century B.C. made promises to the people of Judah. They promised that God would help the Judeans return to their own land. God would help them have a new start as a nation. The nation of Persia helped God carry out His plans. The return of the Exiles was like a second exodus. Thus, the returned exiles were called "the redeemed of the Lord."

Prophecy was usually one of two types. Prophecies of judgment warned people that God was about to punish them for their sins. These prophecies did not simply predict the future. If the people repented, God would change His plans. Prophets in the eighth century B.C. warned sinful Israel that it would be punished. The nation of Assyria carried out God's plans. They destroyed cities of Israel and made the people slaves. Prophets in the sixth century B.C. gave Judah the same warning. The nation of Babylon carried out the plans of God. The Babylonians made slaves of the people of Judah. This is called the Exile.

Prophecy in the New Testament was like Old Testament prophecies in most ways. Prophecy was one of the more important spiritual gifts (1 Corinthians 14). The messages of New Testament prophets helped people understand God's will. Their prophecies were like sermons in many ways. Perhaps they did not have to study to prepare their messages as modern preachers do. Somehow God inspired them to speak His word clearly and correctly.

People today think of prophecy as telling about future events. Thus, they think that the gift of prophecy is the ability to do this. They think that this was the main purpose of the prophets' messages. This does not seem to be the main biblical meaning.

Isaiah 6:1-13; Jeremiah 1:4-19; Amos 7:10-17; Jonah 1:1-3; Micah 1:1; Zechariah 1:1-6

See **Assyria, Babylon, exhortation, Exile, Exodus, future, gifts, inspire, inspiration, Isaiah, Israel, Judah, Judea, judgment, Malachi, message, Persia, preacher, prophet, redeem, salvation, sermon, slave, spiritual, word, will**

prophesy (PRAHF-uh-sie) *verb:*

To prophesy is to deliver a message from God to people. The message urges people to repent and obey God. To prophesy sometimes means to tell of judgment that God will send. To prophesy can also mean to predict future events.

Ezekiel 25:2; 28:21; Joel 2:28; Amos 2:12; 7:15; 1 Corinthians 14:1-40

See **exhort, proclamation, prophecy, prophet**

prophet (PRAH-fut) *noun:*

A prophet is one who speaks for God. A prophet delivers the message of God to the people. A false prophet is a person whose claim to speak for God is a lie.

There were many prophets in the Old Testament. Some were called "former prophets" and some "latter prophets." The former prophets included Abraham, Moses, Samuel, Elijah, and Elisha. The latter prophets were the writing prophets.

The writing prophets were those for whom books of the Old Testament are named. These prophets are divided into the Major and the Minor

Prophets. The Major Prophets were Isaiah, Jeremiah, Lamentations, Ezekiel, and Daniel. The Minor Prophets were Hosea, Joel, Amos, Obadiah, Jonah, Micah, Nahum, Habukkuk, Zephaniah, Haggai, Zechariah, and Malachi.

There were also prophets in the Early Christian Church.

Deuteronomy 18:15, 18, 20, 22; Judges 6:8; 1 Samuel 3:20; Jeremiah 1:5; 5:31; Amos 2:11-12; Matthew 1:22; Acts 13:1; 1 Corinthians 12:28; Ephesians 4:11

See **Abraham, Amos, Daniel, Elijah, Elisha, Ezekiel, God, Habakkuk, Haggai, Hosea, Isaiah, Jeremiah, Joel, Jonah, Malachi, Micah, Moses, Nahum, Obadiah, prophecy, prophesy, Zechariah, Zephaniah**

prophetess (PHAH-fuh-tus) *noun:*

A prophetess is a woman who is a prophet. Miriam and Deborah are biblical examples of prophetesses.

Exodus 15:20; Judges 4:4-16

See **Deborah, Miriam, prophecy, prophet,**

prophetic (pruh-FET-ik) *adjective:*

Prophetic describes someone or something as related to a prophet or prophecy. For example, a prophetic oracle is a message from God spoken by a prophet.

See **God, message, oracle, prophecy, prophet**

propitiate (proh-PISH-ee-ayt) *verb:*

To propitiate is to remove the cause for judgment against a person. To propitiate means also to lessen a person's anger and thus become a friend.

The death of Jesus Christ propitiated God's anger for the sins of all people. Thus, sinners were reconciled to God and became His friends.

See **death, judgment, propitiation, reconcile, sin, sinners**

propitiation (proh-PISH-ee-AY-shun) *noun:*

Propitiation is the act of atoning for the sins of another. Propitiation provides a way to turn aside the punishment a person deserves. It means to turn away the wrath of God. The Greek word for propitiation is related to the mercy seat in the Temple.

The doctrine of propitiation is based on these facts: Sin separates people from God. It offends His holiness. The justice of God must be satisfied to provide reconciliation. His anger against sin must be set aside. Therefore, the death of Jesus Christ propitiated the wrath of God. God himself provided the sacrifice His justice demanded. He offered His only Son as the atoning sacrifice for sin. This shows that God is just and also loving and forgiving.

Propitiation is one way the doctrine of the Atonement has been explained.

Romans 3:21-26; 1 John 2:1-2

See **ark, atonement, Christ, death, doctrine, expiation, forgiveness, God, holi-**

ness, Jesus, justice, love, mercy, mercy seat, propitiate, reconciliation, sacrifice, salvation, Septuagint, sin, Son of God

propositional truth (PRAHP-uh-ZISH-uh-nul TREWTH) *noun phrase:*

Propositional truth is the way some people believe revelation and inspiration happened. Revelation is understood as true information about God. It is claimed that this information is recorded in the Bible. This truth about God can be understood through reason.

Propositional truth also includes ideas about the beginning of the world and of history. The information in the Bible is believed to be true to the facts of science. Propositional truths are revealed facts about God and the world. These facts form the basis of Christian faith. God is the source of these facts. The Bible contains these truths that are believed to be the thoughts of God.

Fundamentalism puts special stress on propositional truth. Wesleyan scholars do not deny that there are propositional truths in the Bible. But the difference is that they do not stress them. Rather, Wesleyans stress that God reveals *himself,* not truths *about* himself, in Scripture. Wesleyans believe the purpose of revelation is to reveal God as Creator and Redeemer.

See **Bible, Creator, fundamentalism, inerrant, inspiration of the Bible, reason, redeemer, revelation, truth, Wesleyanism**

proselyte (PRAHS-uh-liet)

1. *noun:* A proselyte is a convert from one religion or denomination to another. Many early Christians were Gentile proselytes to Judaism (Acts 2:5, 10; 6:5; 13:43, 50).

2. *verb:* To proselyte is to convert someone to a new religion or denomination.

See **Christian, convert, denomination, Gentile, God-fearer, Judaism, religion**

prostitute (PRAHS-tuh-tewt) *noun:*

See **harlot**

Protestant (PRAH-tuh-stunt)

1. *proper adjective:* Protestant describes the part of Christianity that stresses justification by grace through faith alone.

2. *proper noun:* A Protestant was one who protested against errors in the Roman Catholic church. This began in the 1500s. Leaders of the early Protestant Reformation included Martin Luther, John Calvin, and Huldreich Zwingli. They said that any beliefs not taught in Scripture should be rejected. That is why they rejected certain Roman Catholic doctrines. The doctrine of purgatory and the doctrine of salvation through good works were two doctrines they refused to accept. Protestants stress the priesthood of all believers and the importance of Scripture over tradition.

See **John Calvin, doctrine, good works, indulgence, justification by grace through faith alone, Martin Luther, merit, pope, priesthood, purgatory, Roman Catholic, salvation, Scripture, tradition, Huldreich Zwingli**

Protestant Reformation (PRAH-tuh-stunt REF-ohr-MAY-shun) *proper noun phrase:*

See **Protestant, reformation**

Protestantism (PRAH-tuh-stunt-IZ-um) *proper noun:*

Protestantism is the group of denominations and doctrines that came from the 16th-century Protestant Reformation. The denominations that form Protestantism teach justification by grace through faith alone. They teach that human efforts have nothing to do with reconciliation with God. They teach that the Bible is the most important source for what Christians should believe. All other sources must submit to the Bible.

Romans 3:21-26; 5:1-5; Galatians 3:10-29

See **Bible, denomination, doctrine, new birth, justification, justification by grace through faith alone, Protestant, Protestant Reformation, regeneration, reformation, reconciliation**

proverb (PRAH-verb) *noun:*

A proverb is a short, wise saying that gives helpful guidance based on experience. The Hebrew word for *proverb* refers to teaching by using figures of speech. Old Testament proverbs include riddles, parables, and difficult sayings. Israel borrowed many of its proverbs from other nations. But Israel believed that reverence for God was the source of all wisdom.

Israel used proverbs to teach young people the wisdom learned from earlier generations. Proverbs help those who follow their guidance to find success. The best examples of Hebrew proverbs are found in the Book of Proverbs.

See **Hebrew, Israel, parable, Proverbs, reverence, Solomon, wisdom**

Proverbs (PRAH-verbz) *proper noun:*

Proverbs is the name of a book in the Old Testament. It is one of the five books of wisdom poetry. The book is a collection of the proverbs of the wise men of Israel across many years. King Solomon and King Hezekiah helped collect the proverbs in this book.

See **Hezekiah, Israel, Old Testament, proverb, Solomon, wisdom**

providence (PRAH-vuh-duns) *noun:*

Providence is the care and direction that God gives to the world. It is the way He shows His love and concern for His creation. God created the world, and He continues to support and guide it. People do not always understand the ways that God works in the world. But Christians know He is never absent from it. God desires the best for His creation. He governs and supports the world through His love and power. "Providence" is a name sometimes given for God.

Ruth; Esther; Psalm 24:1-2; Matthew 6:24-33; 10:29-31

See **creation, deism, grace, love, pantheism, sovereign, theism, theodicy, world**

psalm (SAHM or SAHLM) *noun:*

A psalm is a hymn that was usually sung to the music of a harp. The example of Hebrew psalms are in the Book of Psalms. King David wrote many psalms.

See **David, Hebrew, hymn, Psalms**

psalmist (SAHM-ist or SAHLM-ist) *noun:*

A psalmist was a person who wrote a psalm. For example, King David was a psalmist.

See **David, Psalms**

Psalms (SAHMZ or SAHLMZ) *proper noun:*

Psalms is the name of a book of poems in the Old Testament. It is one of the five poetry or wisdom books. The Book of Psalms is also called the Psalter.

King David wrote many of the psalms in the book. Many other psalms were written in his honor. Psalms was used as a book of hymns in Temple worship. The Psalms were usually sung to the music of a harp. Psalms is from a Hebrew word that means "songs of praise."

There are several types of psalms in the book. Some psalms are prayers for God to forgive and free the people from their troubles. Other psalms thank and praise God for His salvation. Some psalms express trust in God. Still others were written for special times of worship.

Some psalms praise the kings of Israel. Others are wisdom psalms that talk about the life and ways of God. There are also teaching psalms and psalms that praise Jerusalem.

See **David, faith, forgiveness, freedom, Hebrew, hymn, Jerusalem, Jerusalem (map 7), Old Testament, praise, prayer, psalmist, salvation, temple, wisdom, worship**

Psalter (SAHL-ter) *proper noun:*

The Psalter is another name for the Book of Psalms.

See **Psalms**

Pseudepigrapha (SOO-duh-PIG-ruh-fuh) *proper noun:*

The Pseudepigrapha are religious books not included in the Bible or the Apocrypha. The books claim to be written by people such as Adam, Abraham, Enoch, Moses, and Isaiah. The people named as authors of the books did not really write them. The books were written by Jews between 200 B.C. and A.D. 100. This explains the term Pseudepigrapha. It comes from Greek words that mean "false writings."

Many of the books are very much like the books of the Bible. The Pseudepigrapha provide important help for understanding the Jews between the Old and New Testaments. But many of the books contain strange and false doctrines.

See **Apocrypha, Bible, doctrine, Greek, Jew, New Testament, Old Testament**

publican (PUB-li-kun) *noun:*

Publicans were people, usually Jews, who collected taxes for Rome from other Jews. They often cheated the people and made themselves rich. Publicans were hated by their fellow Jews. Most Jews believed that the publicans had turned against them to serve Rome. They were often viewed as pagans (Matthew 18:17). They were viewed as sinners who had no hope of forgiveness. But Jesus said that God would forgive even publicans.

There were two groups of publicans. First, there were the chief publicans, of whom Zacchaeus was an example. Second, there were common publicans, who worked for the chief publicans. Levi, who became the apostle Matthew, was one of these.

Matthew 5:46-47; 9:10-11; 10:3; 11:9; 18:17; 21:31; Mark 2:15-16; Luke 3:12; 5:27-30; 7:29; 15:1; 18:10-13; 19:1-2

See **forgiveness, Jew, Levi, Matthew, pagan, sinner, Rome, Zacchaeus**

pure (PYOOR) *adjective:*

Pure describes someone or something that is clean and free from a foreign substance. It describes something that is not mixed with anything else.

Pure in the Bible sometimes describes something or someone that has been cleansed. The bad substances have been removed. Things used in the Temple had to be made ritually pure. Pure also describes what has been cleansed from sin and made holy by God. A pure person is one who is righteous. He or she walks in the way of the Lord. A person who obeys God is pure in heart.

Exodus 25:11, 17, 24; Leviticus 24:7; Job 8:6; Psalm 12:6; Proverbs 15:26; 30:5; Matthew 5:8; Philippians 4:8; Titus 1:15; James 3:17

See **cleanse, entire sanctification, heart purity, holiness, holy, imparted righteous, righteousness, ritual, sacrifice, sanctification, sin, temple, walk**

purgatory (PER-guh-TOHR-ee) *noun:*

Purgatory is a place where people are believed to be purified enough to enter heaven.

Roman Catholics believe that penitent souls go to purgatory after death. They are cleansed in purgatory from their venial sins. Thus, they are made ready to enter heaven. Souls in purgatory may be helped by the prayers of people on earth. Only saints go directly to heaven.

Protestants and Eastern Orthodox Christians do not believe in purgatory. The doctrine of justification by grace alone through faith makes purgatory unnecessary. Purgatory is not taught by the Scriptures. It has some support in the Apocrypha (2 Maccabees 12:39-45). The Bible offers only two possible fates for people—heaven or hell.

See **Apocrypha, cleanse, Eastern Orthodoxy, fate, heaven, hell, justification, mortal sin, penitence, perfect, Protestant, pure, Roman Catholic, saint, sin, soul, venial sin**

purification (PYOOR-uh-fuh-KAY-shun) *noun:*

Purification is the process of making pure.

See **pure**

Purim (POOR-um or PYOOR-um) *proper noun:*

Purim is one of the major Jewish festivals. Purim celebrated the escape of the Jews from total destruction. This feast began during the time of Esther.

See **Esther, festival, Jew, Jewish**

purity of heart (PYOOR-uh-tee uv HAHRT) *noun phrase:*

See heart purity

Q q

Queen of Sheba (KWEEN uv SHEE-buh) *proper noun phrase:*

See **Sheba**

Qumran (kewm-RAHN) *proper noun:*

Qumran was a small community of Essenes in the desert near the northern part of the Dead Sea. The Dead Sea Scrolls were found in caves near Qumran.

See **Dead Sea, Dead Sea Scrolls, Essenes, Qumran (map 8), scroll**

Qur'an (kuh-RAN, kuh-RAHN, or KOH-run) *proper noun:*

See **Koran**

R r

rabbi (RAB-ie) *noun:*

Rabbi is the name used for a Jewish teacher of the Torah. It means "master." Rabboni is another word for rabbi (John 21:16).

A rabbi is a respected teacher who explains the law to the people. The disciples of Jesus sometimes called Him Rabbi. The chief religious leader and teacher in a Jewish congregation today is called a rabbi.

Matthew 23:7-8; John 1:38, 49; 3:2, 26; 6:25; 20:16

See **Jesus, Jew, law, synagogue, Torah**

rabboni (rab-BOHN-ie) *noun:*

See **rabbi**

raca (RAYK-uh or RAH-kuh) *noun:*

Raca was an Aramaic term used to describe people whom a person hated. The term meant that such people were completely stupid and worth nothing. Jesus said that calling another person "raca" was a very serious wrong.

Matthew 5:21-22

See **Aramaic, fool, hate**

Rachel (RAY-chul) *proper noun:*

Rachel was the second and favorite wife of Jacob. She was the mother of two sons who became tribes of Israel. Her sons were Joseph and Benjamin.

Jeremiah pictures Rachel as weeping for her children as they are taken into exile (Jeremiah 31:15).

Genesis 29—31; 35:16-20; Matthew 2:18

See **Benjamin, exile, Israel, Jacob, Jeremiah, Joseph, tribes of Israel**

Rahab (RAY-hab) *proper noun:*

Rahab was a harlot or prostitute who helped the Israelites conquer Jericho. She helped two Israelite spies to escape from Jericho. Her life was spared when Joshua and the army destroyed Jericho. Rahab was an ancestor of Jesus (Matthew 1:5). She was mentioned as a person of great faith (Hebrews 11:31).

Joshua 2:1-24; 6:17-25; James 2:25

See **faith, harlot, Israelite, Jericho, Joshua**

Ramah (RAY-muh) *proper noun:*

Ramah was a town a few miles north of Jerusalem. It was the birthplace and home of the prophet Samuel. Samuel is buried there.

Ramah was the scene of national grief after Jesus was born. Matthew relates the grief to King Herod killing the children around Bethlehem.

1 Samuel 1:1, 19-20; 2:11; 7:15-17; 8:4; 25:1; 28:3, Jeremiah 31:15; Matthew 2:16-18

See **Herod, Jerusalem, prophet, Samuel**

ransom (RAN-sum)

1. *verb:* To ransom means to make a payment to gain freedom for a captive. Jesus died and rose again to ransom sinners held captive by Satan. All who will accept His salvation can be freed from the power of sin. It is not correct to say that Jesus' death was a price paid to Satan. It was a costly sacrifice for humanity's redemption.

2. *noun:* A ransom is the price paid to gain freedom for a captive.

Exodus 21:30; Job 33:24; Psalm 49:7; Isaiah 35:10; 51:10; Matthew 20:28; Mark 10:45; 1 Timothy 2:6

See **atonement, exile, freedom, propitiation, redeem, redemption, salvation, sin**

rapture (RAP-cher)

1. *noun:* Rapture is a condition of being carried away with the emotion of joy.

2. *proper noun:* The Rapture is what will happen to living believers when Christ comes again. They will be "caught up . . . to meet the Lord" (1 Thessalonians 4:17). They will be completely changed so as to become immortal. Dead Christians will be resurrected at the same time. Thus, all believers will be forever with the Lord (1 Corinthians 15:51-53; Philippians 3:20-21; 1 John 3:2-3). The rapture of living Christians happens at the time of the second coming of Christ. They are two parts of the same event.

Dispensationalism says that the Rapture is the secret return of Christ before the Great Tribulation. The Parousia is to be expected seven years later. Many believe that Scripture does not support this view of the Second Coming.

See **dispensationalism, immortality, parousia, resurrection, Second Coming, tribulation**

reason (REE-zun)

1. *noun:* Reason is the ability humans have to think and make decisions. Humans use reason to understand the world and each other. Reason helps people settle differences.

2. *verb:* To reason means to think carefully. God reasons as well as people. But the way God thinks is far above people's reasoning. He knows and understands all things.

See **God, philosophy, propositional truth, revelation, world**

Rebecca (ruh-BEK-uh) *proper noun:*

Rebecca was the wife of Isaac and mother of twin sons, Jacob and Esau.

Genesis 24—27; Romans 9:10-13

See **Esau, Isaac, Jacob**

rebirth (ree-BERTH) *noun:*

See **new birth**

reconcile (REK-un-siel) *verb:*

To reconcile is to bring enemies together as friends. It is to create peace where there once was fighting.

The Bible teaches that sin separates people from God. Sinners have made themselves His enemies. But God loves all people and wants to make them His friends. The death of Christ showed how far God would go to reconcile sinners to himself. Sinners are made right with God when they put their faith in Jesus Christ. Thus, Christ is the means of reconciliation between people and God.

Romans 5:1-11; 2 Corinthians 5:14-21; Ephesians 2:11-22; Colossians 1:15-23

See **atonement, death, expiation, faith, justification, peace, reconciliation, right, salvation, sin**

reconciliation (REK-un-SIL-ee-AY-shun) *noun:*

Reconciliation is the act or process of reconciling.

Reconciliation is an important part of the Christian doctrine of salvation. Reconciliation with God is one result of forgiveness and justification. The relation between sinners and God is not right. Sinners have wronged God and are separated from Him.

Jesus Christ has done all that was needed to bring sinners back to God. Christ is the means of reconciliation. Reconciliation brings God and humanity together in friendship and peace. It also helps bring together all people who are reconciled to God.

Romans 5:10-11; 2 Corinthians 5:18-21; Ephesians 2:16; Colossians 1:15-23

See **atonement, doctrine, forgiveness, justification, peace, reconcile, right, salvation, sinner**

redeem (ree-DEEM) *verb:*

To redeem means to buy back. It means to return something or someone to a position that had been lost. To redeem is to set something or someone free to fulfill his or her purpose. God redeemed the children of Israel from slavery in Egypt. Slaves were sometimes redeemed from their masters for a certain price.

Christ came into the world to redeem sinners. He came to set them free from sin and return them to fellowship with God. Paul says that Christ can redeem all people from sin and death.

Exodus 6:6; 15:13; Psalms 44:26; 107:2; Isaiah 43:1; 63:9; Hosea 7:13; 13:14; Galatians 3:13; 4:5; Revelation 5:9; 14:3-4

See **atonement, fellowship, freedom, lost, ransom, salvation, sin, slave**

redeemer (ree-DEEM-er) *noun:*

A redeemer is someone who redeems others. He helps those who cannot redeem, or free, themselves. Christ is the Redeemer of the world.

Job 19:25; Isaiah 41:14; 43:14; 48:17; 54:5; Jeremiah 50:34

See **atonement, Christ, freedom, redeem, redemption, Savior**

redemption (ree-DEMP-shun) *noun:*

Redemption is the process of redeeming someone or something. Redemption is another word for salvation.

1 Corinthians 1:30; Ephesians 1:7; 4:30; Colossians 1:14; Hebrews 9:12, 15

See **forgiveness, new birth, reconciliation, redeem, redeemer, salvation**

Red Sea (RED SEE) *proper noun:*

The Red Sea is a long gulf of the Indian Ocean. The Red Sea is southwest of Israel between Africa and Arabia.

The water that the Israelites crossed on their way from Egypt to Canaan was the Sea of Reeds. The Sea of Reeds was one of two northern branches of the Red Sea. The Sea of Reeds was more shallow than the Red Sea. (This story is told in Exodus 13:17—14:29.)

Exodus 15:4, 22; Numbers 14:25; 21:4; 33:10-11; Deuteronomy 1:40; 2:1; Joshua 2:10; 4:23; 24:6; Acts 7:36; Hebrews 11:29

See **Canaan, Egypt, Exodus, Israelites, Moses, Red Sea (map 2), Sea of Reeds (map 2)**

reformation (REF-ohr-MAY-shun) *noun:*

Reformation is the act of correcting what is wrong in a person or organized group.

The Reformation was an attempt to correct errors in the Church in the 1500s. There had been a number of attempts to reform the Church before then. Some of the attempts succeeded but only in a limited way. Martin Luther, John Calvin, John Knox, and Huldreich Zwingli were important leaders of the Reformation. They pointed out errors in what was taught about salvation, the Bible, and the Church. The Reformers and their supporters finally had to leave the Roman Catholic Church. Those Christians who started the Reformation were called Protestants, from the verb "protest."

See **Bible, John Calvin, church, Martin Luther, Protestant, Roman Catholic, sacrament, salvation, Huldreich Zwingli**

Reformed tradition (ree-FOHRMD truh-DI-shun) *noun phrase:*

The Reformed tradition was one of the four groups that developed from the Reformation. They were the Lutheran, the Reformed, the Anabaptist, and the Anglican. Other groups developed later. The Reformed tradition developed from the theology of Huldreich Zwingli and especially John Calvin. The theology of the Reformed tradition is often called Calvinism. But the theology of the Reformed tradition is not exactly the same as the theology of Calvin. Today the Reformed tradition is represented by a number of denominations.

See **Anabaptist, Anglican, John Calvin, Calvinism, denomination, Lutheran, Protestant, reformation, theology, tradition, Huldreich Zwingli**

regenerate

1. (ree-JEN-er-ayt) *verb:* To regenerate is to cause someone to be born again spiritually. Sinners are spiritually dead. They receive spiritual life from God when they are converted. It is as if their lives are started over again. It is as if they are created new. This is what it means for God to regenerate a sinner.

2. (ree-JEN-er-it) *adjective:* Regenerate describes a person who has been born again. A regenerate person is one who has become a born-again Christian (Titus 3:5).

See **born again, convert, life, regeneration, sin, sinner, spiritual**

regeneration (REE-jen-er-AY-shun) *noun:*

Regeneration is the result of the saving work of God in the hearts of sinners. He causes them to be born again. Regeneration is the spiritual work of God that completely changes sinners. Regeneration refers to the same religious experience as justification, adoption, conversion, and initial sanctification.

John 3:1-8; Ephesians 2:1-10; Titus 3:4-7; 1 Peter 1:23

See **adoption, born again, conversion, heart, initial sanctification, justification, new birth, regenerate, spiritual**

Rehoboam (REE-huh-BOH-um) *proper noun:*

Rehoboam was the first king of Judah, the Southern Kingdom. He was the son of Solomon who became king after his father. The united kingdom of Israel divided after the death of Solomon. Thus, Rehoboam became the first king of the Southern Kingdom of Judah. He ruled for 17 years. He was an evil king.

1 Kings 11:41—12:24; 14:21-31; 2 Chronicles 9:31—12:16

See **Israel, Jeroboam, Judah, Solomon, Rehoboam (time line)**

religion (ree-LI-jun) *noun:*

Religion is an attitude and practice of complete devotion to a god. This god may be an idol or just the forces of nature. However, not all religions have a god as their object of worship. Some religions speak of a "highest reality" that they worship. This highest reality is not personal deity. Some religions worship more than one god.

There are five major world religions: Buddhism, Christianity, Hinduism, Islam, and Judaism.

See **Buddhism, Christianity, deity, devotion, God, god, Hinduism, idol, Islam, Judaism, theism, worship**

religious (ree-LI-jus) *adjective:*

Religious describes someone or something marked by its relation to religion. For example, a religious belief is a belief about religion. A religious person is one who follows closely his or her religion.

See **Christian, monk, nun, religion, saint**

remnant (REM-nunt) *noun:*

A remnant is a part of something that is left behind.

The Old Testament prophets used the term *remnant* in a special way. The prophets warned Israel and Judah that many of them would be taken into exile. This would be the judgment of God for their sin. But God promised that some of the people would later return to their home country. These people were the remnant.

The people of Judah were taken into exile, and a remnant did return to Palestine. The prophets gave hope that this small remnant would form a new Israel.

Early Christians believed that the Church fulfilled the promise of the remnant.

1 Chronicles 11:8; Isaiah 4:2-6; 6:13; 7:3; 10:19; Ezekiel 6:7-10; 9:8; 36:24-32; Amos 9:8-15; Micah 2:12; Haggai 1:12-14; Zechariah 8:12; 13:9; Matthew 3:9; 22:14; Romans 9:24-33; 11:1-12; Galatians 6:16; Ephesians 2:18-22; 1 Peter 2:9

See **branch, church, exile, Israel, Judah, judgment, prophet**

Reorganized Church of Jesus Christ of Latter Day Saints (ree-OHR-guh-niezd CHERCH uv JEE-zus KRIEST uv LAT-er DAY SAYNTS) *proper noun phrase:*

See **Mormon**

repent (ree-PENT) *verb:*

To repent is to turn from sin toward God. One who repents shows sorrow for the sins he or she has committed. But to repent is more than just to be sorry. A person who repents asks God for forgiveness. He or she asks God to help him or her stop sinning and to obey Him. To repent is to change completely, not simply to regret past sins. Repentance is possible because of the prevenient grace of God.

The Old Testament says that God repented about creating man (Genesis 6:6). This means God was sorry He had made man. Sometimes He changed His course of action in the way He dealt with Israel.

Genesis 6:5, 7; Exodus 32:1-35; Judges 2:18; 1 Samuel 15:11, 35; Jeremiah 18:8; 26:19; Ezekiel 14:6; 18:30; Matthew 3:2; 4:17; 12:41; John 3:1-9; Acts 2:38; Revelation 2:5, 16, 21

See **conversion, forgiveness, grace, justification, mercy, new birth, prevenient grace, reconciliation, sin**

repentance (ree-PEN-tuns) *noun:*

Repentance is the act of repenting. Repentance is an important part of the Christian faith. Repentance means to confess one's sins to God. Repentance includes turning away from a life of sin. It means turning toward God.

See **confess, conversion, faith, forgiveness, repent, salvation, sin**

reprobate (REP-ruh-bayt)

1. *adjective:* Reprobate describes people who are so evil that they cut themselves off from God. They have rejected the love of God time after time. Finally God leaves them alone. They go on to the destruction they have chosen.

2. *noun:* A reprobate is a person whose evil causes God to finally leave them alone to the destruction he or she has chosen.

Jeremiah 6:30; Romans 1:28; 1 Corinthians 9:27; 2 Timothy 3:8; Titus 1:16

See **accursed, condemnation, damnation, evil, hell, lost, wages of sin**

responsibility (ree-SPAHN-suh-BIL-uh-tee) *noun:*

Responsibility is a task someone is given to carry out. It also means being able to act in the way one knows to be right.

Responsibility starts with a knowledge of what is morally or religiously correct. It includes the freedom to do what is good. Responsibility is the ability to act on that knowledge. To accept responsibility means to accept the results of one's actions. This may be praise or it may be blame. This is called moral responsibility.

Ezekiel 18:19-23; Romans 1:18—3:20

See **conscience, ethics, freedom, morality, right, sin, tree of knowledge**

rest of faith (REST uv FAYTH) *noun phrase:*

Rest of faith is a phrase sometimes used in the Holiness Movement. It means entire sanctification. The phrase comes from the Hebrews 4:1-12.

See **entire sanctification, Hebrews, Holiness Movement**

restitution (RES-tuh-TEW-shun) *noun:*

Restitution is an act in which something wrong is made right. Sometimes it means returning to its owner something that was stolen. Something that has been taken wrongly is put back in its proper place. Sometimes it means correcting a wrong done to the good name of another.

For example, Zacchaeus promised to return any money that he had falsely taken from anyone. People who become Christians will try to make restitution whenever possible.

Leviticus 24:18; Luke 19:1-10

See **justice, reconciliation, repent, right, righteousness, Zacchaeus**

resurrection (REZ-uh-REK-shun) *noun:*

Resurrection is a return to life after death. The Old Testament refers to resurrection in two places: Isaiah and Daniel.

Resurrection is an important doctrine in the New Testament. It teaches that the dead, both the righteous and the sinful, will experience resurrection. It is not completely clear how this will happen. But God will make it happen at the end of the world. Then He will judge all people. The righteous will be raised to eternal life. Sinners will go to eternal punishment.

The resurrection of Christ is the source of the Christian hope for resurrection. Jesus called himself "the resurrection and the life" (John 11:25). The resurrection will happen at the second coming of Christ. Christians who have died will be raised to a new life. They will be given a spiritual body that cannot die. No one fully knows what the spiritual body will be like. But it will be like the body Christ had when He rose from the dead. Death will have no power over the resurrected body.

The new birth is also a kind of resurrection. The old life of sin is crucified with Christ. Christians are given eternal life through the Holy Spirit.

Jesus raised a few people from the dead during His ministry on earth. These were not resurrections in the full sense. All of these people died again at a later time. They, too, hope for the final resurrection to immortality.

Isaiah 25:8; 26:29; Daniel 12:2; Matthew 22:31-32; 27:50-53; Mark 12:26-27; Luke 7:11-17; 20:37-38; John 5:25-29; 11:25; Acts 24:15; 1 Corinthians 15:12-28; Revelation 20:4-15

See **doctrine, eternal punishment, eternal life, hope, immortality, judgment, new birth, righteous, Second Coming**

retribution (RE-truh-BYEW-shun) *noun:*

Retribution is punishment that someone receives because of the evil he or she has done. Retribution is given only to punish. Its purpose is not to make the person good who did wrong. Its purpose is to do justice so that right wins over wrong. The death penalty is a severe form of retribution by a society. Hell is the final retribution of sinners who refuse to repent.

Matthew 11:20-24; Romans 26:6-11; 12:19—13:4; 2 Thessalonians 1:4-10; Revelation 9:20-21

See **death, hell, justice, penalty, repent, revenge, right, wages of sin, wrath**

Reuben (REW-bun) *proper noun:*

1. Reuben was the oldest of the 12 sons of Jacob. The descendants of Reuben became one of the 12 tribes of Israel.

2. Reuben was the name of the land occupied by the tribe of Reuben.

Genesis 30; 35; 37; 42; 49

See **Canaan, Israel, Jacob, Reuben (map 3), tribes of Israel**

reveal (ree-VEEL) *verb:*

To reveal means to make someone or something known. To reveal is to make a revelation. God revealed himself to His creation in many ways. The most important and complete way that He revealed himself was through Jesus Christ, His Son.

See **creation, revelation, son**

revelation (REV-uh-LAY-shun)

1. *noun:* Revelation is the process of making something known that has been hidden. Revelation is the process God used to make himself

known to His creation. God shows who He is through what He does. God has also shown who He is through His acts in creation and redemption.

God acted in history to show His love. He made a covenant with Abraham. He acted in the Exodus events to redeem Israel from slavery in Egypt.

God spoke through the prophets to show that He defends the oppressed. He showed that He loves justice and mercy. He also showed that He judges evil. He judged His people when they were not faithful to Him.

But God made the most perfect revelation of His love in Jesus Christ. God became incarnate in Christ. Christ showed that God could create the world and could redeem it as well. The love of God for the world has no limit. It is so great that He gave His Son for the sins of the world. God fully showed us who He is in Christ. The second coming of Christ will complete the revelation of God as Redeemer.

The Bible is the inspired record of how God revealed himself. The revelation of God is perfect. The way of salvation is revealed without error in the Bible. The Bible is not the revelation. God is the Revelation. But the Bible is the final and faithful record of God's revelation.

Some scholars speak of general and special revelation. By general revelation they mean that creation reveals certain things about God. This is seen in nature. By special revelation they mean the special acts of redemption that reveal God. This is seen in the Bible. Some say that special revelation can be understood only through faith.

2. *proper noun:* The Book of Revelation is the last book in the New Testament. It was written by a prophet called John (Revelation 1:1-3; 22:6-9). Most people believe this is the same one who wrote the Gospel of John. The book was addressed to Christians of Asia Minor who were being persecuted. The book is a revelation from Jesus Christ of hope for the future.

Revelation is a difficult book to understand. The word pictures it uses to describe future events may be explained in different ways. This strange, apocalyptic language helps people imagine what the future will be like. Scholars have never completely agreed on all that the book means. But the Book of Revelation makes it clear that the future is under the control of God. The return of Christ will be the final revelation of the victory of God.

Isaiah 40:5; John 1:1-5; Romans 1:17-18; 2:5; 16:25; Galatians 1:12; Ephesians 3:3; 1 Peter 1:13; Revelation 1:1

See **Abraham, apocalyptic, covenant, creation, exile, Exodus, faith, future, God, holiness, Incarnation, inspiration, John, justice, love, mercy, millennium, propositional truth, redemption, righteousness, salvation, Second Coming, word**

revenge (ree-VENJ)

1. *verb:* To revenge is to cause other people harm in return for their evil deeds.

2. *noun:* Revenge is the harm done to other people to pay back their evil deeds. Revenge is a way of trying to bring justice when wrong has been done. The nations around Israel generally demanded punishment that was greater than the crime. But the law in Israel, an "eye for eye," sets limits on revenge (Exodus 21:23-25; Leviticus 24:17-22; Deuteronomy 19:21). The New Testament teaches that no person should seek revenge (Matthew 5:38-42; Romans 12:19-21).

See **evil, judgment, justice, law, retribution**

reverence (REV-er-uns) *noun:*

Reverence is a feeling or attitude of deep respect, love, and adoration. This usually refers to a person's attitude toward God. This may be shown through kneeling before Him or simply being obedient to Him. Reverence shows that people know that God is holy and worthy of worship.

Reverence may also refer to respect for people in authority.

Leviticus 19:30; 2 Samuel 9:6; Psalm 89:7

See **adoration, fear, God, holiness, holy, love, worship**

Revised Standard Version (ree-VIEZD STAN-derd VER-zhun) *proper noun phrase:*

See **Bible, translate, version**

revival (ree-VIE-vul) *noun:*

Revival is the giving of new life to something that is dying. A revival of religion is a fresh religious life given to those who serve God. Interest in God and the desire to serve Him are greatly increased in revival. No human can make revival happen. The Holy Spirit brings revival. But people must obey the Holy Spirit before He can bring revival. Believers must repent of their failures to obey God. They must ask for forgiveness and turn to God completely.

Revival makes people more aware of the holiness and love of God. It makes them more aware of what love for God means.

Revival may also lead to the conversion of people who have not been Christians. It may happen in one person. It may happen in one church. Or it may include a whole community or country.

Revivals have often happened in the history of the church. One great revival happened in England in the 1700s. John Wesley was one of its leaders. Two great revivals have happened in the United States. They were called the First Great Awakening (1700s) and the Second Great Awakening (1800s). Other great American revivals have been led by Charles G. Finney and Dwight L. Moody. Billy Sunday and Billy Graham are also known as great leaders of revivals.

See **confess, conversion, evangelism, growth in grace, Josiah, life, love, piety, religion, repent, sin, spirit, John Wesley**

reward (ree-WOHRD)

1. *noun:* A reward is usually something that is given to a person for some good done. It is a prize or payment that one earns and deserves for being good. It may also be the natural result of good behavior. Sometimes the punishment for bad behavior is called a reward.

The New Testament teaches that Christians will receive rewards for the good they do (Matthew 5:12; 6:4-6, 18; 10:41-42; Romans 2:1-11; 4:4; 6:23; 1 Corinthians 3:14; 1 Timothy 5:18; 2 John 1:8). These rewards include hope, joy, love, peace, and life with God. But Christians do not obey God simply to get rewards. They do not earn rewards as payment for good deeds. Rewards result when Christians allow God to do what He desires in their lives.

2. *verb:* To reward is to give something to a person who has done a worthy deed.

Genesis 15:1; 1 Kings 13:6-10; Psalms 19:7-11; 58:10-11; 91:8; 137:8; Proverbs 11:18-21; Isaiah 40:10; Matthew 5:46; 10:41-42; Luke 6:23, 35; 1 Corinthians 3:14; 9:17-18; Colossians 3:24; 2 Timothy 4:14; Hebrews 11:6; Revelation 22:12

See **eternal death, eternal life, gift, hope, joy, love, obedience, peace**

right (RIET)

1. *adjective:* Right describes someone or something that is just, fair, proper, and good. The Hebrew and Greek words for *right* mean "just" and "righteous." People who have been reconciled are often described as being right with God (see Exodus 9:27; Deuteronomy 32:4; Psalm 7:9; Proverbs 12:5; Revelation 16:7).

Right is the side opposite the left. One on the right hand is considered to hold a position of power and honor (Psalm 110:1; Matthew 25:31-46; Acts 2:33).

2. *verb:* To right is to put someone or something back into its proper place or position. It means to do justice to a person who has been wronged.

3. *noun:* A right is something that properly belongs to a person. It is something he or she may justly claim as his or her own. For example, a person has a right to live (Isaiah 10:2; Jeremiah 5:28).

The phrase *the right* usually means what is just, fair, proper, and good. The right includes what people do to honor and obey God.

See **birthright, just, justice, justify, reconcile, righteous, righteousness, values**

righteous (RIE-chus)

1. *adjective:* Righteous describes something or someone who is right or just. Righteous sometimes describes what agrees with the law (Genesis 38:26).

Righteous people are those whose character and conduct are just and right. Their behavior agrees with the will of God. They are in right relation to Him. Sinners who repent of their sins and receive justification by faith are made righteous. The grace of God helps them to live righteous lives.

2. *noun:* The righteous are people who live righteous lives. The righteous are people who are in a right relation to God. Thus, the righteous are people who have been justified by God.

Genesis 18:23-28; Ezra 9:15; Job 17:9; Psalms 1:1-6; 5:12; 7:10-17; 34:15-22; 37:39; 107:42; 145:17-21; Ezekiel 18:20-26; Habakkuk 1:4, 13; 2:4; Matthew 9:13; 13:43; 23:28; 25:37, 46; Luke 18:9-14; Romans 2:5; 3:10; 5:7, 19; 1 Timothy 1:9; 2 Timothy 4:8; James 5:16; 1 John 2:1

See **Bible, God, grace, judge, just, justification, justify, law, obedience, repent, right, righteousness, scripture, will, worship**

righteousness (RIE-chus-nes) *noun:*

Righteousness is the quality or condition or being right or good. Righteousness may also mean justice.

The Bible teaches that God is righteous. But the righteousness of God does not refer to His moral character. And it does not refer to His command that people live morally. It refers instead to His saving acts. He is the Source of all righteousness. The same Greek word is used for righteousness and for justification.

The righteousness of God reconciles His fallen creation to himself. The world is brought back to its proper Lord. True worship and obedience are made possible. The righteousness of God shows that the same God is Creator, Judge, and Savior.

Deuteronomy 6:25; 9:4-6; Psalms 9:7-8; 23:3; 45:7; 71:1-24; 98:9; 103:1-18; Isaiah 11:1-5; 45:8, 22-25; 64:6; Jeremiah 9:23-24; Hosea 10:12-15; Amos 5:24; Matthew 3:15; 5:6, 10, 20; 6:33; 21:32; Luke 1:75; Romans 1:17; 3:21-26; 4:1-25; 5:17-21; 6:13-22; 8:10; 14:17; 1 Corinthians 1:26-31; 2 Corinthians 5:21; Galatians 2:15-21; 3:6, 21; 5:5; Ephesians 4:24; Philippians 1:11; 3:4-21; Titus 3:5

See **character, Christ, Christian, creation, faith, forgiveness, God, grace, Jesus, judge, just, justice, justification, justify, Lord, morality, obedience, reconcile, reconciliation, right, righteous, salvation, sanctification, sin, worship**

Rimmon (RIM-ahn) *proper noun:*

Rimmon was the personal name of the god Baal that was worshiped in Syria.

2 Kings 5:15-19

See **Baal, god, idol, Syria**

rite (RIET) *noun:*

A rite is the way a ceremony is conducted. It includes both the words and the actions. A rite is also the liturgy of a church of group of churches.

See **ceremony, liturgy, ritual**

ritual (RICH-ew-wul) *noun:*

A ritual is a ceremony repeated in a group. A ritual has special meaning for those who take part in it. A ritual is usually one of several related acts. These acts and their meanings are central to the life of the community. They explain why the community came to be and why it exists.

The meaning of a ritual is learned by taking part in the life of the community. It is related to the past. Each generation keeps alive the meaning of ritual. It also passes the meaning of ritual along to the future community.

Ritual is usually practiced in a religious group such as a church. But some groups that are not religious also practice rituals.

Rituals played an important part in Israel. For example, the ritual of Passover reminded Israel of how God freed them from Egypt. Each denomination today has some rituals of its own. Some rituals are practiced by most Christians, such as the Lord's Supper and baptism. The meaning of each of these comes from things that Jesus did and said. These rituals help people know the meaning of Christ and the Church. They also give direction for the Christian life.

Exodus 12:3-28; Numbers 9:5; Joshua 5:10; 2 Kings 23:21; 2 Chronicles 30:13; Matthew 26:26-30; 28:19; Luke 22:14-20; Acts 8:12, 38; 9:18; 10:48

See **baptism, celebrate, ceremony, community, Eucharist, festival, liturgy, Lord's Supper, Passover, ritual, sacrament, sacrifice, worship**

Roman (ROH-mun)

1. *proper adjective:* Roman describes a person or thing that is related to Rome. For example, a Roman soldier was a man who served in the army of Rome. All of the area ruled by Rome was known as the Roman Empire.

2. *proper noun:* A Roman is a citizen of Rome. Romans were the people who lived in the city of Rome. Romans were also all the citizens of Rome who lived in the Roman empire.

Acts 25:16; 16:21, 37-38; 22:25-29; 23:27; 25:16

See **Roman Catholic, Rome, Rome (map 11)**

Roman Catholic (ROH-mun KATH-uh-lik)

1. *proper adjective:* Roman Catholic describes that branch of Christianity whose leader is the pope, the bishop of Rome. It is called the Roman Catholic Church.

2. *proper noun:* A Roman Catholic is a member of the Roman Catholic Church.

See **Catholic, Christianity, church, pope**

Romans (ROH-munz) *proper noun:*

Romans is the name of a book in the New Testament. It is one of the epistles. It is a letter written by the apostle Paul to the Christians in Rome in Italy. It was written about A.D. 60. He wrote to let them know about his plans to visit Rome. He hoped they would help support him in his planned mission to evangelize Spain.

The letter reminds Paul's readers about the character of the gospel. It stresses justification by grace through faith alone as the center of the gospel. It also stresses sanctification as the true fruit of righteousness through faith in Christ.

See **epistle, evangelism, faith, gospel, grace, Italy, justification, mission, Paul, righteousness, Rome (map 11), sanctification**

Rome (ROHM) *proper noun:*

Rome is an important city and capital of Italy today. In Bible times, Rome was also an important city. It became the capital of a world empire. Rome ruled all of the Middle East and Mediterranean world. It was during the time of the great Roman Empire that Jesus was born. Also the events of the New Testament took place during the Roman Empire.

Acts 2:10; 18:2; 19:21; 23:11; Romans 1:7, 15; 2 Timothy 1:17

See **Augustus, Caesar, Herod, Mediterranean Sea, Middle East, Roman, Rome (map 11)**

Rosh Hashanah (RAHSH hah-SHAH-nuh) *proper noun phrase:*

See **festival**

RSV, *abbreviation:*

RSV is an abbreviation for the *Revised Standard Version* of the Bible.

See **Bible, translate, version**

rule of faith (REWL uv FAYTH) *noun phrase:*

Some Early Church fathers used the phrase "rule of faith" to mean the central Christian doctrines. The rule of faith was believed to be the teachings of the apostles. The early fathers believed these teachings agreed with the Scriptures and were without error. The fathers used the rule of faith to respond to the errors of heretics. Later, the rule of faith came to include the creeds of the Church. All of this is a part of what is called tradition.

See **apostle, creed, doctrine, heretic, scripture, tradition**

rule of faith and practice (REWL uv FAYTH and PRAK-tus) *noun phrase:*

The rule of faith and practice is the Bible. The Bible is the measure by which Christians know what to believe about God. It is also the measure by which Christians know how to live. Most Protestants believe that the Bible is the measure for judging all doctrines and ethics. Roman Catholics also stress the importance of the Bible. But they believe that the teachings of the Church are equally important.

See **Bible, doctrine, ethics, faith, inspiration, morality, Protestant, Revelation, Roman Catholic**

Ruth (REWTH) *proper noun:*

1. Ruth is the name of a woman in the Old Testament. A book in the Old Testament is named for her. Ruth was a native of the land of Moab. Her husband died and thus left her a widow. She moved to the land of Israel

and married Boaz, an Israelite. They became the great-grandparents of King David. Thus, Ruth was an ancestor of Jesus. Perhaps the Bible told her story to teach the Jews an important lesson. God was able to use Gentiles to fulfill His purposes.

2. Ruth is a book in the Old Testament. It is one of the history books.

See **Boaz, David, Gentile, Israelite, Jesus, Moab, Old Testament**

S s

Sabaoth (SAB-ee-ohth or SAB-ay-oth) *proper noun:*

Sabaoth is a Greek word that means "hosts." A host is a great crowd of people, such as soldiers. The Bible sometimes refers to God as the "Lord of Sabaoth" or "Lord of Hosts" (Romans 9:29; James 5:4, KJV, RSV). The phrase probably means that all created things and beings are under God's control.

See **God, Lord**

Sabbath (SAB-uth) *proper noun:*

Sabbath means "rest." It refers to the weekly day of rest and worship for Jews. The Bible says God rested on the seventh day of creation. So Saturday is the Jewish day of rest, that is, their Sabbath. It is also called the Seventh Day. God told the Jews to keep the Sabbath holy. This was the fourth of the Ten Commandments (Exodus 16:23; Leviticus 23:3). The Sabbath began at sunset on Friday and ended at sunset on Saturday.

Special sacrifices were offered to God on the Sabbath. Limits were put on what the people could do on the Sabbath. Pharisees in the time of Jesus applied Sabbath laws to every detail of life. The Sabbath became a burden to the people. Jesus did some things on the Sabbath that made the Pharisees angry. He said that the Sabbath should be a time of worship, joy, and service.

God told the people of Israel to let their land rest once every seven years. The fields were not plowed, and the vines were not trimmed. This was called the Sabbath Year. The poor people received all that grew on the land in the Sabbath Year.

The first day of the week became the day of worship for the early Christians. It celebrated the resurrection of Christ, which took place on this day. They called it "the Lord's Day." Christians later began thinking of Sunday as the Christian Sabbath.

Exodus 16:23; 23:10-11; Leviticus 23:3; 25:3-7; Deuteronomy 15:1-8; Matthew 12:9-13; Mark 2:23-28; Luke 13:10-17; Acts 2:1; 13:14; Revelation 1:10

See **Christian, Lord's Day, Pharisee, rest of faith, resurrection, sacrifice, Ten Commandments, worship**

Sabbath Rest (SAB-uth REST) *proper noun phrase:*

See **rest of faith, Sabbath**

Sabbath Year (SAB-uth YEER) *proper noun phrase:*

See **Sabbath**

sackcloth (SAK-KLAHTH) *noun:*

Sackcloth was clothing of dark, coarse cloth made of goat hair. It was usually worn during times of mourning. Sacks were usually made of the same material.

People wore sackcloth in Bible times to show their grief, sorrow, mourning, or penitence. It was worn next to the skin. It meant the same as wearing black sometimes means today. Prophets often wore sackcloth when they warned the people of the coming judgment of God.

Genesis 37:34; 2 Samuel 3:31; 1 Kings 20:31; 2 Kings 6:30; 19:1-2; Isaiah 20:2; 32:11; Revelation 6:12; 11:3

See **Bible, God, judgment, penitence, prophet**

sacrament (SAK-ruh-munt) *noun:*

A sacrament is a special act Christians do as a sign of grace. Sacraments are outward signs of an inward grace given by Christ to Christians.

Sacraments are usually based on special events in the life of Jesus. He was baptized by John the Baptist. He ate a final Passover meal with His disciples. The sacraments of baptism and the Lord's Supper are based on these events. Christians remember the meaning of these events when they worship together in these sacraments. Christ is present to Christians in a special way through the sacraments.

Protestants usually practice two sacraments. They are baptism and the Lord's Supper. The Roman Catholic Church and the Eastern Orthodox churches practice seven sacraments. Some Protestant groups do not observe any sacraments. Protestants who observe sacraments believe that the benefits of the sacraments can be received only through faith.

Christians do not always agree on the part that the sacraments play in salvation. Some Christians believe that people are saved through the sacrament of baptism. Others believe that sacraments are only for people who have already become Christians.

The sacraments are usually given to Christians by priests or ministers.

Matthew 3:6-16; 26:20-29; Mark 1:9-11; 14:12-25; Luke 3:21-22; 22:14-23; John 2:1-10; 13:1-11; Acts 2:38-41; 8:16

See **baptism, Christ, church, disciple, Eastern Orthodoxy, Eucharist, faith, grace, Jesus, John, Lord's Supper, minister, Passover, priest, Protestant, Roman Catholic, salvation**

sacred (SAY-krud) *adjective:*

Sacred describes someone or something that belongs to a god. Thus, sacred describes someone or something that is holy. Sacred things are related to religion or religious practices. Thus, a building or a song may be called sacred.

See **consecration, God, god, holiness, holy, religion, sanctify**

sacrifice (SAK-ruh-fies)

1. *verb:* To sacrifice is to make or offer a sacrifice.

2. *noun:* A sacrifice is something valuable that is offered to God. It was usually an animal, fruit, or grain in the Old Testament. The word *sacrifice* comes from a Latin word meaning "made sacred."

Sacrifices were an important part of the celebration of worship in Israel. The people were supposed to bring perfect offerings to the Tabernacle or Temple for sacrifice. These offerings became sacred to God.

There were many kinds of sacrifices offered in Old Testament times. These included the burnt offering, cereal offering, sin offering, guilt offering, and peace offering (Leviticus 6:8—7:18).

Cattle, sheep, and doves were killed as a part of the ritual of animal sacrifices. The priests used bowls to collect the blood that they sprinkled on the altar (Exodus 24:6-8; 1 Samuel 14:31-35; 1 Kings 6:15). All or part of the animal was then burned. The part of the animal that was not burned became food for the priests. Sometimes the worshipers also shared in a communion meal of the sacrificed animal.

Sacrifices were made daily in the Tabernacle and, later, in the Temple. But they were especially offered on the Sabbath and feast days. Jews no longer offered sacrifices after the Temple was destroyed in A.D. 70.

Sacrifices were a part of the covenant between God and the people of Israel. They were one means God chose to provide atonement. Sacrifices in the Old Testament were offered to celebrate the grace and forgiveness of God. They were not to be offered to try to gain the favor of God. The people of Israel sometimes failed to understand this. They accepted the false belief of their pagan neighbors that sacrifices made God gracious. Thus, their sacrifices became merely empty rituals. This explains why the prophets and Jesus often spoke against offering only sacrifices. They knew that what God really wanted was obedience, not just sacrifices (1 Samuel 15:22; Psalm 51:16-17; Jeremiah 7:21-26; Hosea 6:6; Amos 5:21-25; Matthew 9:13; 12:7).

The New Testament uses the language of sacrifice to refer to the death of Christ. He is the "Lamb of God" who takes away the sins of the world (John 1:29, 36; 1 Peter 1:18-19; Revelation 5:6-10; 13:8). He is the true Passover Lamb, whom God made a sin offering (Romans 8:3; 1 Corinthians 5:6-8; 2 Corinthians 5:14—6:1; Hebrews 9—10). The Book of Hebrews especially stresses Christ as the perfect sacrifice (Hebrews 1:3; 2:9, 14; 9:12, 17, 22, 25-28; 10:10, 12-14, 18; 13:12, 20). He provides atonement and reconciliation with God. Christ's death shows that God loves sinners. He wants them to trust in Christ for salvation.

The apostle Paul urged Christians to give themselves to God as living sacrifices (Romans 12:1-2). Paul meant that Christians should give their lives in complete worship and obedience to God. Their lives should show their thanks for His forgiveness. Christians do not live simply to please themselves. They give themselves freely to serve God and all those for whom Christ died (2 Corinthians 5:11—6:10).

Sometimes sacrifices refer to the things people do without or give up. They usually do this because they want to, but sometimes they are forced to.

See **altar, atonement, blood, celebrate, covenant, expiation, festival, forgiveness, grace, Holy Communion, Lamb of God, offering, pagan, propitiation, reconciliation, ritual, Sabbath, sacred, tabernacle, temple, worship**

sacrificial death (SAK-ruh-FISH-ul DETH) *noun phrase:*

Sacrificial death refers to the death of Christ as an atonement for sin.

See **atonement, death, expiation, propitiation, sacrifice**

Sadducee (SAD-yew-see) *proper noun:*

The Sadducees were a group of Jewish leaders during the time of Jesus. The Sadducees believed that only the Torah should be accepted as having authority. They said that the rest of the Old Testament was not Scripture. The Sadducees did not believe in the resurrection nor in a final judgment.

The Sadducees controlled the priesthood and the Temple. They represented the Jews to the Romans. They cooperated with the Romans who ruled Palestine. The Sadducees were wealthy and were not liked by the people. Jesus opposed the Sadducees. The Sadducees disappeared after Jerusalem was destroyed in A.D. 70.

Matthew 3:7; 16:1; 22:23; Mark 12:18; Luke 20:27; Acts 4:1; 5:17; 23:6

See **judgment, Old Testament, Palestine (map 8), Pentateuch, Pharisee, priest, resurrection, Roman, Scripture, sect, Temple, Torah**

saint (SAYNT) *noun:*

A saint is a person who is holy because he or she belongs to God. Saints are known for their pure lives and devotion to God. *Saint* in the New Testament was a name given to all Christians.

Saint is used today in two special ways. (1) It is used to refer to a person of great virtue, piety, and moral character. (2) Roman Catholics use the term for people known for their great holiness of life. They may also be called saints because they died as martyrs, or miracles were done through them. They are called saints only after their deaths.

Daniel 7:18-21; 8:31; Matthew 27:52; Acts 9:13; 26:10; Romans 8:27; 1 Corinthians 6:2; Ephesians 1:1; 5:3; 1 Thessalonians 3:13; Revelation 5:8; 13:7-10

See **godliness, holiness, initial sanctification, martyr, miracle, piety, pure, purgatory, regeneration, Roman Catholic, testimony, virtue**

Salem (SAY-lum) *proper noun:*

See **Jerusalem**

Salt Sea (SALT SEE) *proper noun:*

See **Dead Sea**

salvation (sal-VAY-shun) *noun:*

Salvation is the complete process by which God redeems His creation. The Bible tells the many ways God acted to bring salvation to His world.

Salvation is the love of God at work in the world. It is the way God takes away sins and reconciles people to himself. Salvation is for all who call upon God for forgiveness.

God completed His work of salvation through His Son, Jesus Christ. Full reconciliation with God is possible through Christ, who sets people free from sin. The Holy Spirit works through the Church to make Christ known to the world. Salvation makes possible the holy fellowship of the Church.

All Christians agree that there are two parts to salvation. They are justification and sanctification. Christian do not fully agree on the order or content of these parts. Protestants believe the justification returns believers to favor with God. Sanctification is the method God uses to make Christians holy. This begins in justification. Wesleyans speak of initial and entire sanctification. These are two crises or stages within the total process of salvation. Salvation will be completed at the second coming of Christ and the final resurrection.

Genesis 49:18; Exodus 12:31—15:21; 1 Samuel 2:1; Psalms 3:8; 74:12; 89:26; Isaiah 12:2-3; Luke 1:69, 77; 19:9; Acts 13:26, 47; Romans 1:16; 10:10; 13:11; 2 Corinthians 6:2; 7:10; Philippians 2:12-13; Revelation 12:10

See **atonement, bondage, Christ, Christian perfection, church, creation, Exodus, fellowship, forgiveness, glorification, God, holiness, Jesus, justification, love, process in sanctification, reconcile, reconciliation, redemption, sanctification, save, Second Coming, sin**

Salvation Army (sal-VAY-shun AHR-mee) *proper noun phrase:*

See **Holiness Movement**

Samaria (suh-MAIR-ee-uh) *proper noun:*

Samaria was the name of three geographic places in Israel. (1) Samaria was a hill in the central part of Palestine (1 Kings 16:23-24). (2) Samaria was a city that became the capital of Israel, the Northern Kingdom. (3) Samaria was a whole region of Israel between Jerusalem and Galilee. The king of Assyria sent people from Assyria to live in Samaria after defeating them.

1 Kings 16:32; 18:19; 2 Kings 17:24; Luke 17:11; John 4:4-43; Acts 8:1-13; 9:31; 15:3

See **Assyria, Galilee, Israel, Jersusalem, Judah, Palestine, Samaria (map 8)**

Samaritan (suh-MAIR-uh-tun) *proper noun:*

A Samaritan was a person who lived in the region of Samaria. Samaritans were hated by Jews in the time of Jesus. The Samaritans were descendants of Jews who had married Gentiles. These Gentiles were mostly from Assyria. The Samaritans worshiped Israel's God, but not in Jerusalem.

Two well-known Samaritans mentioned in the Bible are (1) the Good Samaritan in a parable of Jesus (Luke 10:25-37); (2) the Samaritan woman whom Jesus talked to at a well (John 4:1-26).

Matthew 10:5; Luke 9:52; 17:16

See **Assyria, Gentile, Jew, parable, Samaria**

Samson (SAM-sun) *proper noun:*

Samson was one of the judges of Israel. Samson was a Nazirite and was known for his great strength. His story is told in Judges 13—16.

See **Israel, judge, Judges, Nazirite**

Samuel (SAM-yew-wul) *proper noun:*

1. Samuel was one of the great leaders of the people of Israel. He was a Nazirite, a priest, a judge, and a prophet. He anointed Saul and David as the first two kings of Israel.

2. First and Second Samuel are books in the Old Testament. They report the history of Israel from about 1050 to 950 B.C. They especially tell about events in the lives of Samuel, Saul, and David.

1 Samuel 1:1-4; 7:3—12:25; 15:1—16:13; 28:3-25

See **David, Israel, judge, Nazirite, Old Testament, priest, prophet, Saul**

sanctification (SANG-tuh-fuh-KAY-shun) *noun:*

Sanctification is God's act by which He makes people holy. Wesleyans believe that sanctification includes the two crises of initial and entire sanctification. Initial sanctification takes place when a person is born again. They also believe in entire sanctification, as a second work of grace. Sanctification includes a lifelong process of spiritual growth.

1 Corinthians 1:30; 1 Thessalonians 4:3-4; 5:23; 2 Thessalonians 2:13; 2 Timothy 2:21; Hebrews 2:11; 10:10, 14, 29; 1 Peter 1:2

See **Christian perfection, church, crisis, entire sanctification, God, growth in grace, holiness, holy, initial sanctification, process in sanctification, salvation, second work of grace, Wesleyanism**

sanctify (SANG-tuh-fie) *verb:*

Sanctify means to set apart someone or something for a holy purpose. The Hebrew and Greek words translated *sanctify* mean "to make holy." To sanctify means to separate from sin and dedicate to God. God sanctifies the persons who consecrate themselves completely to Him.

Genesis 2:3; Exodus 29:44; 30:29; Leviticus 8:30; 21:8; Nehemiah 3:1; Joel 1:14; 2:16; Hebrews 2:11; 13:12

See **consecrate, dedication, entire sanctification, Greek, Hebrew, holy, sanctification, sin**

sanctuary (SANG-chew-AIR-ee) *noun:*

A sanctuary is any place set apart for the worship of a god. The Tabernacle in the wilderness was the earliest sanctuary of Israel. The Temple became the center of worship after the Israelites settled in Canaan.

The word *sanctuary* refers to the inner parts of the Tabernacle and Temple (Leviticus 4:6). God was present with His people in these holy places in a special way. But God could not be limited to sanctuaries. The prophets warned their people against trusting the sanctuary instead of God himself (Jeremiah 7 and 26).

Today sanctuary means the part of a church building where people gather for worship. Sanctuary may refer especially to the part where the altar is located.

Exodus 15:17; 25:8; Leviticus 19:30; 1 Chronicles 22:19; 2 Chronicles 5:1—7:22; Psalms 73:17; 96:6

See **altar, Canaan, church, God, god, holy, Israel, prophet, tabernacle, temple, worship**

Sanhedrin (san-HED-run or san-HEE-drum) *proper noun:*

The Sanhedrin was the highest ruling council of the Jews. It came into existence about 200 years before the birth of Christ. It came to an end in A.D. 70 when the Romans destroyed Jerusalem.

The Sanhedrin was led by the high priest and met in Jerusalem. The Sanhedrin included the high priests, members of wealthy families, elders, and scribes. Most members of the Sanhedrin were Sadducees. There were about 70 members.

The Sanhedrin could order arrests. This group could judge cases whose punishment did not involve putting a person to death. But a person could be put to death if he or she did wrong to the Temple. Jesus was tried before the Sanhedrin, who said that Jesus had blasphemed God. Stephen was stoned as a result of judgment by the Sanhedrin.

2 Chronicles 19:5-11; Matthew 26:59; Mark 14:55; 15:1; Luke 22:66; John 11:47; Acts 4:5-21; 5:17-41; 6:12-15

See **blasphemy, elder, high priest, Jerusalem, Jew, judgment, Pharisee, Rome, Roman, Sadducee, scribe, Stephen, temple**

Sapphira (suh-FIE-ruh) *proper noun:*

See **Ananias**

Sarah (SAIR-uh) *proper noun:*

Sarah was the wife of Abraham and the mother of Isaac. Her name at first was Sarai, but God changed it (Genesis 17:15).

Genesis 11:29-31; 17:15-27; 20:1-18, Romans 4:19; 9:9; Hebrews 11:11

See **Abraham, Isaac**

Sarai (SAIR-ie) *proper noun:*

See **Sarah**

Satan (SAY-tun) *proper noun:*

Satan is a spiritual being opposed to God and His people. He tries to prevent God's purposes in the world from being completed. The word *Satan* in Hebrew means "the accuser."

Satan is mentioned only three times in the entire Old Testament. The Book of Job describes him as one who tests the faithfulness of the people of God (Job 1:16—2:10). Both God and Satan are said to have tested the faithfulness of David (2 Samuel 24:1-25; 1 Chronicles 21:1-27). God reproved Satan for accusing Joshua, the high priest, in the vision of Zechariah (Zechariah 3:1-10).

The Old Testament speaks of God using Satan for His purposes. He is an accuser of the people of God. The Old Testament does not name Satan as the serpent who tempted Adam and Eve. The Book of Revelation in the New Testament does this (Revelation 12:9; 20:1). Satan is called "the tempter."

The view of Satan changed between the two Testaments. Satan is referred to more often in the New Testament. There it says that Satan is the devil. He is the leader of the demons. He is the one who tempts people to do evil. Satan tempted Jesus (Matthew 4:1-11; 12:24-26). He is blamed for sickness and opposing the purposes of God (Mark 4:15; Luke 13:16).

The Bible does not say clearly who or what Satan is. This much is said: Satan is an evil creature who is limited in his knowledge and power. He cannot force people to obey him and disobey God. Satan has been defeated by Jesus Christ. He will be finally destroyed at the second coming of Christ.

Luke 10:18; 22:3; John 12:31; 14:30; 16:11; Acts 5:3; 26:18; 2 Corinthians 2:11; 4:4; 2 Thessalonians 2:9; Revelation 12:9; 20:1-3, 7-10

See **angel, Beelzebub, Christ, demon, devil, dualism, exorcism, faith, faithfulness, Jesus, Job, New Testament, Old Testament, principalities and powers, Second Coming, serpent, tempt, temptation**

Saul (SAWL) *proper noun:*

Two men in the Bible were named Saul:

1. Saul in the Old Testament was the first king of united Israel. He was from the tribe of Benjamin. Saul was king for 40 years. He was a righteous king in the early years of his reign. But he turned away from God in later years. His son, therefore, did not become king after him (1 Samuel 9—31).

2. Saul was the Hebrew name of the New Testament man better known as Paul. He was also from the tribe of Benjamin (Acts 8:1-3; 9:1-31; 11:19—28:31; Philippians 3:4-7).

See **Benjamin, Bible, forty years, Hebrew, Israel, Jonathan, Paul, righteous, Saul (time line), tribes of Israel**

save (SAYV) *verb:*

To save is to bring salvation to someone. To save means to free from the power of sin and evil. It also means to heal or make whole.

People who accept Christ as Savior are saved. But they are also continuing to be saved as they obey God. They will be finally saved when Jesus returns. The proof of salvation is that Christians are being healed from the disease of sin. They are being made whole.

Luke 8:12; 19:2-10; John 10:7-11; 14:6; Acts 2:43-47; Romans 5:1-11; 13:11; 1 Peter 1:3-12; 1 John 1:1-7; 3:1-3

See **born again, Christ, conversion, growth in grace, healing, Holy Spirit, justification, salvation, Savior, Second Coming**

saved (SAYVD) *adjective:*

Saved describes a person who has become a Christian. A saved person is a disciple of Jesus Christ. Christ sets the person free from the power of sin and evil. A saved person has been born again. This individual has accepted Jesus Christ as his or her Savior.

See **born again, conversion, disciple, Jesus, salvation, Savior, save**

Savior (SAYV-yer) *proper noun:*

Savior is a title that is sometimes used for God in the Old Testament. He is called Savior because of His acts of redemption.

Christ is called the Savior in the New Testament. The New Testament says that Christ was the Savior God promised through the prophets. God made salvation possible for all people through Jesus Christ. Christ is sometimes referred to in the New Testament as Lord and Savior.

2 Samuel 22:3; Psalm 106:21; Isaiah 19:20; 43:3, 11; 60:16; Luke 1:47; 2:11; Acts 5:31; 13:23; Titus 1:4; 2:13; 2 Peter 1:1, 11; 2:20; 3:2, 18; 1 John 4:14

See **Christ, deliverance, God, Lord, redeem, redemption, righteousness, salvation, save**

scourge (SKERJ)

1. *noun:* A scourge was a whip used to punish those who had done wrong. The whip was made of strips of cord or leather fastened to a handle. Sometimes pieces of bone or metal were fastened to the strips. Punishment by scourging was severe and painful. Jesus and Paul were scourged by those who falsely accused them.

2. *verb:* To scourge is to whip someone with a scourge.

Matthew 20:19; 27:26; Luke 18:33; John 2:15; 19:1; Acts 16:22-24; 22:25

See **Jesus, Paul, suffering**

scribe (SKRIEB) *noun:*

Scribes were secretaries who made their living by reading and writing for others. Few people in Old Testament times could read or write. Thus, scribes were an important part of both public and private life.

Scribes after the time of the Exile copied and explained the Torah. They were teachers of the law. The Gospels mention that most scribes opposed Jesus. Some scribes, however, became His followers.

2 Samuel 8:16; 1 Kings 4:3; 2 Chronicles 24:11; 34:8; Ezra 4:8; Jeremiah 32:12; 36:8, 26; Matthew 5:20; 8:19; 12:38; 15:1; 23:2, 13-29; Acts 6:12; 23:9; 1 Corinthians 1:20

See **exile, gospel, Jesus, law, Old Testament, Pharisee, Torah**

Scripture (SKRIP-cher) *proper noun:*

Scripture is the Bible. Scripture comes from a Greek word that means "what is written." Scripture means the written Word of God. The word *Scripture* in the New Testament refers to the Old Testament. Christians also view as Scripture the books that now make up the New Testament. Christians believe that both the Old and New Testaments are God's holy Scripture.

Matthew 21:42; 22:29; 26:56; Mark 12:24; 14:49; Luke 4:21; 24:27; John 5:39; 17:12; Romans 15:4; 2 Timothy 3:15-16; 2 Peter 1:20-21

See **authority of Scripture, Bible, holy, inspiration, New Testament, Old Testament, rule of faith and practice**

scroll (SKROHL) *noun:*

A scroll was a "book" made in the form of a long roll. Some scrolls were made of material like paper. Some were made of leather called parchment. Books as they appear today did not exist in Bible times. Scribes copied the Scriptures by hand onto these scrolls. A scroll was read as the reader wound the roll from one roll to another.

Psalm 40:7-8; Isaiah 34:4; Jeremiah 36:1-32; Ezekiel 2:9; Revelation 6:14

See **Bible, scribe, Scripture**

Sea of Reeds (SEE uv REEDZ) *proper noun phrase:*

The Sea of Reeds is one of the two northern branches of the Red Sea. This was the body of water that the Israelites crossed to escape the armies of Pharaoh. The Sea of Reeds is often confused with the Red Sea.

See **Israelite, pharaoh, Red Sea, Sea of Reeds (map 2)**

Second Adam (SEK-unk AD-um) *proper noun:*

See **Adam, Jesus**

second blessing (SEK-und BLES-ing) *noun phrase:*

Second blessing is a phrase used by some people in the Holiness Movement. It refers to entire sanctification. The term stresses entire sanctification as a second work of grace.

See **Christian perfection, entire sanctification, holiness, Holiness Movement, perfect love, second work of grace**

Second Coming (SEK-und KUM-ing) *proper noun phrase:*

The Second Coming is the return of Jesus Christ to earth. The Second Coming is also called the Parousia, or appearing of Christ. Jesus told His disciples that He was going to His Father. But He said that He would return. Christ is now with the Church through the Holy Spirit. But He will again be personally present at the Second Coming.

The Second Coming has two parts. (1) Jesus Christ will be revealed to the world in all His power and glory. (2) The righteous dead will be raised to new life. The mortal natures of Christians will be changed. They will become immortal. Thus, the Second Coming is a source of hope for Christians.

The Second Coming is the time when the kingdom of God will be made complete. This will be the end of the age. Evil will be destroyed. Salvation will be made complete.

Christians do not agree on the details of the Second Coming. But they do agree that Jesus will return. The Bible gives no exact knowledge of the events related to the Second Coming. The return of Christ is important to Christian faith. But it is not important how Christ will return. The Second Coming should be a source of hope for the Church. It should not be a matter of argument about how it will happen.

Matthew 24:3-44; Acts 1:11; 1 Corinthians 5:5; 15:23; 2 Corinthians 1:14; 1 Thessalonians 2:19; 3:13; 4:15; 5:23; 2 Thessalonians 2:1-2; 2 Peter 1:16

See **Bible, Christ, Christian, Day of the Lord, eschatology, Holy Spirit, hope, immortality, Jesus, kingdom of God, millennium, parousia**

second work of grace (SEK-und WERK uv GRAYS) *noun phrase:*

Second work of grace is a phrase some people use for entire sanctification. The Holiness Movement uses this phrase to stress several things about the doctrine. Entire sanctification is a work that God does in Christians through His Holy Spirit. This spiritual experience is not something people earn by doing good works. It is free, a gift of God's grace.

Entire sanctification happens after a person has been converted. The phrase stresses the crisis rather than the process in sanctification.

John 17; Romans 6:19-22; 1 Thessalonians 4:2-5; 5:23-24

See **baptism with the Holy Spirit, Christian, conversion, crisis, entire sanctification, good works, grace, Holiness Movement, Holy Spirit, initial sanctification, process in sanctification, salvation, sanctification, second blessing, spiritual**

sect (SEKT) *noun:*

A sect is a group within an organized religion. Roman Catholics say sects are heresies. Protestants identify sects as small groups that stress their differences from the rest of Christianity. Denominations do not do this. They seek to find their places within the Christian Church as a whole. Sects believe that their understanding of Christianity is the only true one. Sects are not the same as cults. Cults reject certain basic doctrines of the Christian faith.

Acts 5:17; 15:5; 24:5; 26:5; 28:22

See **Christian, Christianity, church, cult, denomination, doctrine, faith, Protestant, religion, Roman Catholic**

sectarian (sek-TAIR-ee-un)

1. *adjective:* Sectarian describes someone or something as related to a sect. For example, a sectarian group or a sectarian belief.

2. *noun:* A sectarian is a person who belongs to a sect. Sectarians may be those who understand their churches or groups to be sects.

A sectarian is also someone who divides the church by quarreling.

See **sect**

secular humanism (SEK-yew-ler HYEW-mun-iz-um) *noun phrase:*

Secular humanism is the view of human life that is based on secularism. It stresses the value of people over things. It stresses the good that people can do through reason. But secular humanism also says that belief in God harms humanity. Thus, secular humanism is a form of atheism. But not all atheists share the view of secular humanism. Secular humanism has great hopes for what humanity can do to improve the world. Some atheists believe that there is not much hope for the human race.

See **atheism, secularism**

secularism (SEK-yew-ler-IZ-um) *noun:*

Secularism is a modern view of the world that believes God does not exist. It is a form of atheism. Secularism believes that the world and human life were not created by God. It says that a person is alone in the world. The only source of help for humanity is humanity.

Secularism teaches that history has no divine purpose. It says that all religions and morality are made by humans. Secularism holds that humanity alone must make life good since there is no God. The most complete statement of secularism is made by secular humanism.

See **atheism, creation, God, morality, religion, secular humanism**

security (see-KYOOR-uh-tee) *noun:*

See **eternal security**

seder (SAY-der) *noun:*

Seder means order of service. The word *seder* is the English form of a Hebrew word. Seder is the traditional ritual of a Passover meal in modern Jewish practice. The ritual meal tells the story of Israel's exodus from Egypt.

Exodus 12:3-30; Matthew 26:17-29; Luke 22:7-8

See **bondage, Egypt, Exodus, festival, Israel, Passover, ritual, tradition**

seed (SEED) *noun:*

A seed is the part of a plant that can make more plants. Seed also means a part of anything living that can reproduce itself. Sometimes seed means what the seed creates. For example, the Bible speaks of Abraham's children as his seed.

The Bible describes the children of God as His seed.

The Bible refers to sin as a seed. It reproduces itself as evil.

Genesis 1:11-29; 3:15; 9:9; 12:7, 15-16; Exodus 16:31; Deuteronomy 1:8; Jeremiah 31:36; Matthew 13:3-9; Mark 4:26-29; Romans 9:7-8, 1 Peter 1:23; 1 John 3:9

See **Abraham, creation, fruit, harvest**

selah (SEE-luh) *interjection:*

Selah is a Hebrew term that appears often in the Psalms and in Habakkuk. The Hebrew poetry of both books was set to music and sung in worship. The word *selah* probably marked where the singer was to pause while the music continued. Thus, the word was not meant to be read aloud in public worship.

Psalm 3:2, 4, 8; 7:5; 9:16, 20, etc.; Habakkuk 3:3, 9, 13

See **Habakkuk, Hebrews, Psalms, worship**

self (SELF) *noun:*

The self is the person as he or she really is. Today self usually refers to the identity of a person. It is what makes one person different from another.

There is no single term for self in the Bible. All the different terms that are translated "self" refer to persons as wholes. The word does not refer to only the inner person.

The Holiness Movement sometimes speaks of a "death to self" in entire sanctification (Romans 6:13, 19; 7:14-25; 12:1-2; Galatians 2:19-20). This does not mean that the self of the consecrated Christian really dies. He or she would no longer exist if this happened. Death to self means that Christians no longer put their will above God's will. Entire sanctification brings the end of self-rule, not the end of self.

See **Christian, consecrate, consecration, death, entire sanctification, flesh, man, soul, will**

self-control (SELF-kun-TROHL) *noun:*

Self-control means being able to govern one's desires, emotions, or actions. The New Testament includes self-control among the fruit of the Spirit (Galatians 5:23). But self-control is also a Christian discipline. People must allow God to help them live lives that are pure.

Acts 24:25; 1 Corinthians 9:25; Titus 2:2; 2 Peter 1:6

See **Christian, discipline, fruit of the Spirit, God, pure, self, temperance**

self-discipline (SELF-DIS-uh-plun) *noun:*

See **discipline, self, self-control**

Septuagint (sep-TEW-uh-jint) *proper noun:*

The Septuagint was a Greek translation of the Hebrew Old Testament. It was begun about 250 B.C. and completed sometime during the first century A.D. The Septuagint includes the books of the Apocrypha. It was the Bible of early Christians outside of Palestine.

The term *Septuagint* comes from the Greek work for 70. Thus, it is sometimes referred to as LXX, the Roman number for 70.

See **Apocrypha, Bible, Christian, Greek, Hebrew, Latin, Palestine**

sepulcher (SEP-ul-ker) *noun:*

A sepulcher was a grave or tomb. It was a place where dead people were buried. Most often, a sepulcher was a natural cave. The sepulcher was closed by placing a large stone in front of the opening. Sepulchers were usually outside the town. The mouths of sepulchers were often painted white to call attention to them. Jewish people were not to touch sepulchers.

1 Samuel 10:2; 2 Chronicles 16:14; 21:20; 32:33; Matthew 23:27; Luke 11:47; 23:53; Acts 2:29

See **Jesus, Joseph**

seraph (SAIR-uf) *noun:*

A seraph is a heavenly being, perhaps a kind of angel. Seraphim is the plural form of seraph. Isaiah describes the seraphim as having six wings. They stood close to the throne of God. Thus, they were spiritual messengers who were quick to do the will of God.

Isaiah 6:2, 6

See **angel, cherub, God, heaven, Isaiah, will**

seraphim (SAIR-uh-fim) *plural noun:*

See **seraph**

sermon (SER-mun) *noun:*

A sermon is a religious speech usually given during a Christian worship gathering. A sermon is often called a message. Its purpose can be to evangelize, teach, encourage, or celebrate.

Matthew 5—7; Acts 2:14-41; 7:2-53

See **evangelism, gospel, kerygma, message, preach, Sermon on the Mount, worship**

Sermon on the Mount (SER-mun ahn thuh MOUNT) *proper noun phrase:*

Sermon on the Mount is the name given to one of Jesus' greatest sermons. It is recorded in Matthew 5—7. The Sermon on the Mount contains teachings by Jesus about the kingdom of God. It tells how those in the kingdom of God should live.

See **Jesus, kingdom of God, Matthew, preach, sermon**

serpent (SER-punt) *noun:*

A serpent is a snake. A serpent suggested to Adam and Eve that they disobey God (Genesis 3:1-24). The Book of Revelation identifies this serpent as the devil (Revelation 12:9; 20:1).

Images of serpents were commonly worshiped in the religion of Baal.

Genesis 49:17; Number 21:4-9; 2 Kings 18:4; Isaiah 27:1; Matthew 23:33; Romans 16:20; 2 Corinthians 11:3; Revelation 12:9, 14-15; 20:1

See **Adam, Baal, devil, dragon, Eve, Satan, tempt, worship**

servant (SER-vunt) *noun:*

A servant is a person who works for another person. Servants may be slaves, or they may be paid for their services.

The Old Testament uses the title *servant* in a number of different ways. Servant was a title that humble persons sometimes used to refer to themselves (Exodus 4:10; Psalms 119:17; 143:12). But servant could be a title of great honor. The servant of a king was an important person in the government.

Servants of the Lord could simply be people who did what God wanted. But a number of important leaders of Israel were also called servants of the Lord. They included Moses, David, other kings, and the prophets.

The prophecies about the Servant of the Lord in Isaiah are difficult to explain (Isaiah 42:1-7; 49:1-6; 50:4-9; 52:13—53:12; 61:1-3). The Servant may refer to the prophet, a king, Israel, or the Messiah. The Servant would bring redemption by accepting suffering that He did not deserve.

Christians generally believe that Jesus filled the role of the Suffering Servant (Matthew 12:15-21; Acts 8:26-35). Jesus said that He came to be a servant and not to be served (Matthew 20:28; Mark 10:45; Romans 15:8). He told His followers, "Whoever wants to become great among you must be your servant" (Mark 10:43).

All Christians should be the servants of God and of one another. But some Christians are called to be His special servants or ministers. The Greek word for servant may also be translated "minister."

Genesis 9:25; 32:4; Exodus 14:31; Judges 2:8; 2 Samuel 7:5, 8, 20-29; Psalm 113:1; Isaiah 20:3; Amos 3:7; Haggai 2:23; Zechariah 1:6; Romans 15:8; 16:1; 2 Corinthians 3:6; 6:4; 11:23; Ephesians 3:7; 4:11-12

See **Christian, David, disciple, humility, Jesus, Lord, Messiah, Moses, minister, prophecy, prophet, redeem, redemption, slave, suffering**

service (SER-vus) *noun:*

The English word *service* has two major Christian uses. Both uses come from the same Greek word that appears in Romans 12:1. The King James Version translates the word "service." The *New International Version* translates it "worship."

1. A church service is a meeting of believers for worship. One purpose of worship gatherings is to equip believers to serve. As believers worship God, He serves them. He gives them the grace they need to serve others.

An order of service is the plan for a worship gathering. A pastor decides how things will be done during a church service. This may include songs, testimonies, prayer, offering, and a sermon. The order of service lists what is done first, second, and so on.

2. Service is serving. Service refers to what people do to help others. Christian service is the work believers do for the church. Ministry is service. But not all service is done for the church. Christian service is often done outside of the church for the needy world.

Romans 12:6-8; 1 Corinthians 12:5; 2 Corinthians 9:12-13; Ephesians 4:11-13; 1 Peter 4:10-11

See **Christian, church, compassion, compassionate ministry, grace, Greek, hymn, liturgy, ministry, pastor, prayer, sermon, testimony, translate, work, world**

Seth (SETH) *proper noun:*

Seth was the third son of Adam and Eve. Luke lists him as an ancestor of Jesus Christ.

Genesis 4:25-26; 5:3-8; Luke 3:23-38

See **Adam, Eve, genealogy, Genesis**

Seventh Day (SEV-unth DAY) *proper noun:*

See **Sabbath**

Shallum (SHAL-um) *proper noun:*

1. Shallum was a common name in Old Testament times. More than a dozen men in the Bible have this name.

2. Shallum was king of Israel, the Northern Kingdom. He killed Zechariah and then ruled in his place. Shallum was killed one month later by Menahem.

2 Kings 15:10, 13-15

See **Israel, Menahem, Shallum (time line), Zechariah**

shalom (shah-LOHM) *noun:*

Shalom is the Hebrew word for peace. It is used as a greeting.

See **Hebrew, peace**

Sheba (SHEE-buh) *proper noun:*

1. Sheba is the name of several men in the Bible. One was the grandson of Abraham (Genesis 25:3).

2. Sheba is also the name of a city in Israel (Joshua 19:2). It is also known as Beersheba.

3. Sheba is the name of a country in Arabia. The queen of Sheba visited King Solomon to see his wealth. She also wanted to test Solomon's great wisdom (1 Kings 10:1-13).

See **Abraham, Beersheba, Israel, Solomon, wisdom**

Shechem (SHEE-kum) *proper noun:*

Shechem was an important religious and political center in Israel during Old Testament times. Shechem was at first an important Canaanite city. It was the first place visited by Abraham (Genesis 12:6-7). Joseph was buried at Shechem (Joshua 24:32). Joshua led Israel to renew its covenant with God at Shechem (Joshua 24:1-28). King Rehoboam was crowned as king at Shechem, and he made it his capital city (1 Kings 12:1, 25). Shechem was probably the same as Sychar, the site of Jacob's well (John 4:5-7).

See **Abraham, Canaan, covenant, Jacob, Joseph, Joshua, Rehoboam, Shechem (maps 3, 4), Sychar**

shekinah (shuh-KIE-nuh) *noun:*

Shekinah means "dwelling." The English word comes from a Hebrew word that refers to God's presence in the Temple. The term *shekinah* does not appear in the Bible. But the Bible does refer to signs that God was with His people. Rabbis used shekinah to mean that the glory of God was near His people. God was especially close when His people studied the law and worshiped Him.

Exodus 13:21-22; Deuteronomy 12:5; 1 Samuel 4:4; Ezekiel 43:1-5; Matthew 18:20

See **glory, God, immanence, law, rabbi, sign, temple, worship**

Shema (shuh-MAH) *proper noun:*

The Shema is the creed of Judaism. It is made up of a confession quoting Deuteronomy 6:4-9; 11:13-21; and Numbers 15:37-41. The Hebrew word *Shema,* the first word of Deuteronomy 6:4, means "hear."

See **confess, creed, Deuteronomy, Judaism, Numbers**

Sheol (SHE-ohl) *proper noun:*

Sheol was the region to which dead people went. It was described as a place of great sadness, where there was no hope. Those who were in Sheol did not know they were there.

Sometimes Sheol refers to the sorrows of death. *Hades* is the Greek word for Sheol. Sheol came to mean the place where the dead waited for the resurrection. Sheol does not mean the same as hell or Gehenna.

Deuteronomy 32:22; 2 Samuel 22:6; Psalms 9:17; 18:5; Isaiah 5:14; 14:15; Ezekiel 31:6, 17; Amos 9:2; Matthew 16:18; Luke 10:15

See **Hades, hell, resurrection**

shepherd (SHEP-erd) *noun:*

A shepherd is someone who leads and cares for sheep. The Bible often compares human leaders to shepherds. Leaders are to care for their followers just as shepherds care for sheep. Kings, prophets, and priests were referred to as shepherds in the Old Testament.

Psalm 23 calls God a shepherd. Isaiah said that God would be a shepherd to His people. Jesus spoke of himself as the Good Shepherd.

The Greek word for *shepherd* also means "pastor." Pastors are shepherds to their people.

Exodus 2:17; Psalms 23:1; 80:1; Isaiah 40:11; Jeremiah 23:4; 50:6; Ezekiel 34:2, 5; Luke 2:8-20; John 10:2-16; 1 Peter 2:25

See **Israel, king, pastor, priest, prophet, psalm**

Shiloh (SHIE-loh) *proper noun:*

Shiloh was an important town in Israel during Old Testament times. It became a religious center for the tribes under Joshua's leadership (Joshua 18:1). The Tabernacle remained at Shiloh until the time of Samuel. Samuel spent his boyhood at Shiloh with Eli the priest (1 Samuel 1:1-3, 11, 20, 28).

Joshua 19:51; 21:1-2; Judges 18:31

See **Joshua, Samuel, Shiloh (map 3), tabernacle**

shrine (SHRIEN) *noun:*

A shrine is a place where a god is worshiped. A shrine can be a place where a saint or sacred person is buried. A shrine may also be an idol or image of a god.

Acts 19:24

See **god, idol, sacred, saint, worship**

sickness (SIK-nus) *noun:*

See **healing, health**

Sidon (SIE-dun) *proper noun:*

Sidon was a city on the Mediterranean Sea coast in Bible times. It was located in the country of Phoenicia. It was an important city for trade. The people of Sidon were idol worshipers (1 Kings 11:1, 5, 33). Jesus visited the area of Sidon and healed a girl (Mark 15:21-28). Sidon is often mentioned with the city of Tyre (Matthew 15:21; Acts 12:20).

Genesis 10:19; Matthew 11:21-22; Acts 27:3

See **Ashtoreth, idol, Mediterranean Sea, Phoenicia, Sidon (maps 7, 8), Tyre**

sign (SIEN) *noun:*

A sign is an outward event or object that has meaning beyond itself. A sign points to something else that is greater than the sign itself. For example, Noah was told that the rainbow was a promise. God would not destroy the earth again by water.

Signs are sometimes acts of God. He sends a message through the sign. The plagues on Egypt were signs of the power of God over the Pharaoh.

The miracles done by Christ were called signs. They showed that the kingdom of God had come. Sometimes Jesus would not do a miracle. This was because people refused His message even though they saw the signs.

Signs happened on the Day of Pentecost. These were wind and tongues of fire. These signs showed that the Holy Spirit had come.

Genesis 17:11; Joshua 4:6; Isaiah 7:11; Jeremiah 9:12; Matthew 16:3; 24:3, 10; Luke 21:11, 25; Acts 2:43; 4:30; Romans 4:11

See **Holy Spirit, message, miracle, Pentecost, plague, promise, tongues of fire**

Silas (SIE-lus) *proper noun:*

Silas was a member of the Jerusalem church and a citizen of Rome. He traveled with Paul for a time on Paul's missionary journeys. He is also called Silvanus.

Acts 15:22, 39-41; 16:16—17:15; 2 Corinthians 1:19; 1 Peter 5:12

See **Jerusalem, missionary, Paul, Rome**

Simeon (SIM-ee-un) *proper noun:*

1. Simeon is the name of two men in the Bible.

   a. Simeon was the second son of Jacob (Genesis 34:25-31; 42:24; 49:5-7). His descendants became one of the 12 tribes of Israel (46:10).

b. Simeon was a righteous man in the New Testament. He was given a special promise by the Holy Spirit. The promise was that he would not die before he saw the Messiah. This was fulfilled when he saw the infant Jesus in the Temple (Luke 2:25-35).

2. Simeon was the name of the land occupied by the tribe of Simeon.

See **Canaan, Jacob, Messiah, promise, righteous, Simeon (map 3), tribes of Israel, Temple**

Simon (SIE-mun) *proper noun:*

Simon was the name of several men in the New Testament.

1. Simon Peter was an important disciple of Christ (Matthew 17:1-5; Luke 22:31-32; John 13:6-9). He was also a leader in the Early Christian Church (Acts 2:14-41; 3:1-10).

2. Simon the Zealot was one of the 12 disciples (Matthew 10:4; Luke 6:15).

3. Simon was a brother of Jesus (Matthew 13:55).

4. Simon was a Pharisee at whose house Jesus one time ate (Luke 7:36-50).

5. Simon of Cyrene was forced by the Romans to carry Jesus' cross to Calvary (Matthew 27:32).

6. Simon Magus was a man who did magic. He tried to buy the gift of the Holy Spirit (Acts 8:9-24).

7. Simon was the name of a man in Joppa. Peter stayed for a time with him (Acts 9:43; 10:6, 17, 32).

See **Calvary, Cephas, cross, disciple, Peter, Pharisee, zealot**

simultaneous (SIE-mul-TAY-nee-us) *adjective:*

Simultaneous means that two or more events happen at the same time.

Justification, regeneration, and adoption into the family of God are simultaneous events. These terms refer to the act of God in which a person is born again. The new birth and initial sanctification happen simultaneously.

See **adoption, born again, initial sanctification, justification, new birth, regeneration**

sin (SIN)

1. *verb:* To sin is to commit a sin.

2. *noun:* Sin is refusing to worship God as God. It is the opposite of holiness. Sin is opposing God as Lord of His creation. Sin is a person's attempt to take the place of God in the world. Sin means worshiping the creature instead of the Creator. It is refusing to believe God. Sin means missing the purpose God has for people and the world. Sin has left its mark on every part of our world. The Bible tells us that sin entered the human race through Adam and Eve.

Sin destroyed the fellowship that existed between God and humanity. It severely harmed the image of God in humanity. It made people wicked in all their ways and in all parts of their lives. Sin separated God and humanity. It has brought physical and spiritual death upon the human race.

Sin refers to the nature of sinners and to the sinful acts they do. Sin shows itself in acts that oppose the will and rule of God. Thus, the wrath of God is directed against sin.

Sin in it broadest sense means any transgression against the law of God. It is any failure to do the perfect will of God. This is the way the Reformed tradition defines sin. But Wesleyanism defines sin in a more narrow sense. To sin is to choose to disobey what one knows to be the will of God.

Genesis 3:1-24; Romans 1:18-32; 3:9-20; 5:12-19; 6:15-23; 1 John 3:4

See **Adam, creation, death, depravity, dominion of sin, fall, fellowship, God, grace, holiness, image of God, Lord, mortal sin, nature, original sin, Reformed tradition, pride, righteousness, transgress, Wesleyanism, will, worship**

Sinai (SIE-nie) *proper noun:*

1. The Sinai is the large region of land east of Egypt and southwest of Palestine. It lies between the two arms of the Red Sea. God led the people of Israel to Sinai after the Exodus. Most of the Sinai is wilderness or desert land.

2. Mount Sinai is in the southern part of the region of Sinai. The Bible sometimes refers to Mount Sinai as Horeb.

God made a covenant with the Israelites at Mount Sinai. He gave His law to Moses at Sinai. Thus, Sinai in the New Testament represents the law of God.

Exodus 3:1; 16:1; 19:1-23; Deuteronomy 5:2; 29:1; Galatians 4:24-25

See **covenant, Egypt, Exodus, Israelites, law, Sinai (map 2), Ten Commandments**

sinful nature (SIN-ful NAY-cher) *noun phrase:*

The sinful nature is the fallen human nature. The sinful nature makes it easier to sin against God than to obey Him.

See **carnal, depravity, entire sanctification, flesh, indwelling sin, nature, original sin**

sinless perfection (SIN-les per-FEK-shun) *noun phrase:*

Sinless perfection is a state of such perfection that one never sins. The people who oppose the doctrine of Christian perfection sometimes accuse Wesleyanism of saying this. But the Holiness Movement has never claimed that sinless perfection is possible. Only God has this.

Wesleyanism denies that Christian perfection is total or final. It is evangelical perfection, not sinless perfection. Wesleyanism says that only perfection in love is possible in the present world. Christian perfection in this sense may be a present experience for Christians. It teaches that entirely sanctified Christians are never free from temptation.

No human being can be completely free from mistakes and wrong actions. Only God is totally perfect. Even those who have been perfected in love must pray, "Forgive us our debts [trespasses]" (see Matthew 6:12-15, KJV). Even entirely sanctified people still "fall short" of God's perfect law of righteousness and holiness (Romans 3:23).

***See* Christian perfection, entire sanctification, heart, Holiness Movement, original sin, perfect, perfect love, perfection, sanctify, sin, temptation, trespass, Wesleyanism**

sinner (SIN-er) *noun:*

A sinner is a person who sins. A sinner transgresses the law of God.

Psalm 51:5; Matthew 9:13; Luke 18:3; Romans 5:8; 1 Timothy 1:15

***See* depravity, dominion of sin, original sin, sin, sinful nature, transgress, trespass**

sinning religion (SIN-ing ree-LI-jun) *noun phrase:*

Sinning religion is a term meaning that Christians sin daily in "thought, word, and deed." It means that daily obedience to God is not possible.

The doctrine of sin in Reformed theology has been wrongly thought of as teaching this. It is true, however, that Reformed theology states that Christians cannot be free from sin. Wesleyanism believes that Christians can live without sinning. The differences are largely due to the two group's definitions of sin. Reformed theology says sin is any failure to follow God's perfect law. Wesleyanism says sin is a willful act against a known law of God.

Reformed theology stresses the sinfulness of the human condition even for Christians. But it also stresses the demand of God for total obedience. It does not usually make a clear difference between sins and mistakes. Sometimes it also identifies the sinful nature with the human nature. It does not show the difference between original sin and the effects of sinful habits. Reformed theology denies that Christian perfection is possible. This is because it understands Christian perfection to mean sinless perfection. All these views make freedom from sin impossible. Wesleyans reject these views. They believe Scripture teaches that Christian should live without sinning against God.

Some Calvinists claim that Wesleyanism believes in "sinless perfection." Some Wesleyans claim that Calvinism teaches a "sinning religion." Neither claim is a correct or fair statement of the views of the other. The claims are often based on the mistaken understandings held by supporters of both positions.

Reformed theology holds that those who are truly converted do not sin on purpose. It does not teach a "sinning religion." But true Wesleyans do not teach "sinless perfection" either. Scriptural freedom from sin is not "sinless perfection."

See **Calvinism, Christian perfection, elect, election, freedom, grace, original sin, perfection, Reformed tradition, sin, sinful nature, sinless perfection, transgress, Wesleyanism**

skeptic (SKEP-tik) *noun:*

A skeptic is someone who doubts. A skeptic may be someone who doubts that God is real or that God exists. A skeptic may doubt that people can know God or the way He works. For some skeptics, doubt can be removed.

Thomas, one of Jesus' disciples, was a skeptic about the resurrection of Christ. Christ removed Thomas's doubts.

See **atheist, agnostic, disciple, faith, resurrection, skepticism, Thomas**

skepticism (SKEP-tuh-SIZ-um) *noun:*

Skepticism is the belief that people cannot know God even if He does exist. It says that the mind is simply not able to know whether or not God exists. Skepticism holds that if God exists He is beyond human knowledge. It neither denies the existence of God nor claims knowledge of His existence.

See **atheism, belief, Ecclesiastes, faith, God, religion, revelation, secularism, theism**

slander (SLAN-der)

1. *verb:* To slander is to say bad and false things about someone. To slander is to harm the name of another person by telling lies about him or her. It means to accuse someone falsely.

2. *noun:* Slander is the act and result of slandering someone. It is the act of charging someone falsely. Slander is also the false charges that are made.

Psalm 101:5; Proverbs 10:18; Jeremiah 6:28; 9:4

See **condemn, hate, inveigh, judge, lie**

slave (SLAYV) *noun:*

A slave is someone who serves another person because he or she is the property of that person. Slaves have few rights. They can be used in almost any way that pleases their masters. A slave is the opposite of a free person. Sometimes people choose to be slaves.

The Israelites were slaves in Egypt for many years. The Egyptians were their masters and treated the Israelites harshly. The Israelites did not have freedom while in slavery.

The apostle Paul said that sinners are slaves to sin. They serve evil. This slavery finally leads to death.

Paul said that there is also a form of slavery that leads to eternal life. He urges people to become slaves to Christ. Those who become slaves to Christ find that they are truly free.

Exodus 1:1-22; Matthew 8:9; 10:25; 18:28; Romans 6:16-20; 8:12-17; 1 Corinthians 7:21-23; Ephesians 6:5; Philemon 16

See **bondage, Christ, death, disciple, Egypt, eternal life, evil, freedom, fruit of the Spirit, holiness, Moses, Paul, righteousness, servant, sin**

slavery (SLAY-ver-ee) *noun:*

Slavery is the condition of one who is a slave.

A person is born into slavery to sin because of original sin. A person also chooses to be in slavery to sin. God can free a person to choose to be in slavery to Jesus Christ.

See **bondage, original sin, sin, slave**

Smith, Joseph (SMITH, JOH-suf) *proper noun:*

See **Mormon**

Sodom and Gomorrah (SAH-dum and guh-MAWR-uh) *proper noun phrase:*

Sodom and Gomorrah were two cities located in southern Palestine. They were probably located at the southern end of the Dead Sea. The cities were known for their wickedness. God destroyed Sodom and Gomorrah with fire and brimstone.

Genesis 18:16—19:29

See **Abraham, brimstone, Dead Sea, Lot**

sodomy (SAH-duh-mee) *noun:*

Sodomy usually means sexual relations between men or having sexual relations with an animal. Sodomy sometimes means the rape of one male by another.

The word *sodomy* comes from an event that happened in the Old Testament city of Sodom.

Genesis 19:1-11

See **adultery, fornication, immoral, Sodom and Gomorrah**

Solomon (SAHL-uh-mun) *proper noun:*

Solomon was the third king of the united kingdom of Israel. He followed his father, King David. Solomon was king for 40 years. Solomon had the Temple built in Jerusalem. He was known for his great wisdom. God blessed him with great wealth.

Solomon finally made some foolish mistakes in the way he governed the kingdom. The united kingdom was divided after his death.

Solomon made it possible for false gods to become a part of life in Judah. He married many foreign wives, and he had many concubines. All of them brought their gods with them to Jerusalem.

2 Samuel 1—11

See **concubine, David, Ecclesiastes, god, Jerusalem, Judah, Israel, Proverbs, Solomon (time line), Song of Solomon, temple, wisdom**

son (SUN)

1. *noun:* A son is a male child of a mother and father.

2. *proper noun:* The Son is the second person of the Trinity. The Son is eternal with the Father. The Son is God just like the Father is God. The Son does not have a mother. The Son does not come from the Father as an earthly son does. The Son of God comes from the Father in a special way. He comes from the Father as a word comes from a voice. The Son is the Father's voice.

The Son of God was born in human form by Mary. The Holy Spirit made Mary become pregnant in a special way. This child was named Jesus.

Matthew 1:18-25; Luke 1:26-38; John 1:1-5, 9-18; Philippians 2:4-11; Colossians 1:15-20

See **Christ, eternal, father, God, Holy Spirit, incarnation, Jesus, Mary, Son of God, Trinity**

Son of God (SUN uv GAHD) *proper noun phrase:*

Son of God is one of the titles used in the New Testament for Jesus. Jesus is also called the Son of the Most High. This means the same as Son of God.

He is not God's Son in the human sense. He is called Son of God because He is the Second Person of the Trinity. He comes from the Father eternally. Christ is the Word of God made flesh. He is eternally with the Father and the Holy Spirit. He is God even as the Father and the Holy Spirit are God. They are one.

The Gospel of John says that the Word of God became incarnate in Jesus. The Word (that is, Jesus) obeyed His Father by taking on the form of man. He showed the love of God for the world through His death on the Cross. He ascended to the Father after the Resurrection. He will reign eternally with the Father.

Christians become sons of God through the adoption that Christ makes possible. Christians may be sons of God when they live by His grace.

The Old Testament refers to David as a son of God (2 Samuel 7:14; Psalm 89:26). It also uses "Son of God" to refer to the Messiah.

Psalm 2:7; Matthew 3:17; 4:3; Mark 1:1, 11; Luke 1:32, 35; John 1:18, 34, 49; 3:16-18, 35-36; Acts 13:33; Romans 1:3-4, 9; 1 John 1:3; Revelation 2:18

See **child of God, Christ, cross, crucifixion, David, father, God, Holy Spirit, Incarnation, Jesus, revelation, resurrection, son, Son of Man, Trinity, word**

Son of Man (SUN uv MAN) *proper noun phrase:*

Son of Man is a common title used for Jesus in the Gospels.

"Son of man" in the Hebrew Old Testament often means simply "man." The phrase stresses that humans are weak creatures as compared to God. But they are honored as compared to the rest of creation (Numbers 23:19; Psalms 4:2; 8:4; 144:3; 146:3; Proverbs 8:4, 31; Isaiah 51:12; Jeremiah 49:18; Micah 5:7). The prophet Ezekiel frequently used this phrase to identify himself (Ezekiel 2:1, 3, 6, 8).

The use of the phrase in Daniel 7 is especially important. God destroys the rule of four evil kings in the vision of the prophet. These kings were like beasts. Then God gives eternal rule to "one like a son of man." This human ruler comes on the clouds of heaven (verses 13-14). The prophet learns that the human king is a symbol for the people of Israel (verses 18, 22, 25, 27). Several books in the Old Testament, Apocrypha, and Pseudepigrapha further develop this idea.

Jesus is the only one to use the phrase in the Gospels. "Son of Man" is used only four times outside the Gospels (Acts 7:56; Hebrews 2:6-8; Revelation 1:13; 14:14). The phrase always refers to Jesus Christ wherever it appears in the New Testament.

Jews of the first century sometimes referred to themselves as "son of man" rather than "I." Jesus also did this. But the Gospels tell us that Jesus used the phrase as no Jew ever had. He made it a title. (Compare Matthew 16:13-28 and Mark 8:27—9:1.)

The title is most frequently used in the Synoptic Gospels. It is used in three special kinds of sayings. (1) Jesus refers to His present work on earth calling himself the Son of Man (Matthew 8:20; 11:18-19). (2) He predicts His crucifixion as the suffering Son of Man (Mark 8:31; 9:31; 10:33-34; 14:21, 41). (3) He refers to the future coming of the Son of Man (Matthew 24:27, 37, 39; Mark 8:38; Luke 12:8-10; 11:30; 17:30).

Christians sometimes use "Son of Man" as the opposite of "Son of God." They mean that Jesus is both God and man.

***See* Apocrypha, Christ, crucifixion, Daniel, Ezekiel, God, Jesus, man, Messiah, pseudepigrapha, Second Coming, servant, suffering, symbol, Synoptic Gospels, vision**

Song of Solomon (SAHNG uv SAHL-uh-mun) *proper noun phrase:* The Song of Solomon is a book of the Old Testament. It is sometimes called the Song of Songs. A song is a canticle. Therefore, this book is sometimes called the Canticle of Canticles.

The Song of Solomon seems to be a collection of wedding poems used in Israel. Brides and grooms were sometimes treated as queens and kings at wedding ceremonies. The book celebrates the physical love of husbands and wives for each other.

Some Jews have understood the book as a poem about the love of God for Israel. Some Christians explain it as describing the love of Christ for the Church. It seems more natural to understand the book as about human love. The book teaches that God is the Creator of marriage and sex. These are among His good gifts to the human race.

***See* ceremony, Christ, Christian, church, gift, Israel, love**

Song of Songs (SAHNG uv SAHNGZ) *proper noun phrase:*

See **Song of Solomon**

sons of the prophets (SUNZ uv thuh PRAHF-its) *noun phrase:*

The sons of the prophets were the disciples of the prophets.

1 Kings 20:35; 2 Kings 2:3, 5, 7, 15; 4:1, 38; 5:22; 6:1; Amos 7:14

See **disciple, prophet**

soothsayer (SEWTH-SAY-er) *noun:*

A soothsayer was a person who predited the future by using signs in nature. This pagan practice was against the law of God and was not allowed in Israel.

Soothsaying is the practice of a soothsayer.

Deuteronomy 18:14; Joshua 13:22; 2 Kings 21:6; Isaiah 2:6; Micah 5:12; Daniel 2:27; 4:7; 5:7, 11; Acts 16:16

See **astrology, false prophet, magic, pagan, prophet, sorcery**

sorcery (SOHR-ser-ee) *noun:*

Sorcery is an attempt to use evil, supernatural means to influence people and events. Sorcery uses magic charms, drugs, and spells to try to produce evil results. The Bible rejects the practice of sorcery. A person who practiced sorcery was called a sorcerer.

Exodus 22:18; Deuteronomy 18:10; Isaiah 47:9, 12; Jeremiah 27:9; Acts 8:9, 11; 13:6, 8; Galatians 5:20; Revelation 9:21; 18:23; 21:8; 22:15

See **astrology, evil, false prophet, magic, soothsayer, supernatural, witch**

soteriology (soh-TIR-ee-AHL-uh-jee) *noun:*

Soteriology is the doctrine of salvation. The term comes from two Greek words meaning "salvation" and "word."

See **adoption, assurance, atonement, eschatology, grace, redemption, regeneration, salvation, sanctification, sin**

soul (SOHL) *noun:*

Soul is a way of describing a person as a living being. Sometimes soul refers to the part of a person that lives on after death.

The Hebrew word that is translated *soul* means "breath" or "possessing life." The Old Testament uses the word to speak of both humans and animals. Soul can mean living beings, self, and person. The Hebrew word suggests that the soul is the source of human emotion, will, and action. Soul sometimes means the same as mind.

The Old Testament usually speaks of the soul as departing at death. This simply means that the person is no longer alive. It does not mean that souls live on as spirits without bodies. Later, Judaism came to believe that the soul went to Sheol after death. A difference is made between soul and spirit in later parts of the Old Testament. There is a separate Hebrew word for spirit. But the relation between soul and spirit is not clear.

One Greek word for *life* is translated "soul" in the New Testament. The Greek word for *soul* does not mean life apart from a body. The New Testament does not give one clear meaning to the word *soul.* Sometimes the New Testament talks about a person as body and soul. It also talks about a person as body, soul, mind, and strength. These are not separate parts of people. They are ways of describing a human as a whole person.

Some Greeks taught that the soul and body were sharply different. The body was earthly and physical; the soul was eternal. The Greeks taught that the soul existed before the body. They said that the soul became trapped in a physical body at birth. But the soul would escape to the eternal world. This view has greatly influenced what Christians think about the soul.

The Bible does not teach the Greek view of the immortality of the soul. It stresses the resurrection of the dead. Those who are raised from the dead by Christ will receive a spiritual body. This will happen at the second coming of Christ.

The Christian faith teaches the resurrection of the whole person. This will happen to people when Christ returns in glory and judgment. But Christians believe that they will continue to exist as persons even after death. Christians go to be with Christ when they die (Philippians 1:21-23).

Genesis 1:20; 2:7; Job 10:1; Isaiah 14:9-17; Matthew 10:28; 16:25-27; Luke 23:40-43; Romans 8:38-39; 1 Corinthians 15:12-57; 2 Corinthians 5:1-8; 2 Timothy 1:9-10

***See* death, eternal, glorification, heaven, immortality, judgment, man, mind, resurrection, Second Coming, self, Sheol, spirit, will**

soul winning (SOHL WIN-ing) *noun phrase:*

Soul winning is the act of leading someone to faith in Christ. Soul winning refers to personal evangelism.

***See* confess, conversion, evangelical, evangelism, faith, gospel, Holy Spirit, salvation, soul, witness**

sovereign (SAHV-run) *adjective:*

Sovereign describes a person or country whose power to rule is not limited. A sovereign king or nation is not controlled by any other person or nation. A sovereign is a ruler of a nation.

Only God is sovereign in the full sense. All other powers are limited in some way. God is not limited by any power outside himself. God is sovereign in His acts of creation and redemption. His sovereignty was shown in the life, death, and resurrection of Jesus. The power of God can be limited only if God places limits on himself. He did this when He created Adam and Eve and gave them freedom. God limits himself when He enters into covenant with humanity. God does not force people to serve Him. The limits that God places on himself show how sovereign He really is.

2 Samuel 22:33; 1 Chronicles 29:11; Psalm 21:13; Isaiah 40:26, 29; Matthew 6:13; Romans 1:16; 1 Corinthians 1:18-25; Revelation 15:8

See **attribute, Calvinism, covenant, creation, election, freedom, God, holiness, Reformed tradition, resurrection, revelation, Second Coming, theism**

sovereignty (SAHV-run-tee) *noun:*

See **attribute, God, sovereign**

spirit (SPIR-ut) *noun:*

Spirit is the quality, power, or force that makes a person alive and acting. Spirit cannot be seen, but it is real. This is true of both the Spirit of God and the spirit of people. The Bible refers to human spirit, evil spirits, and the Divine Spirit. Both the Hebrew and Greek words translated *spirit* have a number of different meanings.

1. Both the Hebrew and Greek words that are usually translated *spirit* sometimes mean "blowing wind" (Exodus 10:13; Psalm 107:25; John 3:8). They may also mean "breath" (Ezekiel 37:5-6, 8, 10; 2 Thessalonians 2:8). The English word *spirit* comes from a Latin word meaning "breath."

2. The human spirit may refer to the attitude or character of a person. Sometimes the spirit of a person means simply the person as he or she really is (Number 14:24; Deuteronomy 34:9; Luke 1:80; Romans 1:9; 8:16; 1 Corinthians 2:11).

3. The term *spirit* may mean the whole person. Spirit and body together may refer to a whole person. Or spirit, soul, and body may refer to the unity that is one person. Spirit is merely one way of looking at and describing a person. A human cannot be divided into parts and remain a fully human person (2 Corinthians 7:1; Colossians 2:5; 1 Thessalonians 5:23).

The spirit of a human refers to his or her capacity to know God. Apart from Christ, the spirit of people is dead in sin. They cannot know God or be fully human until they are born again. Also, God wills that the Christian's spirit be filled with the Holy Spirit. Then the human spirit is set free from all that is opposed to God (John 3:3-8; 1 Corinthians 2:9-16; Galatians 5:16-25; Ephesians 3:14-21; 5:17-20).

4. Some scriptures seem to suggest that the spirit may be separated from the whole person. Spirit may refer to the part of a person that lives on after death (Ecclesiastes 12:7; Luke 8:55; 23:46; Acts 7:59; 1 Peter 3:18-20).

5. Sometimes *spirit* or *evil spirit* may refer to the sinful character of a person (1 Samuel 16:14-23; Hosea 5:4; Matthew 10:1; 12:43; Mark 1:23-27; 1 Timothy 4:1; 1 John 4:1-3).

6. The Old Testament refers only a few times to the Spirit of God. But this is the most frequent use of the term *spirit* in the New Testament. The phrase *Holy Spirit* appears only three times in the Old Testament. But this

is a very common way of referring to the Spirit of God in the New Testament. The King James Version usually uses *Holy Ghost* instead of *Holy Spirit* (Isaiah 63:10-11; Matthew 3:11; 28:19; John 20:22; Acts 1:2, 5, 8, 16; Romans 5:5; 1 Corinthians 6:19; Titus 3:5).

The Old Testament does not view the Spirit of God as a separate being. The *spirit of God* is simply "God," who is present, powerful, and acting in His world. It is usually just a way of speaking of His immanence.

Often the Spirit means the power of God that helps people to do His will. The Spirit is the way God inspired prophets and the Scriptures (Genesis 1:2; 6:3; Numbers 11:25; 1 Samuel 11:6; 16:13-14; Job 33:4; Psalm 139:7-12; Isaiah 11:1-3; Micah 3:8; 2 Timothy 3:16).

The Old Testament stresses the power that God's Spirit gives to a few special people. He gave strength even to people like Samson, whose behavior was not righteous (Judges 13—16). The New Testament is different. There Jesus is the example of life in the power of the Spirit. The New Testament stresses the power the Spirit gives all Christians to become like Christ. The New Testament especially stresses the Spirit as the Source of righteousness and holy living. The Holy Spirit is the sanctifying Spirit (Romans 8:2-4; 2 Corinthians 3:17-18; 2 Thessalonians 2:13; 1 Peter 1:2).

The New Testament refers to the Spirit in several important ways. He is the Spirit of God. He is the Spirit of the Lord. He is the Spirit of Christ (Romans 8:9-11). Sometimes the Spirit is named along with the Father and the Son (Matthew 28:19; 2 Corinthians 13:14). Both God the Father and the risen Christ are spirit. The Holy Spirit is spirit in the same way Father and Son are spirit (John 4:23-29; Acts 16:7; Romans 8:9-17; 2 Corinthians 3:17-18).

The New Testament provides the major basis for the Christian doctrine of the Holy Spirit. Scholars in the Church raised difficult questions about what the New Testament meant. Thus, the doctrine of the Holy Spirit developed as the Church matured. The Church came to understand the Holy Spirit as the Third Person of the Trinity. The Holy Spirit was seen as the Agent of all God does in the world. He is God acting to bring redemption. He is God continuing the work of Christ in the world. He is God as close to people as their breath.

The Holy Spirit presents sinners with the claims of Christ and the gospel. He draws people to salvation (John 16:7-15). He makes faith possible and completely changes those who will believe (2 Thessalonians 2:13; 1 Peter 1:2). Christians are former sinners who have been "born of the Spirit" (John 3:5-8). The Holy Spirit is the divine Agent in sanctifying believers. He sets them free from the power of sin. He produces in them the character of Christ. Thus, Christian moral virtues are the "fruit of the Spirit" (Romans 8:2; 1 Corinthians 6:11; 2 Corinthians 1:21-22; Galatians 5:22-23).

The Spirit is also the Christians' first taste and promise of glory. This is the glory they will receive when Christ returns (Romans 5:1-5; 8:22-23; 2 Corinthians 1:21-22; Ephesians 4:30). The Holy Spirit is the basis of the hope believers have for the future resurrection.

The Holy Spirit helps Christians to pray. The Bible says that the Spirit intercedes for us (Romans 8:26-27).

The Holy Spirit creates the Church and makes it one in Christ. The Holy Spirit makes the Church able to fulfill its first calling. This is to worship God and enjoy Him forever (Ephesians 3:14; 4:3-16).

See **body, born again, Christ, church, divine, doctrine, evil, fruit of the Spirit, glorification, God, holy, Holy Spirit, immanence, intercession, inspiration, life, Lord, power, prophet, regeneration, resurrection, righteous, soul, version, virtue, worship**

spiritual (SPIR-uh-chuh-wul or SPIR-uh-chwul) *adjective:*

Spiritual describes someone or something that is related to spirit, especially the Spirit of God. For example, spiritual gifts are gifts given to Christians by the Holy Spirit.

Sometimes *spiritual* means the same as "religious" or "pious." A spiritual person is one who is devoted to God and religious matters. A spiritual person is one who is led by the Holy Spirit.

Spiritual needs describe the things people need that only the Holy Spirit can provide. They include such things as salvation, sanctification, and hope. People who are sinners, backslidden, or not disciplined have serious spiritual needs.

A spiritual being is one whose existence does not depend on a physical body. Thus, God, angels, and demons are called spiritual beings.

Hosea 9:7; Romans 1:11; 7:14; 15:27; 1 Corinthians 2:13—3:1; 14:1, 37; 15:44-46; Galatians 6:1; 1 Peter 2:5

See **angel, backslide, body, demon, gift, God, Holy Spirit, hope, piety, salvation, sanctification**

spiritual death (SPIR-uh-chuh-wul or SPIR-uh-chwul DETH) *noun phrase:*

See **death, spiritual**

spiritual gifts (SPIR-uh-chuh-wul or SPIR-uh-chwul GIFTS) *noun phrase:*

See **gift**

sprinkling (SPRINGK-ling) *noun:*

Sprinkling is one way the sacrament of water baptism is done. The minister allows drops of water to fall from his or her fingers onto the person's head.

See **baptism, minister, ritual, sacrament**

steadfast love (STED-fast LUV) *noun phrase:*

See **lovingkindness**

Stephen (STEE-vun) *proper noun:*

Stephen was a Jewish Christian in the Early Church. He was one of the seven deacons.

Stephen preached boldly, and he did great signs and wonders in Jerusalem. The enemies of the Church accused Stephen of blasphemy. The Jewish leaders had Stephen stoned to death by the people. Stephen was the first Christian martyr.

Acts 6:1—7:60

See **blasphemy, deacon, martyr, sign**

steward (STEW-erd) *noun:*

A steward is one who is trusted to care for what belongs to another. Stewards in the Old Testament were people who cared for houses belonging to others. Steward in the New Testament has two meanings. (1) A steward may be one who takes care of another person. (2) A steward may be the one who manages the property of another person.

Christians are sometimes called stewards in the New Testament. They are stewards of the grace of God. The care for the gospel has been given to them. They are stewards of the gifts God gives to the Church.

Genesis 43:19; 44:4; Luke 16:2-4; 12:42; 16:1, 3, 8; 1 Corinthians 4:1-2; Titus 1:7; 1 Peter 4:10

See **Christian, disciple, faithful, gift, gospel, grace, offering, servant, tithe**

stewardship (STEW-erd-ship) *noun:*

Stewardship is the act of fulfilling the duties of a steward. The Christian life should be one of stewardship. All that a Christian is and has belongs to God. He trusts Christians to care for what belongs to Him. Thus, stewardship is a way of caring for what God has entrusted to Christians. Such care seeks to bring honor to God.

Stewardship usually refers to giving money to care for the church. But stewardship is much more than this. It includes all parts of life, such as one's time, talents, and possessions.

See **steward**

stumbling block (STUM-bling BLAHK) *noun phrase:*

A stumbling block is anything that causes a person to trip and fall. It especially refers to something that traps the one who falls. The Old Testament refers to idols as stumbling blocks. Idols caused Israel to sin and fall away from God (Isaiah 57:13-14; Ezekiel 7:19-20; 14:3-5).

Paul warned certain strong Christians against eating meat offered to idols. Their example could cause weak Christians to go against what they felt was right. The wrong use of freedom was a sin against fellow Christians. It could cause weak persons to lose their faith. Thus, Paul called such persons stumbling blocks (Romans 14:13-23; 1 Corinthians 8:1-13).

The New Testament says that Jesus Christ was a stumbling block to the Jews. Christians claimed that Jesus of Nazareth was the Messiah. But the Jews said that He had died on the Cross because He broke the law. Thus, they refused to accept Him as their Messiah. They thought that those who believed in Him had fallen into a dangerous trap. But Christians claimed that the *block* the Jews rejected was precious. Christians believed God had made Jesus the most important *block* in the spiritual *temple.* The Church was this spiritual temple. It was made up of the people of God.

Matthew 21:42-43; Romans 9:30-33; 1 Corinthians 1:18-25; Galatians 3:10-14; 6:16; Ephesians 2:19-22; Philippians 3:3-21; 1 Peter 2:4-10

See **Christ, Christian, church, cross, faith, freedom, idol, Israel, Jesus, Jew, law, Messiah, temple**

subsequent to regeneration (SUB-suh-kwent tew ree-JEN-er-AY-shun) *adjective phrase:*

Subsequent to regeneration describes when entire sanctification happens. The word *subsequent* means that one event happens after an earlier one. Entire sanctification occurs after the experience of regeneration. That is, it is subsequent to regeneration.

Romans 12:1-2; 1 Thessalonians 4:3; 5:23-24

See **entire sanctification, Holiness Movement, new birth, regeneration, sanctification, Wesleyanism**

substitutionary theory of the Atonement (SUB-stuh-TEW-shun-nair-ree THEE-uh-ree uv thee un-TOHN-ment) *noun phrase:*

The substitutionary theory of the Atonement is one view of how the death of Christ provides salvation. It views the Atonement as meeting the demands of divine justice. Divine justice demands that sin be punished and justice satisfied. The death of Christ satisfied the demands of justice that sin be punished. The sinless Christ accepted the punishment for sin that sinful people should have received. This view shows how the Atonement reveals both God's love and His justice. The substitutionary theory of the Atonement is the view held by most Calvinists.

See **atonement, John Calvin, Calvinism, Christ, cross, forgiveness, justice, love, penalty, propitiation, Reformed tradition, sacrifice, salvation, sin**

suffering (SUF-er-ing) *noun:*

Suffering is the experience of physical, mental, or spiritual pain or stress. Both humans and animals can experience suffering. A person may choose to suffer, or suffering may be forced on him or her.

People experience suffering for many reasons. There are also many kinds of suffering or afflictions. Suffering may come from persecution, sickness, war, hunger, disease, bad habits, or foolish decisions.

Suffering was not a part of the plan God had for the world. God does not want anyone to suffer. Suffering came into the world because of sin. But this does not mean that all suffering is a direct result of sin. Many times the reasons for suffering are not known. God will do away with all suffering in the new heaven and earth.

The New Testament says that Christians should expect to share in the sufferings of Christ. They should identify with the work and purposes of Christ, the Suffering Servant. Christians become instruments of redemption in this way.

Genesis 3:15; 47:9; Isaiah 53; 63:9; Matthew 16:24; Mark 10:39; John 16:21; Romans 8:17-18; 1 Corinthians 15:26; Philippians 1:29; Colossians 1:24; 1 Thessalonians 3:1-5; Hebrews 10:14; 12:1-2; Revelation 12:1-2, 13-17

See **alien, bereave, death, fall, persecution, redeem, redemption, servant, temptation, tribulation**

Suffering Servant (SUF-er-ing SER-vunt) *proper noun phrase:*

See **Jesus, suffering**

Sunday (SUN-day or SUN-dee) *proper noun:*

Sunday is the usual day of Christian worship. The first day of the week became the day of worship for the early Christians. It celebrates the resurrection of Christ, which took place on that day.

See **Christian, Lord's Day, resurrection, Sabbath, Seventh Day, worship**

Sunday, Billy (SUN-day or SUN-dee, BIL-ee) *proper noun:*

See **revival**

supernatural (SEW-per-NACH-er-ul) *adjective:*

Supernatural describes powers and events that cannot be explained through human or natural causes. Many things are called supernatural simply because people do not understand them. Sometimes magic is described as supernatural. Sometimes supernatural is used to describe the works of evil.

Supernatural should properly refer only to God. Only the acts of God are beyond nature. All powers other than God are created ones. Thus, they are natural. Only the Creator is beyond the creation. Only He is supernatural.

See **creation, demon, evil, faith, God, magic, miracle, nature, Satan, sorcery, sovereign, spiritual**

superstition (SEW-per-STI-shun) *noun:*

A superstition is a belief about why things happen without good reason. A superstition has no basis in fact. Superstitions result from fear of what is not known, or from lack of knowledge.

See **magic**

Sychar (SIE-kahr) *proper noun:*

Sychar was a town in Samaria near Jacob's well. Jesus talked to a Samaritan woman at Jacob's well (John 4:3-42). Sychar was probably the same place as Shechem.

See **Jacob, Samaria, Samaritan, Shechem, Sychar (map 8)**

symbol (SIM-bul) *noun:*

A symbol is something that stands for or suggests something else. A symbol can stand for something else when people agree to give it that meaning. Symbols usually exist in a community and have real importance only for the community. The community shares the meaning of the symbol and keeps the symbol alive.

Some examples of symbol follow. The flag of a nation is a symbol shared by the citizens of that nation. The flag stands for all that the nation means to its citizens. Wild beasts symbolize pagan nations in the Book of Daniel. The cross on a church is a symbol that it is a Christian church. It stands for all God did in Christ to bring salvation to the world.

See **Christian, cross, Daniel, pagan, Protestant, Roman Catholic, sacrament, sign**

synagogue (SIN-uh-gahg) *noun:*

A synagogue is a place of worship for Jews. A synagogue can be organized wherever 10 or more males meet for worship. Jews gather at the synagogue to worship God and study the Hebrew Scriptures.

Synagogues came into existence during the Exile. They have been the only place of worship for Jews since A.D. 70. The second Temple was destroyed at that time. It has never been rebuilt.

Worship in a synagogue in the time of Jesus included lessons from the Torah. It also included lessons from the prophets, the Shema, Psalms, and 18 benedictions. Some synagogues today are called temples.

Matthew 4:23; 12:9-14; Mark 1:21-25; Luke 4:15-21; 13:10-17; John 9:22; Acts 13:15

See **benediction, dispersion, exile, Jerusalem, Jew, Judaism, prophet, Psalms, scripture, Shema, temple, Torah, worship**

Synoptic Gospels (suh-NAHP-tik GAHS-pulz) *proper noun phrase:*

The Synoptic Gospels are the Gospels of Matthew, Mark, and Luke. The word *synoptic* comes from two Greek words meaning seen together. The Synoptic Gospels tell the good news about Jesus in very similar ways. Their words and order of events are very much alike. Most scholars today believe that Mark was the earliest Gospel. Matthew and Luke may have used Mark in writing their Gospels. They also seem to have used another common source for the sayings of Jesus.

See **gospel, Jesus, Luke, Mark, Matthew, New Testament**

Syria (SIR-ee-uh) *proper noun:*

Syria was a small nation located north and east of the Sea of Galilee. Syria often caused trouble for Israel. Syria is called Aram in some versions of the Bible. The capital city of Syria was Damascus.

See **Damascus (map 3), Galilee, Syria (maps 4 and 8)**

systematic theology (SIS-tuh-MAT-ik thee-AHL-uh-jee) *noun phrase:*

Systematic theology is a complete statement of the nature and content of the Christian faith. All the important Christian doctrines are stated in an orderly and connected way. The central subject of systematic theology is God. Some of the other major doctrines are hamartiology, Christiology, soteriology, pneumatology, eschatology, and ethics.

Systematic theology is a service done for the church by scholars called systematic theologians. They help the church understand its faith. They also explain the Christian faith to those who are not Christians.

See **apologetics, Christology, church, doctrine, eschatology, ethics, God, hamartiology, pneumatology, revelation, soteriology, theism, theology**

T t

tabernacle (TAB-ber-NAK-ul) *noun:*

A tabernacle was a house, like a tent or hut, that could be moved (Psalm 76:1-2). The people of Israel lived in tabernacles as they moved from Egypt to Canaan.

The most important tabernacle in the Old Testament was Israel's house of worship. God told Moses to build a special tent as a sanctuary. The Tabernacle was about 45 feet (14 meters) long by 15 feet (4.5 meters) wide. It was divided into two parts. The outer room was called the holy place. It was 30 (9 meters) feet long by 15 feet (4.5 meters) wide. The inner room was called the most holy place, or holy of holies. The ark of the covenant was kept in this inner part. The altar, where sacrifices were offered, was placed outside in front of the Tabernacle. The Tabernacle was the house of God in a special way. God met His people there as they worshiped Him (Exodus 35:4-19; Deuteronomy 31:15; Psalm 61:4; Isaiah 33:20; Hebrews 8:2; 9:11).

The people of Israel moved the Tabernacle as they traveled from place to place. The Levites set up the tent sanctuary in each place that Israel camped. Solomon built the Temple in Jerusalem to take the place of this Tabernacle.

The New Testament uses the word *tabernacle* as a figure of speech. The physical body is like a tabernacle where the spirit dwells. The spiritual body will take the place of the physical body after the resurrection (2 Corinthians 4:16—5:20; 2 Peter 1:13-14).

***See* altar, ark, Canaan (map 3), Egypt (map 2), Exodus, festival, holy of holies, holy place, Jerusalem (map 5), Levite, Moses, Old Testament, Philistine, resurrection, sanctuary, Solomon, spiritual, temple, worship**

Tabor (TAY-ber) *proper noun:*

Tabor is a mountain in the southern part of Galilee. It is mentioned several times in the Old Testament. Some Bible scholars believe Mount Tabor is the place of the Transfiguration.

Judges 4:6, 12, 14; Psalm 89:12; Jeremiah 46:18; Hosea 5:1

***See* Galilee, Tabor (map 8), Transfiguration**

talent (TAL-unt) *noun:*

A talent was a way people in the Bible weighed things. The talent let them know how heavy something was. A talent was the largest weight mentioned in the Old Testament. A talent was used to measure gold, silver, lead, iron, and bronze (see Exodus 38:29; 1 Kings 9:14; 2 Kings 5:22-23; 1 Chronicles 29:1-9; Zechariah 5:7; Matthew 18:24).

A talent can mean the way a debt is figured (Matthew 18:23-25).

A talent also means a spiritual gift that God gives to Christians

(1 Corinthians 12:4-10). People should use their talents to serve God (Matthew 25:15-28).

See **gift, spiritual, steward**

Tamar (TAY-mahr) *proper noun:*

Tamar is the name of three women in the Old Testament.

1. Tamar was the daughter-in-law of Judah, who was a son of Jacob. Tamar was childless. Through deceit, she became pregnant by Judah. She had twin sons, Perez and Zerah. Perez was an ancestor of King David (see Genesis 38; Ruth 4:12). Tamar is one of four women who are listed as an ancestor of Jesus (Matthew 1:3).

2. Tamar was a daughter of King David (2 Samuel 13:1).

3. Tamar was the daughter of Absolom and granddaughter of King David (2 Samuel 14:27).

See **David, Jacob, Judah**

tares (TAIRZ) *noun:*

Tares are a kind of weed that looks like wheat. It is difficult to tell the difference between tares and the wheat until harvest time.

Matthew 13:24-30, 36-43

See **parable**

Tarsus (TAHR-sus) *proper noun:*

Tarsus was a city in Asia Minor. It was a harbor city on the Mediterranean Sea. It was an important city in the Roman Empire in New Testament times.

The apostle Paul was born and raised in Tarsus. After his conversion, He lived several years in Tarsus.

Acts 9:11; 11:25; 21:39; 22:3; Galatians 1:21; 2:1

See **apostle, Asia Minor, Mediterranean Sea, Paul, Rome, Tarsus (maps 9, 11)**

temperance (TEM-pruns or TEM-puh-runs) *noun:*

Temperance is the exercise of self-control in matters that relate to human desires. Temperance means controlling the desire for and use of physical things. For example, food is not evil. But people should not eat too much of it. Temperance includes controlling the desire to eat too much.

The New Testament calls temperance a Christian virtue. Temperance or self-control is also a fruit of the Spirit (Galatians 5:22-23).

Sometimes temperance means refusing to use drinks that have alcohol in them.

Acts 24:25; 1 Corinthians 9:25; Titus 1:8; 2:2; 2 Peter 1:6

See **abstinence, disciple, discipline, drunkenness, fruit of the Spirit, gossip, growth in grace, modesty, obedience, piety, self-control, virtue**

temple (TEM-pul) *noun:*

A temple is a building for the worship of a god or gods (1 Samuel 5:2; 1 Chronicles 10:10; Acts 19:27).

Solomon had a beautiful temple for the worship of God built in Jerusalem. It was dedicated about 950 B.C. It took the place of the simple Tabernacle used earlier. It was built to house the ark of the covenant. Like the Tabernacle, it also had the holy place and the holy of holies. It was to be a special house of God.

Solomon knew that God was too great to be limited to the Temple. But it was the special place where God had chosen to make himself known. The people of Judah began to rely too much on the Temple. The prophets told them that God did not need the Temple or their sacrifices. He wanted their obedience and worship. The prophets warned the people to repent or the Temple would be destroyed. The people refused to believe the prophets. The Temple and the ark were destroyed by Babylon in 586 B.C. (1 Kings 5—9; 2 Kings 25:8-12).

The Jews who returned after the Exile built another, less beautiful Temple. This second Temple was dedicated to the worship of God in 515 B.C. (Ezra 1:1-5; 3:7-13; Haggai 1:1-11).

Herod had the Temple completely rebuilt on a grand scale. The building was not finished until about 60 years after his death. It was perhaps more beautiful than even Solomon's Temple was (John 2:20).

Jesus visited this Temple and taught there. He chased out the money changers. He predicted that the Temple would be destroyed. Early Jewish Christians continued to worship at the Temple. The Romans destroyed the Temple in A.D. 70, not long after it was completed.

Matthew 21:12-13; 24:1-2; John 2:13-22; 7:14-15; 10:22-39; Acts 5:42

See **ark, Babylon, covenant, exile, God, Herod, holy of holies, holy place, Jerusalem (map 10), Jew, prophet, Rome, sacrifice, Solomon, tabernacle, temple of the Holy Spirit, worship**

temple of the Holy Spirit (TEM-pul uv thuh HOH-lee SPIR-ut) *noun phrase:*

The temple of the Holy Spirit is a phrase used by the apostle Paul. It refers to the Church, which is the Body of Christ. The Holy Spirit lives in the Church through its members. Christians make up the Body of Christ.

God no longer has the Temple in Jerusalem as His dwelling place. Now He lives in people who have been born again through Christ. They are His temple.

The Jerusalem Temple was a place where God was worshiped. Sacrifices of praise were made to Him there. Now Christians daily give themselves to God as an act of worship. They worship God through all they do. They are to bring glory to God through their bodies. They are the temple of the Holy Spirit.

1 Corinthians 3:16-17; 6:13-20; 2 Corinthians 6:16; 1 Peter 2:4-10

***See* apostle, body of Christ, Christ, church, 1 and 2 Corinthians, glory, Holy Spirit, Jerusalem, new birth, pagan, Paul, sanctification, temple, worship**

tempt (TEMPT) *verb:*

To tempt means "to test" or "to prove." God tested the faith of Abraham to see how strong his obedience was. The people of Israel tested God because they did not believe His promises. They acted as though they did not believe that He was truly God. They sinned when they tested God.

Satan tested or tempted Jesus. He tried to get Jesus to disobey His Heavenly Father. He tried to get Jesus to bring the kingdom of God through wrong ways. Satan is called "the tempter."

Satan sometimes tempts people to disobey God and do what is wrong. He tests the faith a person has in God. The Bible sometimes speaks of temptation without blaming it on the devil. People cannot be tempted unless what they are tempted to do appeals to them.

Genesis 22:1; Exodus 17:2, 7; Psalm 78:18, 41; Matthew 4:7; 16:1; Mark 1:13; Galatians 6:1; James 1:13-15

***See* Abraham, devil, faith, Jew, obedience, Satan, sin, temptation, trial**

temptation (temp-TAY-shun) *noun:*

Temptation is the experience of being enticed by something attractive, which can draw the person away. A temptation may lead someone's attention away from God and His will. It may be an experience of severe suffering or a problem. It may be something that is evil.

The temptation of Jesus was His time of testing by Satan in the desert.

A temptation is not a sin. But it can lead to sin if a person gives in to it.

Matthew 4:1-11; 6:13; 26:41; Luke 4:13; 1 Corinthians 10:13; James 1:13-15

***See* faith, Jesus, obedience, Satan, sin, suffering, tempt, tribulation, will**

tempter (TEMP-ter) *noun:*

***See* Satan, tempt**

Ten Commandments (TEN kuh-MAND-munts) *proper noun phrase:*

The Ten Commandments are the laws that God gave to Israel through Moses. The 10 religious and moral laws were given to him on Mount Sinai.

The Ten Commandments were written on tablets of stone. These were kept in the ark of the covenant. These laws were the foundation of many other laws of the people. The Ten Commandments are for everyone. They refer to all people of all places of all times. The Ten Commandments are found in Exodus 20:1-17 and Deuteronomy 5:6-21.

The Ten Commandments tell how the people were to live in fulfilling their covenant with God.

The New Testament says that Christians are to obey the Ten Commandments. Both Testaments agree that all the commandments are summed up in one Great Commandment. This is to love God and one's neighbor as oneself.

Deuteronomy 6:4-6; Matthew 22:34-40; Mark 10:17-22; 12:28-33; Romans 13:8-10; Galatians 5:14

***See* ark, commandment, covenant, Deuteronomy, Exodus, God, Great Commandment, law, love, mediator, morality, Moses, New Testament, religious, testament**

teraphim (TAIR-uh-fim) *plural noun:*

Teraphim were images or idols owned by ancient Israel. One idol was called a *teraph.*

Rachel took teraphim from her father, Laban. Teraphim were idols people had in their houses. People used teraphim to find out what God was thinking. The prophets often said that teraphim were wrong. They said the Jews should not own or use teraphim.

Genesis 31:19, 30, 32; Judges 18:17, 24; 2 Kings 23:24; Ezekiel 21:21; Hosea 3:4; Zechariah 10:2

***See* idol, Israel, Jew, prophet, Rachel**

testament (TES-tuh-munt) *noun:*

A testament is a covenant or agreement. Testament comes from a word that means "covenant."

Testament is the term used for the two main divisions of the Bible. The two divisions are the Old Testament and the New Testament. *Old* refers to the covenant that God made with Israel at Sinai. *New* refers to the new covenant that God made with the world through Jesus Christ.

Matthew 26:28; Mark 14:24; Luke 22:20; 1 Corinthians 11:25; 2 Corinthians 3:6, 14; Hebrews 7:22; 9:15-20; Revelation 11:19

***See* Christ, covenant, Lord's Supper, Moses, New Testament, Old Testament, Sinai (map 2)**

testimony (TES-tuh-moh-nee) *noun:*

A testimony is a witness to or proof of an agreement or covenant. A testimony is a way of showing that one is faithful to an agreement or covenant.

God gave the Ten Commandments as a way of showing His faithfulness to Israel. Israel was to give testimony to the covenant by obeying the Ten Commandments. The Ten Commandments were kept in the ark of the covenant. The ark of the covenant was also called the ark of the testimony.

Jesus Christ is the testimony or witness of the new covenant. He is the testimony through His life, death, and resurrection. Those who receive Christ as Savior receive Him as the testimony of God. The Holy Spirit gives witness to Christians that Christ is the true testimony. Christians then become testimonies to Christ. They witness for Christ through what they say and do. Believers may give testimony by telling others what Jesus means to them.

The word *martyr* comes from the Greek word that means "witness" or "testimony." A martyr gives testimony to Christ when he or she is killed because of his or her faith.

Exodus 30:26; 31:7; 32:15; Deuteronomy 4:45; Nehemiah 9:34; Psalms 19:7; 25:10; 93:5; 119:146; John 3:32-33; 5:33-47; 8:17-18; 1 Corinthians 1:6; 2:1

See **Apostles' Creed, ark, Christ, covenant, Eucharist, faith, faithfulness, Great Commission, martyr, mission, preach, tabernacle, temple, Ten Commandments, witness, witness of the Spirit**

tetragrammaton (TET-ruh-GRAM-uh-tahn) *noun:*

Tetragrammaton means the four-letter name for God. The name of Yahweh in Hebrew had four letters, YHWH. Sometimes the tetragrammaton JHVH is used for Jehovah.

See **God, Jehovah, Yahweh**

text (TEKST) *noun:*

Text usually means the written or printed material on pages in books. It can also mean the subject or title of a speech. Text can refer to a very old copy of Scripture written by hand. A text can mean the scripture that provides the basis for a sermon.

See **Bible, preach, sermon, translate**

Thaddeus (THAD-ee-us) *proper noun:*

Thaddeus was one of the 12 disciples of Jesus (Matthew 10:3; Mark 3:18). He is same person as Judas, the son of James (Luke 6:16; Acts 1:13). In some Bible translations, his first name is Lebbeus.

See **apostle, disciple, Judas**

thanksgiving (THANGKS-GIV-ing) *noun:*

Thanksgiving is the act of giving thanks for blessings one has received. It is to say or to show that one is grateful to another. Thanks that is given to God is a form of praise and worship.

A day of thanksgiving is celebrated as a national holiday in some countries. For example, Thanksgiving is a major holiday in the United States and Canada. It occurs on the fourth Thursday of November in the United States. It occurs on the second Monday of October in Canada.

Matthew 26:27; Luke 22:17; 1 Corinthians 1:4; Ephesians 1:15-23

See **praise, worship**

theism (THEE-iz-um) *noun:*

Theism refers to a group of religions that are based on belief in one God. They are monotheistic religions. The major theistic religions are Christianity, Judaism, and Islam.

These religions believe that God is real and that He created the world.

Theism says that God is active in the world. It says that there are no gods beside Him. Theism teaches that all that exists depends on God for that existence.

Isaiah 46

See **attribute, Christianity, deism, God, god, henotheism, Islam, Judaism, monotheism, pantheism, polytheism, revelation**

theodicy (thee-AHD-uh-see) *noun:*

Theodicy is an attempt to explain why evil exists in the world. Theodicy shows how God can be all-good and all-powerful and still allow evil. Theodicy shows that evil in the world does not mean God does not exist. It tries to show how God acts in the world. The Book of Job is an early example of theodicy.

See **covenant, evil, fall, freedom, grace, Job, justice, loving-kindness, omnipotence, providence**

theology (thee-AHL-uh-jee) *noun:*

Theology is the study of God as He has made himself known. Theology also studies how the people of God have responded to revelation. It tries to interpret revelation.

There are several kinds of theology: (1) biblical theology, which studies what the Bible teaches; (2) historical theology, which studies the growth of the Church and its doctrines; (3) systematic theology, which studies and relates all the doctrines of the Church; (4) moral theology, which looks into the meaning of Christian ethics; and (5) pastoral theology, which studies the life of faith in the Church today.

See **Apostles' Creed, belief, divinity, doctrine, ethics, evangelism, faith, heretic, orthodox, systematic theology**

Theophilus (thee-AHF-uh-lus) *proper noun:*

Theophilus is a man in the New Testament. Luke wrote the Gospel of Luke (Luke 1:3) and the Book of Acts (Acts 1:1) to Theophilus. His name means "friend of God."

See **Acts, gospel, Luke**

Thessalonians (THES-uh-LOH-nee-unz) *proper noun phrase:*

1. The Thessalonians were people who lived in the city of Thessalonica in Greece. The apostle Paul wrote two letters to the Christian converts in that city.

2. First and Second Thessalonians are two books in the New Testament. They are two of the epistles. They were written by the apostle Paul. They may be the earliest New Testament writings. They were written about A.D. 50.

Paul had to leave his converts in Thessalonica soon after they became Christians. He had been severely persecuted there and knew that they would be also. He feared that their suffering might cause them to reject their Christian faith. So Paul sent Timothy to encourage them. Timothy returned to the apostle with good news. The Thessalonians were still faithful and model Christians in spite of their troubles.

Paul wrote 1 Thessalonians to let them know how grateful he was to God for them. He praised them for their faithfulness. He reminded them of the call of God to holy living. He also reminded them that God was faithful to sanctify them completely. He wrote about the Second Coming. Second Thessalonians was written to correct wrong views some people held about the Second Coming.

See **convert, epistle, faithfulness, good news, Greece, Paul, sanctify, Second Coming, suffering, Thessalonica (map 11), Timothy**

Thessalonica (THES-uh-luh-NIE-kuh) *proper noun:*

Thessalonica was a city in Macedonia. The apostle Paul visited Thessalonica on his second missionary trip. He preached in the synagogue and helped to start a Christian church there. Paul wrote two letters to the Christians in this city.

See **apostle, Macedonia, missionary, Paul, synagogue, 1 and 2 Thessalonians, Thessalonica (map 11)**

Thomas (TAHM-us) *proper noun:*

Thomas was one of the 12 disciples of Jesus. People call him "doubting Thomas" because he refused to believe that Jesus had risen until he had physical proof. The Greek name of Thomas was Didymus. Both the names Thomas and Didymus mean "twin."

Matthew 10:3; Mark 3:18; John 14:1-6; 20:24-29

See **apostle, disciple, skeptic**

thorn in the flesh (THOHRN in thuh FLESH) *noun phrase:*

A thorn in the flesh is thought to be a physical affliction of some kind. The apostle Paul wrote about his thorn in the flesh. It is not known what kind of problem this may have been. Biblical scholars can only guess what it was.

Paul believed his thorn in the flesh was caused by Satan. But he also believed that God had a purpose in allowing it. It kept Paul from having too high an opinion of himself. He prayed three times that God would heal him. But God assured Paul that His grace was enough to help him overcome it. Paul learned from this experience to accept joyfully his difficulties.

The Old Testament speaks of a thorn in the side or in the eye (Numbers 33:55; Joshua 23:13). The pagan people of Canaan were a continuing source of problems for Israel. Canaanites were like thorns in Israel's side.

2 Corinthians 12:1-10

See **affliction, apostle, Canaan, Christ, flesh, grace, heal, healing, Israel, joy, Old Testament, pagan, Paul, prayer, Satan**

throne of God (THROHN uv GAHD) *noun phrase:*

Throne of God is a way the Bible describes the rule of God. He is Lord over all people and all things.

Earthly kings sat on special chairs called thrones. The throne was a symbol of their power and authority. The Bible speaks of God sitting on a throne. God does not really sit on a physical throne. But He does rule over all the earth.

Psalms 45:6; 47:8; Ezekiel 1:26; 10:1

See **God, heaven, holiness, kingdom of God, sovereign, symbol**

Tiberias (tie-BEE-ree-us) *proper noun:*

1. Tiberias was a ruler of the empire of Rome. He was ruler during the time of John the Baptist and Jesus (Luke 3:1). He was one of the Caesars.

2. Tiberias is a city on the western shore of the Sea of Galilee (John 6:23). It was built by Herod Antipas during the time of Christ. It was named for Caesar Tiberias. Tiberias is an important city in Israel today.

See **Caesar, Galilee, Herod, John, Jesus, Rome, Tiberias (map 8)**

Tigris (TIE-grus) *proper noun:*

Tigris is one of the two large rivers in Mesopotamia. It flowed from the Garden of Eden. It is mentioned with the Euphrates and two other rivers (Genesis 2:10-14). The Hebrew name for Tigris is *Hiddekel.*

See **Eden, Euphrates, Mesopotamia, Tigris (maps 1, 6)**

Timothy (TIM-uh-thee) *proper noun:*

1. Timothy was a young fellow worker of the apostle Paul. He traveled with Paul on some of his missionary journeys. Paul left him in charge of the church at Ephesus. Sometimes his name is spelled Timotheus in the King James Version.

2. First and Second Timothy are two books in the New Testament. They are epistles. They were letters written to Paul's young helper Timothy. They contain teachings concerning the daily life of a local church. They give rules for proper Christian worship. They give rules for church leaders, such as bishops, deacons, and elders. They also contain warnings against dangerous heresies in the Church, especially gnosticism. First and Second Timothy and Titus are sometimes called the Pastoral Epistles.

Acts 16:1—20:6; Romans 16:21; 1 Corinthians 4:17; 16:10; 2 Corinthians 1:19; Philippians 2:19-24; 1 Thessalonians 3:1-10; 1 and 2 Timothy

See **apostle, bishop, Christian, church, deacon, elder, Ephesus (map 11), epistle, gnosticism, heresy, missionary, New Testament, Pastoral Epistles, Paul, Titus, version, worship**

tithe (TIETH) *noun:*

A tithe is the tenth of a person's income paid to support the church. A tithe can be paid in money, crops, or animals.

Tithes in the Old Testament were paid to support a government or a religion (Leviticus 27:30-33; 1 Samuel 8:15-17). Most often, tithes were paid to support priests, Levites, and the Temple. Sometimes they were used for people with needs.

Abraham paid a tithe of his goods to Melchizedek. Jacob paid a tithe when he made a covenant with God at Bethel. Malachi accused the Jews of not bringing their tithes to the Temple. The Pharisees tithed even the herbs used to season food.

Jesus taught that His people should tithe. But the New Testament idea of stewardship goes beyond just the simple tithe.

Genesis 14:20; 28:16-22; Numbers 18:24-28; Deuteronomy 12:17-19; 14:22-29; Nehemiah 10:36-38

See **Abraham, Jacob, Levite, Malachi, Melchizedek, Pharisee, priest, stewardship, temple**

Titus (TIE-tus) *proper noun:*

1. Titus was a young fellow worker of the apostle Paul. He is not mentioned in the Book of Acts. But his importance to Paul is very clear in Galatians and 2 Corinthians. Titus later served as a leader of the churches of Crete.

2. Titus is a book in the New Testament. It was a letter written to Titus by Paul. It is similar to 1 and 2 Timothy in many ways. It is also called a pastoral epistle. The letter gives the pastoral guidance of the apostle Paul to his young helper.

2 Corinthians 2:12-13; 7:6-14; 8:6; 12:18; Galatians 2:1-3; 2 Timothy 4:10; Titus 1:4-5

See **Acts, apostle, church, 1 and 2 Corinthians, Crete, Crete (map 11), epistle, Galatians, New Testament, Pastoral Epistles, Paul, 1 and 2 Timothy**

tongue (TUNG) *noun:*

A tongue is that part of the human body that makes a person able to speak and taste (Judges 7:5; Mark 7:33-35).

The word *tongue* sometimes means speech. Speech is what a person says using his or her tongue (James 1:26; 3:5-8).

Tongue may mean a special kind of speech, that is, a certain natural language (Genesis 10:5, 20, 31; Deuteronomy 28:49; 2 Samuel 23:2; Isaiah 45:23; Daniel 1:4; Mark 16:17).

Tongues (plural) also means languages. Sometimes a Christian is given the power to speak in a language he or she had not learned. Those who received the Holy Spirit on the first Christian Pentecost were given this gift. Those who heard them speak understood them clearly in their own languages (Acts 2:4-11). Thus, the Holy Spirit helped the Church take the gospel to the whole world.

Acts tells of others who spoke in tongues when they received the Holy

Spirit. The Spirit helped them praise God and preach the gospel (Acts 10:46; 19:6).

Tongues seem to be used in another sense in 1 Corinthians 12—14. The Corinthians perhaps believed that the Holy Spirit allowed them to speak the language of angels (13:1). People could not understand them when they spoke in tongues. They could not even understand themselves (14:1-13).

Paul said that people who heard them speak in tongues would think they were crazy. This is why there needed to be a person who had the gift of explaining tongues. But Paul said that it would be much better if they prophesied instead (1 Corinthians 14:20-25). Paul told them that the gift of prophecy was more important than tongues. Prophecy was the ability given by the Spirit to preach the gospel (chapter 14). Paul said that not everyone who received the Holy Spirit would speak in tongues (12:27-30).

See **angel, 1 and 2 Corinthians, gift, glossolalia, gospel, Holy Spirit, love, Pentecost, praise, preach, prophesy, spirit**

tongues of fire (TUNGZ uv FIER) *noun phrase:*

Tongues of fire were flames of fire that appeared at the first Christian Pentecost. Something that looked like flames rested on each person present. The flames were in the shape of pointed tongues. Thus, they were called tongues of fire. The tongues of fire were signs of the coming of the Holy Spirit. He came to cleanse and give power to the disciples.

Acts 2:3-4

See **cleanse, disciple, Holy Spirit, Pentecost, sign**

topical (TAHP-uh-kul) *adjective:*

Topical describes a kind of sermon. A topical sermon is based on a topic instead of an exposition of the Scriptures.

See **exposition, Scripture, sermon**

Torah (TOH-ruh) *proper noun:*

Torah is the most general term for the law of God. *Torah* comes from the Hebrew word that means "law," "direction," or "teaching." The Pentateuch, the first five books of the Bible, is known as the Torah. But Torah sometimes refers to the whole Old Testament. Later the Hebrew Scriptures were divided into the Torah, the Prophets, and the Writings.

Genesis 26:5; Deuteronomy 4:8, 44; Joshua 1:7; 2 Kings 10:31; 2 Chronicles 6:16; 34:14; Psalms 19:7; 37:31; 119:77, 92; Isaiah 1:10; Amos 2:4; Malachi 2:6-9

See **covenant, law, Pentateuch, prophet, scripture**

total depravity (TOH-tul duh-PRAV-uh-tee) *noun phrase:*

Total depravity refers to the complete loss of the image of God in humanity. Reformed Christians teach that fallen humans have no divine life whatever. Only the grace of God can restore the divine image. But God offers this possibility to only a few. This is to show that He is sovereign. All others are totally without hope and cannot return to the image of God.

Wesleyans understand total depravity differently. They teach that the Fall did affect every part of humanity. Depravity is total in this sense only. They believe also that the prevenient grace of God is given to every fallen person. This makes it possible for even totally depraved people to repent, believe, and be saved (Romans 5:17-18; Philippians 2:12-13). The Holy Spirit convicts people of their sins through prevenient grace.

See **Calvinism, depravity, fall, grace, hope, image, original sin, prevenient grace, Reformed tradition, repent, salvation, save, sin, sinning religion, sovereign, Wesleyanism**

Tower of Babel (TOU-er uv BAY-bul) *proper noun phrase:*

See **Babel, Babylon**

Tower of Babylon (TOU-er uv BAB-uh-lun) *proper noun phrase:*

See **Babel, Babylon**

tradition (truh-DISH-un) *noun:*

Tradition is handing something on to one who follows. Tradition is what is given from one generation to the next. This includes beliefs, practices, and values. Tradition makes it possible that what one generation's values will be valued by the next. Tradition helps the new generation understand itself and its past. It also helps the new generation face the future. Tradition helps a person know his or her place in the community.

Tradition has a number of uses in the Bible and Christian doctrine. The stories of the patriarchs were part of the Jewish tradition. The teachers of the law applied the laws of Moses to life. The traditions they started were considered as important as the law itself. The Pharisees were angry with Jesus because He did not always obey their traditions.

Paul used the word *tradition* to describe the truths of the gospel that he taught. Tradition refers to the teachings that the apostles passed on to the Church. These truths concerning Christ and the gospel are the Christian tradition.

1 Chronicles 4:22; Matthew 15:2-6; Mark 7:1-13; 1 Corinthians 11:2; 15:1-8; Galatians 1:14; 2 Thessalonians 2:15; 3:6

See **Apostles' Creed, authority of Scripture, Catholic, Christ, Christian, church, creed, doctrine, elder, faith, gospel, Israel, Moses, patriarch, Pharisee, Protestant, Roman Catholic, scripture, Torah, truth, Wesleyan**

transcendence (tran-SEN-duns) *noun:*

Transcendence means the greatness of God in relation to His creation. He is above the world in every respect. He is the Creator of the world. The world depends on Him daily for existence. God is not limited by space and time as are His creatures. He is above the world in power and glory. He is the Cause of His own being.

The transcendence of God does not mean that He is separated from the world. He is very much involved in it. This is His immanence. But His very closeness to the world does not change His transcendence. The person who knows the closeness of God also knows that God alone is God. The transcendence of God is an important part of His holiness.

Deuteronomy 4:39; Joshua 2:11; 1 Kings 8:23; Isaiah 6:1-8; 46:1-13; Ezekiel 10:19; 11:22; Luke 11:2; Romans 1:18-25; 11:33-36

See **creation, deism, deity, God, holiness, Holy Spirit, immanence, infinite, Lord, pantheism, sovereign, theism, Yahweh**

Transfiguration (trans-FIG-yuh-RAY-shun) *proper noun:*

The Transfiguration was an event in the life of Jesus Christ that showed His deity. This event is recorded in all the Synoptic Gospels.

The Transfiguration happened on a mountain in the presence of three disciples. Jesus took Peter, James, and John to the top of a mountain to pray. The face of Jesus changed when He was praying. His face shone like the sun, and His clothes became very bright. Then God's voice said, "This is my Son . . . listen to him!" The disciples saw the glory of Christ.

Matthew 17:1-8; Mark 9:2-8; Luke 9:28-36

See **Christ, deity, glorify, glory, God, James, Jesus, John, Peter, resurrection, supernatural, Synoptic Gospels**

transgress (tranz-GRES) *verb:*

To trangress is to sin by disobeying or rejecting the law of God. To transgress is to resist God and to refuse to do His will. It is to disobey God willingly and knowingly.

Wesleyans teach that it is possible to transgress without doing it on purpose. Such transgressions are not properly called sins. All Christians fall short of the perfect law of God. They need the forgiveness of God and of other people when they do.

Numbers 14:41; Deuteronomy 17:2-7; Joshua 7:11-15; Psalm 51:1-14; Isaiah 24:5; 43:25-27; Jeremiah 3:11-14; Matthew 15:2-3; Galatians 2:21

See **faithful, God, law, mortal sin, sin, trespass, Wesleyanism, willful**

transgression (tranz-GRE-shun) *noun:*

Transgression is the act of trangressing. It is breaking the law of God.

Proverbs 17:11; Romans 4:15

See **law, sin, transgress**

translate (TRANZ-layt) *verb:*

To translate is to change something or someone from one position or condition to another. The word *translate* is used in various ways.

1. The Book of Hebrews says that Enoch was translated or taken to heaven before he died (Genesis 5:18-23; Hebrews 11:5).

2. Christians are those who have been translated from darkness to light.

They move from Satan's kingdom to the kingdom of Christ. This is one way Paul spoke of becoming a Christian. He meant that God changes the condition of those who accept Christ (Colossians 1:13).

3. To translate is to change from one language into another. The meaning of what is said in one language can be put into another. This process is called *translation*. A book written in one language can be translated into another language. The Bible is the best example of a book that has been translated.

See **Bible, darkness, Enoch, heaven, kingdom of God, light, Satan, scripture, translation, version**

translation (trans-LAY-shun) *noun:*

A translation is the result of translating. The Bible is the best example of a translation. It was written in languages that are no longer spoken. Thus, it had to be translated into the languages of today. There are over 1,500 translations of the Bible in the world.

New Bible translations are being made all the time. These are needed for various reasons. (1) The Bible has not yet been translated into some languages. Scholars are working on this. (2) Languages change. Words change their meaning. People do not use language exactly as those before them did. (3) The original writings of the authors of the Bible do not exist. They have been lost. Scholars continue to find earlier and better copies of these originals. Scholars also continue to learn more about what biblical writers meant by their words.

See **Bible, scripture, tongue, translate, version**

tree of knowledge (TREE uv NAHL-ij) *noun phrase:*

The tree of knowledge was a special tree in the Garden of Eden. God told Adam and Eve they could eat the fruit of every other tree. But He told them not to eat the fruit of this one tree. The tree was a symbol for the limits God sets on people.

The serpent told Eve that eating from the tree would make her wise. It would make her like God, knowing good and evil. The serpent deceived Adam and Eve, and they disobeyed God. Their transgression caused them to be separated from God. It caused them to experience shame. It caused them to blame each other and God for this. They had to leave the Garden of Eden.

Genesis 2:15-17; 3:1-24; Romans 1:18-25; 5:12-20; 7:7-11

See **Adam, Eden, Eve, evil, fall, God, original sin, serpent, sin, spiritual, symbol, transgress**

tree of life (TREE uv LIEF) *noun phrase:*

The tree of life was a special tree in the Garden of Eden. God caused Adam and Eve to leave the garden after they sinned. The tree of life is a symbol of eternal life. Eternal life is a special gift of God.

The Book of Revelation says that the tree of life will be in heaven. Eternal life remains a gift even in heaven.

Genesis 3:22-24; Revelation 2:7; 22:2, 14, 19

See **Eden, eternal, gift, God, immortality, life, sin, symbol, tree of knowledge**

trespass (TRES-PAS)

1. *verb:* To trespass means to sin. It means to disobey God, knowing it is wrong to do so. Sometimes to trespass means to sin without meaning to or without knowing it.

Sometimes people use the word *trespass* when they pray the Lord's Prayer. *Trespass* is the word used in the Anglican Book of Common Prayer. The word used in Matthew 6:12 is *debt*. The word used in Luke 11:4 is *sin*.

2. *noun:* A trespass is a wrong act. It is the act of trespassing.

Leviticus 5:6-19; 7:1-7; Numbers 5:6, 12, 27; 1 Samuel 6:3-17; 2 Chronicles 24:18; Ezra 9:6-15; Matthew 6:14-15; Mark 11:25-26; Ephesians 2:1

See **Anglican, debt, Lord's Prayer, offering, repent, sacrifice, sin, transgress**

trial (TRIE-ul) *noun:*

A trial is a test of the quality of someone or something. Difficult times that test the faithfulness of a person to God are called trials. Those who pass the test are proven to be true followers. The word temptation in the Bible sometimes means "trial." Trials often take the form of suffering or tribulation (Matthew 6:13; 26:41; Luke 4:13; 22:28; 2 Corinthians 8:2; Galatians 4:14; James 1:2, 12; 1 Peter 1:7; Revelation 3:10).

Trials are also a part of the legal system. They are conducted to find out whether a person is innocent or guilty. The trial of Jesus was the test by law that led to His crucifixion. The trial was not fair. The charges against Jesus were false (Matthew 26:57—27:31; Mark 14:53—15:20; Luke 22:54—23:25; John 18:12—19:16).

See **crucifixion, faithful, follower, suffering, temptation, tribulation**

tribes of Israel (TRIEBZ uv IZ-ree-ul) *noun phrase:*

The tribes of Israel were groups of families. The tribes formed one nation. They shared a common history and religion. The 12 tribes were descendants of the 12 sons of Jacob. They are Reuben, Simeon, Levi, Judah, Zebulun, Issachar, Dan, Gad, Asher, Naphtali, Joseph, and Benjamin. See Genesis 49:2-28.

The land of Palestine was divided among the 12 tribes. But the priestly tribe of Levi was to serve all tribes. So it was not given a separate area. Two of the areas were named after Joseph's sons to make up the 12. They were Ephraim and Manasseh. No part was named after Joseph himself.

The Book of Revelation uses the phrase *tribes of Israel*. It means all the people of God of all time (Revelation 7:4-8). The New Testament also uses *twelve tribes* to represent the whole Christian Church.

The so-called 10 lost tribes were those of the Northern Kingdom. Most of them became a part of the kingdom of Assyria after 721 B.C.

Joshua 13—19; Deuteronomy 33:6-25; 2 Kings 17; Ezekiel 48; Matthew 19:28; Luke 22:30; James 1:1

See **Asher, Assyria (map 6), Benjamin, Dan, Ephraim, Gad, Israel, Issachar, Jacob, Joseph, Judah, Levi, Manasseh, Naphtali, Palestine (map 3), patriarch, Reuben, Simeon, Zebulun**

tribulation (TRIB-yew-LAY-shun) *noun:*

Tribulation means severe oppression, affliction, suffering, or trouble of any kind. The word *tribulation* in both Hebrew and Greek means being pressed by difficult experiences. Tribulation includes such things as war, exile, being hated, being persecuted, or being put in prison. Sometimes such suffering is just a natural part of a person's life (Romans 12:12; James 1:27). It may be the result of living in a sinful world. Sometimes the Lord uses suffering as a punishment for sin (Romans 1:18-32; 2:9).

At other times, tribulation results when evil people persecute righteous people (1 Thessalonians 1:6; 2:14-16; 3:1-5; 2 Thessalonians 1:4-8).

The New Testament refers to a time of "great tribulation." It is a time of trouble that will cover the world near the end of time. Christians understand this in different ways depending on their views of eschatology. They place it at different times in relation to the Second Coming and the millenium.

The Great Tribulation may not even refer to the events of the Second Coming. It may simply predict the awful sufferings people experienced when Jerusalem was destroyed in A.D. 70 (Matthew 24:5-22; Mark 13:1-23; Luke 21:5-24).

Judges 10:14; Matthew 13:21; 24:21-22; Mark 13:19-20; Luke 21:16-19, 36; Romans 8:35-39; 1 Thessalonians 3:4; Revelation 2:9-11; 3:10-12; 6:1—9:21

See **affliction, eschatology, exile, millennium, persecution, righteous, Second Coming, sin, suffering, trial**

trichotomy (trie-KAHT-uh-mee) *noun:*

Trichotomy is the belief that people are made up of three parts. These are body, soul, and spirit. There are scriptures that seem to support this view. Other scriptures seem to support dichotomy (two parts). The Bible stresses the unity of the whole person.

See **body, dichotomy, man, person, soul, spirit**

Trinity (TRIN-uh-tee) *proper noun:*

Trinity is a central Christian doctrine. It states that the one true God reveals himself as Father, Son, and Holy Spirit. The Trinity is not three gods who act as one. The Trinity is one God who reveals himself as three Persons.

The word *Trinity* does not appear in the New Testament. But the doctrine of the Trinity is true to the way God is spoken of in the Bible. It speaks of the Father, the Son, and the Holy Spirit as each being God. The doctrine of the Trinity is a mystery. No one completely understands it. But the Bible and Christian experience make the doctrine necessary.

Deuteronomy 6:4; Matthew 28:19-20; John 1:18; 14:16; 17:3; 1 Corinthians 8:5-6; 2 Corinthians 13:14; Galatians 1:1-5; Ephesians 2:18; Hebrews 1:8; 9:14; 1 Peter 1:21-22; 3:18; 2 Peter 1:21

***See* doctrine, father, God, monotheism, person, Son of God, spirit, theism**

Triumphal Entry (trie-UM-ful EN-tree) *proper noun phrase:*

The Triumphal Entry was the event when Jesus rode into Jerusalem on a donkey. The people waved palm branches and shouted, "Hosanna!" which means "God, save us!" This happened just a few days before He was crucified. Early Christians saw this event as fulfilling the words of Isaiah 62:11 and Zechariah 9:9.

Today Christians celebrate the triumphal entry of Jesus on Palm Sunday. This is the Sunday before Easter Sunday.

Matthew 21:1-9; Mark 11:1-10; Luke 19:28-38; John 12:12-18

***See* Easter, Jesus, Palm Sunday**

triune (TRIE-yewn) *adjective:*

Trine describes God as Trinity. Triune is a way to speak of God. He is God in three persons eternally. He is one God. Yet He is Father, Son, and Holy Spirit.

Matthew 3:11; John 16:14; 17:21; Acts 2:32-33; 1 Corinthians 12:4-6; Ephesians 3:13; 1 Peter 1:2

***See* doctrine, eternal, Father, God, Holy Spirit, Jesus, Son of God, Trinity**

trust (TRUST) *noun:*

***See* faith, faithful, obedience**

truth (TREWTH) *noun:*

Truth is that which is real or correct. Truth is also that which agrees with what is real or correct. A person can depend on the truth. Truth can be trusted. Truth sometimes means to state the facts as they really are.

Jesus called himself the Truth in that He is the Revelation of God. The gospel is the truth because it is the message about Jesus. The words and deeds of Jesus were true. He did the truth. He preached grace, and He forgave sinners. His deeds showed that His words could be depended on. Jesus used *truth* to mean the opposite of hypocrisy.

Paul used *truth* to mean the gospel of Jesus Christ. The gospel is the truth of God, the message of salvation. Truth can also mean the true doctrines taught by the apostles.

Genesis 24:49; 32:10; 42:16; Deuteronomy 32:4; Psalm 25:10; 57:3; 115:1; Proverbs 3:3; 16:6; Luke 4:25; 9:27; 12:44; John 1:14, 17; 3:21; 4:23

***See* amen, apostle, doctrine, God, gospel, grace, hypocrisy, loving-kindness, obedience, revelation**

Tyre (TIER) *proper noun:*

Tyre was an important city on the Mediterranean Sea coast during Bible times. The king of Tyre provided building materials for kings David and Solomon (2 Samuel 5:11; 1 Kings 5:1-12). Jesus visited the area of Tyre (Mark 7:24-31). Paul visited Tyre on his third missionary journey (Acts 21:3-7). Tyre is often mentioned with the city of Sidon (Matthew 15:21; Acts 12:20).

See **David, Mediterranean Sea, missionary, Paul, Sidon, Solomon, Tyre (maps 7, 8)**

U u

unclean (un-KLEEN) *adjective:*

Unclean describes someone or something that is not clean—physically, ritually, or ethically.

The difference between *clean* and *unclean* was closely connected with Israel's faith in God. In Israel, God and something that was unclean were seen as opposites. Someone or something unclean could have no part in the worship of God. Such people or things had to be either cleansed or destroyed.

The Old Testament law identified certain things or actions as unclean. For example, certain sex acts made people unclean. People became unclean if they touched dead bodies. Some kinds of meat, like pork, were considered unclean and thus were not eaten. People had to be cleansed if they became unclean in any of these ways.

Some laws against unclean things were meant to protect the health of the people (Deuteronomy 28:58-61). But most laws against unclean things concerned the pagan practices of Israel's neighbors. For example, sex with temple prostitutes was a central part of Baal worship. The pig, which Israel considered unclean, was a sacred animal in Baal worship.

The New Testament continues this concern of Judaism about the clean and the unclean. Christians are warned to separate themselves from the unclean behavior of pagans.

2 Corinthians 6:14—7:1

See **Baal, cleanse, God, harlot, holiness, Israel, Jesus, Jew, law, morals, pagan, Paul, prophesy, prophet**

unction (UNGK-shun) *noun:*

Unction means "anointing." It comes from the Latin term that means "to anoint." Unction is a gift of the Holy Spirit. Unction is usually thought of as the power to preach what the Holy Spirit gives.

1 John 2:20, 27

See **anoint, exhort, Holy Spirit, preach**

unitarianism (YEW-nuh-TAIR-ee-un-IZ-um) *noun:*

See **Unitarian Universal Association**

Unitarian Universalist Association (YEW-nuh-TAIR-ee-un YEW-nuh-VER-sul-ist uh-SOH-see-AY-shun) *proper noun:*

The Unitarian Universalist Association is a religious organization. It is the result of two groups that came together in 1961. The two groups were the American Unitarian Association and the Universalist Church of America.

The Unitarian movement arose in the 18th century. It came from an American denomination called the Congregationalists. The Unitarians denied the doctrine of the Trinity.

The Universalists also arose in the 18th century. They became an organization about 1800. The Universalists believed that God will save all persons, that no one will ever be lost forever.

The Unitarian Universalist Association does not accept Christian creeds, such as the Apostles' Creed and the Nicene Creed. A person does not have to believe Christian doctrines to be a part of the Unitarian Universalist Association. The Unitarian Universalist Association is not a Christian denomination.

See **Apostles' Creed, creed, deity, denomination, doctrine, Nicene Creed, Trinity**

United Methodist Church (yew-NIE-tud METH-uh-dist CHERCH) *proper noun phrase:*

See **Holiness Movement, Methodist**

unity (YEW-nuh-tee) *noun:*

Unity is the quality of being one. Unity is a whole made of different parts that have a single purpose.

The unity of the Church refers to its shared life in Jesus Christ. It is like a body with many members working together for a common goal.

The unity of God is the belief that the Holy Trinity is one God. The one God reveals himself as Father, Son, and Holy Spirit.

See **Body of Christ, church, community, ecumenical, father, God, Holy Spirit, koinonia, monotheism, Son of God, Trinity**

universalism (YEW-nuh-VER-suh-LIZ-um):

1. *noun:* Universalism is the belief that all people will be saved. It is the belief that God will not allow anyone to go to hell. Universalism believes that the love and mercy of God will overcome all sin.

2. *proper noun:* Universalism is a religious movement that started in the 1800s. The Universalists joined with the Unitarians in 1961 to create the Unitarian Universalist Association.

Romans 5:12, 18-19; 11:15, 32

See **Christ, election, faith, fall, hell, predestination, salvation, sin, Unitarian Universalist Association**

Universalist (YEW-nuh-VER-suh-list):

1. *noun:* A universalist is a believer in universalism.

2. *proper noun:* A Universalist is a member of the religious movement known as Universalism.

See **Unitarian Universalist Association, universalism**

unknown tongue (un-NOHN TUNG) *noun phrase:*

Unknown tongue is the way the King James Version sometimes translates *tongue* in 1 Corinthians.

1 Corinthians 14:2, 4, 13-14, 19, 27

See **glossalalia, tongue**

unleavened bread (un-LEV-und BRED) *noun phrase:*

Unleavened bread is bread that is baked without leaven. Jews eat unleavened bread during the Passover Week. This was the kind of bread Israel ate at the time of the Exodus. Thus, Passover is also called the Festival of Unleavened Bread.

The last meal Jesus ate with His disciples was probably a Passover supper. The bread He ate with them was unleavened. This is why Christians usually eat unleavened bread in celebrating Holy Communion.

Exodus 12:1-17; 23:15; Matthew 26:17; Luke 22:14-20

See **Christian, Exodus, festival, Holy Communion, Israel, Jesus, leaven, Passover**

unpardonable sin (un-PAHR-dun-uh-bul SIN) *noun phrase:*

The unpardonable sin is a sin that cannot be forgiven. The phrase refers to blasphemy against the Holy Spirit. It is to refuse to accept the fact that Jesus is the Christ. The person who finally rejects Christ rejects the witness of the Holy Spirit to Christ. A person cannot be forgiven as long as he or she rejects Christ.

Matthew 12:31-32; Mark 3:28-30; Luke 12:10

See **blasphemy, Christ, forgiveness, Holy Spirit, sin, spirit**

Upper Room (UP-er REWM) *proper noun phrase:*

Jesus and His disciples celebrated their last Passover meal together in the Upper Room (Mark 14:15). This was possibly an upstairs guest room. Jesus' followers probably stayed in this same room in Jerusalem after He ascended into heaven (Acts 1:12-14). Christian tradition says that about 120 of Jesus' followers gathered there to pray. It was in this room that the Holy Spirit came upon the 120. The Book of Acts reports these events but does not say where they happened.

Acts 1:15; 2:1

See **Acts, Ascension, Christian, disciple, Holy Spirit, Jerusalem (map 10), Jesus, Passover, Pentecost, tradition**

upright (up-RIET) *adjective:*

Upright describes a person who is godly or righteous. For example, the Bible says that Job was blameless and upright (Job 1:1).

Psalm 64:10; 97:11; Proverbs 14:2; 15:8; Titus 1:2; 2:12

See **godly, Job, just, pious, right, righteous**

Ur (ER) *proper noun:*

Ur was a city in Babylonia or Chaldea on the Euphrates River. Ur was the home of Abraham. He and his family left Ur for the land of Canaan.

Genesis 11:27-31; 15:7; Nehemiah 9:7

See **Abraham, Babylon, Canaan, Chaldea, Euphrates, Ur (maps 1, 6)**

Urim and Thummim (YEWR-um and THUH-mum) *proper noun phrase:*

Urim and Thummim were objects placed in the clothes of the high priest.

He wore these when he went before the Lord to pray for the people. The Urim and Thummim were supposed to help him learn the will of God. No one knows for certain what the Urim and Thummim looked like.

Exodus 28:30; Leviticus 8:8; 1 Samuel 10:19-22; 14:37-42

See **high priest, prayer, vestment, will**

usury (YEW-zhuh-ree or YEWZH-ree) *noun:*

Usury is interest that must be paid on money that is borrowed. Usury usually means an amount of money that is unfair or unjust. Old Testament law commanded the people not to demand usury of their fellow Israelites. But they could charge usury to others. The New Testament neither approves nor rejects the practice of usury.

Exodus 22:25; Leviticus 25:36-37; Deuteronomy 23:19-20; Psalm 15:5; Proverbs 28:8; Ezekiel 18:8, 13, 17; Matthew 25:27

See **Israel, New Testament, Old Testament**

Uzziah (uh-ZIE-uh) *proper noun:*

Uzziah was a king of the nation of Judah. He became king at the age of 16 when his father was killed. He ruled Judah for more than 50 years. He was known as a righteous king. Uzziah was also known as Azariah.

2 Kings 15:1-7; 2 Chronicles 26:1-23; Isaiah 6:1; Hosea 1:1; Amos 1:1

See **Azariah, Judah, king, Uzziah (time line)**

V v

vain (VAYN) *adjective:*

Vain describes a person, action, or thing that has no real value. This is true even though value is claimed. Vain describes something that is worthless, not important, or that cannot reach its goal.

Vain also describes a person who claims importance for himself or herself that he or she does not have. Thus, the person's pride is vain because he or she claims something that does not exist.

Exodus 20:7; 1 Samuel 12:21; Psalms 2:1; 39:6; Proverbs 12:11; 28:19; 31:30; Jeremiah 10:3; Acts 4:25; Galatians 2:2; 1 Thessalonians 2:1; James 2:20

See **pride, values, vanity, virtue**

values (VAL-yewz) *noun:*

Values are qualities that people hold to be most real and of highest worth. Values are qualities that people hold important and to which they give support through action. Honesty and kindness are examples of values. Some values are more important than others.

God is of highest value for Christians. All other religious and moral values must come from and be judged by God. Christ reveals who God is. Thus, Christian values should have Jesus Christ as their Source.

Not all values have religious and moral importance. Some values are simply a matter of taste or desire. For example, a person might like one kind of art and not another.

Romans 2:18; Philippians 1:10-11

See **character, ethics, God, Jesus, materialism, modesty, morality, virtue**

vanity (VAN-uh-tee) *noun:*

Vanity means that which is without worth in itself. Vanity means that which is useless or empty. Vanity refers to that which people consider important but which will fail or disappear. Idolatry, false prophets, physical life, and wealth are biblical examples of vanity. Vanity is all of life apart from God. Vanity is worship of anything other than God.

Job 15:35; Proverbs 22:8; Ecclesiastes 1:2, 14; Isaiah 41:29; Jeremiah 8:19; Zechariah 10:2; Acts 14:15; Romans 8:20; Ephesians 4:17

See **deceive, false prophet, flesh, idol, idolatry, life, materialism, pride, vain, worship**

veil (VAYL)

1. *verb:* To veil is to cover or hide as with a veil.

2. *noun:* A veil was a special cloth women used to cover their heads and faces. This was the main difference between the clothing of men and women in Israel (Genesis 24:65; Deuteronomy 22:5; Ruth 3:15; Song of Solomon 5:7; Isaiah 3:23; 47:2; Nahum 3:5). The practice of women wearing veils continued into New Testament times (1 Corinthians 11:2-16). It is

still practiced in Arab countries today. Moses covered his face with a cloth veil after he was in God's presence. His face shone too brightly without it (Exodus 34:29-35; 2 Corinthians 3:13-16).

The veil in the Tabernacle was a special curtain dividing it into two parts. There was a similar veil in the Temple. These veils were used to hide the most holy place in the sanctuary (Exodus 26:31-36; 33:20; 35:12; 40:3, 21). The most holy place was not to be seen or entered by anyone. Only the high priest entered there. And he went in only once a year on the Day of Atonement.

The Synoptic Gospels report that the Temple veil was torn into two pieces when Jesus died (Matthew 27:51; Mark 15:38; Luke 23:45). His death allows all people to come to God directly, not through a priest (Hebrews 6:19; 9:3; 10:20).

The apostle Paul said that the unbelief of Jews was like a veil. They were unable to see Christ in the Old Testament (2 Corinthians 3:12-18).

***See* atonement, festival, high priest, holy place, Moses, priest, sanctuary, Synoptic Gospels, tabernacle, temple**

vengeance (VEN-juns) *noun:*

***See* revenge, wrath**

venial sin (VEE-nee-ul SIN) *noun phrase:*

A venial sin is the name Roman Catholics give to one type of sin. A venial sin is a sin done with less than full knowledge and desire. It does not come from a desire of the heart to disobey God. Venial sins are not as serious as mortal sins. Thus venial sins can be forgiven without the sacrament of penance.

***See* Catholic, mortal sin, penance, Roman Catholic, sacrament, sin**

version (VER-zhun) *noun:*

A version is a translation. The word *version* is usually used to refer to a translation of the Bible. The Hebrew Old Testament and Greek New Testament are not versions. These are the languages in which the books were first written.

The earliest translation of the Old Testament was the Greek Septuagint (LXX). The earliest version of the entire Bible was the Peshitta, which means "simple." It was a translation into the language of Syria.

The Latin Vulgate was another important early translation of the entire Bible. Latin was the language of Rome. Most Christians used it when the Vulgate was translated. The Vulgate became the standard Bible of the Church. But most Christians by the time of the Reformation could not understand Latin.

The first English translation of the New Testament was made by John Wycliffe. He lived during the 1300s. His version was translated from the Latin Vulgate. William Tyndale was the first to produce an English translation from the Greek and Hebrew. He lived during the 1500s. Many other English translations were made during this century. The most important was the Bishop's Bible.

The King James Version (KJV) was made by over 40 scholars early in the 1600s. It was made from the original Hebrew and Greek. Its form was greatly influenced by the earlier English versions. The *American Standard Version* (ASV) was made by a number of scholars about the year 1900. It tried to make the KJV more modern. The *New American Standard Bible* (NASB) was made some years later. It attempted to improve on the ASV. The *Revised Standard Version* (RSV) was made in the 1950s by another group of scholars. It was another attempt to improve on KJV. The *New King James Version* (NKJV) also attempted in the 1980s to improve on the KJV. But it made fewer changes than any of the earlier versions. The *New Revised Standard Version* (NRSV) was translated in the 1980s to improve the RSV.

Most new English translations have not tried to follow the original KJV. The *New English Bible* (NEB) was made by British scholars in the 1960s. The *New International Version* (NIV) was made by evangelical Protestants during the 1970s.

Two widely used modern English translations were made first by a single person. They were then changed and improved by groups of scholars. Both were made during the 1960s and 1970s. They are free translations that try to give the thoughts in modern English. They are *The Living Bible* (TLB) and the *Good New Bible, Today's English Version* (TEV). Some versions try to keep as close as possible to a word-for-word translation. Sometimes such versions are more difficult to understand. The *New American Standard Bible* is such a translation.

There are two important modern English translations made by Roman Catholic scholars. They were completed during the 1950s and the 1960s. They are *The Jerusalem Bible* (JB) and the *New American Bible* (NAB).

Several modern translations have been written in simple English. These Bibles are useful for children, youth, new readers, and people who are learning English. Three of these Bibles are the *Contemporary English Version* (CEV), the *New Life Bible* (NLB), and *New Century Version* (NCV).

Many other good English versions could be named. But those mentioned are the best and the most widely used.

***See* Bible, evangelical, Greek, Hebrew, New Testament, Old Testament, Protestant, Roman Catholicism, Septuagint, translate, Vulgate**

vestment (VEST-munt) *noun:*

A vestment is special clothing of some kind. It was an outer garment or robe. The word usually refers to the clothing worn by priests during ceremonies. Another word for vestment is vesture.

Leviticus 8:6-19; Deuteronomy 22:12; 2 Kings 10:22

***See* ceremony, priest**

vesture (VES-cher) *noun:*

See **vestment**

vicarious (vie-KAIR-ee-us) *adjective:*

Vicarious describes an act as experienced or done for the good of another person. The good that comes from a vicarious act is counted to the other person's credit.

The sacrifice of Jesus on the Cross for sinners was a vicarious act. He gave His life to provide salvation for all who will trust Him. His death provided the Atonement for the sins of the world.

Wesleyans accept the doctrine of the vicarious atonement of Christ. The Reformed tradition understands vicarious atonement to mean substitutionary atonement.

Mark 14:24; Luke 22:19; John 10:11; Romans 5:6-8; Galatians 3:13; 1 Timothy 2:6; 1 Peter 3:18

See **atonement, cross, death, doctrine, expiation, propitiation, Reformed tradition, sacrifice, salvation, substitutionary theory of the Atonement, Wesleyanism**

vice (VIES) *noun:*

Vice means evil habits that destroy moral character. Vice is the opposite of virtue.

Theologians in the Middle Ages named seven deadly vices or sins. They were pride, covetousness, lust, envy, gluttony, anger, and laziness. They believed that these sins were the sources of all other sins.

Romans 1:29-32; 1 Corinthians 5:1, 8; 6:13; Ephesians 4:19; 1 Thessalonians 4:3-8

See **anger, character, covet, envy, lust, moral, morality, pride, sin, virtue**

virgin (VER-jun) *noun:*

Virgin usually meant a young woman who had not had sex with a man (Genesis 24:16; Leviticus 21:3). But virgin sometimes simply meant a woman who was able to bear children (Genesis 24:3; Isaiah 7:14). The Old Testament uses two different words to show the difference between these two meanings.

Matthew and Luke say that Mary, the mother of Jesus, was a virgin. They meant that she had not had sex with any man. This is the meaning of the Greek word they used.

Matthew 1:18-25; Luke 1:26-38

See **marriage, Mary, Virgin Birth**

Virgin Birth (VER-jun BERTH) *proper noun phrase:*

The Virgin Birth is the birth of Jesus by His mother, Mary. Mary was a virgin. Jesus was a special creation of the Holy Spirit in the womb of Mary. The Gospels of Matthew and Luke are the basis for this belief.

Matthew 1:18-25; Luke 1:26-38

See **creation, Incarnation, Jesus, Luke, Mary, Matthew, spirit, virgin, word**

Virgin Mary (VER-jun MAIR-ee) *proper noun phrase:*

See **Mary, virgin, Virgin Birth**

virtue (VER-chew) *noun:*

The Hebrew word for virtue means "ability." It usually refers to moral character of high quality in a person. It refers to someone of high moral worth.

Two Greek words for virtue are used in the New Testament. One word means the high moral quality of a person. Goodness, kindness, and self-discipline are examples of such virtue. These result from the work of God in the Christian (1 Peter 2:9; 2 Peter 1:3, 5). The other word means power, influence, or strength (Mark 5:30; Luke 6:19; 8:46).

Ruth 3:11; Proverbs 12:4; 31:10, 29; 2 Corinthians 12:9; Hebrews 11:11

See **character, moral, morality, temperance, vice**

vision (VIZH-un) *noun:*

A vision in the Bible referred to a special experience that revealed God to someone. Prophets or other people especially chosen by God sometimes had visions. Biblical visions gave messages from God about the present and future. A vision is not the same as a dream. It is not imagination.

Christians sometimes use *vision* to mean a goal that is set. A church may have a vision of helping people in another country build a church building.

Numbers 12:6; 1 Samuel 3:15; Isaiah 1:1; Ezekiel 12:27; Daniel 2:19; 10:7; Obadiah 1; Nahum 1:1; Luke 1:22; Acts 9:10, 12; 10:3, 17, 19; 2 Corinthians 12:1

See **message, oracle, prophet, revelation**

vocation (voh-KAY-shun) *noun:*

A vocation is an activity or a calling. A vocation is the task one does in response to a calling.

A vocation is usually what a person does to earn a living. But the Bible teaches that discipleship is the vocation of all Christians. It is the right response to the call of God.

God calls only a few people to a vocation in the ministry. But God calls all people to serve Him and to do His will. Thus, any work done to bring glory to God is a divine vocation.

Romans 11:29; 1 Corinthians 1:26-29; Ephesians 4:1-12; 6:5-8; Philippians 3:14; 1 Thessalonians 4:1-8; Hebrews 3:1-2; 2 Peter 1:10-11

See **call, disciple, divine, election, glory, minister, ministry, stewardship, will**

vow (VOU) *noun:*

A vow is a promise to do something or not to do it. A vow in the Bible was made freely and as a sign of devotion to God. A vow is a promise one must keep.

Genesis 28:20-22; Deuteronomy 23:23; 1 Samuel 1:11; Psalm 22:25

See **covenant, offering, promise, worship**

Vulgate (VUL-gayt) *proper noun:*

The Vulgate is the translation of the Bible and the Apocrypha into Latin. The word *Vulgate* came from a Latin term meaning "common." Latin was the common language of the Roman Empire at the time. This translation was made by Jerome late in the A.D. 300s. It became the official version of the Roman Catholic Church.

See **Apocrypha, Latin, Rome, Roman Catholic, translate, version**

W w

wages of sin (WAY-juz uv SIN) *noun phrase:*

The wages of sin is the death that sin finally brings. Death is the pay sinners justly earn for rejecting the forgiveness Christ offers.

Romans 3:21-26; 6:23

See **death, faith, forgiveness, grace, hell, judgment, sin**

walk (WAWK)

1. *verb:* To walk means to move by foot. In the Bible, to walk often means to live in a certain way. To "walk in the Spirit" is to live in obedience to the Holy Spirit (Galatians 5:16, KJV). To "walk in the light" is to live in obedience to the revelation of God (1 John 1:6-7). To "walk in the flesh" is simply to live as a human being (2 Corinthians 10:3; see Galatians 2:20, KJV). But to "walk after the flesh" is to live in a way that opposes God (Romans 8:4-8, KJV).

2. *noun:* The Bible often refers to a person's walk as his or her usual way of living. Thus, walk refers to ethical and religious behavior. The Christian life is a walk. It is a way of life. Sometimes the Christian walk is called a pilgrimage.

Genesis 3:8; 5:22-24; 6:9; 13:17; 17:1; 24:40; Leviticus 26:12; Deuteronomy 8:19; 23:14; 1 Kings 8:23; 2 Kings 21:22; Job 31:5-7; Psalms 1:1; 119:45; Micah 6:8; Matthew 4:18; Romans 6:4; 8:4; 13:13; 14:15; 2 Corinthians 5:7; 10:2-3; Galatians 5:16; Ephesians 4:1; 5:2, 8, 15; Philippians 3:17-18

See **Bible, ethics, flesh, Holy Spirit, life, pilgrimage, revelation, spirit, way**

way (WAY) *noun:*

A way is a path or road. The Bible often uses *way* to describe the manner of conduct of a person. The way a person lives shows his or her goals and purposes in life.

The Bible suggests that there are really only two ways. One way is right and pleasing to God. It leads to salvation. The other way leads to death. Jesus is "the Way" in that He shows people how to find God.

Christians are called "people of the Way" in the Book of Acts. They followed Jesus and lived as He taught them.

Exodus 33:13; Job 21:14, 31; Psalms 1:1, 6; 67:2; Proverbs 8:22; 30:19-20; Isaiah 40:3, 10-11; Ezekiel 18:25; Matthew 7:13-14; Acts 9:2; 19:9, 23; 22:4; 24:14, 22

See **Acts, death, God, life, right, salvation, walk**

Wesley, Charles (WES-lee, CHAHRLZ) *proper noun phrase:*

Charles Wesley was a brother of John Wesley. He wrote many hymns.

See **Holiness Movement, hymn, Methodist, John Wesley**

Wesley, John (WES-lee, JAHN) *proper noun phrase:*

John Wesley was an important Protestant leader who lived in England in the 1700s. He was a priest in the Church of England. Later he became the founder of the Methodist Church. Wesley was a missionary to Georgia, in the American colonies, for a short time. He was an important leader of what is called the English Evangelical Revival.

John Wesley preached that all people could know the grace of God. He preached to the poor and to those oppressed by society. Wesley fought to change evil social conditions. But his main message was that people could be completely changed by the grace of God. He believed that by the help of God, Christians could live holy lives. He believed that this was possible through entire sanctification. This is a second work of grace.

See **Anglican, entire sanctification, Episcopal, evangelical, grace, holy, holiness, Methodist, Protestant, revival, second work of grace, Wesleyanism, Charles Wesley**

Wesleyan (WES-lee-un)

1. *proper adjective:* Wesleyan describes a person or doctrine that holds to the teachings of John Wesley.

2. *proper noun:* A Wesleyan is one who holds to such doctrines. Also, a Wesleyan is a member of The Wesleyan Church.

See **John Wesley, Wesleyan church, Wesleyanism**

Wesleyan Church (WES-lee-un CHERCH) *proper noun phrase:*

See **Holiness Movement, Wesleyanism**

Wesleyanism (WES-lee-un-IZ-um) *proper noun:*

Wesleyanism is the doctrinal tradition that stems from John and Charles Wesley. Wesleyanism is a part of Protestant Christianity. The Methodist Church resulted from the work of the Wesley brothers. It is the oldest and largest part of Wesleyanism. Many other smaller denominations make up the larger family of Wesleyanism.

Wesleyanism in North America developed into two major groups. These are Methodism and the Holiness Movement. Many different denominations are included in these.

There are some small differences in their doctrines. There are also differences in their church government. But Wesleyanism is generally marked by belief in the following doctrines.

1. Wesleyanism stresses the Arminian doctrine that salvation is for all people. It denies the doctrine of special election.

2. Wesleyanism teaches the doctrine of prevenient grace. Wesley taught that the grace of God reaches out to sinners before they are aware of it. He viewed the sovereignty of God as the sovereignty of grace. The grace of God awakens people to their sinful conditions. This grace makes it possible for people to seek forgiveness. Prevenient grace is provided to all by the death and resurrection of Christ. Wesley taught that the Spirit of God draws all people toward salvation. But no person is forced to be saved.

3. Wesleyanism teaches the doctrine of initial sanctification. The Spirit really changes all who confess their sins and receive Christ as Savior.

4. Wesleyans teach the doctrine of assurance. Wesley taught that the Holy Spirit witnesses to believers. He assures them that they are adopted into the family of God.

5. Wesleyanism also teaches the doctrine of entire sanctification. The Wesleys taught that Christians could and should be cleansed from original sin. They could and should be made perfect in love toward God and man.

6. Wesleyanism teaches the unity of the Church. It is not sectarian.

7. Wesleyanism accepts the authority of the Scriptures in all matters of faith and practice.

8. Wesleyanism values Christian traditions as important.

9. Most Wesleyans observe the sacraments of baptism and the Lord's Supper.

See **adoption, Arminianism, assurance, baptism, Calvinism, church, election, entire sanctification, forgiveness, Holiness Movement, initial sanctification, Lord's Supper, Methodist, new birth, original sin, predestination, prevenient grace, Protestant, Reformed tradition, resurrection, sacrament, salvation, sect, sovereignty, tradition, unity, John Wesley, Wesleyans, witness of the Spirit**

Westminster Confession (WEST-MIN-ster kun-FESH-un) *proper noun phrase:*

See **Presbyterian**

wicked (WIK-ud)

1. *adjective:* Wicked describes someone or something as very bad or evil. Wicked persons and things cause trouble and destruction. Satan is sometimes called "the wicked one" (Ephesians 6:16; 1 John 2:13).

2. *noun:* The wicked are wicked or evil people.

Genesis 6:5; Psalms 9:15; 10:1-11; 18:21; 37:35-36; Proverbs 15:14; 21:10; Jeremiah 16:4; Matthew 16:4; Acts 2:23; Romans 1:29; Colossians 1:2

See **evil, Satan, sin**

will (WIL)

1. *noun:* Will is the ability of a person to make a choice or express a desire. It is the ability to decide between two or more choices. Will is the power of the mind to act in one way and not another.

The will of fallen people is controlled by evil. Christ must free the human will from its slavery to sin. People can turn to Christ for salvation only by the grace of God. Wesleyanism believes this is the work of prevenient grace.

The will of God is what He wants for His creation. He made known His will through Jesus Christ.

2. *verb:* To will is to decide between two or more choices. It is to exercise the will.

Luke 11:2; John 4:34; 7:17; Acts 13:22; 1 Corinthians 7:37; Ephesians 6:6; Hebrews 10:36; 1 John 2:17

See **Fall, freedom, human, man, mind, nature, person, prevenient grace, salvation, slavery, Wesleyanism**

willful (WIL-ful) *adjective:*

Willful describes an act that is done on purpose. The one who acts knows exactly what he or she is doing. The person does it because he or she wants to. Wesleyanism defines sin as willfully disobeying God's law.

See **law, obedience, sin, transgress, Wesleyanism, will**

wine (WIEN) *noun:*

Wine is a drink made from the juice of grapes. It changes naturally so as to contain alcohol. The Bible uses a number of different terms for wine. Wine was usually made weaker with water. *New* wine was especially high in alcohol content (Acts 2:13-15).

Wine differed from strong drink or beer (Isaiah 28:7; Luke 1:25). Strong drink was made from grain or fruit other than grapes.

The Bible speaks of wine as a drink that made people happy (Psalm 104:15; Ecclesiastes 10:19; John 2:1-11). Wine was sometimes used as a medicine (Luke 10:34; 1 Timothy 5:23). But wine could also cause people to do evil or foolish things. It caused great harm and wrong (Genesis 9:21; Proverbs 23:29-35; Isaiah 5:11-17; 28:7). The Bible strongly condemns drunkenness (Proverbs 23:19-21; Romans 13:13; Galatians 5:19-21; 1 Peter 4:3).

The Bible says it is better to drink no wine than to drink too much. It is better to practice total abstinence than to influence someone wrongly by drinking wine (Romans 13:13; 14:21; Ephesians 5:18; 1 Timothy 3:8; Titus 2:3).

See **abstinence, drunkenness, evil, Holy Communion**

wisdom (WIZ-dum) *noun:*

Wisdom is a person's knowledge and understanding for daily living. It is the knowledge gained from experience that makes proper choices in life possible. It is knowing the right thing to do. It helps people to make correct plans to gain the results they desire. It helps them to live happy lives.

A special group of wise men lived in Israel while the kings ruled. The prophets, priests, and the wise men were important influences on the society and religion of Israel. The wise collected the wisdom of earlier generations and of Israel's neighbor nations. King Solomon and King Hezekiah especially encouraged the wise to collect books of wisdom (1 Kings 4:29-34; Proverbs 25:1). The Old Testament wisdom books include Proverbs, Job, and Ecclesiastes. James in the New Testament is like the wisdom books in some ways.

Israel understood that the advice of the wisdom teachers came from God. Wisdom in the fullest sense belonged to Him alone (Job 12:13-15). Thus, human wisdom was a gift of His grace. Reverence and obedience to God were the beginning of all true wisdom. He was the Judge of right and wrong. There was no success in life apart from Him.

Success is not a goal of wisdom. But it is sometimes the result of wisdom. Ecclesiastes teaches that wisdom does not always lead to earthly success. Even wise and faithful men suffer, as Job and Jesus prove.

Wisdom is treated as if it were a person in a few places in the Old Testament (Job 28; Proverbs 8). God used this wisdom to create the world and to reveal himself to people. This idea of wisdom influenced the idea of the Logos in John's Gospel.

The New Testament stresses that wisdom is a gift of God. Human wisdom apart from the revelation of God is foolish and of little value. The Holy Spirit gives the wisdom of God to those who accept the gospel (1 Corinthians 1:18—2:16).

This should not suggest that the Bible is opposed to education or human knowledge. It simply claims that human wisdom is very limited apart from the wisdom of God. Human wisdom cannot give people what they need most, the knowledge of God. It cannot give them salvation and an understanding of life. Only God can give these.

***See* Christ, Ecclesiastes, gift, grace, Hezekiah, Israel, James, Job, judge, logos, obedience, priest, prophet, Proverbs, revelation, right, salvation, Solomon, wise men, word**

wise men (WIEZ MEN) *noun phrase:*

The wise men were visitors who came to Bethlehem to worship Jesus. They were Gentiles who came to give honor to the King of the Jews. They brought valuable gifts to Jesus. Christian tradition says that there were three wise men who were kings from Persia. The Greek term *magi* used to describe them in Matthew suggests that they practiced astrology.

Wise men were important to kings during Old Testament times. The kings asked for advice from those who were considered to be wise (see wisdom).

Matthew 2:1-18

***See* astrology, Bethlehem (map 8), Christmas, Gentile, magi, Matthew, Persia, tradition, wisdom**

witch (WICH) *noun:*

A witch is a person who claims to possess magical powers. A witch claims to be able to talk with evil spirits. A witch practices sorcery, magic, and witchcraft.

Deuteronomy 18:10; Exodus 22:18; 2 Chronicles 33:6

See **evil, exorcism, magic, occult, soothsayer, sorcery, witchcraft**

witchcraft (WICH-kraft) *noun:*

Witchcraft is the practice of sorcery and magic with the aid of evil spirits. Witchcraft is practiced by witches.

1 Samuel 15:23; 28:3-14; 2 Kings 9:22; Micah 5:12; Nahum 3:4

See **evil, exorcism, magic, occult, soothsayer, sorcery, spirit, witch**

witness (WIT-nus)

1. *noun:* A witness is a person who gives testimony. The word *witness* is used in a number of ways. It is the report of what a person has experienced. Thus the person knows it to be true. A witness tells what he or she has experienced.

Christians are witnesses. They know that Christ is the resurrected Lord. Thus, Christians are prepared to give a report of what they know.

2. *verb:* A person who witnesses tells others of what he or she has seen or experienced. The person tells what God means to him or her.

Deuteronomy 4:26; 1 Kings 21:10; Malachi 2:14; Matthew 23:31; Luke 4:22; John 1:7-8, 15; 5:31, 37; Romans 2:15; 8:16; 9:1; Hebrews 10:15, 28; 12:1-2

See **Christian, evangelist, judge, testimony**

witness of the Spirit (WIT-nus uv thuh SPIR-it) *noun phrase:*

The witness of the Spirit is the assurance the Holy Spirit gives to believers. He assures them that their sins are forgiven. He witnesses to them that they have been adopted into the family of God. This witness is the Holy Spirit himself.

The fact that Christians have the Holy Spirit proves that they are Christians. It is also the basis of their hope for final salvation.

John 7:37-39; Romans 8:15-17; 1 John 5:6

See **adoption, assurance, Christian, forgiveness, Holy Spirit, hope, initial sanctification, new birth, regeneration, salvation, Wesleyanism, witness**

word (WERD) *noun:*

1. A word is something that is said or written that has a meaning. *Word* may refer to a single unit of meaning. It may also refer to one or more phrases or sentences.

2. The Old Testament prophets often refer to "the word of the Lord." This *word* was a statement of God that prophets delivered in His name. It was generally a message of judgment or hope, or a call to repentance (Isaiah 16:13; 28:13; Jeremiah 1:2, 4, 11, 13; Ezekiel 12:17, 21, 26).

3. The Word of God sometimes means the Scriptures or the law of God (Psalm 119; Hebrews 4:12). This Word reveals what God wants for His creation. The entire Bible is called the Word of God. This is true even though it contains many words that God did not say himself.

4. The Gospel of John uses *Word* to refer to the eternal Son of God. The Word is God as He makes himself known to people. He is the eternal, living Word of God made incarnate in Jesus Christ.

5. The gospel message is sometimes called *the word of God* (1 Thessalonians 1:5-6; 2:13). This word may take the form of preaching or the celebration of the sacraments (1 Corinthians 11:23-26).

See **Bible, God, gospel, hope, Incarnation, judgment, law, logos, message, name, oracle, repentance, revelation, sacrament, scripture, Son of God**

Word of God (WERD uv GAHD) *proper noun phrase:*

See **Bible, Jesus, word**

works (WERKS) *noun:*

See **good works, justification, second work of grace**

works of the flesh (WERKS uv thuh FLESH) *noun phrase:*

Works of the flesh are deeds that people do under the power of sin. Works of the flesh oppose the Spirit of God. These deeds use the created world as a means of sin. People do these works when they make the flesh the source of their lives. They depend on themselves for life and not on the Holy Spirit.

The works of the flesh are deeds done in service to sin. They result when people allow sin to rule their lives. Works of the flesh are vices. They arise from the sinful nature.

Works of the flesh are the opposite of the fruit of the Spirit. The works of the flesh are listed by Paul in Galatians 5:19-21.

Romans 8:5-8; Galatians 5:13, 16-24; Ephesians 2:3, 11; Philippians 1:22; Colossians 2:11; 2 Peter 2:18; 1 John 2:16

See **deeds of darkness, depravity, flesh, fruit of the Spirit, idolatry, sin, sinful nature, vice, witchcraft**

world (WERLD) *noun:*

World in the Bible has a number of meanings.

1. World means the creation that God made. It includes all living things. It includes things such as the stars that do not live. The Bible says that the world is good and that it belongs to God. Bad things have happened to the world because of sin. And bad things happen in the world because of sin.

2. World means the many normal human relations that form everyday life. This includes human groups, such as families, clans, and kingdoms. It includes communities. World includes the needs and activities of ordinary life. It includes social activities, such as business and making money.

3. World means heaven, the next world. It is the world to come.

4. World means God's creation under the influence of sin. This includes persons who are separated from God because of their sins. World is the

evil in the world that makes war against God. The world needs to be set free from bondage to sin by Jesus.

5. World means the kingdom of evil over which Satan has control. He is the god of this world. Christians can overcome this world through Jesus. The Spirit of Christ comes to live in them and give them victory over evil.

God loves His creation and all the people in it. Jesus came into the world to save it. He came to redeem all the people in the world. He also came to redeem His creation.

1 Samuel 2:8; 2 Samuel 22:16; 1 Chronicles 16:30; Job 18:18; Psalms 9:8; 17:14; Isaiah 13:11; 14:17; Matthew 13:5; 24:14; Luke 2:1; 20:34-45; John 3:16; 6:51; 7:4; 17:14; Romans 1:20; 5:12; 1 Corinthians 2:6-8; 8:13; 2 Timothy 1:9; James 1:27; 1 John 4:1-3

***See* bondage, creation, freedom, heaven, salvation, Satan, sin, spirit, worldliness**

worldliness (WERLD-lee-nes) *noun:*

Worldliness means treating the world and its contents as if they are God. Worldliness means worshiping something in place of God. It means serving sin and the powers of evil. Worldliness means setting our minds and affections on things that try to stand against God. It means loving what God hates. It means loving wickedness instead of righteousness. Worldliness means having a heart that bends in the direction of evil instead of bending in the direction of the Holy God. To be worldly is to be spiritually dead.

The gospel of Jesus Christ sets people free from slavery to this world. The Holy Spirit gives Christians power to live above worldliness and in obedience to God.

Psalms 49:16-18; 73:2-22; Proverbs 23:20-21; Amos 8:10; Matthew 16:26; John 5:44; 12:43; Romans 12:2; Colossians 3:2-5; 2 Timothy 3:2-7; 2 Peter 2:12-18; 1 John 2:15-17

***See* carnal, evil, flesh, God, godliness, righteousness, sin, slavery, spirit, wicked, world, worship**

worship (WER-shup) *noun:*

Worship is the reverence, honor, and service shown to a divine being.

The Bible says that people sometimes worship false gods. They worship idols or other created things. Only the true God who created all things is worthy of worship.

Worship of God is a form of ministry or service to Him. It is a confession that He is Creator and that people are His creatures. It reminds people that they depend totally on God. Worship is a means by which people show faith in God.

Worship of God can happen in private. It also occurs when the members of a church come together to worship. People worship God through adoration, prayers, thanksgiving, and preaching. People also worship God by singing hymns and by receiving the sacraments. Public worship prepares people to serve God in the world. This service is also a kind of worship.

Genesis 24:26, 52; Exodus 34:14; 2 Kings 10:19-23; 1 Chronicles 16:29; Psalms 5:7; 29:2; 66:4; 99:5, 9; Isaiah 2:8; Jeremiah 44:19; Daniel 3:5-28; Micah 6:6-8; John 4:23-24; Romans 12:1-2; Philippians 3:3; Revelation 1:12-18

***See* adoration, confess, creation, faith, God, god, holiness, hymn, idol, ministry, praise, prayer, preach, reverence, sacrament, sacrifice, service, thanksgiving**

wrath (RATH) *noun:*

Wrath is a kind of anger. The Bible speaks of both the wrath of people and the wrath of God.

The wrath of God is rejection of sin. It is the way God, the righteous Judge, attacks wrong and creates justice. The wrath of God is one way He shows His holy love even to evil people. Wrath is one way He shows sinners their need to change their behavior. He allows them to suffer the awful results their sins bring. His wrath has the final purpose of saving sinners, not destroying them. But God cannot save those who continue to reject Him.

The Bible often warns people against the violent anger that is wrath. People are not to take revenge into their own hands. They are to trust God instead. He is the only Judge who can punish with justice.

Genesis 49:5-7; Matthew 5:9, 21-22; Romans 1:18—2:11; 12:19—13:7; Galatians 5:19-20; Ephesians 2:3; 4:26-31; Colossians 3:8; 1 Thessalonians 1:10; James 1:19-20

***See* anger, evil, God, holiness, holy, judge, justice, love, retribution, revenge, righteous, save, sin, suffering, trust, unclean**

X x

Xerxes (ZERK-zeez) *proper noun:*

Xerxes was a king of Persia 400 years before Christ. Most scholars believe he is the same king as Ahasuerus (Ezra 4:6). He chose Esther, a Jewish woman, as a wife.

Esther 1:1-2, 9-10, 15-19; 2:17-18

See **Esther, Jew, Persia**

Y y

Yahweh (YAH-way or YAH-vay) *proper noun:*

Yahweh is the personal name of the God of Israel. Jews considered the name too holy to speak. So they read "Lord" when they came to "Yahweh" in the Scriptures. The men who translated the Hebrew Old Testament into Greek followed this practice. Most English translations use "LORD" (capital letters) where the Hebrew Scriptures have the name Yahweh. Some older translations use the name Jehovah for Yahweh. Most scholars today believe that the name is correctly said "Yahweh," not "Jehovah."

See **God, heaven, Lord, name, tetragammaton, transcendence**

YHWH (YAH) *proper noun:*

YHWH is the four-letter personal name of Israel's God. The Hebrew language originally used only consonants. We do not know for sure how this name was pronounced at first.

The Jews tried not to take God's name in vain even when they read the Scriptures. When they came to YHWH, they read "adonai" instead. This Hebrew word means "lord." The Septuagint uses "kurios" (KEW-ree-ahs) for YHWH. This is a Greek word that also means "lord."

The King James Version sometimes uses "Jehovah" for YHWH. The translators tried to use the vowels of "adonai" with the consonants of YHWH. This was a mistake. The name was probably pronounced Yahweh (YAH-way or YAH-vay).

See **Adonai, God, Greek, Hebrew, Jehovah, kurios, Lord, name, Septuagint, tetragrammaton, version, Yahweh**

Yom Kippur (YOHM kuh-POOR or YAHM KIP-er) *proper noun:*

See **atonement, festival**

Z z

Zacchaeus (zak-KEE-us) *proper noun:*

Zacchaeus was a rich, chief tax collector who met Jesus. The Jews of Jesus' day thought that people such as Zacchaeus were hopeless sinners. But Jesus said that He had come to save sinners like Zacchaeus.

Luke 19:1-10

See **publican**

Zacharias (ZAK-uh-RIE-us) *proper noun:*

Zacharias is the same name as Zechariah. He was the father of John the Baptist.

Luke 1:5-25; 67-80

See **Zechariah**

zeal (ZEEL) *noun:*

Zeal means eagerness to reach a goal. It means a strong interest in something. Zeal is strong devotion to a cause. A person can have zeal for good or bad goals.

The Bible speaks of the zeal of God. He is a jealous God who wants His will to be done among people. He reveals His will and loves His people with zeal.

Deuteronomy 4:24; 29:20; Psalm 69:9; Proverbs 6:34; 2 Corinthians 7:7; 11:2

See **piety, God, will**

zealot (ZEL-ut) *noun:*

A zealot was a member of the people called Zealots. The Zealots were a sect of Judaism in the first century A.D. They were like the Pharisees in many important ways. But they used violent means to try to free the Jews from Roman rule. They had great zeal for the rule of God and the freedom of His people.

Luke 6:15

See **Judaism, kingdom of God, Pharisee, Rome, sect, Simon**

Zebedee (ZEB-uh-dee) *proper noun:*

Zebedee was the father of James and John, two of Jesus' disciples. Zebedee was a fisherman.

Matthew 4:21; 10:2; 26:37; Mark 1:19

See **disciple, James, John**

Zebulun (ZEB-yew-lun) *proper noun:*

1. Zebulun was one of the 12 sons of Jacob. The Bible says little about him. His descendants were known as the tribe of Zebulun.

2. Zebulun was the name of the land occupied by the tribe of Zebulun.

Genesis 30:19-20; Numbers 1:31; 2:7

See **Canaan, Israel, Jacob, tribes of Israel, Zebulun (map 3)**

Zechariah (ZEK-uh-RIE-uh) *proper noun:*

1. Zechariah is the name of more than 30 different men in the Scriptures. Only the most important ones are mentioned here:

a. Zechariah was a Judean prophet and priest who was stoned to death. He lived during the 800s B.C. (2 Chronicles 24:20-22).

b. Zechariah was one of the kings of Israel, the Northern Kingdom. He was a son of Jeroboam II. He had ruled for only six months when he was killed by Shallum (2 Kings 14:29; 15:8-12).

c. Zechariah was a priest and prophet who lived during the 500s B.C. He urged the Jews to build a new Temple after the return from the Exile. He was joined in this by the prophet Haggai. A book in the Old Testament was written by this Zechariah.

d. Zechariah was a godly priest of the first century A.D. He was a father of John the Baptist (Luke 1:5-25, 67-80).

2. Zechariah is the name of a book in the Old Testament. It is one of the 12 Minor Prophets. The book contains visions the prophet had about building the Temple. It includes oracles about the cleansing of the people of God. It predicts the coming of the Messiah as a humble King. It also includes visions about the last judgment.

See **exile, Haggai, Jeroboam, John, oracle, priest, prophet, temple, vision, Zechariah (time line)**

Zedekiah (ZED-uh-KIE-uh) *proper noun:*

Zedekiah was the last king of the nation of Judah, the Southern Kingdom. He was also known as Mattaniah. He was the son of Josiah and a brother of Jehoahaz and Jehoiakim. He was the uncle of Jehoiachin. Zedekiah ruled for 11 years. He was an evil king. Nebuchadnezzar took him to Babylon as a captive.

2 Kings 24:17-20; 25:2-7; 1 Chronicles 3:15

See **Babylon, exile, Jehoahaz, Jehoichin, Jehoiakim, Josiah, Judah, Nebuchadnezzar, Zedekiah (time line)**

Zephaniah (ZEF-uh-NIE-uh) *proper noun:*

1. Zephaniah is the name of a Judean prophet who lived during the 600s B.C. He was a descendant of King Hezekiah. Zephaniah prophesied during the time of King Josiah. He wrote one of the books of the Old Testament.

2. Zephaniah is the name of a book in the Old Testament. It is one of the 12 Minor Prophets. Zephaniah's prophecy stresses "the day of the LORD." The prophet predicts that the idolatry of Judah will bring the judgment of God.

See **day of the Lord, Hezekiah, idolatry, Josiah, judgment, prophet**

See **also time line**

Zerubbabel (zuh-RUB-buh-bul) *proper noun:*

Zerubbabel was a governor of Judah after the Exile. He was put in this position by Cyrus of Persia. Zerubbabel was a descendant of David. Zechariah the prophet perhaps hoped that Zerubbabel would be the Messiah.

1 Chronicles 3:17-19; Ezra 1:8-11; 5:14

See **Cyrus, David, exile, Messiah, Persia**

Zeus (ZEWS) *proper noun:*

Zeus was the father of gods and men for the ancient Greeks. Zeus was known as Jupiter by the Romans.

Barnabas was called Zeus by the people of Lystra (Acts 14:12-13). This happened when he and the apostle Paul were on a missionary trip.

See **apostle, god, Greece, Jupiter, missionary, Paul, Rome**

Zimri (ZIM-ree) *proper noun:*

Zimri was a king of Israel, the Northern Kingdom. He killed Elah and all the male relatives of Baasha. Zimri ruled for only seven days. He was then killed by Omri.

1 Kings 16:8-20

See **Baasha, Elah, Israel, Omri, Zimri (time line)**

Zion (ZIE-un) *proper noun:*

Zion means "fort." Zion was originally a rocky hill to the west of Mount Moriah. It became a part of Jerusalem. David captured the hill and built his palace there. Later the name Zion was given to the hill where Solomon built the Temple. This was really Mount Moriah. Zion also became another name for Jerusalem.

Sometimes Christians use the word Zion to refer to the Church or their denominations.

2 Samuel 5:7; Psalms 48:11; 74:2; 87:2; Isaiah 1:8, 27; 2:3; Joel 2:1, 15, 23, 32

See **church, denomination, Jerusalem, Moriah, Solomon, temple**

Zwingli, Huldreich (ZWING-glee, HUL-drik) *proper noun:*

Huldreich Zwingli was a Protestant Reformer from Switzerland. He lived from 1484 to 1531. He taught that the Scriptures were the most important authority for Christians. Zwingli believed that both the church and state are ruled by God. They are closely related. He taught that only certain people are chosen for salvation.

One of Zwingli's most important teachings concerned the Lord's Supper. He taught that the Eucharist is a way of remembering Christ's sacrifice. Faithful Christians have real fellowship with Christ during the meal.

Zwingli and Calvin became the chief sources of the Reformed tradition.

See **John Calvin, Eucharist, fellowship, Lord's Supper, Martin Luther, predestination, Protestant, Reformation, Reformed tradition, sacrament**

Appendix

Time Line and Maps

CHRONOLOGY OF THE BIBLE

B.C. = Before Christ
c. = circa (around)*

DATE	Time scales represent varied number of years.
PREHISTORY	**THE BEGINNINGS: EVENTS IN PREHISTORY** Creation Adam and Eve in the Garden Cain and Abel Noah and the Flood The Tower of Babylon
2000 B.C.	**THE ANCESTORS OF THE ISRAELITES** Abraham comes to Palestine. *c.* 1900 Isaac is born to Abraham. Jacob is born to Isaac.
1800 B.C.	Jacob has 12 sons, who become the ancestors of the 12 tribes of Israel. The most prominent of these sons is Joseph, who becomes adviser to the King of Egypt. **THE ISRAELITES IN EGYPT** The descendants of Jacob are enslaved in Egypt. *c.* 1700—*c.* 1250
1600 B.C.	Moses leads the Israelites out of Egypt. *c.* 1250-
1250 B.C.	The Israelites wander in the wilderness. During this time Moses receives the Law on Mount Sinai. *c.* 1250—*c.* 1210 **THE CONQUEST AND SETTLEMENT OF CANAAN** Joshua leads the first stage of the invasion of Canaan. *c.* 1210 Israel remains a loose confederation of tribes, and leadership is exercised by heroic figures known as the Judges. **THE UNITED ISRAELITE KINGDOM**
1000 B.C.	Reign of Saul *c.* 1030—*c.* 1010 Reign of David *c.* 1010—*c.* 970 Reign of Solomon *c.* 970—931

*A circa date is only an approximation. Generally speaking, the earlier the time, the less precise is the dating. From the time of the death of Solomon in 931 B.C. to the edict of Cyrus in 538 B.C., the dates given are fairly accurate, but even in this epoch a possible error of a year or two must be allowed for.

CHRONOLOGY OF THE BIBLE

Date			
	THE TWO ISRAELITE KINGDOMS		
	JUDAH (Southern Kingdom)		ISRAEL (Northern Kingdom)
	Kings		*Kings*
950 B.C.	Rehoboam 931-913		Jeroboam 931-910
	Abijah 913-911		Nadab 910-909
900 B.C.	Asa 911-870		Baasha 909-886
			Elah 886-885
		Prophets	Zimri 7 days in 885
	Jehosphahat 870-848	Elijah	Omri 885-874
			Ahab 874-853
850 B.C.	Jehoram 848-841		Ahaziah 853-852
	Ahaziah 841		Joram 852-841
	Queen Athaliah 841-835	Elisha	Jehu 841-814
	Joash 835-796		Jehoahaz 814-798
800 B.C.	Amaziah 796-781		Jehoash 798-783
	Uzziah 781-740	Jonah	Jeroboam II 783-743
		Amos	
750 B.C.	Jothan 740-736	Hosea	Zechariah 6 mo. in 743
			Shallum 1 mo. in 743
	Ahaz 736-716	Micah	Menahem 743-738
		Isaiah	Pekahiah 738-737
			Pekah 737-732
	Hezekiah 716-687		Hoshea 732-723
			Fall of Samaria 722
700 B.C.	**THE LAST YEARS OF THE KINGDOM OF JUDAH**		
	Manasseh 687-642		
650 B.C.	Amon 642-640		
		Prophets	
	Josiah 640-609	Zephaniah	
	Joahaz 3 mon. in 609	Nahum	
	Jehoiakim 609-598	Jeremiah	
600 B.C.	Jehoiachin 3 mon. in 598	Habakkuk?	
	Zedekiah 598-587		
	Fall of Jerusalem July 587 or 586	Ezekiel	

CHRONOLOGY OF THE BIBLE

DATE	
550 B.C.	**THE EXILE AND THE RESTORATION** The Jews taken into exile in Babylonia after the fall of Jerusalem Persian rule begins. 539 Edict of Cyrus allows Jews to return. 538 Foundations of New Temple laid. 520 Restoration of the walls of Jerusalem 445-443 *Prophets*: Haggai, Zechariah, Obadiah, Daniel, Malachi, Joel?
400 B.C.	**THE TIME BETWEEN THE TESTAMENTS** Alexander the Great establishes Greek rule in Palestine. 333 Palestine is ruled by the Ptolemies, descendants of one of Alexander's generals, who had been given the position of ruler over Egypt, 323 to 198
200 B.C.	Palestine is ruled by the Seleucids, descendants of one of Alexander's generals, who had acquired the rule of Syria. 198 to 166 Jewish revolt under Judas Maccabeus reestablishes Jewish independence. Palestine is ruled by Judas' family and descendants, the Hasmoneans. 166 to 63 The Roman general Pompey takes Jerusalem 63 B.C. Palestine is ruled by puppet kings appointed by Rome. One of these is Herod the Great, who rules from 37 B.C. to 4 B.C. **THE TIME OF THE NEW TESTAMENT**
A.D. 1	Birth of Jesus* Ministry of John the Baptist: baptism of Jesus and beginning of his public ministry
A.D. 30	Death and resurrection of Jesus Conversion of Paul (Saul of Tarsus) *c.* A.D. 37 Ministry of Paul *c.* A.D. 41 to A.D. 65 Final imprisonment of Paul *c.* A.D. 65

*The present era was calculated to begin with the birth of Jesus Christ, that is, in A.D. 1 (A.D. standing for Anno Domini, "in the year of the Lord"). However, the original calculation was later found to be wrong by a few years, so that the birth of Christ took place perhaps about 6 B.C.

Map 1

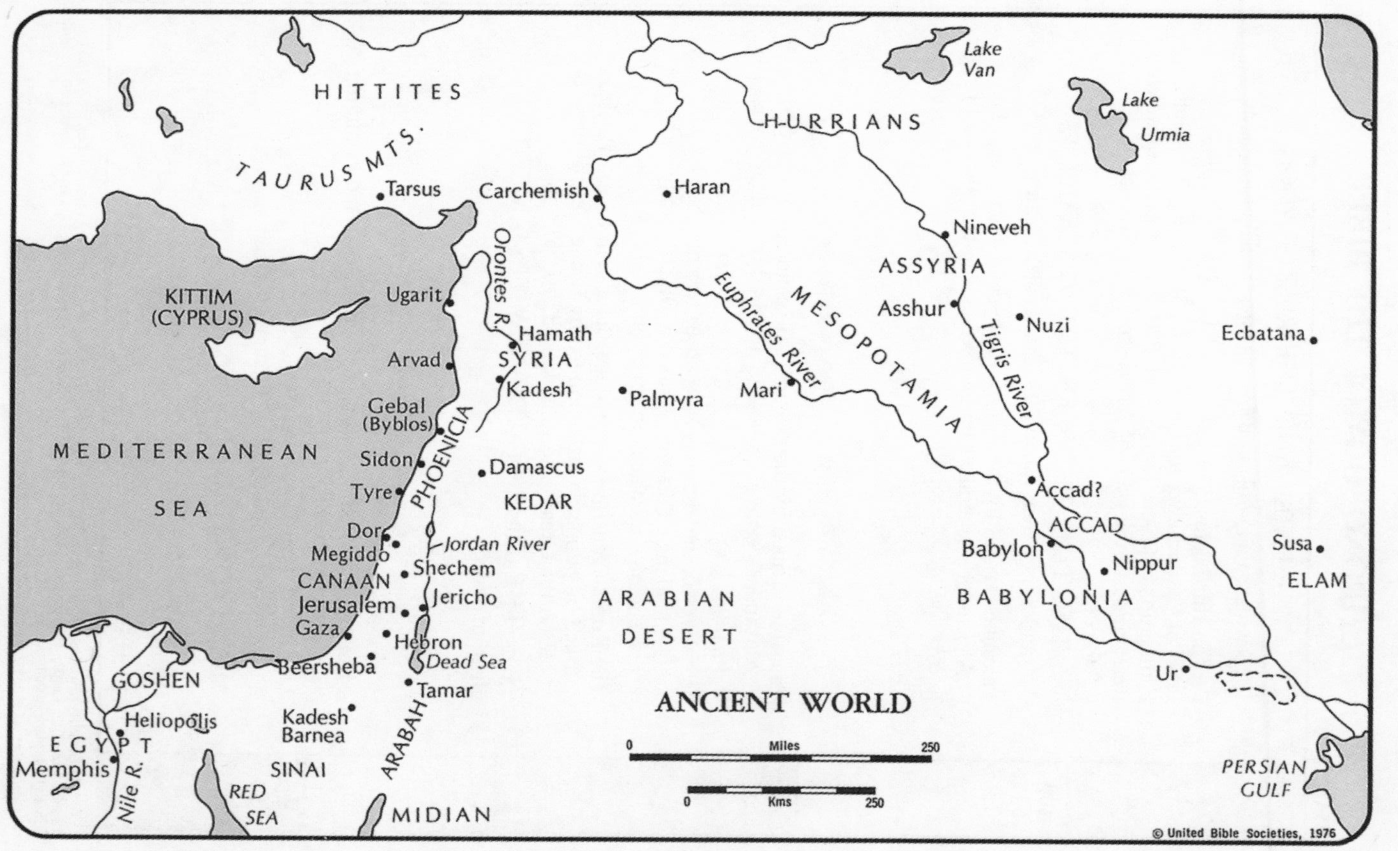

HITTITES
TAURUS MTS.
Tarsus
Carchemish
Haran
HURRIANS
Lake Van
Lake Urmia
Nineveh
ASSYRIA
Asshur
Nuzi
Ecbatana
KITTIM (CYPRUS)
Ugarit
Orontes R.
Hamath
SYRIA
Arvad
Kadesh
Palmyra
Mari
Euphrates River
MESOPOTAMIA
Tigris River
Gebal (Byblos)
PHOENICIA
MEDITERRANEAN SEA
Sidon
Damascus
Tyre
KEDAR
Dor
Megiddo
Jordan River
Shechem
CANAAN
Jerusalem
Jericho
Gaza
Hebron
Dead Sea
Beersheba
Tamar
ARABIAN DESERT
Accad?
ACCAD
Babylon
Nippur
BABYLONIA
Susa
ELAM
Ur
GOSHEN
Heliopolis
EGYPT
Memphis
Nile R.
Kadesh Barnea
SINAI
RED SEA
ARABAH
MIDIAN
ANCIENT WORLD
0
Miles
250
0
Kms
250
PERSIAN GULF
© United Bible Societies, 1976

Map 2

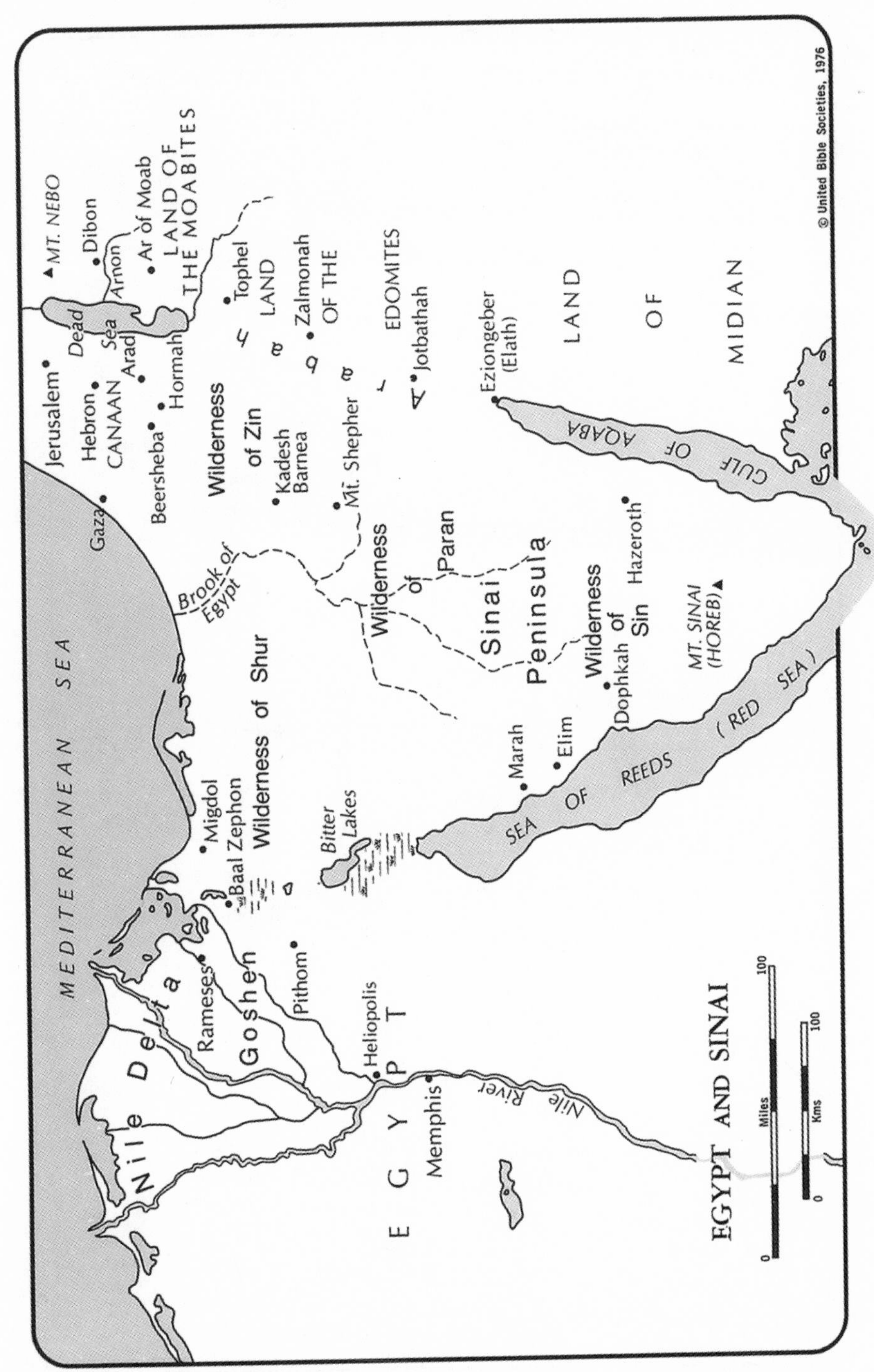

MEDITERRANEAN SEA
MT. NEBO
Dibon
Arnon
Ar of Moab
LAND OF THE MOABITES
Jerusalem
Dead Sea
Hebron
CANAAN
Arad
Hormah
Beersheba
Gaza
Tophel
LAND OF THE EDOMITES
Zalmonah
Wilderness of Zin
Kadesh Barnea
Mt. Shepher
Jotbathah
Eziongeber (Elath)
LAND OF MIDIAN
GULF OF AQABA
Brook of Egypt
Wilderness of Paran
Sinai Peninsula
Hazeroth
Wilderness of Sin
MT. SINAI (HOREB)
Dophkah
Elim
Marah
SEA OF REEDS (RED SEA)
Wilderness of Shur
Migdol
Baal Zephon
Bitter Lakes
Nile Delta
Rameses
Goshen
Pithom
Heliopolis
EGYPT
Memphis
Nile River
EGYPT AND SINAI
Miles
Kms
0
100
© United Bible Societies, 1976

Map 3

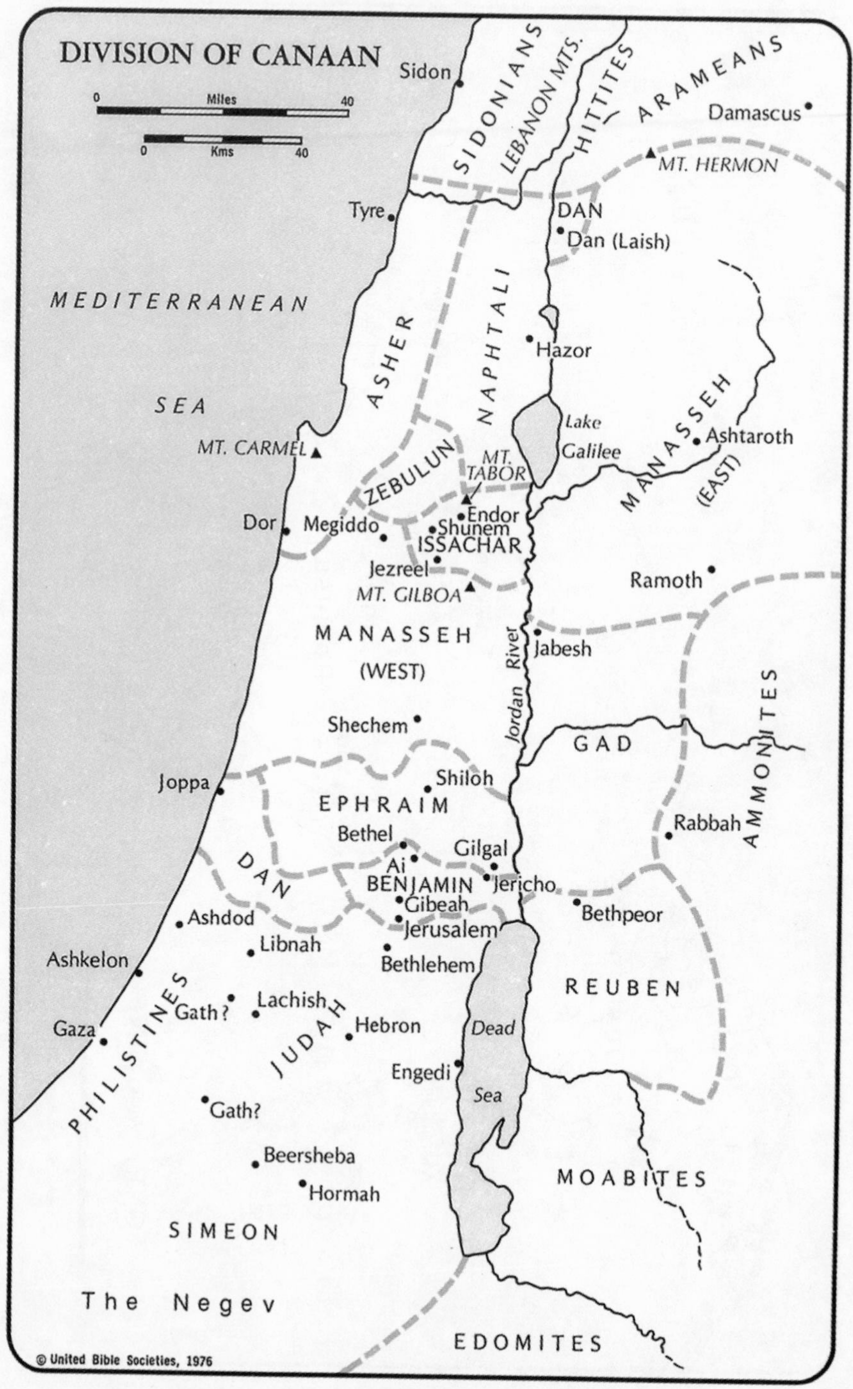
DIVISION OF CANAAN
0 Miles 40
0 Kms 40
Sidon
SIDONIANS
LEBANON MTS.
HITTITES
ARAMEANS
Damascus
MT. HERMON
Tyre
DAN
Dan (Laish)
MEDITERRANEAN
SEA
ASHER
NAPHTALI
Hazor
MANASSEH
(EAST)
Ashtaroth
Lake
Galilee
MT. CARMEL
ZEBULUN
MT. TABOR
Endor
Shunem
ISSACHAR
Dor
Megiddo
Jezreel
MT. GILBOA
Ramoth
MANASSEH
(WEST)
Jabesh
Jordan River
Shechem
GAD
AMMONITES
Joppa
Shiloh
EPHRAIM
Bethel
Rabbah
Gilgal
Ai
DAN
BENJAMIN
Jericho
Gibeah
Bethpeor
Ashdod
Jerusalem
Libnah
Bethlehem
Ashkelon
REUBEN
Gath?
Lachish
Gaza
JUDAH
Hebron
Dead
Sea
Engedi
PHILISTINES
Gath?
Beersheba
MOABITES
Hormah
SIMEON
The Negev
EDOMITES
© United Bible Societies, 1976

Map 4

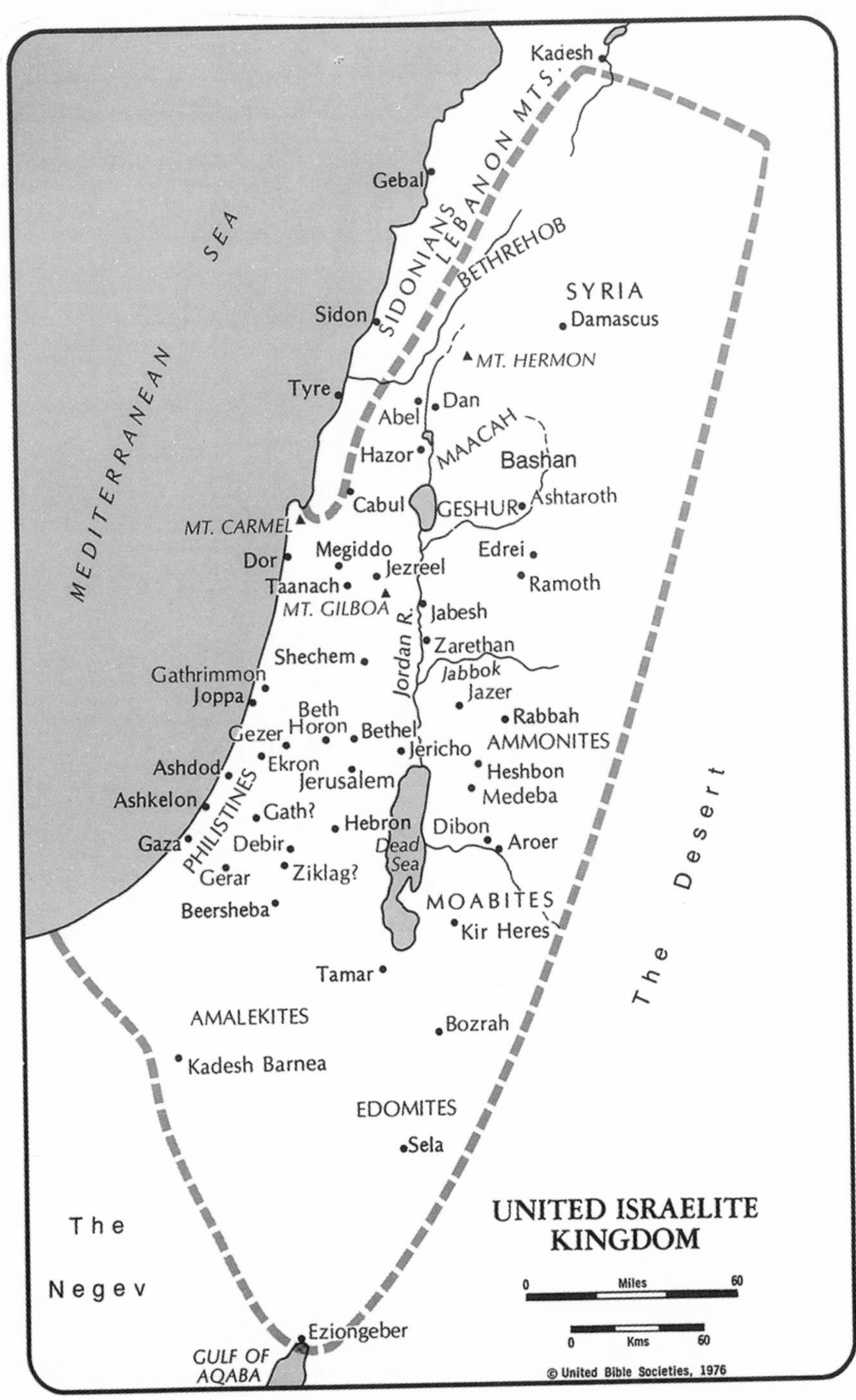

Kadesh
LEBANON MTS.
Gebal
MEDITERRANEAN SEA
SIDONIANS
BETHREHOB
SYRIA
Damascus
Sidon
MT. HERMON
Tyre
Dan
Abel
MAACAH
Hazor
Bashan
Cabul
GESHUR
Ashtaroth
MT. CARMEL
Dor
Megiddo
Edrei
Jezreel
Taanach
Ramoth
MT. GILBOA
Jabesh
Jordan R.
Zarethan
Shechem
Jabbok
Gathrimmon
Jazer
Joppa
Rabbah
Beth Horon
Gezer
Bethel
Jericho
AMMONITES
Ashdod
Ekron
Heshbon
Jerusalem
Medeba
Ashkelon
PHILISTINES
Gath?
Hebron
Dibon
Gaza
Debir
Dead Sea
Aroer
Gerar
Ziklag?
MOABITES
Beersheba
Kir Heres
Tamar
The Desert
AMALEKITES
Bozrah
Kadesh Barnea
EDOMITES
Sela
The Negev
UNITED ISRAELITE KINGDOM
0 Miles 60
0 Kms 60
Eziongeber
GULF OF AQABA
© United Bible Societies, 1976

Map 5

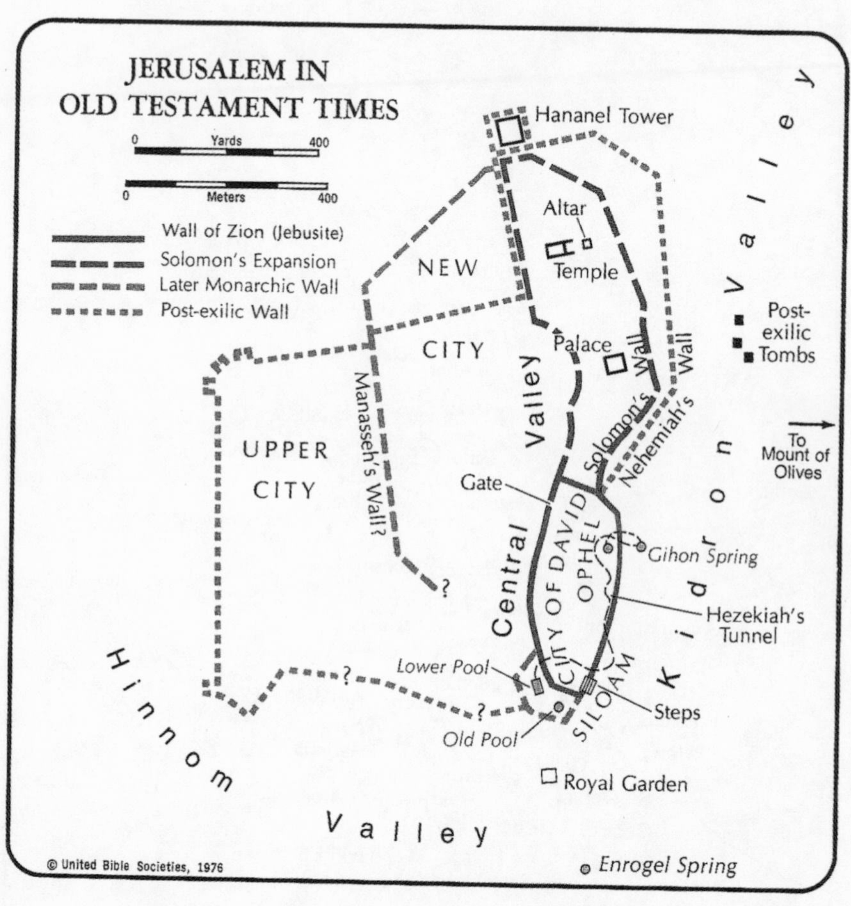
JERUSALEM IN
OLD TESTAMENT TIMES
0 Yards 400
0 Meters 400
Wall of Zion (Jebusite)
Solomon's Expansion
Later Monarchic Wall
Post-exilic Wall
Hananel Tower
Altar
Temple
NEW
CITY
Palace
Solomon's Wall
Nehemiah's Wall
Post-exilic Tombs
To Mount of Olives
Kidron Valley
Central Valley
UPPER
CITY
Manasseh's Wall?
Gate
CITY OF DAVID
OPHEL
Gihon Spring
Hezekiah's Tunnel
Lower Pool
SILOAM
Steps
Old Pool
Royal Garden
Hinnom Valley
Enrogel Spring
© United Bible Societies, 1976

Map 6

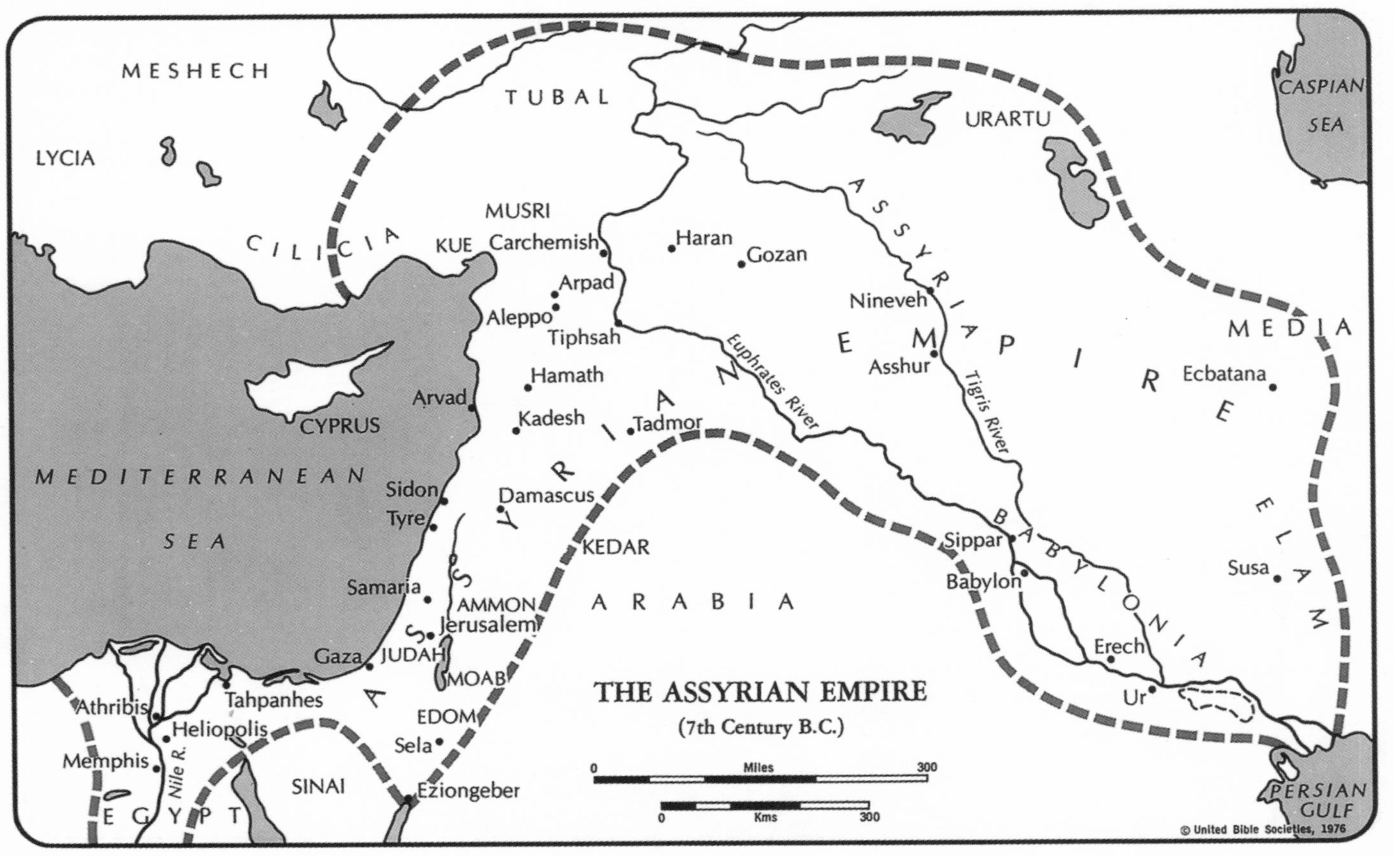

THE ASSYRIAN EMPIRE
(7th Century B.C.)
0
Miles
300
0
Kms
300
© United Bible Societies, 1976
MESHECH
LYCIA
TUBAL
URARTU
CASPIAN SEA
CILICIA
MUSRI
KUE
Carchemish
Haran
Gozan
ASSYRIA
Nineveh
Arpad
Aleppo
Tiphsah
Asshur
MEDIA
Ecbatana
EMPIRE
ASSYRIAN
Euphrates River
Tigris River
Hamath
Kadesh
Tadmor
Arvad
CYPRUS
MEDITERRANEAN SEA
Sidon
Tyre
Damascus
KEDAR
ELAM
Susa
Sippar
Babylon
BABYLONIA
Samaria
AMMON
Jerusalem
ARABIA
Gaza
JUDAH
MOAB
Erech
Ur
Athribis
Tahpanhes
Heliopolis
EDOM
Sela
Memphis
Nile R.
SINAI
Eziongeber
EGYPT
PERSIAN GULF

Map 7

THE KINGDOMS OF ISRAEL AND JUDAH
0 Miles 40
0 Kms 40
Sidon
LEBANON MTS.
Damascus
PHOENICIA
Zerephath
MT. HERMON
SYRIA
Tyre
Dan
Kedesh
MEDITERRANEAN
Hazor
SEA
GALILEE
BASHAN
Lake Galilee
MT. CARMEL
Megiddo
Shunem
Jezreel
Ramoth
Jordan River
ISRAEL
GILEAD
Samaria
Shechem
AMMON
Shiloh
Joppa
Bethel
Gilgal
Ekron
Geba
Jericho
Ashdod
Jerusalem
Libnah
Bethlehem
Ashkelon
PHILISTIA
Gath?
Lachish
Hebron
Gaza
Dead Sea
JUDAH
Gath?
Beersheba
MOAB
EDOM
© United Bible Societies 1978

Map 8

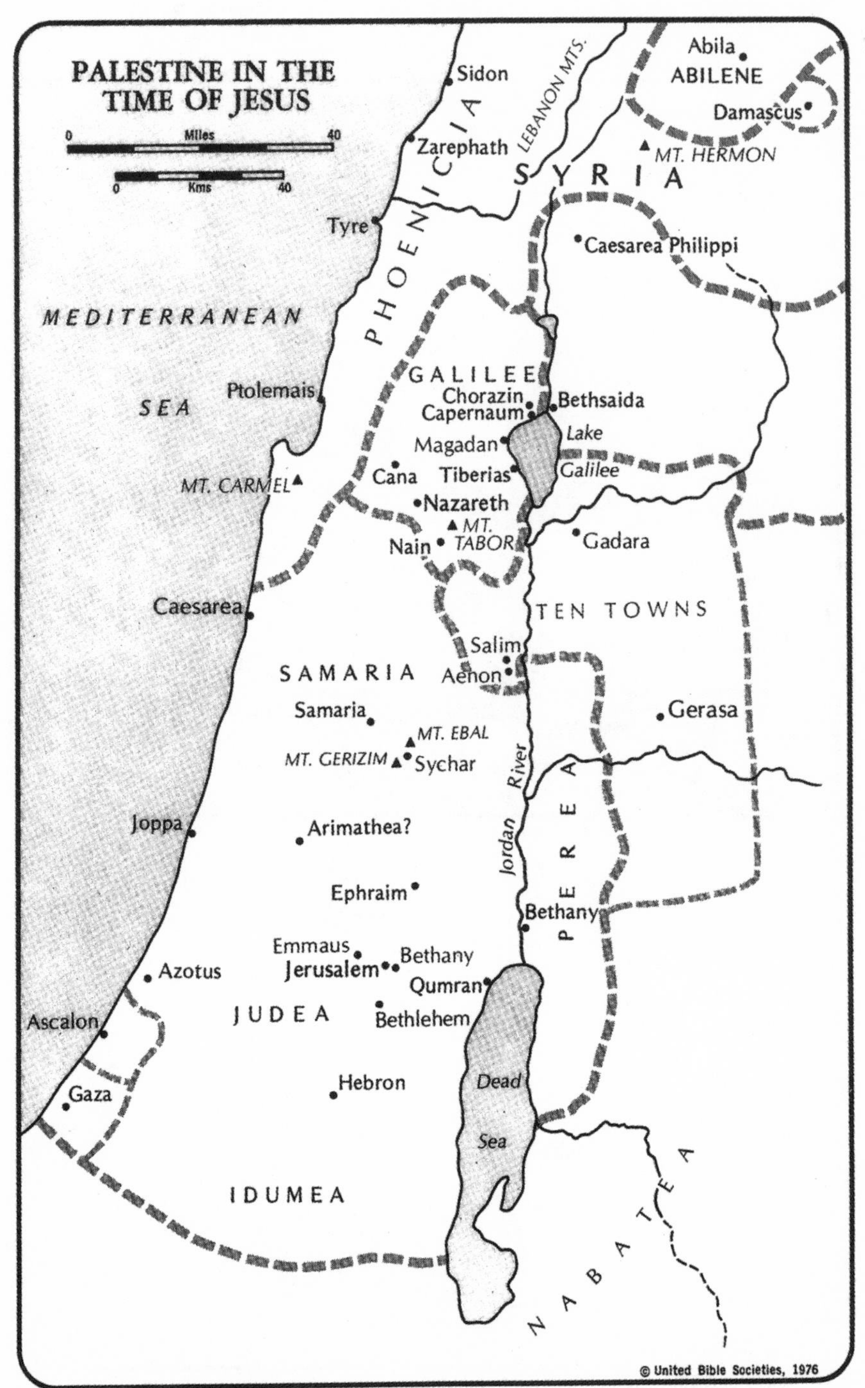
PALESTINE IN THE TIME OF JESUS
0 Miles 40
0 Kms 40
Sidon
LEBANON MTS.
Abila
ABILENE
Damascus
Zarephath
MT. HERMON
PHOENICIA
SYRIA
Tyre
Caesarea Philippi
MEDITERRANEAN
SEA
GALILEE
Ptolemais
Chorazin
Capernaum
Bethsaida
Lake
Magadan
Galilee
MT. CARMEL
Cana
Tiberias
Nazareth
MT. TABOR
Nain
Gadara
Caesarea
TEN TOWNS
Salim
SAMARIA
Aenon
Samaria
Gerasa
MT. EBAL
MT. GERIZIM
Sychar
Jordan River
PEREA
Joppa
Arimathea?
Ephraim
Bethany
Emmaus
Jerusalem
Bethany
Azotus
Qumran
JUDEA
Bethlehem
Ascalon
Hebron
Dead Sea
Gaza
IDUMEA
NABATEA
© United Bible Societies, 1976

Map 9

Antioch
Iconium
PISIDIA
Lystra
CILICIA
Derbe
PAMPHYLIA
Attalia
Perga
Tarsus
Euphrates R.
LYCIA
Patara
Myra
Antioch
Seleucia
CYPRUS
SYRIA
Salamis
Paphos
PHOENICIA
MEDITERRANEAN
SEA
Sidon
Tyre
Damascus
Ptolemais
PALESTINE AND SYRIA
Caesarea
Samaria
0 Miles 200
Joppa
Lydda
0 Kms 200
Azotus
Jerusalem
Gaza
JUDEA
Alexandria
© United Bible Societies, 1976

Map 10

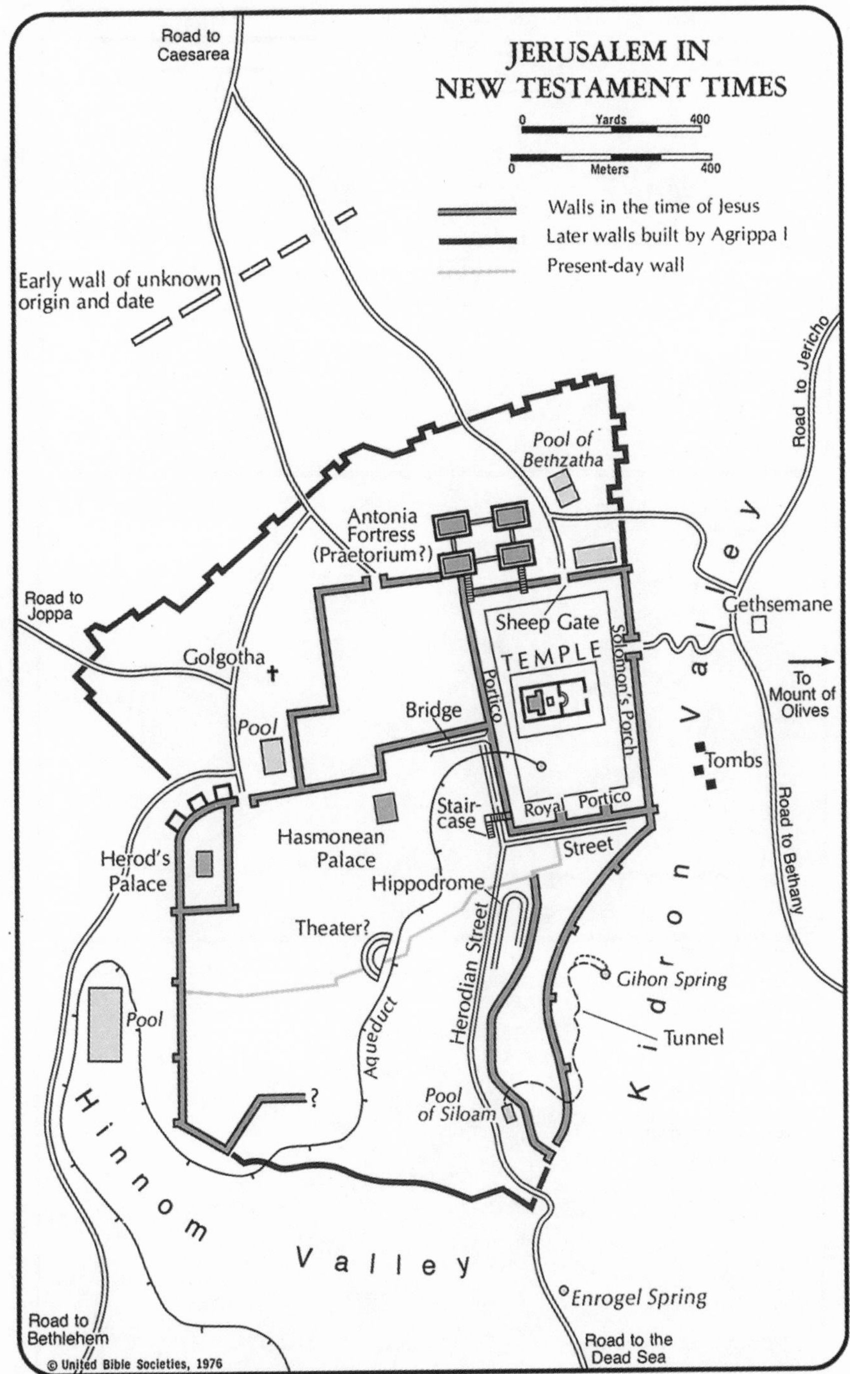

JERUSALEM IN NEW TESTAMENT TIMES
0 Yards 400
0 Meters 400
Walls in the time of Jesus
Later walls built by Agrippa I
Present-day wall
Road to Caesarea
Early wall of unknown origin and date
Road to Jericho
Pool of Bethzatha
Antonia Fortress (Praetorium?)
Road to Joppa
Gethsemane
Sheep Gate
TEMPLE
Solomon's Porch
Portico
Golgotha
To Mount of Olives
Bridge
Pool
Tombs
Stair-case
Royal Portico
Road to Bethany
Street
Hasmonean Palace
Herod's Palace
Hippodrome
Theater?
Herodian Street
Gihon Spring
Aqueduct
Pool
Tunnel
Kidron Valley
Hinnom
Pool of Siloam
?
Valley
Enrogel Spring
Road to Bethlehem
Road to the Dead Sea
© United Bible Societies, 1976

Map 11

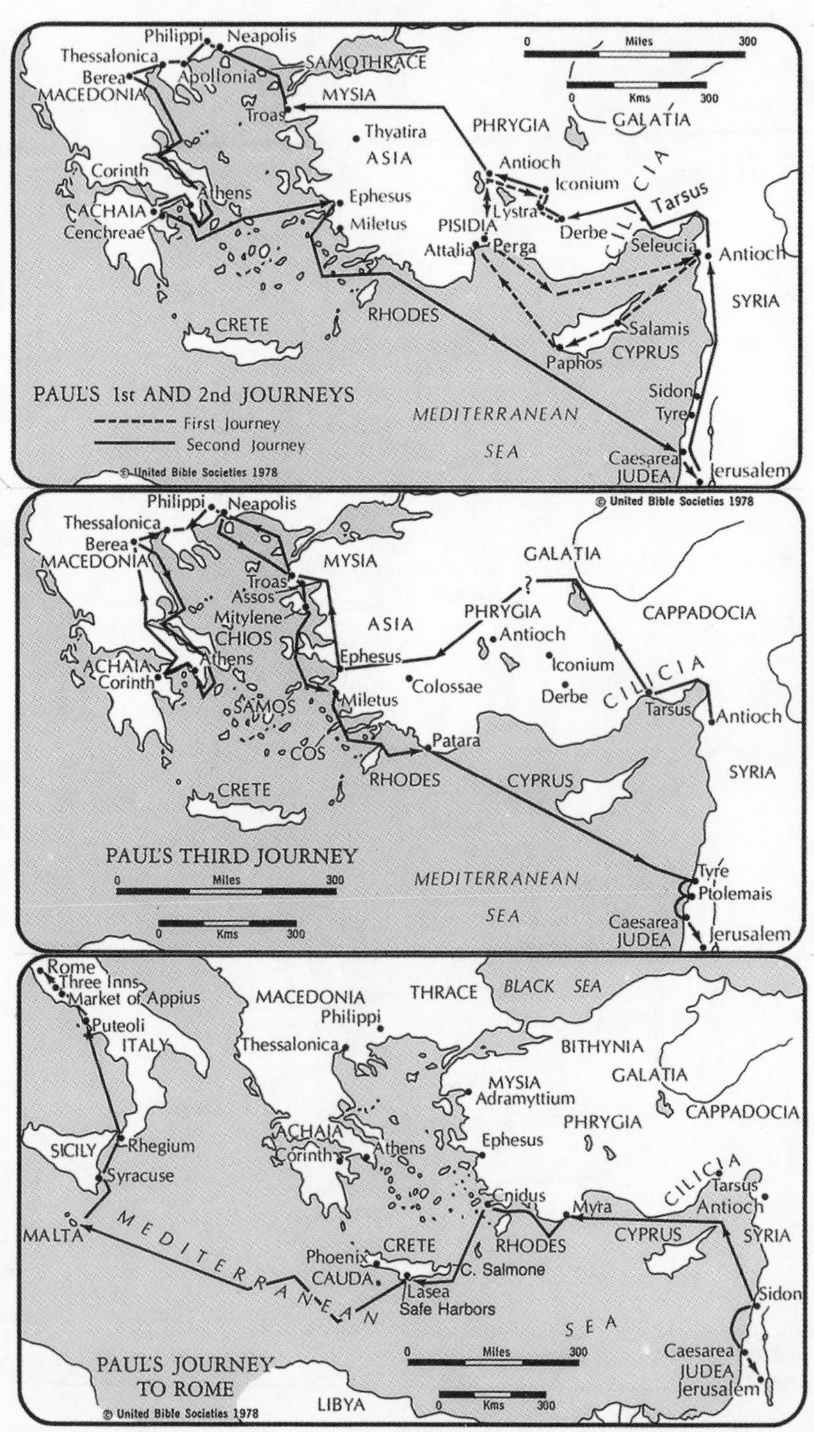

PAUL'S 1st AND 2nd JOURNEYS
First Journey
Second Journey
Philippi
Neapolis
Thessalonica
SAMOTHRACE
Berea
Apollonia
MACEDONIA
MYSIA
Troas
Thyatira
PHRYGIA
GALATIA
ASIA
Antioch
Iconium
CILICIA
Tarsus
Corinth
Athens
Ephesus
Lystra
ACHAIA
Cenchreae
Miletus
PISIDIA
Derbe
Attalia
Perga
Seleucia
Antioch
SYRIA
CRETE
RHODES
Salamis
CYPRUS
Paphos
Sidon
Tyre
MEDITERRANEAN
SEA
Caesarea
JUDEA
Jerusalem
Miles
Kms
© United Bible Societies 1978
PAUL'S THIRD JOURNEY
Philippi
Neapolis
Thessalonica
Berea
MACEDONIA
MYSIA
GALATIA
Troas
Assos
Mitylene
CHIOS
PHRYGIA
CAPPADOCIA
ASIA
Antioch
ACHAIA
Corinth
Athens
Ephesus
Iconium
Colossae
Derbe
CILICIA
SAMOS
Miletus
Tarsus
Antioch
Patara
COS
RHODES
CYPRUS
SYRIA
CRETE
MEDITERRANEAN
SEA
Tyre
Ptolemais
Caesarea
JUDEA
Jerusalem
Miles
Kms
© United Bible Societies 1978
PAUL'S JOURNEY TO ROME
Rome
Three Inns
Market of Appius
Puteoli
ITALY
MACEDONIA
THRACE
BLACK SEA
Philippi
Thessalonica
BITHYNIA
MYSIA
Adramyttium
GALATIA
PHRYGIA
CAPPADOCIA
SICILY
Rhegium
Syracuse
ACHAIA
Corinth
Athens
Ephesus
CILICIA
Tarsus
Antioch
Cnidus
Myra
MALTA
MEDITERRANEAN
CRETE
RHODES
CYPRUS
SYRIA
Phoenix
CAUDA
C. Salmone
Lasea
Safe Harbors
SEA
Sidon
Caesarea
JUDEA
Jerusalem
LIBYA
Miles
Kms
© United Bible Societies 1978